Get the eBook FREE!

(PDF, ePub, Kindle, and liveBook all included)

We believe that once you buy a book from us, you should be able to read it in any format we have available. To get electronic versions of this book at no additional cost to you, purchase and then register this book at the Manning website.

Go to https://www.manning.com/freebook and follow the instructions to complete your pBook registration.

That's it!
Thanks from Manning!

Operations Anti-patterns, DevOps Solutions

JEFFERY SMITH

MANNING

SHELTER ISLAND

For online information and ordering of this and other Manning books, please visit www.manning.com. The publisher offers discounts on this book when ordered in quantity. For more information, please contact

    Special Sales Department
    Manning Publications Co.
    20 Baldwin Road
    PO Box 761
    Shelter Island, NY 11964
    Email: orders@manning.com

Manning Publications Co.
20 Baldwin Road
PO Box 761
Shelter Island, NY 11964

Development editor:	Toni Arritola
Technical development editor:	Karl Geoghagen
Review editor:	Aleksandar Dragosavljević
Production editor:	Deirdre S. Hiam
Copy editor:	Sharon Wilkey
Proofreader:	Keri Hales
Typesetter:	Gordan Salinovic
Cover designer:	Marija Tudor

ISBN 9781617296987
Printed in the United States of America

To my children, Ella and Xander.
You can change the world.

contents

preface

I'm an avid reader of things related to the DevOps space. I came up in the technology field in a regional insurance office in upstate New York. The company was a pretty good size for the local economy but wouldn't exactly be considered a powerhouse in the world of technology. Many of my friends worked in similar companies where technology was important, but it wasn't the product the company sold. It was a means to deliver the goods and services that their customers paid for.

Fast-forward 10 years. I've moved to Chicago and become involved in the local technology scene. There are a lot more companies in Chicago that have technology as the product. As a result, many of the companies are more technologically sophisticated and at the forefront of new ideas and practices than I'd previously experienced.

But in these tech circles, you're surrounded by people who are in a similar space. This homogeny creates a sort of bubble or echo chamber. You quickly begin thinking everyone is at the same stage of evolution in their journey. That couldn't be further from the truth. That disconnect is what inspired this book.

People read blog posts from Facebook, Apple, Netflix, Uber, and Spotify and assume that because these wildly successful and popular companies are doing things in a certain way, matching that success requires following the same pattern. The same is happening with regards to DevOps practices. After having a few conversations with people doing DevOps, you conclude that you need to be running Docker in a public cloud provider, deploying 30 times per day in order to be doing DevOps right.

But DevOps is an iterative journey. The journey starts similarly in most companies, but where it ultimately heads depends greatly on your situation and circumstances.

Maybe deploying 30 times per day isn't the end goal for your organization. Maybe your company can't adopt Kubernetes because of problems running legacy applications. That doesn't mean that you can't achieve some of the benefits of a DevOps transformation.

DevOps is as much about people as it is about technology and tools. I wanted to write this book as a toolkit to show how some of the common problems that besiege teams have DevOps solutions that don't require rewriting your entire technical stack. You can find positive change in DevOps by modifying the way teams interact, communicate, and share goals and resources. I hope that you recognize these patterns in your organization and that the book provides you with the tools necessary to break them.

acknowledgments

There are so many people in my life who have contributed to this book in ways both large and small. I'll start by thanking my biggest fan, my best friend, and my partner in life. My wife, Stephanie, endured my absenteeism, my frustrations, and my doubts with support, love, and understanding. You are my rock, and this book doesn't exist without you. I love you deeply.

I'd like to thank my mother, Evelyn, for all that she has done and continues to do for me. For seeing my love for computers and encouraging it. For stretching our checking account to buy me my first computer. For not getting angry when I kept the phone line busy for hours at a time. For teaching me right from wrong. For bragging for me when I was too embarrassed to do it. For making me stand up and speak in church. For making me do all the other things that I hated then but made me who I am now. I am forever grateful.

To my sister, Gloria, for always being in my corner. You carry the weight of our family, and your heart is so large, your love so bottomless that you don't even realize it. It isn't your selflessness that impresses me most, but how effortlessly it comes to you. You are the example that drives me to be a better person every single day.

To Debbie Maxwell, my high school math teacher. You wouldn't give up on me no matter how many reasons I gave you to. I graduated high school because of your tutelage, your support, and continued belief in me. Thank you.

And last but not least, to Mickey McDonald, my first manager and mentor. You saw me reading a book on TCP/IP that I barely understood. But you took a shot. You

hired a black kid doing data entry who had no formal schooling, no formal training, but a ton of desire. You helped change my life.

I would also like to thank the awesome team at Manning for making this book possible. In particular, I thank Toni Arritola, the development editor, for her patience and support. I also thank Karl Geoghagen, the technical development editor, for his review and feedback. Thank you also to review editor Aleksandar Dragosavljevic, project editor Deirdre Hiam, copy editor Sharon Wilkey, proofreader Keri Hales, and typesetter Gordan Salinovic.

To all the reviewers—your suggestions helped make this a better book: Adam Wendell, Alain Couniot, Andrew Courter, Asif Iqbal, Chris Viner, Christian Thoudahl, Clifford Thurber, Colin Joyce, Conor Redmond, Daniel Lamblin, Douglas Sparling, Eric Platon, Foster Haines, Gregory Reshetniak, Imanol Valiente, James Woodruff, Justin Coulston, Kent R. Spillner, Max Almonte, Michele Adduci, Milorad Imbra, Richard Tobias, Roman Levchenko, Roman Pavlov, Simon Seyag, Slavomir Furman, Stephen Goodman, Steve Atchue, Thorsten Weber, and Hong Wei Zhuo.

about this book

Operations Anti-patterns, DevOps Solutions was written to help individual contributors and team leads begin a series of actions that lead to a DevOps transformation. It begins by setting up the primary pillars of any DevOps transformation and attempts to frame organizational problems within those contexts.

Who should read this book

This book is intended for engineers from either the operations or development side of the technology team. It's aimed at team leads and individual contributors. Higher-level managers and senior leaders will find many useful takeaways in this book, but the solutions and the approaches outlined take into account the limited role of the reader. Leaders further up the organization's hierarchy will have a much wider set of tools available to them that are not covered in this book.

If you're an executive looking to implement DevOps, this book will be helpful but incomplete. As an executive, you have access to options for cultural change that are beyond my target reader. While I still recommend reading this book (and purchasing a copy for every member of your staff and optionally as stocking stuffers for your friends and family), I'd be remiss if I didn't point you to other books that take the scope of your hard power into account as an agent for change. Two good options are *The Phoenix Project* by Gene Kim, Kevin Behr, and George Spafford (IT Revolution Press, 2018) and *The DevOps Handbook* by Gene Kim, John Willis, Patrick Debois, and Jez Humble (IT Revolution Press, 2016).

How this book is organized: A roadmap

This book is organized around a series of antipatterns that are commonly found in organizations. Each chapter starts with a definition of the antipattern and begins to explain methods and solutions for reversing said patterns:

- Chapter 1 discusses the ingredients of a DevOps organization and sets up common terminology in the DevOps community.
- Chapter 2 presents the first antipattern, the *paternalist syndrome*, and dives into the impact of low-trust organizations. It examines the role of gatekeepers in processes and their impact on the speed of change. The chapter tackles ways to automate these gatekeeper concerns to empower staff members and increase the rate of change safely.
- Chapter 3 describes the *operational blindness* antipattern and discusses the need to have operational visibility into our systems. It walks through processes for confirming that systems are working as expected through systems understanding, data, and metrics.
- Chapter 4 covers the *data instead of information* antipattern. It discusses how data can be structured and presented in a way that makes it more useful to its audience. Sometimes data is useful, but other times it needs to be presented in a way to convey a specific story.
- Chapter 5 introduces the *quality as a condiment* antipattern and discusses the need for ensuring that the quality of the system is part of all the individual ingredients. Attempting to ensure quality at the complete end of the process leads to a sort of quality theatrics.
- Chapter 6 defines the *alert fatigue* antipattern. When teams support production systems, they often set up a wide array of alerting. But those alerts can be detrimental when they are noisy without always needing remediation. This chapter discusses approaches to solving for this condition by being more deliberate in alert creation and understanding the alert's true goal.
- Chapter 7 explains the empty toolbox antipattern. As teams expand in their roles or duties, it's important that time and energy is invested in the tools they use to perform those duties. The process of adding responsibility without the corresponding tooling results in a general slowdown of the team as they perform repetitive tasks.
- Chapter 8 presents the *off-hours deployment* antipattern and discusses the fear around the deployment process. Instead of managing the fears, this chapter discusses how your approach to the deployment process can create safety in the process. By using automation, you can create repeatable deployment processes with defined rollback checkpoints.
- Chapter 9 covers the *wasting a perfectly good incident* antipattern. Many incidents get resolved but never discussed. Incidents occur when our understanding of the system collides with the reality of the system. This chapter gives a structured

approach to tackling those moments to create continuous learning in your organization.

- Chapter 10 deals with the *information hoarding* antipattern. Sometimes information hoarding is accidental, based on permissions in tools, lack of opportunities for sharing, and other innocuous causes. This chapter walks through practices to reduce information hoarding and increase sharing among teams.
- Chapter 11 talks about organizational culture and how it is formed. The culture is created not through slogans and value statements, but through actions, rituals, and behaviors that are rewarded and/or punished.
- Chapter 12 talks about how organizations measure teams and set their goals. Sometimes these measurements create conflict among teams. If one team is measured by stability and another team is measured by a rate of change, you create conflict between the teams. This chapter covers sharing goals and priorities to better align teams.

In general, the chapters can be read individually in any order, although some concepts do occasionally build on others. The focus may sound as if the burden lays more on the operations teams or the development teams, but I encourage you to read all of the chapters at some point in order to understand how their concepts are interconnected across teams.

About the code

This book contains only a handful of code examples, and all of the code is really only for illustrative purposes. The code that is displayed does follow a standard formatting.

liveBook discussion forum

Purchase of *Operations Anti-patterns, DevOps Solutions* includes free access to a private web forum run by Manning Publications where you can make comments about the book, ask technical questions, and receive help from the author and from other users. To access the forum, go to https://livebook.manning.com/book/operations-anti-patterns-devops-solutions/welcome/v-6/. You can also learn more about Manning's forums and the rules of conduct at https://livebook.manning.com/#!/discussion.

Manning's commitment to our readers is to provide a venue where a meaningful dialogue between individual readers and between readers and the author can take place. It is not a commitment to any specific amount of participation on the part of the author, whose contribution to the forum remains voluntary (and unpaid). We suggest you try asking the author some challenging questions lest his interest stray! The forum and the archives of previous discussions will be accessible from the publisher's website as long as the book is in print.

about the author

Jeffery Smith has been in the technology industry for more than 20 years, oscillating between management and individual contributor. Jeff currently serves as the director of production operations for Centro, an advertising software company headquartered in Chicago, Illinois.

Jeffery is passionate about DevOps transformations in organizations large and small, with a particular interest in the psychological aspects of problems in companies. He lives in Chicago with his wife, Stephanie, and their two children, Ella and Xander.

about the cover illustration

The figure on the cover of *Operations Anti-patterns, DevOps Solutions* is captioned "Indien du Mexique en voyage," or Mexican Indian traveling. The illustration is taken from a collection of dress costumes from various countries by Jacques Grasset de Saint-Sauveur (1757–1810), titled *Costumes de Différents Pays*, published in France in 1797. Each illustration is finely drawn and colored by hand. The rich variety of Grasset de Saint-Sauveur's collection reminds us vividly of how culturally apart the world's towns and regions were just 200 years ago. Isolated from each other, people spoke different dialects and languages. In the streets or in the countryside, it was easy to identify where they lived and what their trade or station in life was just by their dress.

The way we dress has changed since then, and the diversity by region, so rich at the time, has faded away. It is now hard to tell apart the inhabitants of different continents, let alone different towns, regions, or countries. Perhaps we have traded cultural diversity for a more varied personal life—certainly for a more varied and fast-paced technological life.

At a time when it is hard to tell one computer book from another, Manning celebrates the inventiveness and initiative of the computer business with book covers based on the rich diversity of regional life of two centuries ago, brought back to life by Grasset de Saint-Sauveur's pictures.

The DevOps ingredients

It's 11:30 p.m. on a Friday, when John, the IT operations manager, hears his phone ring. The ringtone is distinct, one that John has programmed so that he can instantly recognize a call from the office. He answers the phone, and on the other end is Valentina, one of the senior software developers at John's office. There's a problem in the production environment.

The last software release included additional functionality that changed how the application interacted with the database. But because of a lack of adequate hardware in the testing environments, the entire application couldn't be tested prior to release. Around 10:30 this evening, a scheduled task that runs only quarterly began executing. The job was missed during the testing phase, and even if it wasn't, there isn't enough data in the test environment to create an accurate test. Valentina needs to stop the process, but she doesn't have access to the production servers. She's spent the last 45 minutes searching through the company intranet site to find John's contact information. John is the only person Valentina knows who has the production access she needs.

1

Killing the scheduled task isn't straightforward. The task usually runs overnight and wasn't designed to be stopped midway through processing. Because Valentina doesn't have production access, her only alternative is to dictate a series of cryptic commands to John over the phone. After a few missteps, John and Valentina finally manage to stop the task. The two plan to regroup on Monday to figure out what went wrong and how to fix it for the next quarter. Now both John and Valentina must stay on guard over the weekend in case the behavior repeats itself with another job.

Chances are this story feels familiar to you. Having production code that hasn't been properly tested feels like a scenario that could have been avoided, especially when it interrupts a team member on their off-time. Why is the testing environment insufficient for the needs of the development group? Why wasn't the scheduled task written in such a way to make stopping and restarting it straightforward? What's the value of the interaction between John and Valentina if John is just going to blindly type what Valentina dictates? Not to mention the two probably skipped the organization's change approval process. Nothing raises the safety of a change like five people approving something they don't understand!

The questions raised here have become so commonplace that many organizations don't even think to examine them in detail. The dysfunction detailed is often accepted as inescapable, due to the difference in roles between development and IT operations teams. Instead of addressing the core issues, organizations continue to heap more approvals, more processes, and tighter restrictions onto the problem. Leadership thinks that they're trading agility for safety, but in reality, they're getting neither. (When was the last time you said, "Thank goodness for change control"?) These negative and sometimes wasteful interactions between teams and processes is exactly what DevOps is attempting to solve.

1.1 What is DevOps?

These days, "What is DevOps?" feels like a question you should ask a philosopher more than an engineer. I'll give you the story and the history of DevOps before presenting my definition. If you ever want to start a fight at a conference, though, you can ask the "What is DevOps?" question to a group of five people, and then walk away and watch the carnage. Luckily, you're reading this and not talking to me in the hallway, so I don't mind putting my definition out there and seeing what happens. But first, the story.

1.1.1 A little DevOps history

In 2007, a systems administrator by the name of Patrick Debois was consulting on a large data center migration project for the Belgium government. He was in charge of the testing for this migration, so he spent a fair amount of time working and coordinating with both the development and operations teams. Seeing the stark contrast between how development and operations teams functioned, Debois got frustrated and started thinking of solutions to this problem.

Fast-forward to 2008. Developer Andrew Clay Shafer, attending the Agile Conference in Toronto, proposes an ad hoc discussion session called "Agile Infrastructure." He received such poor feedback on his proposal that he didn't even attend the session himself. In fact, only a single attendee joined the session, Patrick Debois. But because Debois was so passionate about discussing this topic, he tracked Shafer down in the hallway, where they had an extensive discussion about their ideas and goals. Directly out of those conversations, they formed the Agile Systems Administrator Group.

In June 2009, Debois was back in Belgium, watching a live stream of the O'Reilly Velocity 09 conference. At this conference, two employees from Flickr, John Allspaw and Paul Hammond, gave a talk titled "10 Deploys per Day: Dev & Ops Cooperation at Flickr." Debois, moved by the talk, was inspired to start his own conference in Ghent, Belgium. He invited developers and operations professionals to discuss various approaches to working together, managing infrastructure, and rethinking the way the teams worked together. Debois called this two-day conference *DevOps Days*. A lot of the conversations about the conference were happening on Twitter, which then limited the number of characters per message to 140. To save as many precious characters as possible, Debois shortened the conference's Twitter hashtag from #devopsdays to just plain #devops, and with that, DevOps was born.

> **DEFINITION** *DevOps* is a set of software-development practices that combines a software development mentality with other functions in the organization. DevOps puts a heavy emphasis on shared responsibilities across all teams throughout the software development life cycle. The edges of job functions soften, as operations team members take on tasks that were traditionally more developer-focused, and development team members do the same. The term *DevOps* is most commonly associated with development (Dev) and IT operations (Ops), but the approach can be extended to other groups as well, including but not limited to security (DevSecOps), QA, database operations, and networking.

It's been more than 10 years since that fateful meeting. Since then, DevOps has moved beyond small web startups and has begun to penetrate larger enterprises. The success of DevOps, however, has brought the most cantankerous enemy of any movement: market forces.

According to LinkedIn Talent Solutions, in 2018 the most recruited job overall, not just in tech, was DevOps engineer. Considering we've defined DevOps as a set of practices, it's strange how a style of work quickly became a job title. You've never heard of an Agile engineer, because it just sounds silly. As transformational as DevOps is, it couldn't escape market forces. With that much demand, the job title of DevOps has led to scores of candidates rebranding themselves as DevOps engineers.

Product marketers are looking to cash in on the DevOps craze. Simple products like metrics and monitoring get rebranded into "DevOps dashboards," further diluting the meaning of the word. With the market pulling the term "DevOps" in different directions, it has splintered into different meanings for different people. I could spend an entire chapter arguing about what DevOps should and shouldn't mean; instead, I'll use the definition that I proposed previously. But if you ever see me at a conference and want to see me go on a tirade, ask me what it's like being a "DevOps manager."

1.1.2   *What DevOps is not*

Ironically it might be easier to define what DevOps is not rather than what it is. Thanks to market forces, these details will probably fall on deaf ears, but since this is my book, I figure I might as well go for it! For starters, it's not about tools. If you purchased this book hoping to learn about Jenkins or Docker or Kubernetes or AWS, you're going to be sorely disappointed. I don't do refunds, but you can feel free to scream into the ether with your disdain.

DevOps isn't about tools, but about how teams work together. Technology is definitely involved, but, honestly, the tools are less important than the people. You can install the latest version of Jenkins or sign up for CircleCI, but if you don't have a solid test suite, it's useless. If you don't have a culture that considers automated testing valuable, the tool doesn't provide value. DevOps is about people first, then process, *then* tools.

You need the people on-board and ready for change. Once the people are on-board, they need to be involved and engaged with creating the process. Once a process is created, you now have the necessary input to pick the right tool!

So many people focus on the tool first and try to work backward from there. This is probably one of the top DevOps follies. You can't choose a tool and then tell the people that they have to change all their processes. Our brains are wired to immediately be hostile to that type of approach. When tools are launched like that, the tool feels like it's happening *to* them, not *through* them. That approach differs significantly from the way people accept new ideas. You have to have buy-in.

In addition, when you get excited about a new tool, you begin applying it to problems you never had. When you buy a new table saw, suddenly everything in your home becomes a construction project. It's the same thing with software tools.

All this is to say that the major focus of this book and DevOps is about people and their interactions. While I may reference specific tools here and there, the book avoids giving specific examples based on architecture. Instead, the examples focus on capabilities, regardless of which tool provides that capability. To highlight this approach, the DevOps philosophy is structured on top of the CAMS model, which aims to place people first when addressing problems.

DevOps as the "new" systems administrator

When I attend technology events, I'm often greeted by someone who believes that the popularity of DevOps means certain doom for the "traditional" systems administrator. With the rise of virtual machines, software-defined networking, and API access for creating infrastructure, it is no surprise that software development skills are becoming increasingly important for systems administrators and, in many companies, is already a strict requirement. This push toward more development-focused systems administrators has led many to speculate that DevOps is the beginning of the end for systems administration.

But the demise of the operations function has been greatly exaggerated. The way operations teams go about their work is definitely in a state of flux, but it has been since about 1960. I agree that developers will take more of a role in operations work, but operations work will continue to be separate and distinct from the work that developers do on a daily basis.

Regardless of who does that work, tasks like infrastructure architecture planning, capacity planning, operating the system at runtime, monitoring, implementing patches, overseeing security, developing internal tools, and managing the platform will continue to exist. Operations engineering will continue to be a specialized form of engineering. There is no doubt that system administrators have a new set of skills that they'll need to learn, but again, this is nothing new. If system administrators survived the transition from token ring to IPX/SPX, to TCP/IP, to IPv6, I'm sure learning Python is not an insurmountable task.

1.2 CAMS, the pillars of DevOps

DevOps is structured around four pillars of attention and focus. Those pillars are culture, automation, metrics, and sharing: *CAMS*, as it's called for short. As illustrated in figure 1.1, these pillars for DevOps are crucial to holding up the entire structure.

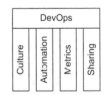

The details of the four pillars are as follows:

Figure 1.1 Culture, automation, metrics, and sharing are all necessary for a successful DevOps transformation.

- *Culture* is about changing the norms by which your teams operate. These norms might be new communication patterns between teams or completely new team structures. Cultural changes are dictated by the type of cultural problems you have. I outline specific examples in this book, but you'll also learn how to identify these problem areas yourself so that you can apply the problems beyond the examples highlighted here. Don't underestimate the value and impact of a company's culture on its technology outcomes. As you'll find in this book, most problems are people problems, not technology problems.

- *Automation* is not just about writing shell scripts. (I mean, that's definitely part of it, but stick with me.) Automation is about freeing human capital from the mundane. It's about empowering people to do their jobs safely and autonomously. Automation should be used as a cultural re-enforcer of the way work gets done within your organization. Simply saying, "Automated testing is a cultural value" is one thing, but embedding that cultural value into your processes through automated checks and merge requirements enforces that cultural norm. When implemented properly, it sets a new standard for how work is completed.
- *Metrics* are the way you tell whether or not something is working. The absence of errors is not sufficient. Metrics should also be used as a cultural re-enforcer for the way we evaluate our systems. It's not enough for order processing to not produce errors; we should be able to show successful orders flowing through the system as well.
- *Sharing* is based on the idea that knowledge wants to be free! Humans often learn best when they're teaching something to someone else. Sharing is about creating that—ready for it—cultural re-enforcer! Knowledge management is incredibly important in a world where we continue to build more and more complex systems.

While my focus on CAMS varies throughout the book, understand that these four pillars are the underpinning for everything in a DevOps transformation. If you think back to these four pillars, you can solve a lot of problems inside your organization.

Why are you leaving out the "L" in CALMS?

Recently some people, including Andrew Clay Shafer himself, have taken to using the term CALMS, with the "L" standing for "lean." I prefer the original version and will be sticking to it. I highlight this difference in case you hear the term in the wild.

The idea behind CALMS is that delivering smaller, more frequent software updates is a preferred approach and that sometimes a minimal product in the hands of a customer is better than waiting six months for a more fleshed-out version.

I completely agree with this approach, but at the same time I recognize that your mileage may vary, depending on your industry. Some companies have customers who don't want frequent updates. Maybe they have a hardware certification process that makes allowing the latest updates a bit more cumbersome in smaller organizations. Maybe you're in an industry where a minimal product just isn't functional enough for customers to even experiment with. If you're in an already entrenched market, it's tough to get people to even consider your tool without meeting a wide range of capabilities.

I think a lean approach is incredibly smart. But I also think the cultural benefits of DevOps can apply even to sectors where the lean approach isn't practical. I leave out the "L" to divorce the two approaches and ensure that people can still benefit from DevOps, even if they're not releasing software to customers on a frequent basis.

1.3　*Another DevOps book?*

You're probably looking at this book and asking yourself, "Do I need another book that's going to tell me my company culture is toxic?" You probably don't. In all my years in this industry, I've never "enlightened" someone by saying that their company has a bad culture. Instead, most employees fall short in the understanding of *why* their company has a bad culture.

It's true that culture often comes from the top of the organizational chart, but it is equally true that various cultures exist within the same organization—some good, some bad. I can't promise that I can help you transform your entire organization with a few sips from the DevOps Kool-Aid, but I can promise you that I can help you transform your corner of the organization.

My motivation for writing this was driven by the number of people I meet who feel that because their manager isn't on board, they can't do DevOps. To some extent, that's true. For some areas, you need senior leadership buy-in. But there's still a lot of change that an individual contributor or a team lead can push through to make your lives and processes better. A little bit of investment will also free up some of your time that's currently spent on wasteful, low-value tasks and unleash that freed time on more productive work. This book takes a lot of the lessons that I've learned and distills them into a specific set of actions that you can take to bring the DevOps transformation out of the C-suite and down into the trenches.

Lastly, this book will be a little more prescriptive about the changes that are needed in your corner of the organization. Together we'll dive deeper than just case studies about how things are handled at Company X. Instead, we will come up with a specific set of actions that you will implement, tweak, and iterate on within your organization. Notice that I said "you." This isn't a book that will paint you as a hapless victim of poor management. You have the power to make your situation better. You will be the change agent that your organization needs to start this DevOps journey. All you need is a plan. Let's get started on that.

Summary

- DevOps is more than just a new set of tools. DevOps is truly about redefining the way you look at work and the relationship between tasks across different teams. The changes that a DevOps transformation brings will go beyond pure technology and stretch into the fabric of how we look at the nature of our work.
- To introduce change, you need a way to examine the problems within your organization and address these productivity killers. That's the meat of this book.
- Despite the need for culture, I recognize that most of you reading this will be engineers, biased toward action. I open up the first part of the book with examples of problems your organization is most likely experiencing and a few concrete approaches to solving them. Even in these scenarios, I highlight how company culture influences the current state of affairs. Let's start with the reasons Valentina has to call John in the middle of the night.

The paternalist syndrome

This chapter covers

- Replacing barriers in your process with safeguards
- Understanding the concept of gatekeeping
- Eliminating gatekeepers through automation
- Addressing key items when building approval automation

In some organizations, a group or groups seem to wield outsized power relative to their peers. The power is sometimes granted or enforced through things like access controls or approvals. The operations group may refuse to allow changes to systems without an extensive review process. The security team may prevent other teams from adopting technology created after 1984. The development group may refuse to build tools that allow people to make changes without their watchful eye.

The rules or mandates can typically be traced back to some inciting event that justified draconian action. But the very thing that was supposed to make the teams more effective instead drags them to a crawl. If you've seen this in your own company or teams, you're not alone.

I call this the *paternalist syndrome*, named after the parental relationship one group assumes over others. The paternalistic syndrome relies on gatekeepers to decide how and when work gets done. This concentration in power initially seems like a prudent decision but can quickly devolve into a productivity strain.

In this chapter, I'll walk you through a common example of how gatekeepers get introduced into a process. Then I'll break down the often-overlooked negative impact that introducing gatekeepers to a process can have. Stepping through the example, I'll challenge the expected gains in safety that the process and gatekeepers were intending to add.

Next, I'll discuss using automation to achieve the same goals more effectively. Automation is incredibly valuable because of its repeatability. Performing the same tasks in exactly the same way through scripts and programs will reduce variability and make your processes more audit friendly because of their consistent approach. I'll break down the true purpose of the approval process, followed by steps on following an automation approach to each of those core concerns.

2.1 *Creating barriers instead of safeguards*

Sometimes approval processes from other teams or groups adds real value. But often the involvement of another team is about something else. It's about a lack of trust between each other and a lack of safety inside your systems. Imagine I tell you to eat soup, but I give you no silverware to do it. My justification is that you might cut your mouth open when you try to eat your soup with a steak knife. It sounds insane, but that's the metaphor for what many companies do—and it's lazy. The better option, if I'm concerned about system safety, would be to give you a spoon and only a spoon: the best tool you need for a specific task.

For some of you, this idea of system safety might be a new concept. But I'm sure you've experienced in your career an unforgiving system that might allow you to do something catastrophic. Think of a system that allows you to permanently delete work without a confirmation prompt. (Thanks, Linux!) You become bewildered by how something like this could happen. You take extra precautions like saving multiple copies of the file in case the unexpected behavior happens again. Compare that with the same system that verifies and confirms the dangerous action with the user. That's the type of safety in systems that I'm referring to.

A design approach that prevents you from unknowingly performing a dangerous action should be one of the objectives of system usability. Because so many systems lack these safeguards, organizations compensate by limiting the number of people who can perform these tasks to an anointed few. But being selected as an "authorized" performer of a task doesn't make you infallible. Even an authorized performer can make a mistake, type the wrong command, or misunderstand the impact of an action.

What are you really accomplishing by limiting access to these types of tasks? You're not truly reducing risk, just concentrating the pressures of it on a select few. You also represent the problem as a personnel issue as opposed to a system issue. These engineers are competent enough to understand the impact, while others are not. When safety is missing in your systems, it manifests in the form of handoffs, approvals, and overly restrictive access controls.

Here are some problems that are introduced with overly restrictive access controls:

- Many organizations have teams with overlapping sets of responsibilities. This blurring of lines on technical teams can make it difficult to delineate when one scope of responsibility ends and when another begins between team members. As a developer, if I'm responsible for supporting a test suite, am I allowed to install software to support the test suite? Do I need to inform operations of an installation?
- If that installation breaks the server or is somehow incompatible, who is responsible for resolving the issue?
- Who has the access to actually troubleshoot it?

These are the types of questions that arise when responsibilities overlap. These steps are internally justified as safety protections, which have good intentions but can often spill into the area of the nonsensical.

In the case of an approval process, the process grows with every incident that occurs that isn't specifically handled by the current process. Every incident then leads to an addendum to the approval process, or worse, an extra approver. Before long, you have a heavy, burdensome process that isn't providing the value it's supposed to.

If you've ever attended an approval meeting, you're probably familiar with the situation. A room full of individuals, often managers, tries to assess the risk of a proposal. The meeting over time devolves into a rubber-stamp committee. A large portion of the changes cause zero negative impact, leading to a lower bar for acceptance. In many organizations, it's not long before change approval is considered a hurdle rather than a value-added process. You've been there. Deep down inside, you know it's that bad.

In many traditional organizations, the goal of removing artificial barriers and increasing collaboration is talked about and given a ton of lip service. But this talk is immediately sidelined when an incident occurs. Traditional organizations often reach into the approval toolbox to prevent future incidents. In a DevOps organization, the teams try to resist this urge at all costs. The goal is always to remove the artificial barriers, while still preserving the ones that add value.

Artificial barriers create a power dynamic between teams that can result in a *paternalistic* relationship between the requestor and the approver. Requestors can feel like a child asking their parents to borrow the Ferrari for a date night. This leads to a friction between teams due to an imbalance of power.

You might be reading and recognizing some of the problems discussed and the way they manifest themselves in your own environment. But the question on your mind might be, "Why DevOps?" There are several ways to solve these organizational problems, but the DevOps movement has caught on for a few reasons.

First, it tackles the cultural problems front and center. Some engineers may find it hard to think of things outside technical solutions. But if you take a look at your organization and think critically about what's plaguing it, you'll realize that your problem is more often people (and how they work together) than technology. No technology will solve your prioritization process. No technology will magically align your goals so that teams are working with each other instead of against each other. Email was supposed to solve our communications issues. Then it was cell phones, and now it's instant messaging and chat applications. All these tools have done is allowed us to communicate poorly, faster. This isn't to say that technology isn't part of the DevOps transformation. It just happens to be the easy part.

Another important part of the DevOps movement is its focus on the cost of wasted human potential. If you think about your role, I'm sure you do certain things on a regular basis that could be replaced with a program or a script, freeing you up to do more impactful things. DevOps focuses on maximizing the work you do that will bring lasting value to the organization. It means taking the task that would normally take just five minutes to complete and turning it into a week-long automation task. The value of spending the time on the automation means someone will be waiting a lot longer for their request, but it'll be the last time they'll have to wait. You'll never have to waste those five minutes again. Eliminating the wasted minutes in our workdays leads to a boon in productivity. From a technology viewpoint, it also helps when it comes to retaining talent, as engineers are free to work on more complicated and interesting tasks, versus the common rote tasks of the day.

The goals of DevOps are the following:

- Increase collaboration among teams
- Decrease unnecessary gates and handoffs
- Empower development teams with the tools and authority to own their systems
- Create repeatable, predictable processes
- Share responsibilities for the application production environment

DevOps helps organizations deliver on these areas by following the *CAMS model*. As you learned in the preceding chapter, *CAMS* is an abbreviation for culture, automation, metrics, and sharing (see section 1.2). These four areas help create the conditions necessary for DevOps adoptions to thrive.

A change in *culture* or mindset around how you work can enable people to do their jobs and eliminate wasteful gates. This culture change will lead teams to the need for automation. *Automation* is a powerful tool in creating repeatable processes and, when properly implemented, allows anyone on the team to perform an action consistently. The culture changes and the increase in shared responsibilities creates a need for *metrics* to help everyone understand the state of the systems. Being able to confirm that something is working is more valuable than just being able to confirm there are no errors. Finally, the *sharing* component helps ensure that the DevOps philosophy continues to grow throughout the team as opposed to being constrained to a select few. Sharing knowledge is a requirement for sharing responsibility. You cannot ask for your team members to take additional ownership without some sort of on-ramp for their learning needs. People need to understand parts of the system, at least at a high level, to accommodate the increase in responsibility. You're going to need to create a structure to facilitate that sharing. As the level of automation and the amount of shared responsibility increases, the incentives for information hoarding begin to crumble.

You can't achieve these goals when every interaction between teams is stuck behind layers of approvals, requests, and power trips. These types of activities in processes are *gatekeeper* tasks. If you're not careful, they can add unnecessary delays, create friction among teams, and incentivize people to avoid the gate at any cost, sometimes creating a less-than-optimal solution.

> **DEFINITION** *Gatekeeping* occurs when a person or process serves as an artificial barrier that regulates access to a resource of some kind.

Gatekeepers are at the heart of the paternalist syndrome. The paternalist syndrome happens when a gatekeeper function is introduced because of an absence of trust. That trust could have been eroded by an earlier incident or it may have never existed in the first place. The paternalist syndrome thrives on the idea that *only a certain person or group of people are qualified and trustworthy enough to perform or approve an action.* This creates friction between teams because the gate process creates a barrier for teams to get their work done. When the gate adds no real value, it's viewed as a parental function, with the requestor needing to explain or justify their request.

2.2 *Introducing the gatekeepers*

Stephanie works in the IT operations department for a local health-care organization. She receives a request from Terrance, a developer on the billing team, to deploy the billing application at 4 p.m. this afternoon. Terrance wants to apply a patch before the billing run that is scheduled to happen over the weekend and wants to make sure there's ample time to roll back the application if necessary.

Stephanie gets all the details and agrees that 4 p.m. is a reasonable time for the deployment. She works with the billing team regularly and knows that the group is usually done using the application by noon each day. Stephanie waits until the 4 p.m. start time and begins the deployment. The process is smooth and goes without a hitch. She notices that two people were logged into the application when she began the deployment, but that's not uncommon because many people remain logged in long after they've finished their use of the system. Terrance verifies that the application is functioning as intended, and they consider the deployment a success.

The following morning, Stephanie is pulled into her manager's office. Terrance is already there, head hung low. Stephanie's manager informs her that a couple of billing team members were working in the system later than usual in order to fulfill a last-minute request by the accounts receivable team. Because of the request, they were manually updating a large volume of bills, which is done in a three-step process. The deployment occurred in the middle of that process, and a lot of valuable data-entry time was lost and would need to be reentered. The manager of the billing department is irate and demands that something be done to prevent this from happening again. This gives birth to the company's very first *change management* policy.

> **DEFINITION** *Change management* is an organization's standardized process for introducing changes to an application or system. The process typically involves a statement of the work to be done, which is submitted to a governing body to be approved for a given window of time.

In discussing the situation with the billing and the IT department, it's decided that all deployments should go through a formal review process. Stephanie and the rest of the operations staff will be required to get approval from the billing department before any deployments. The billing department will coordinate among themselves to approve a requested deployment window, but they ask that they get at least a one-day notice, so that they can receive sign-off from everyone in the billing department. Stephanie is responsible for supporting more than just the billing system, so she needs to be able to plan this work out on her end as well.

Stephanie asks that any deployment requests coming from the development teams be submitted at least three days before the requested date. This ensures that Stephanie and her team members have enough time to work the request into their schedules and give the billing team enough notice, so that they can gather the appropriate signatures on their end as well. In addition, the teams agree that a deployment should not continue if users are logged into the system, in order to prevent a user from being disconnected. After a few rounds of discussion, the team agrees to the following process steps:

1 A developer submits a change ticket to Operations.
2 If the change ticket doesn't give the operations department at least a three-day notice, it's immediately rejected, and the developer is asked to resubmit with new dates.
3 The billing team reviews their work schedule. If there is a scheduling conflict with other billing team work, the change is rejected, and the developer is asked to resubmit with new dates.
4 The change is officially approved.
5 The change is implemented.

The process as defined appears to assuage the concerns of the group. But this is a traditional response to a traditional problem. In a DevOps organization, the focus is on removing these types of gated requests and placing a focus on efficient and fast delivery, which is enabled by favoring automated solutions versus adding additional bottlenecks to delivery. Additionally, this process has several subtle side effects that will impact the team. The next section takes a deeper dive at the proposed process and highlights where it falls a bit short.

2.3 Examining the gatekeepers

Everyone agrees that this new process should ensure that they no longer have this problem going forward and that communication regarding these sorts of changes will be greatly enhanced as a by-product of the new policy. But the new policy introduces a few new problems to the equation. Because the team is so focused on preventing future occurrences, they don't think about the additional strain being placed on the organization.

Additionally, gatekeepers are not thinking of the system holistically. Instead, they opt for local optimization of a problem, which might solve one problem but leads to new problems from a complete systems perspective. As an example, the deployment process now requires a three-day notification. In practice, this limits the billing application to being deployed only once per week. This can make addressing pressing items like bug fixes difficult to deploy quickly. In fact, urgent deploys may force you to circumvent the new process. By optimizing for one specific issue (approvals to ensure that work isn't lost), you've slowed and hampered the system as a whole by limiting the ability for the billing application to be deployed quickly.

The new process also requires a lot of extra communication between teams. Talking to team members isn't a bad thing, usually, but the overhead of the approval process can grind the deployment process to a halt if the billing team isn't responsive. These artificial delays build up a resentment toward the process, inviting people to avoid the process at all costs. I personally have never exaggerated a problem so that it could be justified as an emergency change situation and bypass the approval process—all so I could avoid getting paged over the weekend and attend a barbeque in peace. But you could see how someone might do that.

Lastly, another unintended side effect could be that user inaction could result in a deployment being cancelled. If users aren't good about logging off at the end of the day, an innocent mistake could lead to a cancelled deployment. This cancellation deprives customers of new features or functionality with no gain to the business. Plus, it's extremely hard to explain to people why the release was cancelled. "We were ready to deploy, but Frank never replied to our email, so we cancelled the whole release." Sounds a little lame.

If users continue to forget to log off, over time it creates confusion for operations teams as they try to evaluate whether users are genuinely active or merely forgot to log off for the evening. Table 2.1 outlines a few of the new problems introduced by the change management policy that need to be taken into consideration when making a decision on the policy's efficacy..

Table 2.1   New problems introduced by the change management policy

Change	Problem introduced	Discussion
Three days' notification required.	Limits billing application deployment to one per week.	How does this impact the capability to release bug fixes quickly?
Extra communication between teams.	Approval process slows further if the billing team isn't available.	How does the billing team reach consensus? How much does that cost the company in time?
If users are in the system, the deployment is aborted.	Users might forget to log off at the end of their shift.	How does the operations team evaluate whether a user session is valid or a user forgot to log off?

This is the sort of overreaction that fuels the paternalist syndrome. Instead of examining the system and how it contributes to the problem, the team has focused their energy on the individual decisions of team members. This is unproductive and puts the blame on the people instead of the process. Even more damning, it doesn't solve the problem; instead, it just adds more time to the overall workflow.

For starters, we've increased the communication time to at least three days. This means that without careful planning, we're limited to a single deployment per week for the billing application. Depending on how fast the team develops features, this might be acceptable. But we're introducing this delay as the result of a single occurrence. Every other deployment has completed without an issue. Now the teams are forcing every single deployment to go through this process! In addition, we risk every deployment being potentially blocked by users who have not properly logged out at the end of their day. Figure 2.1 illustrates the process and some of the problems that are introduced as a result.

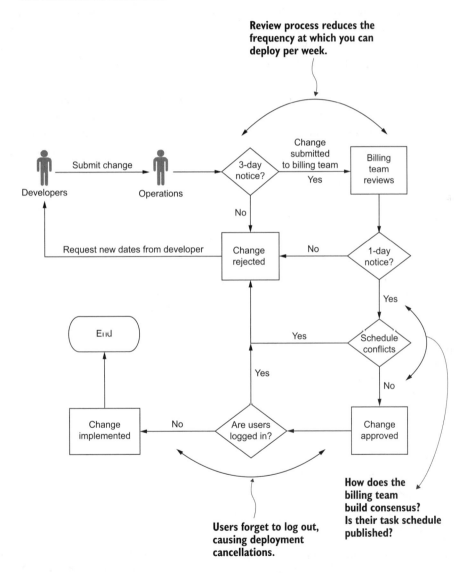

Figure 2.1   The new approval process introduces new issues.

The stated goal of the new process is to prevent a disruption of work due to a deployment of the application. But the process doesn't meet that goal. And it not only doesn't meet the goal, but also actively slows down all future changes in a poor attempt to remove this specific type of failure.

In reality, a simple missed step in the process can create a deployment that disrupts a user's work and results in lost productivity. Figure 2.2 highlights a few points in the process that might be susceptible to human error, resulting in lost or disrupted work.

You may be thinking, "But then that means someone didn't follow the rules!" That's true; the process creates ample opportunity for finger-wagging and telling people just how important the rules are. But I can think of a few scenarios in which an operator follows the process but still risks losing work. Maybe a billing user forgot that today was the day for the deployments. Or perhaps a particular user wasn't consulted about the change. In fact, the entire approval process within the billing department could be highly suspect!

This is why DevOps advocates for automation over manual approvals. The approval process can be easily circumvented and leads to variance in one deployment versus another. This variance is a source of pain when you need to audit a process or when you need to ensure that the exact process is followed every single time it's executed.

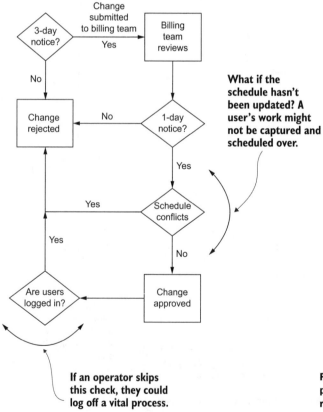

What if the schedule hasn't been updated? A user's work might not be captured and scheduled over.

If an operator skips this check, they could log off a vital process.

Figure 2.2   A few key areas in the process are susceptible to error, resulting in possible data loss.

2.4 *Curing paternalism through automation*

You can use technology to replace a lot of the manual approval processes in a flow. Using the preceding deployment process example, think about how automation might solve some of the problems raised. The three-day notification window is intended to give humans enough time to review the work in progress and make sure things are OK to deploy. But machines can do this instantly, without all of the scheduling and prioritization conflicts that human approvers would have. Automation is a perfect solution for this and many other approval types of processes.

Depending on the nature of your process, some components will be easily automated, while others might require a bit more consideration based on the risks involved. Because the feasibility of automating approvals varies, you'll need to examine the purpose of the approval process.

You'll want to begin by assembling your team. The team needs to extend beyond just the engineers who are looking to automate the process. You want this solution to be holistic, so the team should expand to include the gatekeepers and others involved in the process. This helps to account for all viewpoints of the system.

You also want to be sure that you're including those gatekeepers in the design of the process. Gatekeepers come into existence to help alleviate a perceived risk, real or imagined. They may feel that their concerns are being dismissed or downplayed if they're not involved in the design of a new process or solution. This lack of involvement will make getting their support an uphill battle.

Once your team has been assembled, you'll want to begin to have them commit to the effort of automating the process. It sounds basic, but so many automation efforts fail because the team can't create a mental model of what an automated process flow looks like. They're rooted in these ideas of human evaluation and can't think of how that might be replaced by an automation algorithm and what those steps look like. As a result, the idea of automation is rejected out of hand. "It's too complicated to automate" is a common excuse. If the world can automate a jet-liner landing, I assure you that you're up to the task of automating your approval process.

An initial discussion with the team highlighting the benefits of automating the process is in line. You can focus on topics like the following:

- Reducing time spent in the approval process
- Reducing time spent on administrative tasks
- Reducing iteration time
- Creating consistency in the process flow

Getting consensus that the approval process can be improved is more important than hashing out the solution in this initial discussion. It's not uncommon for members to disagree about the value of the current process (especially the actual gatekeepers). As a group, you cannot solve a problem if you don't all agree on what the problem is. Spend this initial discussion getting the group to understand *why* the approval process needs improvement. This is going to be unique to your organization and specific process, but be sure to examine the unintended side effects of your process. Don't concentrate on the solution at this stage. That's for later. Use this time to get agreement on the problems and the ultimate goal.

Through subsequent meetings, you can begin to work with the team to construct a high-level outline of your approach. You might not tackle everything at once. If there are easy wins you can make, do it! Plenty of value is to be had by iterating on your automation and expanding it over time. You may decide that parts of the process need to remain as manual approvals because of various risks. That's fine, as long as the working group agrees on the risk and the manual approval being the best remedy. Remember, you're not attempting to automate all of the manual approvals, just the ones that aren't adding any real value.

With these items as discussion topics, you can create consensus around the team so that everyone agrees on the deficiencies of the manual process, as opposed to throwing up roadblocks for why automation will fail. Now that the team has consensus, you can take the request to any leadership that needs to approve or prioritize this work.

When bringing the request for prioritization to leadership, be sure to highlight not just the gains in efficiencies that the team expects, but also places where the current process falls short. You can be assured that almost any manual process will involve variability. Automation can help to eliminate or greatly reduce the variability, lowering the chance for any sort of human error or process mistake. If necessary, you can also assign a dollar value to the meetings and coordination necessary for every change. With leadership on board and your work ready to prioritize, you can move on to the details of implementing your change.

In our specific example, approvals are required by a person. This may seem difficult to automate at first. But the gated approval process is just a proxy for another concern. If you can concretely define that concern, automating the concern becomes easier.

2.5   *Capturing the purpose of the approval*

Only a really sick person would create an approval process just for the sake of it. An approval process is typically created to ensure that all necessary concerns surrounding the process have been addressed. Those concerns will vary from process to process. But whenever you're automating an approval step, you should think about the concern that the approval process is a proxy for.

As a nontechnical example, when you go to borrow money from a bank, you must answer a series of questions that may seem a bit invasive. But once you understand that those questions are an attempt to alleviate a larger concern, the questions make sense. If you apply for a loan personally, the loan giver wants to know about your other debts. It's not because they're interested in whom else you owe, but they're using your debt as a proxy to understand your other outstanding commitments and how that might impact your ability to repay their loan.

As a technical example, an approver may want to be sure that a change was peer-reviewed. It's not that the original work is untrustworthy, but it's important to ensure that it's been viewed from multiple angles and perspectives. This is an example of capturing the purpose of an approval.

The approval step in a manual process is typically trying to capture and convey a few facts, as follows:

- All parts of the process are in an appropriate state for the work to continue.
- The necessary people are informed that the work is occurring.
- There are no conflicting actions that should prevent the change from happening.
- The risk of the change is acceptable to the organization.

Each of these concerns can be streamlined to a degree with automation, preventing the need for the tedious approval process.

2.6 *Structuring code for automation*

Continuing our example from earlier in the chapter, the billing deployment process was working fine until a deployment caused the billing team to lose work that was in progress. This deployment incident created the desire for an approval process. In the team's haste to ensure that everything was in order, several manual approval steps and delivery timelines were established. This, however, is an overreaction to the problem.

It may seem faster to quickly implement manual gating, but the team could have focused on making the deployment process smarter and safer. The task may seem daunting initially, but you can start your automation small and modestly. Plan for the case where things are working out as you would normally expect them to. If anything deviates, simply error out with a message and use your manual process as a backup. This section walks through an approach to codifying various approval concerns.

When you attempt to automate the process, it's important that steps be structured appropriately. Every automated workflow will have to handle a series of concerns:

- *Approval process*—What are the checks necessary to ensure that this is allowed to execute?
- *Logging process*—Where does automation log the request, the approval, the execution, and the results?
- *Notification process*—Where does automation notify people that the action was taken? (This notification process can be the same as the logging process, but some people may opt for a notification that gets pushed to the user like email, instead of a passive process like logging, where the user has to proactively look for the notification themselves.)
- *Error handling*—How much automatic recovery do you perform?

The needs of your automation might grow and contract over time as changing requirements and guidelines begin to muddy the waters on your original concept. This is a common problem in application design. The catch here, though, is that the automation of processes is often looked at as a series of simple scripts that are quickly cobbled together. But to echo the immortal words of Admiral Ackbar, "It's a trap!"

By not treating these automation tasks with the respect they demand, you end up with automation that is often inflexible, error prone, and difficult to understand and maintain. Structure even the most mundane of scripts with the thoughtfulness you would afford a full-blown application. Try to think about how the script has different concerns and try to separate those concerns into manageable, maintainable code. Let's start with the approval process.

2.6.1 *Approval process*

When implementing an approval process, you need to think about the reasons the manual approval process came into being. To reiterate, at a minimum, an approval process is typically trying to mitigate four areas of concern:

- All parts of the process are in an appropriate state for the work to continue.
- The necessary people are informed that the work is occurring.
- There are no conflicting actions that should prevent the change from happening.
- The risk of the change is acceptable to the organization.

WORK IS IN THE APPROPRIATE STATE

During the approval process, an approver may want to verify that work steps are in a place so teams can move forward. This is an important concern for approvers and will be one of several checks you'll need to automate. This might be something as simple as ensuring that the request was peer reviewed, or more complex like ensuring that the database is in the correct state before executing.

In our example, the billing team wants to approve deployments to ensure that no scheduling conflicts exist among other billing team members, because a deployment while people are updating the system could result in lost work. A good approval process isn't just a gut check. Deciding whether the deployment should be approved could easily be completed via automation by describing the things that an approver would normally look for. There should be specific states and conditions that an approver evaluates to determine whether to approve or not. What those conditions are will be specific to your solution and organization. I've seen a few common factors in process approvals:

- Any work that exists in the team's work-tracking system has been completed.
- Prerequisites for the task, such as data or file transfers, have been completed.
- Dependent data is in the right state.
- Peer review has occurred.
- The action or change has gone through the appropriate testing cycle.

This list will vary depending on your organization and the actual process you're attempting to automate, but be sure to identify these factors. The best place to get this information is from the approver. Asking the approver questions about the approval process should provide good details about what they look for as part of their process. Ask questions like these:

- What do you look for that would cause you to automatically deny an approval request?
- What are the things you look for that make you question a request?
- What are things that every request you approve must have?

When you question the approver, you'll probably be surprised by the number of things they report to look at versus the number of things they look for in practice. Feel free to push for details on why a component is important or how that need might be satisfied elsewhere. It's all good information to get for the automation of the process.

With the list of items approvers check for, you can begin thinking about how you'll replicate these checks via automation. These items are all simple binary tests—yes or no, right or wrong, approved or not approved. In most cases, any automation you write will mimic these Boolean tests. If the Boolean tests all succeed, the request is approved and the work that was waiting on the approval gate can continue.

THE NECESSARY PEOPLE ARE INFORMED

Ensuring that the necessary people are informed is probably the easiest hurdle to cross and adds the most value, because it will happen consistently, no matter who is executing the process. Your automation scripts can maintain notification lists to be triggered at any stage of the process, or you can send a summary email when things have completed or have changed status. The key is that this task is consistently performed, and if designed correctly, can easily add or remove users from the notification process.

THERE ARE NO CONFLICTING ACTIONS

Coordination and orchestration can be difficult problems to solve, but plenty of well-known patterns can combat this. You tend to not apply these technical solutions, however, when you're dealing with a mixture of humans and automated systems, but locking mechanisms are an excellent solution for this!

In code, you'll often have protected portions or functions that need exclusivity to a resource. You usually solve this through a locking mechanism or semaphore in code. If one piece of code is currently accessing the named semaphore, other pieces of the code need to stop and wait until they can acquire the lock exclusively to move on with their code. There's no reason the same principles can't be applied in processes that have human components.

THE RISK OF CHANGE IS ACCEPTABLE TO THE ORGANIZATION

Making sure that the risk of change is acceptable is probably the most difficult piece to automate holistically. For this, it's important to separate changes into two categories: standard and nonstandard changes.

Borrowing from the language of IT service management (ITSM), "a *standard change* is a change to a service or infrastructure for which the approach is pre-authorized by change management that has an accepted and established procedure." In layman terms, that just means that everyone involved has agreed on the work to be done, understands how to do it, and, understands its impact. Restarting a web service might be considered a standard change, because the approach is well-documented, preapproved, and has a known set of outcomes. Running ad hoc scripts, however, may not be considered a standard change, because the content of the script might change from execution to execution.

This is an area where human approval could be necessary. Just make sure you're separating the action (for example, the deployment or the script execution) from the change when instituting approvals. In a deployment scenario, you might be tempted to think that the deployment of new code is always going to be a nonstandard change. After all, the change is new and different in each release, similar to the previous ad hoc script example. But the primary difference is that the actual change to the code has already gone through an approval process of some sort to get to a position where it can be deployed. Feature requests, user acceptance testing, and pull request reviews are all examples of gates that you place on new code in order to get it to a place where it can be deployed. The actual process of the deployment is standard and should be able to move forward without further approval, assuming the other approval checks have passed, hopefully via automation.

A similar process could apply to script executions. The approval process may dictate that each script, regardless of its actions, is reviewed by a senior engineer. But how the action makes its way through the process could be considered a standard change. How thorough the review process needs to be will ultimately depend on your organization and your comfort level.

2.6.2   *Automating approvals*

With this understanding of the primary approval concerns, you can begin to think about how you would encapsulate these concerns into some form of automation. These four concerns of having work in the appropriate state, informing the necessary people, ensuring there's no conflicting work, and accepting the risk to the organization still need to happen, but by making these checks programmatically, we can greatly reduce the workload on humans in the approval process. Keep in mind that the approval process is something that will change over time. The number of states that you're checking for will change. Continuing with our billing example, today you might be checking only for users being logged into the system. That's a conflicting action that would force the change to be denied. But tomorrow, a new condition could be added. Then you'll need to check for users logged into the system and this new additional condition. Your automation design needs to be able to adapt to these changes in approval criteria.

Designing this portion of the process requires forethought and planning. To start with, you'll want to separate your automation into two areas: one that handles the actual approvals and one that handles whatever command needs to execute if the approvals are granted. In this section, we're going to focus on the actual approvals code.

For starters, think of all of the things that an approver might check when a request is submitted. Earlier in the chapter, I gave a few examples of things approvers might look for:

- Prerequisites for the task, such as data or file transfers, have been completed.
- Dependent data is in the right state.
- Peer review has occurred.
- The action or change has gone through the appropriate testing cycle.

Each of these needs to be represented programmatically somehow. But a major area of concern is that each of these checks might be radically different. Despite these differences, you'll want to be able to treat them more or less the same. This allows you to add new checks easily.

To accomplish this, using a *base class* for approvals is a good idea. The base class can require that all inherited approval classes follow a similar structure. The most useful pattern you'd want is for all approvals to report approval or denial in the same way. This allows you to check many approval types without needing to know the intricacies of the approval you're checking against.

Listing 2.1   Define a base class for your approvals

Defines a base class

```
class BaseApproval:
    def is_approved(self):
        raise NotImplementedError()
    def error_message(self):
        raise NotImplementedError()
```

Defines a standard method to check approval status

In the base class, forces inherited classes to override this method

Has a standard method to retrieve error messages

With the base class defined, you can inherit from this class for your individual approvals. Treat the approval like an abstract class: you'll never instantiate it directly, only via inheritance. The goal with the individual approvals is to create a list of objects that you will be able to instantiate and call in order to ensure that the approvals have been met.

With the base class defined, all approvals inherit from the base class. This makes sure that the approvals all define the is_approved method for easier success checking. For example, the peer-review requirement would be built into its own approval named PeerApproval. This allows you to put all of the logic necessary to check that a request has been peer approved into a single place. The is_approved method for the PeerApproval class performs the approval-checking logic specific to that type of approval and provides a value indicating approval or denial. But this logic is all contained within the PeerApproval class, and thanks to the is_approved method being well-defined, anyone using it doesn't need to know the specific internals of the approval.

As an example, listing 2.2 shows an approval class that checks to ensure that a peer in the group has approved the request. This means that no potential conflicts are present in the state of the system.

Listing 2.2   `PeerApproval` class inheriting from the base class

```
class PeerApproval(BaseApproval):
    def is_approved(self):
        approvers = self.check_approvers()
        if len(approvers) > 0:
            return (True, "")
        else:
            return (False, "No approvals submitted")
```

A helper method you would implement to get the list of approvers

Checks the size of the list of approvers

If approvers are in the list, the check passes with a blank error message.

If it doesn't, returns a false with an error message

You see that the code returns a tuple object, with the first value in the tuple being a Boolean indicating whether the check was approved. The second field contains an error message. This is used for communicating back to the calling program why the check failed, which will ultimately get reported back to the end user. The method is pretty straightforward but can become more or less complicated depending on the situation. The benefit here is all of that complexity is encapsulated in a separate object, away from the actual executed command that the automation is intended to run.

If you wanted to create another approval to check that there are no logged-in users, you might create another class called `SessionsApproval`. This would be a separate class that also inherits from the `BaseApproval` class. By repeating this pattern for every approval concern, you'll have a collection of approvals that need to be checked to ensure that all of the individual concerns have been met. Figure 2.3 shows the relationship between the `BaseApproval` class and an implementation of an inherited class. Then you can group all of those approvals into a collection of some sort, like an array.

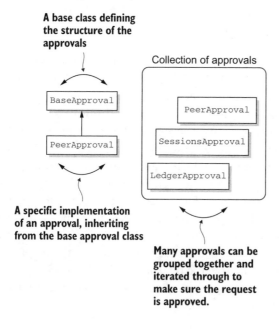

A base class defining the structure of the approvals

Collection of approvals

A specific implementation of an approval, inheriting from the base approval class

Many approvals can be grouped together and iterated through to make sure the request is approved.

Figure 2.3   The composition of classes for the approval process

Now with your separate approvals created, you can implement this collection of approvals by creating a list of all the objects that belong to the approval process and invoke those methods individually in a loop. This makes it easy to add new approval steps without having to make a ton of changes to the main execution code.

```
import sys
def main():
    approval_classes = [PeerApproval,SessionApproval,LedgerApproval]
    for approval_class in approval_classes:
        result = approval_class().is_approved()
        if result[0] == False:
            sys.exit(result[1])
```

List holds all of your Approval objects.

If it's not approved, exits with the error message

Instantiates class and checks whether approval is good

You can repeat this approach across all of the areas of approval concerns, encapsulating each check into a different approval class. This allows you to expand and contract the list of approvals as your system becomes more robust and the approval criteria changes over time.

2.6.3 *Logging process*

Ensuring that your approval is logged helps address the concern of informing the necessary people. This is more of a pull process than a push process, meaning that the information exists for those who want to retrieve it, but it isn't proactively given to the user. You might use a logging process more when the automation's execution has value after the script has been run, either for auditing or troubleshooting purposes. When automation logs to a central location, it becomes much easier for people who did not participate in the change to become aware of it and its details. Murphy's law states that if you're involved with a change, you certainly won't be involved with the incident that gets created as a result of it.

Defining how your application is going to log the various steps it has taken will depend heavily on your organization and its audit requirements. I highly recommend that any automated tasks be backed by a supporting ticket in whatever issue- or work-tracking tool your company uses. The creation of the ticket can be tied into the automation as well, since most issue-tracking software solutions have well-documented APIs. By tying the work that your automation is doing to a ticket, it becomes instantly trackable, visible, and reportable by the same systems, controls, and standards that other processes within your organization are doing today. This can be enormously powerful in communicating to everyone what's happening in the environment.

At my current employer, Centro, we use Jira Software as our automation tracking tool (figure 2.4). Through comments on existing tickets, you can see the progress of the automation code as it progresses through its workload. The automation is responsible for updating the comments in the Jira Software ticket automatically. This eliminates any

Figure 2.4   Automation commenting on a ticket throughout the process

variance in the process, whereas a human might forget to make the appropriate comment or note the wrong time for a change that was made. Automation makes this consistent.

This is the type of system that makes auditors happy. If you want to get a free lunch from your auditor, you're going to want to ensure that as much of the process is requested, approved, tracked, and logged in a single place. Your ticketing system makes the most sense, but even if you split up these activities, you should make sure that the record for each step or transaction flows back into a single system. Don't be that person who has to take screenshots from seven different systems to provide proof that your latest change isn't embezzling money.

2.6.4   *Notification process*

The notification process is one of those superfluous steps that you need to have. When something goes wrong, everyone will be clamoring to make sure they're notified when a process is run. After a handful of successful runs, the notifications will be the victim of email filters that send them into a folder named "Delete after 15 days." The only time they'll be referenced is when someone needs to confirm that they were notified, before they go on a tirade complaining about how they weren't notified. It's a game you'll play, because despite its predictable trajectory, it's still a reasonable request.

When possible, it makes the most sense to use notifications through an existing system that will handle delivery for you. The most common notification is, of course, email, but you might have someone who needs to look extremely concerned and ask for a text message or something. If you have an on-call system like PagerDuty (www.pagerduty .com) or Opsgenie (www.opsgenie.com), it could be worthwhile to interface with that service's APIs. This simplifies the handling of messaging, leaving it to the user to configure how they want the notification, (email, text message, phone call), and up to the service to manage how to make that delivery happen. The drawback to this approach is that it limits your notifications to the few individuals who have accounts with the service. This can become cost prohibitive with a tool that is licensed per user. If this approach doesn't work, you'll want to resort to good old-fashioned email.

When you're designing notification via email, you'll want to take care that you don't sign yourself up for unnecessary work. For starters, try not to maintain individual emails in your application directly. Instead, rely on distribution lists when possible. This helps to prevent a few things:

- You won't have to tinker with email lists as people want to be added or removed.
- When an employee leaves the company, the termination process should handle the removal of that user from the system. That way, you avoid maintaining a list and generating a bunch of bounce-back emails every time someone leaves.
- The management of the notification list can be handled through the organization's service desk process. Unless, of course, you are the service desk, in which case there's no real escape from this pain of user management.

When designing the notification process, you want to be wary of any task that's going to generate more management work for you and the team, taking precious time away from the value-added activities you do. Think about user management, list management, hiring and termination, and notification delivery confirmation, just to name a few. Avoid these problems like the plague! Either make it someone else's problem by outsourcing the process entirely (with organizational tools like PagerDuty) or by using and interfacing with existing processes inside the organization, like the service desk.

2.6.5 *Error handling*

The only thing certain about your job is that you're going to fail at it sooner or later. This includes any code you write around automating tasks. Error handling can be a complicated affair. Your natural instinct will be to handle every error automatically, using the most logical response pattern as the default behavior. My suggestion to you is to resist this urge with every fiber of your being.

It's a good idea to handle the well-known cases of failure. But well-known errors also mean well-known solutions if you intend to auto-remediate things. Maybe the web server commonly gets into a bad state, and you know that you need to restart it when it enters into this state. Sounds straightforward enough, but what if the service is in a bad state for a different reason? What if there's critical, compute-intense code running on the web server, causing excessive load, simulating the behaviors you've commonly associated with a different failure pattern? The list of things that could go wrong is long, but the specific resolution could be more elusive than you think.

When in doubt, the best option in my opinion is to error out, provide the user with as much information as possible, and make sure the task is in a state that can be restarted. Log the error message in the same place you're putting log messages for the automation task (hopefully, in your ticketing system). Be as verbose as you need, but the more information that goes into the ticket, the easier it is to understand what went wrong. The same goes for auto-recovering from an error. If your code is smart enough to detect a failure and choose an appropriate remediation path, that detection of the error, along with the remediation path, should also be posted into your logging solution for the process.

As you become more and more aware of failure scenarios, you can code for them to be handled, slowly building up a reservoir of smart remediation steps. Don't attempt to solve for everything on day one. There's a lot of change happening, and sometimes just erroring out is the best solution.

2.7   *Ensuring continuous improvement*

With an approach laid out, you can begin to implement the automation of the approval process. Remember that you don't have to be perfect right out of the gate! Commit time to iterating on this process and improving each piece little by little. By removing some of these artificial gates, you'll start empowering team members and you'll notice an instant improvement in relationships, whether between development and operations, or development and customer-facing support. By removing manual, low-value gatekeeping tasks, you can increase your cycle time and get things done faster. Think of all the things you can do now that you're not stuck waiting for a day or two for an approval and implementation from another team!

Never assume, however, that this is a one-time commitment. This code that gets created will need to be maintained and updated as new use cases arise. You'll need to continuously build in the appropriate capacity and prioritization processes for your team to ensure that this work gets handled, something this book discusses in the later chapters.

Summary

- Examine processes for unnecessary gatekeeping.
- Understand the drivers for the approvals.
- Create automation to address those approval concerns.
- Structure automation to address concerns for logging, notification, and error handling.
- Commit to continuous improvement of your automation.

Operational blindness 3

This chapter covers

- Making changes in operations functions
- Creating useful system metrics for your application
- Creating useful logging habits

When you launch a system, you expect it to perform a set of tasks, in a certain order, with a few expected results. Sometimes you might expect an error in the process, and you'll need to perform some sort of cleanup process around that error. But the complexity of getting the system to work in the best of times leaves a lot of room for improvement in the way the tool performs in the worst of times.

Creating tools to confirm that work is happening the way you expected gets omitted, leaving you with no clear view as to what's happening in your system. Instead, teams rely on easily obtained metrics that offer no real business context into how the system is performing. While you have generic performance numbers, you're effectively blind from an operational viewpoint. This operational blindness prevents you from making good decisions about your system.

3.1   *War stories*

It's the middle of the day when a notification goes off in the operations group. Almost in lockstep with that page, emails and instant messages begin firing off. People begin popping up from their desks, trying to figure out whether the notification reached just their computer or something larger is going on. The website is down. The external monitoring of the website failed its last three health checks, which triggered the alert.

Unfortunately, the alert isn't descriptive enough to point the teams toward an area to focus on, so they're starting from scratch. The first thing they check are the usual suspects. The system metrics for the web server look fine. Memory is OK, a small spike in CPU seems within limits, and disk performance is within limits. Then they move this same check down to the database layer, and those metrics are equally OK.

The operations team escalates to development since the servers seem to be functioning normally. The development team isn't 100% sure what to look at either. They don't have any access to the production system, so they have to go work alongside the operations group, dictating commands to them. Together they realize there's a large number of queries that are running on the database, most of them in a waiting state. Looking at the web server they see an equally large number of processes, most likely web requests waiting for their corresponding SQL queries to finish. At some point the web servers reached capacity and stopped responding to new requests, like the health check page. After some deeper investigation the team was able to cancel the blocking query, allowing all of the other queries to complete and for the web server to drain its queue and begin processing new requests again.

A lot of time was wasted trying to ascertain the source of the problem. When the issue was escalated, the people who were escalated to were not empowered to see a view of the system that was useful to them in their troubleshooting. Instead they were still heavily reliant on the operations groups. In this scenario, every minute of downtime cost money, so that reliance now has a dollar figure attached to it.

Despite all the graphs, charts and alerts the team members had around system metrics, they were not any closer to understanding when their system was misbehaving. There was a spike in CPU utilization, but was that relevant? If CPU utilization is at 90% does that impact the customer? Teams monitor these metrics because in a lot of cases, that's all that is available to them. In our example above, these system metrics were fine, which exhausted the team's ability to troubleshoot, forcing an escalation. But even after escalating, the metrics that would have been helpful were not being collected and therefore not being alerted against. The system was not asking (and answering) the right questions about its performance. For many organizations, logging contains an incredible amount of insight as to what's going on in the system. For example, long-running queries can be configured to log themselves in your database logs. But for many reasons, this insight remains locked away, untapped for the purposes of understanding system performance. Hopefully I'll be able to help you leverage both metrics and logging more effectively.

In this chapter, you'll learn about the different ways DevOps organizations look at metrics and what they tell you about how your system is performing in a business context. In order to understand these business contexts though, developers and operations staff will need a deeper, more in-depth understanding of the application systems they are supporting. You'll read about different methods for generating metrics that should be tracked in your system. The chapter wraps up with a discussion on logging and log aggregation. With systems becoming broader and more dispersed, centralized logging is a necessity in just about any sized organization.

3.2 *Changing the scope of development and operations*

Throughout this book, I've written about DevOps going beyond just technological change to also change how teams work together and collaborate. There's no greater example of this than the change in roles and responsibilities of the development and operations teams in a DevOps organization.

Traditionally, a bright red line has divided the responsibilities of development and operations. Operations was tasked with the underlying hardware and infrastructure that made application delivery possible. Ironically, the definition of "delivery" was muddled and shortsighted. If the server was up, and networking was functioning, and CPU and memory stats looked OK, any problems that existed in the application must have been the fault of poorly written code. Conversely, developers weren't responsible for their code after it moved into the pearly gates of production. Problems that couldn't be reproduced in a local development environment were clearly infrastructure-related issues. There couldn't possibly be a reason why an application might perform differently in development mode versus production mode! The OPS team just needs to figure out why their application servers are behaving differently!

If these stories sound familiar to you, you're not alone. For years, this is how a lot of organizations functioned. But DevOps is shifting the way both teams work.

With every company essentially being a software company, the applications that operations teams support are no longer just secondary, internal-use applications. In many organizations, these applications are revenue drivers and are core to the company's ability to make a profit. With that shift from internal tools to revenue generation, the pressure to have a deeper understanding of the applications being supported is becoming stronger and stronger.

A disruption in service can cost a company a substantial amount of cash. The famous Knight Capital debacle resulted in a loss of $10 million a minute, due to a software configuration issue that forced the trading platform to make erroneous trades on the stock market (http://mng.bz/aw7X). I'm sure their CPU and memory graphs looked perfectly fine as the application malfunctioned its way into oblivion. CPU and memory level metrics don't always tell the business story!

At the same time, application developers are expected to understand how their systems operate in production in much greater detail. As systems grow and become increasingly more complex, the idea of full and thorough testing in a preproduction environment is becoming less viable. Preproduction environments don't have the same traffic patterns that production has. Preproduction environments don't have the same background processing, third-party interactions, end-user behavior—the list goes on. What this means practically is that a set of actions might very well be tested for the first time in production. Faced with that reality, a developer *must* be able to understand what's happening with their code in production. Without that visibility, their code could be suffering from unknown reactions for a long, painful period of time.

This new reality forces both development and operations to take on a new burden of responsibilities. But to meet these challenges, both teams have to understand what it is that the system does. Then, they have to be able to confirm that it's actually doing what it's supposed to be doing. An absence of errors doesn't mean things are working as expected.

3.3   *Understanding the product*

What is it that your application does? For some, that might be an easy question at first glance. A basic e-commerce company might seem incredibly simple on the face of things. Users come to the site, populate a cart, and check out, and the company ships the product to the customer. But even something as basic as an e-commerce site gets incredibly complicated when you zoom in on it. For example, you might ask the following:

- Is your application responsible for processing credit cards itself or does it interface with a third party?
- Is inventory verified before the purchase is completed or afterward?
- How is order data transmitted to the shipping facilities?
- Are credit card transactions processed synchronously or asynchronously?
- How are recommendations for add-on purchases generated?

These are a few examples of the types of interactions that a system might have. Understanding how each of these works is important to understanding how your application is performing.

Understanding the product you're supporting leads to a better understanding of the types of metrics that you need to generate and monitor in order to verify that your system is functioning as expected. If you know that your application interfaces with a third party to process credit cards, you might create a metric to see how fast your application is able to process credit cards. A drop in this metric could indicate that the third party is having issues, causing the processing time on their end to increase. Are orders that are transmitted to the shipping facility acknowledged? If a large mismatch arises between orders sent and orders acknowledged, some sort of communication issue could be happening between these two sites.

A lot of this information will come naturally to developers, because their job is to build these systems. (Understanding *why* the system does things in a particular way is another topic of conversation.) But this level of understanding has historically been outside the scope of many operations teams. They've focused more on the infrastructure and the network plumbing, leaving the application bits to developers.

This cannot be the case in a DevOps organization. In a DevOps organization, the goal is to continue to push and enable faster delivery of features and products to the end user. This ultimately results in less coordination between teams. (Collaboration and coordination are not the same.) The operations team's ability to respond to anomalies is dependent on the knowledge of what normal is. This knowledge will come only from an understanding of the product and observation of the product over time. Operation engineers who don't understand the product are quickly being replaced by infrastructure-as-a-service solutions like many of the Amazon products. If you're not going to understand my product, what makes you any more useful than a service API? Your expertise of the tools combined with your knowledge of the company's product and business is what makes operation engineers valuable and necessary. Understanding the product is a must in a DevOps organization. If you don't understand and add value from a business perspective, you could be a simple API call away from unemployment.

3.4   *Creating operational visibility*

Operational visibility really stems from two primary sources: metrics and logs. The two may seem interchangeable, but I assure you they're not. A *metric* is a measurement at a point in time of a system resource. *Logs*, on the other hand, are system-generated messages that describe an event that occurred in the system. Logs tend to be much more descriptive about events, offering more nuanced detail than provided by a metric. This section focuses on metrics, but we will come back to logs later in the chapter.

Metrics are a good way to communicate the state of the various activities occurring in a system. Unfortunately, once you get beyond standard system metrics, such as CPU, memory utilization, and disk utilization, it's up to you as an engineer to design, develop, and visualize the metrics that will matter most to your application and the teams supporting it. With this in mind, the first step in creating operational visibility is to go beyond the system metrics and develop custom metrics for your application.

When you're working with a system, three characteristics about the work that the system is doing are almost universally useful. Those metrics are throughput, error rate, and latency. Or to think of it another way, ask yourself three questions about the thing you're measuring: How often is this happening? How often is it failing? How long does it take to complete?

Throughput is defined as the amount of work flowing through your system at any given time. If you're running a web server, your throughput would be the number of requests you're handling at any given time. The time horizon of throughput is heavily influenced by the amount of activity the system sees. In a modestly popular website, you might measure throughput in hits per second. Throughput helps give you an idea of how busy your system is. You can also put these metrics in a more business-centric context, like orders per second. This could be based on the number of users who have finalized their orders (checked out) in a given time period.

Error counts and error rates are quite different. *Error counts* are a metric that most engineers are familiar with. It tallies the number of errors that have happened since a process or system has started. Every system has a unit of work, like a web request. That unit of work is going to be deemed either successful or failed based on criteria inside your application. An error count would be a simple tally of the number of failed units of work your system has encountered.

Error rates are a calculation on error count and are represented as a percentage of the total number of requests. To calculate the error rate, you take the number of failed work units and divide it by the total number of work units. For example, if your work unit is web hits and you receive 100 hits, that would be your total number of work units. If 10 of those web hits resulted in failed requests, your error rate would be 10% (10 divided by 100).

Error rates are more useful than error counts because they give context for people who may not be as familiar with the system. For example, 500 errors per minute sounds like a lot until you realize the total number of hits in that sample period is 100,000. The number 500 can be alarming to people not familiar with normal operating volumes. But 0.005% conveys the scope of the errors in relation to total traffic volume. It also can make alerting easier as traffic volumes fluctuate.

Lastly, *latency* is a measurement of how long it takes a particular action to occur. Sticking with web requests as an example, the latency would be a measure of how long the web request takes to complete. When combined with throughput, latency can give you a signal for future capacity planning. If you can handle five requests concurrently, and your latency for processing each request is one second, then you know that if you're receiving 10 requests per second, you're going to have a backlog that will grow infinitely because you just don't have enough capacity to service your volume of requests! Whenever you're trying to think of what to measure, you can almost always come back to these three types of metrics.

3.4.1   *Creating custom metrics*

Creating custom metrics is a must in order to bring greater operational visibility to your application. The implementation details will vary heavily, depending on the monitoring solution that you have in place. Instead of attempting to enumerate all the possible configurations a company might have, this section focuses on the mechanics of defining these custom metrics. The task of implementing them will be left to you, the reader.

Metrics are most commonly recorded as one of two types: a gauge or a counter. A *gauge* represents a discrete reading in a particular moment in time. Think of a speedometer in your car. When you look down and read your speed, that's a measurement of your current speed at a specific moment in time. An example of a gauge in a system might be something as simple as "disk space available." The metric is read and recorded at a point in time.

A *counter* is an always incrementing value representing the number of times a certain event has occurred. Think of a counter as the odometer in your car. It increases by one every time your car drives a mile. It always increases. An example of a system counter might be something like web page hits. Every time a user visits the website, a counter is increased by one to mark the visit. With a little bit of math, you can calculate the rate at which the events are occurring by measuring the counter at a specific interval. If your first check on the counter is a value of 100, and the second check an hour later is 200, then you can determine that your counter is operating at 100 events/hour. If you want more fine-grained measurements, you just sample more frequently. Other types of counters are available, but these two will give you a lot of mileage.

3.4.2 *Deciding what to measure*

Deciding what to measure can be a difficult task. This section focuses on queueing systems. Most application systems have a queue system of some form or another, and a few well-worn patterns apply to almost any queue system architecture.

Queueing systems are used to break large pieces of work into smaller portions, while also allowing work to be performed in an asynchronous fashion and to separate concerns. In a queueing system, a process that creates work and the process that performs that work can be separated. This allows for flexibility with how fast work gets done and how much strain it puts on the system in terms of resources.

At the center of queueing systems is the message queue itself. Publisher processes are responsible for doing work and creating messages on the queue. Consumer processes are responsible for reading those messages and processing them for whatever specific task they need to do. Figure 3.1 shows a diagram highlighting this process.

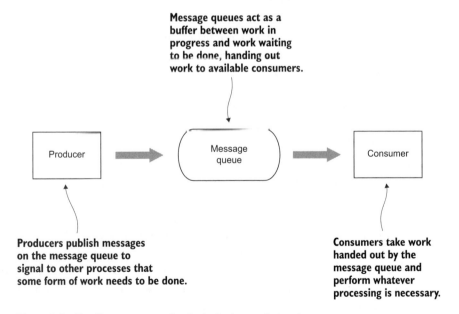

Figure 3.1 The three components of a typical queueing system

A real-world example of a queueing system is a mailbox. When you need to mail a letter, you become the *publisher* portion of the system. You get your message ready and take it to a mailbox. The mailbox acts as the *queue*. It accepts your message and waits for a consumer to come get that message. The *consumer* in this scenario would be the post office. Postal workers stop at the mailbox, empty the queue, and begin the process of getting the letter to its intended recipient. The power of this is that as a publisher, you don't need to know the internals of how the post office gets the mail to your recipient! You just drop the message in the queue, following an agreed-upon protocol. (Sender address, recipient address and a stamp are all required as part of the protocol for mailing a letter.) If the mailbox fills on a regular basis, the post office can increase the frequency at which the mailbox is checked. If the mailbox is often empty, postal workers may check it less frequently.

This queueing system is a common pattern found in applications. For a queuing system, you have several metrics that are important. By looking at each portion of the application structure, you can begin to think about the things that need to be measured. This system has three phases: a message needs to be published, a message needs to be queued, and a message needs to be consumed and processed. These three actions combined represent the throughput of the queue system. But without monitoring, if processing slowed down or stopped, you wouldn't have any visibility into what might be causing the problem. Metrics can help solve this. By adding metrics to these three individual components, you can begin to monitor your systems. Let's start with the producers.

The *producer* is responsible for publishing messages to the queue to be processed by the consumers. To track this, though, you need to know that the producer is doing its job. A metric counter that tracks a published message makes the most sense here. I'll call this metric `messages.published.count`. This will allow you to confirm that your producer application is publishing messages. For every message that gets published, `messages.published.count` increases by one. If you sample this metric every minute, you can compare the values of `messages.published.count` to determine the rate at which messages are being published. This metric allows you to discover three key things at a glance:

- If the number of messages published stops increasing, you know that the overall throughput of the message-processing system is being impacted by the producer side of the process.
- If the number of messages published spikes, you can determine that an influx of messages might be overwhelming the amount of work that the consumer side can handle, generating a backlog.
- If the number of messages published begins to increase at a slower rate, you can determine that the rate of work coming in has slowed, and as a result, the throughput of the message-processing system will also slow.

With just a simple metric, you're able to gather a lot more information of your message-processing system. This could be extremely helpful if your queue is filling up! Are more messages being published faster, or are fewer messages being consumed and processed?

Moving to the queueing portion of the system, you can build and observe two main metrics. First is the *size of the queue*, which will be a gauge metric. Knowing the size of the queue tells you a bit about how your system is behaving. I'll call this metric `messages.queue.size`. It might be useful to have the queue size separated by the name of the queue. For this, you could include the queue name in the metric, like `messages.queue.new_orders.size`. For simplicity, I'll use `messages.queue.size`, but know that the same logic applies.

The queue size is an obvious metric you'll want to graph. Seeing the queue continuously grow could be a sign that consumers are moving slower than the producers. A continuously growing queue can be disastrous for your application. No queue can be completely without bounds. Eventually, the queue will reach capacity, and then your queueing system will begin rejecting new messages. What happens to those messages? Does the publisher retry? How often are retries made? These are all questions you'll need to answer for your own specific application. But knowing when you're approaching this capacity limit is essential for designing whatever your response is. Queue size is a usual metric that is exposed by your message queue system in some way. RabbitMQ, ActiveMQ, Amazon Simple Queue Service (SQS), and Kafka all expose metrics around queue size that can be queried and shipped to your monitoring platform.

Going beyond queue size, *queue latency* is another useful metric to capture. Queue latency represents the average time a message waits in the queue before it gets picked up and processed by a consumer. This is heavily dependent on your application code and requires modifications to the application to emit this metric. But the change is pretty straightforward.

First, you'll need to make sure that messages being published to the queue have some form of date/time stamp associated with them. Most message buses will do this for you automatically, but you can explicitly do it to each individual message for consistency across message bus platforms. A simple modification to your producer code will allow you to tag each message with this data. Then, when the consumer retrieves that message, it does some date math to determine the elapsed time between now and the date/time stamp on the messages published field. Now the consumer emits that metric, before it begins processing the work it needs to do for that message. Figure 3.2 illustrates the process flow.

You might be wondering why you would emit the metric before you do the actual processing. From an operational standpoint, it's good to be able to separate the amount of time it took to get the message (queue time) from the amount of time it took to process the message (processing time). Imagine you emit the metric after you've done your application processing. If the amount of time was 1500 milliseconds (ms), you wouldn't know where to begin optimizing. What if it was in the queue for 1400 ms but took only 100 ms to process? That fix would be very different than if the

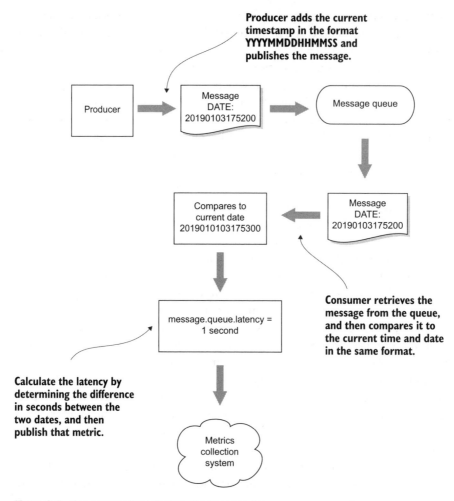

Producer adds the current timestamp in the format YYYYMMDDHHMMSS and publishes the message.

Consumer retrieves the message from the queue, and then compares it to the current time and date in the same format.

Calculate the latency by determining the difference in seconds between the two dates, and then publish that metric.

Figure 3.2   **The process for calculating message latency**

message sat in the queue for 100 ms but took 1400 ms to process. Having the queue time and the processing time metrics split out helps for future troubleshooting.

Now comes the consumer, the final part of the process. Consumer metrics are similar to producer metrics, but in reverse. The consumer metric would be something more like messages.processed.count, which would allow you to gather the same metrics that you did for publishing, only on the consumption side instead. You'll also be able to calculate rates of consumption similarly by sampling the metric more frequently.

This represents the bare minimum of metrics that you should be collecting from a queueing system. But other metrics that are useful to look into are as follows:

- The number of unacknowledged messages in the system
- The number of consumers currently connected to the message bus
- The number of producers currently connected to the message bus

This pattern of message queueing is pretty common, even when a message bus isn't at the center of it. Think of a web server with an application instance running behind it. For example, an Apache HTTP server receives requests from users and proxies those requests to a Tomcat application server running, which handles the dynamic nature of the request. Believe it or not, a queue is at work here!

The Apache HTTP server accepts requests and passes them to the Tomcat instance. But the HTTP server can handle only so many concurrent requests at a time. The Tomcat instance similarly can handle only a set number of concurrent connections at a time. When the HTTP server tries to send the request to the Tomcat instance and that instance is busy, the HTTP server queues that request internally until a Tomcat instance is available. Monitoring the HTTP server queue size would be a way to indicate that the HTTP servers are receiving more work than the Tomcat instances can handle.

Thinking in this component-type way will help you discover new monitoring patterns to apply within your systems. Even though our specific example was detailing a message bus system, the Tomcat and HTTP example highlights how the pattern can be used outside an explicit message bus application context.

3.4.3 Defining healthy metrics

Once you've defined the metrics, you need to also define what makes a metric healthy versus unhealthy. Or at the very least, you need to define when a metric should be reviewed or escalated for deeper examination. This goes beyond just simple alerting, which I'll discuss in a later chapter. It also entails knowing when your service has made a step change in its performance and having something to trigger a reevaluation of "healthy."

Using our example from the beginning of the chapter, let's say that the team was monitoring the average number of concurrent queries executing at any time on the system. An alert above a threshold would have signaled us to this immediate problem and pointed us at the database as the potential source of the problem, reducing the downtime.

But if you zoom out and think about this longer term, it can help with things like capacity planning too. The number of concurrent queries will grow as the website becomes more active. Having a defined line of the number of concurrent queries can serve as a trigger to begin discussions around the size of your database. Is the increase in concurrent queries expected? Or is a bad piece of code running an excessive number of queries erroneously? Or maybe you've reached a growth point and need to evaluate whether your environment is sized correctly. Either way, having a definition of what healthy should look like is important. If not, the number will continue to rise and will serve as a warning only after you've actually experienced a problem, instead of using it as a leading indicator to future problems.

Healthy metrics seems like the domain of development and operations, but I urge you to involve your product teams as well. For some metrics like response time, product teams can be the voice of the customer, knowing which parts of the application absolutely must be responsive, like dashboard loading, and which can be a little slower, like reporting and analytics. The performance of the application is very much a feature of the user experience. It's also bound to the same scarce resource of developer time. Having the product team understand and be part of the healthy metrics definition keeps everyone aligned on what's *acceptable* performance. Defining healthy metrics is a topic that I'll dive deeper into in chapter 6, but it's still worthy of consideration here.

3.4.4   *Failure mode and effects analysis*

Another technique used in the past is borrowed from the manufacturing and safety industries. The process is called *failure mode and effects analysis* (FMEA). The goal of FMEA is to examine a process in detail and identify all of the areas where the process might fail or error out. When adopted to a software approach, the process might be replaced with something like an application method call or an HTTP request, and the various systems that it must interact with to return successfully.

When the team identifies a failure, it is scored on a scale of 1 to 10 across three axes. The *severity* indicates how bad would it be if the error occurred. Each company could rank the scale of severity based on its business. In some cases, like the airline industry, a severity of 10 might be customer death. In other industries, like food delivery, a 10 might mean that the customer never receives their order. The *occurrence factor* indicates how likely it is that the error will occur, with 10 being it will most certainly occur or is already occurring. And lastly, the *detection score* indicates how likely it is that the error will be noticed by customers before internal monitoring or metrics catch it.

These three scores are multiplied together to give the error a *risk priority number* (RPN). The RPN allows you to then prioritize the riskiest gaps. With the errors listed and the RPNs assigned, the goal of the team is to reduce that RPN number by instituting changes to the process that either lower the severity when it happens, decrease the likelihood that the error will occur, or lower the likelihood that a customer will detect the issue before the company does. The last item of detection is the focus on this chapter, because it gives us the necessary criteria to develop monitoring options.

The FMEA process can be quite thorough and often can take several hour-long sessions to complete. But when you're experiencing regular failures and are at a loss for how to prevent them, the FMEA process could be extremely beneficial to your teams. It will often bring to the surface areas of uncertainty around how the application is supposed to behave. With every FMEA process I have run, I've learned something extremely valuable about the system under examination.

GETTING STARTED

First, you'll want to decide on the scope of the process that you're going to examine. Defining the scope of the process up front is important. Is it a particular endpoint that's problematic in your web application? Maybe it's a background processing job. Whatever it is, define its scope—the beginning and the end of the process that you're going to investigate.

Based on the process chosen, you'll want to assemble your team. The team should be cross-functional and made up of operations staff, development staff, business users, and other stakeholders with a level of expertise around the problem. The purpose for this all-encompassing team is to get different perspectives and mental models looking at the process. A developer might think of a failed HTTP call and its downstream technical impacts, while a customer support representative might think of the potential confusion that a partial failure might cause the user. Data analysts might be concerned with the state of a partial database update and how that might impact reporting. Different perspectives will give you a broader list of things that might go wrong in a process.

With the team selected and assembled, the process should be mapped out in as much detail as possible prior to the larger team meeting. This can be done by a smaller team of subject-matter experts (SMEs). An ideal artifact for this pre-meeting would be a swim-lane-based document showing the interactions between systems, processes, and teams.

AN EXAMPLE PROCESS

The team at Webshopper.com has recently experienced numerous failed orders during the checkout process for customers. Since this is such a crucial part of the business, the leadership group has opted to do an FMEA process to either fix the problem or at least get better at detecting it through monitoring and alerting. Several SMEs have gotten together and produced a swim-lane document, shown in figure 3.3.

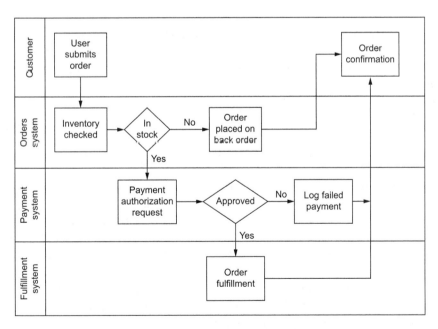

Figure 3.3   A high-level swim-lane diagram of the web checkout process

With the web checkout process documented, the team of SMEs sets out trying to brainstorm potential failure points. Failure points could be anything from a communications failure between the two systems, to an end user putting in garbage information that isn't appropriately sanitized. In the current example, you might look at the communication between the order-processing system and the third-party payment processor. What would happen if the payment processor is offline? The payment process would fail, and the order would be rejected by the system. The team identifies that risk and scores it accordingly:

- *Severity of 10*—This is based on the immediate loss of revenue.
- *Occurrence of 6*—The payment processor has a great history of availability, but everything fails.
- *Detection of 10*—The user would receive the error when the order checkout happens, and the team doesn't currently monitor the health of the payment endpoint.
- *RPN of 600*—This is calculated as follows: Severe 10 × Occurrence 6 × Detection 10 = 600.

With an RPN of 600, this issue will probably rank pretty highly among the errors that the team will generate. Now you have to decide if you can lower any of the three axes with which you scored the error. The severity could be lowered by modifying the system so that it conditionally accepts the order, queuing the payment processing portion until the payment processor comes back online. Lowering the likelihood of occurrence could be handled by having multiple payment processors. Both of these things are solid solutions but will require quite a large chunk of development work.

Detection, however, might be an easier solution. The teams could begin monitoring a few metrics that might help detect problems on the payment provider's end:

- Create a metric for the latency of the payment provider calls. If latency climbs, it could signal a longer performance degradation of the platform.
- Create an error rate metric for the percentage of failed calls to the payment provider.
- Create a health check against the payment provider.

With these metrics, you can get an idea of potential problems on the payment processor's side. This can allow you to be proactive in handling the issue for future orders. You might even be able to change your application's behavior based on these signals to ensure that order taking isn't disrupted, even if you can't immediately process the payment for that order. This is just one high-level example of a failure and how you can use it to generate metrics.

Now that you have the ability to detect this type of failure, the team would score the Detection portion of the RPN again. Maybe the team now feels a bit more confident, and the Detection score is lowered to 6. The new RPN would be 360 (Severe 10 × Occurrence 6 × Detection 6 = 360), making it less of a concern and potentially putting a new issue as the highest risk based on RPN.

How deep should failures go?

The failures could be numerous but should also be within the scope of processes that are in the team's ability to control. For example, the Web HTTP call to the order system could fail because the order system is overloaded. It could also fail because the entire data center is offline. Depending on the scope of your FMEA team, the data center outage might be deemed too big for the scope of the immediate team.

You can continue this FMEA process of error identification and detection mitigation as little or as much as you like. There will most likely always be more that you could be doing, but remember, like anything else, this is a balance. Balancing the usefulness of a metric with the energy that needs to be expended to collect it is something that has to be considered.

METRICS FROM INCIDENTS AND FAILURES

An often-overlooked source for great metrics arises from your system encountering a failure of some sort. Every failure should be accompanied by a retrospective on the outage, sometimes referred to as a *postmortem*. The naming of this meeting changes quite a bit, and by the time you read this, I'm sure a new term will be in vogue. Just know that after a failure, people should get together to discuss the failure.

When you're going through the postmortem process, you should continuously ask the group, "What question about the system and its current state did I have that couldn't be answered?" This usually will highlight many potential gaps in your monitoring solution. If you really needed to know how many requests were being rejected because the web server wasn't accepting any new connections, that's a metric that you can then begin to figure out how to collect and ship to your monitoring solution. Never settle for only the metrics you currently have. You should be continuously asking yourself questions about your system and ensuring that you can answer those questions through metrics.

Sometimes you need information that goes a little deeper than a simple counter can provide. You might need more detailed information about an event. Maybe you need information about requests from a specific customer, information that might get lost in the blandness of metrics. For that, you'll need to rely on your logging infrastructure.

A note on observability

Observability is becoming the latest trend in monitoring circles, and for good reason. Observability gives you the visualization capabilities of metrics along with the fine-grained, detailed information that you get from logging. Being able to look at your HTTP requests and then slice that information based on a customer ID in order to isolate potential problems or hotspots is an amazing and powerful feat.

(continued)
Unfortunately, at the time of this writing, I simply haven't had enough exposure to observability tools, or their pluses and minuses, to write about them and include them in this book. I highly recommend looking at some of the options, however, as I do believe that observability will become a major component in the monitoring toolkit. A few vendors to check out are Wavefront by VMWare (www.wavefront.com), Honeycomb (www.honeycomb.io), and SignalFX, which has been acquired by Splunk (splunk.com).

3.5   *Making logging useful*

Logging is one of the oldest and still extremely useful tools in the monitoring toolkit. It's also regularly done poorly.

3.5.1   *Log aggregation*

The first thing to note is that structured logging is a must. *Structured logs* are placed in a machine-readable format, with fields and values that are clearly defined and parseable. The most widely popular log format to work with is JavaScript Object Notation (JSON), and most languages and frameworks have a library for easily producing your logs in JSON format.

The benefit to machine-readable formats is your ability to ship and ingest logs into log aggregation systems. A *log aggregation system* allows you to combine logs from various, often disparate, systems and create a single location to search from. Many log aggregation systems are out there, from paid software-as-a-service (SaaS) solutions like Splunk (www.splunk.com) or Sumo Logic (https://sumologic.com) to free, open source solutions like the popular Elasticsearch, Logstash, and Kibana stack, commonly referred to as ELK (https://elastic.co/what-is/elk-stack), and Graylog (www.graylog.org). With structured log formats, ingesting logs into any system becomes a much easier task, as it removes the need for complex and typically brittle regular expressions to interpret fields and values. Instead, the well-known format can easily be interpreted by the log shipper or the aggregation server.

The need for log aggregation is as much cultural as it is technical. First, remember that a central tenant of DevOps is to empower teams and to share and democratize as much information as possible. In a world without log aggregation, access to logs is either limited to operations support staff or becomes an incredibly painful burden on those teams, as they're required to copy logs to some other easily accessible location by developers. This gatekeeper function is useful, since you don't want anyone who needs access to logs to also have access to production. But the need for the gatekeeping function can be completely rethought and removed with log aggregation tools, getting the data off the servers that they're generated on and instead shipped to a log aggregation system. This opens up a world of possibilities now that multiple disciplines can gain access to the logs and get a glimpse into how the application is performing in almost real time.

Log aggregation also opens up new business use cases for your logs that you didn't even know were possible. The amount of information conveyed in logs can often tell the story of an entire process flow without you even realizing it. As each function or step in the process logs information about how it's performing, it's inadvertently giving you a glimpse into the business flows as well. Think about it: if a producer process logs that it published a message for order 115, a consumer process logs that it has consumed a message for order 115, and the payment processor logs that it has confirmed payment for order 115, with some clever search criteria, you could watch the entire order flow through the system in real time. This provides value not only to technical teams, but also to business units outside engineering as well.

At a previous job, our engineering department was able to build an entire customer service order portal using nothing but search filters in our logging aggregation tool. No additional programming was necessary outside of creating the necessary search filters, which took about a day's worth of effort. This simply isn't possible in a system without log aggregation because the logs and events are most likely happening on many systems, with no way to combine the logs to paint a complete picture. Logging aggregation can have a significant cultural impact on your organization in terms of who has access to data and what they can design and build with that data.

The benefits aren't just cultural, though. Centralized logging provides many benefits, specifically around the monitoring of your application stack. Logs have traditionally been useless as a source of alerting because in a large system with many servers, examining, parsing, and alerting on those logs can be a heavy lift. You also continue to suffer from the incomplete picture problem. Activity on a single system may not be enough for an alarm state, but the combined behavior of systems might be something you want to act on.

For example, if you wanted to alert on a high level of errors throughout the system, you would have to get creative to calculate how many errors on a single system is problematic. If one node is generating a high level of errors, that might be something that could be caught in an environment with no log aggregation. But if many nodes housed a small percentage of errors, this might not surface in a world where each node is alerting on only its own error load. In a fleet of 20 web nodes, if a single node is generating errors on 1% of its requests, that might not be something you wake somebody up for in the middle of the night. But if all 20 nodes are generating errors on 1% of their requests, it's probably worthy of investigation. Without log aggregation, this sort of alerting and analysis isn't possible.

In addition, log aggregation gives you the ability to create alerting and monitoring around multiple points of interest. Now you can correlate a high number of failed web requests with a high number of failed database logins, because your logs are going to a single place. Many log aggregation tools have advanced calculation capabilities, allowing you to parse the logs across fields, and perform mathematical formulas and transformations to them for graphing and charting purposes. Because the logs enter the system in a structured format, parsing on these becomes as easy as specifying key/value pairs. This is a far cry from the complexity brought about with a tool like grep. This allows ownership of issue investigation during an outage to become further democratized.

3.5.2   *What should I be logging?*

Before identifying what to log, you should identify the various log levels at which you can log to. A well-known pattern of logging levels exists that you should adhere to. The most common levels are DEBUG, INFO, WARN, ERROR, and FATAL. Each error level has specific types of information that are anticipated in each category:

- *DEBUG*—Any information related to things that are going on in the program. These are often messages written by programmers for debugging purposes.
- *INFO*—Any user-initiated action or any system operations such as scheduled tasks executing, or system startup and shutdown.
- *WARN*—Any condition that could become an error state in the future. Library deprecation warnings, low available resources, or slow performance are examples of entries that would go in this level.
- *ERROR*—Any and every error condition should go in this level.
- *FATAL*—Any error condition that causes the system to shut down. For example, if the system needs 32 GB of memory on startup and 16 GB is all that's available, the program should log a FATAL error message and immediately exit.

These level definitions cannot be enforced programmatically, unfortunately. It's up to engineers to log at the appropriate levels. It's important to do this because people parse through logs when they're in search of information. If you're looking for an error, chances are you'll filter based on log entries that have the status of ERROR. But if the error message you're looking for is actually logged at INFO, it becomes bogged down in a sea of unrelated messages.

Getting the log message in the right category is almost as important as logging the message in the first place. Too many downstream actions like searching, filtering, and even monitoring depend on the categorization of the log message being correct. But now that you know which category your log message should go in, what do you want to see in the log?

WHAT MAKES A GOOD LOG MESSAGE

The key to a good log message is *context*. Every log message should be written from the perspective that it is the only log message that someone will see with regards to what's being logged. For example, a "Transaction complete" message is useless. A message like this probably depends on previous messages that came before it, and the details of the transaction are to be inferred by previous log messages. But with many log messages coming in from various servers, and being aggregated to a single instance, tying these two separate log messages together might be problematic. Not to mention, if one of your log messages is logged at INFO, but the subsequent error message is logged at ERROR, then the preceding messages might not even get to the person reading the logs.

The goal is to stuff your log messages with enough context as necessary for the log reader to understand. And not only that, but to continue to do it in a structured field format. If you're processing orders, you might have a file structured as follows:

```
{ "timestamp": "2019-08-01:23:52:44",
"level": "INFO", "order_id": 25521,
"state": "IN PROCESS", "message":
"Paymentverified",
"subsystem": "payments.processors.credit_card"}
```

This log message includes context. You can tie the message to a specific order ID. Depending on your programming language, you can probably add other useful properties that allow you to give further context to the message being displayed. Now, an engineer who sees this log message and wants to know more can filter for log messages based on an `order_id` and get the context around that particular order.

This example leads to another point. You shouldn't log only for troubleshooting purposes. You can think about logging for audit purposes as well as profiling purposes. For example, you might log a message whenever a particular call exceeds a certain threshold. Or you could log changes in state throughout an order process, noting which subsystem changed it and why. User password resets, failed login attempts—the list goes on as to the types of actions that you can log. Through logging, you can build up a detailed story around many actions that occur in your system. Just take special care to log them at the correct log level. This makes it easy to filter and identify later.

When logging error messages, developers should take extra care to explain a little about the error message. Here are some key bits of information:

- What was the action being taken?
- What was the expected outcome of that action?
- What was the actual outcome of that action?
- What are some possible remediation steps to take?
- What are potential consequences of this error (if any)?

The last line requires a bit more explanation. Nothing is worse than seeing an error message along the lines of "Could not complete authorization of credit card." What does this mean? Is the order rejected? Is it in limbo? Does the user get notified? Is there cleanup activity that the operator needs to perform? The error is devoid of information that makes the event useful. Remember, the benefit of logs over metrics is your ability to give more detail around the error. If you're just going to log that the event happened, it might as well be a metric as opposed to a log entry.

Think of the people who will be reading these logs and try to anticipate the questions that they'll be asking as they read the error message. A better example of that message might be "Could not complete authorization of credit card. The order will be rejected, and the customer notified." Now you have a more complete picture of what happened and the resulting actions that the system has taken. And if a different action is taken, the error message can change to suit that particular case. (For example, the system was going to attempt another payment method automatically.)

I've given a few examples of the benefits of aggregated logging. Hopefully, I've convinced you that this is a worthwhile effort and worth the energy. But despite all the promise of efficiencies and glory, nothing comes without downsides.

3.5.3   *The hurdles of log aggregation*

For many readers, the benefits of log aggregation aren't lost on you. The issue has probably centered around time and/or money. Purchasing log aggregation can be an expensive proposition. Most log aggregation tools are charged either by data volume (total number of gigabytes shipped), data throughput (the number of logs you're sending per hour) or total number of events (the number of individual log entries you're sending).

Even when self-hosting with open source software, the software might be free, but the solution isn't! You're still dealing with the employee resources to build and manage the system. The system requires hardware to run on, most notably disk storage. Increases in logging volume result in demands on capacity planning.

Log aggregation sets up a list of perverse incentives to not log as much as you might normally. When your log volume can be directly attributed to the cost of a service, it's easy to begin evaluating the necessity of a log message. That's not always a bad thing. But often the mandate is to reduce spending on the logging platform, which creates a world in which messages might get trimmed not because of their usefulness, but because of their frequency. There are many hurdles to get over, but I implore you to not give up on this much needed piece of the DevOps transformation.

ARGUMENTS FOR SPENDING MONEY

When it comes to the build-versus-buy conversation, I evaluate this in a pretty basic fashion. If a system or service isn't core to your technology solution and you're not using any secret sauce, I always opt to buy the service. Everyone does logging the same. Everyone does email the same. Everyone does directory services the same. There's little need for you to customize these types of services, and as a result, hosting and managing them yourself adds little value.

This is especially true when it comes to logging. Depending on your company, you might have strict rules or requirements around your log data being shipped to a third party, which I'll touch on a bit later. But for a lot of people, shipping logs to a third party is more of a financial hurdle then a policy one. Before I lobby for the buy-versus-build approach, let me first arm you with the tools to get money in the budget in the first place.

Anytime you're looking to spend the company's money, you have to position the purchase in terms of benefit to the business. This could be anything from increased productivity, to revenue protection, to ease of compliance obligations. The key is to understand what it is that your boss (or whomever you need to convince) cares about and how this particular purchase fits into that narrative.

For example, at a previous job, the team I worked on was constantly slowed by requests from other teams. Our projects were consistently late on delivery because developers would need access to logs to troubleshoot customer issues. It was a no-win situation. I wasn't getting my work done, developers were constantly blocked, waiting for my team to deliver logs, and customers were suffering as their problems dragged on and on. When my boss began getting pressed for better project delivery, I used the opportunity to point out just how much time was being wasted grabbing logs for developers to troubleshoot issues. Doing some rough calculations on hours spent per week by my team, and developer time wasted waiting on our team combined with the impact to our project work, the dollar amount of the log aggregation solution seemed quite reasonable. Putting it in terms that my boss could understand, combined with positioning it in the context of how the tool would help get what the company wanted is what ultimately got the funds approved.

Another great tip is to plan for the purchase ahead of time. Know what your department's budget cycle is like and ask for the dollars for your project during that cycle. Organizations typically don't like unplanned expenses. And because many organizations don't have great communication or process around the budget generation procedure, many technical projects get left off the docket, only to become an issue mid-year when the purchase has to fit within the confines of the current budget, which unfortunately doesn't have a huge bucket just for discretionary spending. Making your pitch for a solution and presenting it during the budget process gives you a much greater chance of getting your expenditure approved, albeit at the cost of its rapid implementation.

Lastly, start small and try to control your spending. You don't have to ship all the logs to start with. Ship only your most frequently requested logs. Doing this will help build momentum around the product and help lower your costs. But it won't be long before people on the team are praising the increased access and want more logs available. Now you've got a groundswell of support, and the effort goes from being an operations initiative to a technology department one. Start small, build support, prove value, and then grow the solution over time.

Another way to control spending is to create different retention periods for your logs. Most companies require that logs be kept for a certain amount of time, which increases your storage or SAAS provider costs. But by creating different levels of retention, you can decrease your overall spending by lowering how long certain types of log files are kept. For example, you might need to keep your web access logs for a year, but maybe you can keep logs of users logging in for two weeks. That reduces your overall storage costs and your SAAS cost, as most providers will have different pricing based on the amount of time you need logs available.

BUILD VERSUS BUY

The topic of build versus buy is extremely prevalent in the logging conversation. Plenty of companies run their log aggregation services on-premises. Some companies might have requirements on log data that prohibits its shipping to third-party services. Those prohibitions make this decision a pretty open-and-shut case.

All things being equal, I still advocate for using third-party services for logging when possible. For starters, it's one less thing that your team has to manage. I'm guessing that if you took an honest assessment of your team's operational capacity, you'd find items that should be getting done on a regular basis aren't getting done. Are your servers kept up-to-date on patching? Is your vulnerability management process in a good place? Are you regularly reviewing data to feed into your capacity planning initiatives? Adding another item like logging to the mix can just add to your operational burden.

It's also another internal system that will quickly affect the workflows of many team members. An outage in your logging system will become a high-priority ticket among your team. This isn't to say that third-party hosting providers don't have outages, but the level of effort to recover is significantly less. Not to mention that logging SAAS providers have levels of redundancy that can separate indexing of logs from the ingestion and acceptance of logs, so rarely do you actually lose any logging data. If you do decide to build your log aggregation system yourself, you need to keep a few points in mind:

- Logging volumes can change unexpectedly. An application server that goes into DEBUG mode might log considerably more data. Make sure your infrastructure has a method for dealing with this, either by rate limiting, dropping particular message types, or some sort of elastic scaling.
- Indexing can be an expensive operation, depending on the log field. Be sure you understand your log aggregation system's key performance metrics and keep an eye on them to ensure that indexing isn't delayed.
- If possible, design your storage solution with the idea of hot and cold volumes. Most logs that are searched are within a one- to two-week time period. Designing a system that has those logs on your fastest disks, and moving older logs to slower, more price-conscious disks is another way to save a few dollars on log aggregation.

Of course, there's no such thing as a free lunch. Deciding to buy your log aggregation through a SAAS provider also comes with its own sets of pitfalls.

- Be sure to ask how the SAAS provider charges for overages in your log shipping limits. Some providers may cap your ability to access your data after you've gone over your allotted limit. Ingestion of new logs will continue to function, but that's useless if you can't search the data. Understand how overages affect you.
- Sometimes logs may contain sensitive information. You'll want to have controls in place to scrub this data prior to it being shipped to your SAAS provider. (This is a problem on-premises too, but you don't have the added liability of giving that sensitive data to another company.)
- Be careful that you don't allow the cost of log aggregation to dictate how and what you log. In some cases, it's prudent to trim down logging (debug logging is one example), but you don't want a scenario in which valuable information isn't getting logged in order to save on the cost of logging tools. The added cost will pay for itself (which you'll realize the first time you have an outage and don't have the needed information in the logs to resolve it faster).

Despite the potential issues that can crop up with log aggregation systems, they are without a doubt a large boon to your teams, not only in the technical capabilities they provide, but also in the democratization of information across teams. This shift can lead to a cultural change in the organization around responsibilities and ownership of systems. Now that you understand the importance of having this data available, you're ready to delve into the next chapter, which focuses on how to go about making that data accessible through dashboarding.

Summary

- Understanding the product being supported is key to being able to assist during an incident.
- Error rates, latency, and throughput are potentially useful key metrics that almost any system produces.
- Custom metrics are a great way to show business-specific details on how your system is performing.
- Failure mode effects analysis can be used as a systematic way to figure out what you should be monitoring.
- Messages must be logged at their appropriate log levels to be truly useful.
- Log messages should always give context around the message being logged.

Data instead
of information

This chapter covers

- Scoping dashboards for a specific purpose
- Effectively organizing dashboards
- Prompting the user with context

Sometimes you might have so much data in a system that you're not really sure what's going to be useful in a support type of situation. Instead of starting with a question of "What do I want to know?", people start from the perspective of "What answers do I have?"

This leads to a few problems. First, you don't challenge yourself to come up with ways to get the answers to the questions you have. And second, you tend to think of the data you have as the final answer or response. But data and information are two very different things.

Data is just raw unorganized facts, but when you take that data and give it context and structure, it becomes *information*. When you're looking at your dashboards, you can quickly tell which dashboards are giving you data and which are giving you information.

4.1   *Start with the user, not the data*

Everyone presumes that just having the metrics about a system's status is enough. But the way the status of a system is presented to users is as critical as having the metrics themselves. Poorly visualized metrics are useless, becoming nothing more than a sea of numbers in which the signal gets lost in the noise.

Only a monster or a data scientist would present users with a spreadsheet of metric points in a Microsoft Excel document. Even if given such a document, the first thing the user would do is convert those numbers into some sort of visualization chart. The power of pictures cannot be overstated. It's how humans assimilate knowledge best. The same goes for your metric data.

But just knowing that you need pictures isn't the same as knowing the best way to organize them. The field of data visualization and user experience (UX) design is a topic that could fill volumes of text alone, and since you're not a UX designer, would probably bore you to tears. (If you are a UX designer and you're reading this, job well done!) But you don't need to be an expert to start designing useful dashboards for your team and other stakeholders.

This chapter will give you practical tips for making your dashboards purpose driven and accessible to their audience. I'll give you some guidelines for designing dashboards, organizing them, and calling out key bits of information. But it all starts with understanding who the dashboard is for.

It's a knee-jerk reaction to start your dashboarding process by picking a system or server and looking to see what metrics are available to you so that you can build the ultimate dashboard. That's the mythical single pane of glass that corporate giants have been selling us since the 1970s. That approach is a trap and will most likely lead to a dashboard that isn't incredibly useful to you or anyone else.

Your first step should be identifying the intended audience for your dashboard. This will help you scope your dashboard in terms of which metrics to display, which metrics need accentuation, and the granularity of the data to display. Different audiences need different things, and building a dashboard with that purpose in mind will lead to two very different dashboards. I'll give a brief example.

Think of a database system. The database is sometimes considered the nerve center of the application. That's where all the long-lived data for your application is stored. It also drives decision-making criteria. A reporting team queries the database for various business metrics.

In this fictional company, the database team has decided to create a read replica of the primary database. A *read replica* is another copy of the database that users can only read from (not write to). The database is updated through a replication mechanism from a primary database that it is tied to. As updates are made to the primary, the database system replicates those same changes to the read replica to keep it in sync. The reporting team queries the read replica to help prevent unwanted congestion on the primary database for normal end users of the application.

If you were building a dashboard for the read replica, you should decide which audience you're building the dashboard for—the database administrator or the reporting team. The reporting team probably cares about a few key items when they're running their report:

- How many reports are currently running?
- When was the last time the read replica was updated from the primary?
- How busy is the database overall?

These are similar concerns that a database administrator might have, but the prominence and level of detail necessary might differ wildly. Take the question of "How busy is the database?" The database administrator would probably want that data broken up by CPU utilization, disk input/output (I/O), memory utilization, database buffer cache hit ratio, and more. The administrator wants this detail because their purpose is to understand not only the performance of the system, but the contributing factors to that performance. A reporting team just wants to be able to set expectations around how long their report is going to take to run. In that context, they would be served just as well with a red/yellow/green status indicator on database performance. They just need to know whether the system is going to run slower than usual or on par with typical performance.

This is why starting with your user in mind is a dashboarding best practice. Understand the motivations for what the user will be doing. A troubleshooting dashboard and a status dashboard can look extremely different because the intended use cases are so different. When working on a new dashboard, ask yourself these questions:

- Who is going to be looking at this dashboard?
- What is the intended purpose of the dashboard?
- With that intended purpose in mind, what are the top three to five pieces of information the dashboard needs to convey quickly?

With these bits of information, you can begin tackling your new dashboard.

4.2   Widgets, the dashboard building blocks

After you decide what your new dashboard should display, you have to decide how you're going to display it. Each metric that gets displayed is done so within the context of a widget. A *widget* is a small graphical unit used to display the visualization of a particular metric. A widget can have different display types. The dashboard comprises many widgets.

> **DEFINITION**   *Widgets* are graphical components used to display a metric. The dashboard is a collection of widgets. Widgets can use different display types to express the underlying data.

4.2.1   The line graph

In the technology metrics field, you can almost never go wrong with a basic line graph. A *line graph* gives you current values as well as historical trends, allowing you to see changes over time and the variability of the metric. When in doubt, use a line graph.

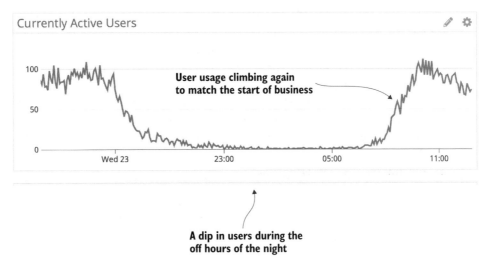

Figure 4.1   A basic line graph widget of the current user's metric

Looking at figure 4.1, you can see how the measured metric, currently active users, goes extremely low overnight but then begins to climb with the start of the workday.

Sometimes you may need to graph multiple values but want them on the same graph. There are two common scenarios for this. In the first scenario, you have multiple processes or servers that you want to see on the same graph. In a web server example, you want to see a graph of each server's CPU utilization or request count to get an idea of whether traffic is balancing evenly across the web cluster. In that case, placing multiple lines on the same graph makes a lot of sense.

In figure 4.2, you can see where a single widget has multiple lines being graphed, each one representing a different server. The tightness of the lines highlights that each node seems to be performing an equal amount of work.

In the second scenario, you may want the ability to see the sum of all of a metric's values, but still be able to isolate a specific aspect. Using our messaging system example from the previous chapter, you may want to know the total number of consumers

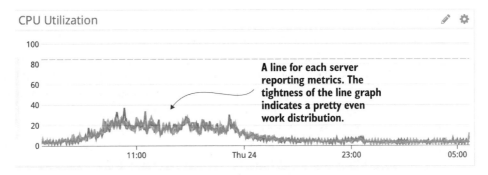

Figure 4.2   Display of multiple servers and their CPU utilization throughout the day

who exist on your messaging platform. But you also want to know where those consumers are coming from, or more precisely, which servers have the most connections.

In this scenario, you may want to consider using an *areas graph* (sometimes referred to as a *stacked line graph*). These graphs function like individual line graphs, but instead of each starting at zero, they stack on top of each other, starting from the high point of the previous line. The area between the two stacked lines is shaded in a contrasting color to highlight the difference between the two workloads.

Because the items are stacked on top of each other, you also get a total count at a quick glance. Figure 4.3 shows a stacked line graph that is displaying the total number of consumers on a messaging bus.

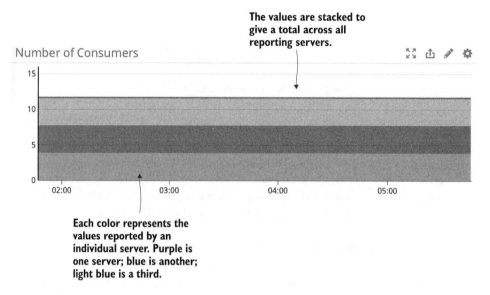

Figure 4.3   Stacked line graph, using different colors to separate the line fields

With this type of graph, you can communicate not only the overall volume, but also which components might be contributing more to the total than the others.

4.2.2   *The bar graph*

Bar graphs are a great option when you have very infrequent data or spots of missing data collection. With a line graph, many tools will draw awkward lines between missing data points, which at first glance look like a series of rising or sinking values. But in truth, the data points are just less frequent. The lack of frequency results in an inaccurate-looking line graph. Bar graphs solve this problem by not needing to draw connecting lines between the two points. Empty values just don't get displayed.

A lot of graphing tools allow you to interpret empty values as zero and plot them accordingly. That might be alright in some cases, but depending on your metrics, a missing value could be distinctly different from a zero value. One example occurs when you're measuring metrics from a server, and the server is responsible for sending the metrics to the metrics collection engine (pushing), instead of the engine connecting to the server and requesting information (pulling).

> **DEFINITION** *Pushing data* happens when an individual agent or server is responsible for shipping data to a centralized collection service. *Pulling data* occurs when the collection service connects to nodes individually to request data. Knowing how data is collected and the direction of data collection can be helpful when troubleshooting collection problems.

If your metric data is being pushed from servers to a metrics collection service, a zero value (the server has sent data and reported a value of zero) is very different from missing data (the server never sent a value, perhaps because it's down). Depending on your environment, you may want to know the difference between the two and graph them appropriately. The bar graph allows you to highlight these differences.

Figure 4.4 shows a bar graph that has missing data. The graph is showing job execution times for a process.

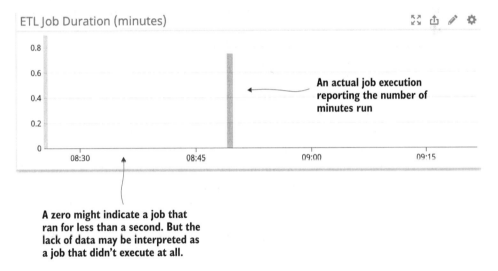

Figure 4.4 A bar graph that has missing data points

The lack of data here tells a very different story. The job being graphed didn't execute during the entire period being displayed. Graphing a zero value here would lead someone to think that the job is executing more frequently than it is. During troubleshooting, this could lead to poorly generated theories and a lot of wasted effort.

I tend to avoid treating no data as zeros. You'll need to make your own decisions on this based on your tools. Sometimes a system just doesn't emit a metric if it doesn't have a value. In cases like that, when no data is regularly expected, converting to zeros might make sense for you.

4.2.3   The gauge

The *gauge* is a great metric when you need to display a single value at a given point in time. It's like the speedometer: when you look at it, it reflects the current value of the metric. Because it displays only a single value, the widgets for this are pretty straightforward.

Some tools allow you to represent the number by using an actual gauge, but in reality, a basic numerical display works just as well in most cases. Unless, of course, the dashboard is going to be displayed to senior management. Then the gauge makes it look more "high-tech." You'll die a little bit inside using it for this reason, but know that you wouldn't be the first person to do it.

4.3   Giving context to your widgets

A widget might display many types of data, from sales numbers to CPU utilization. But those numbers are useless without context. If I gave you a gauge widget titled "Cash on hand" and that number read $2,000,000, is that good or bad? Well, it depends on a lot of factors. Are we normally keeping $18,000,000 on hand? What is cash on hand used for? If it's lunch money, it's probably way too much and could be put to better use through investments.

The point is that sometimes simply displaying data isn't enough. You need to give that data context of whether it's good or bad. I recommend giving context to data in three main ways: through color, threshold lines, and time comparisons.

4.3.1   Giving context through color

Giving context through color can be extremely easy, because most of us are already wired to associate certain colors with a particular meaning. With absolutely no context, if I were to show you a green light, you'd most likely think, "go" or "OK." If I showed you a red light, you'd most likely think, "stop" or "danger." You can use this wiring to your advantage to use color as a means of providing context, specifically with gauge numbers.

Most tools provide an easy way to color-code a value or to annotate the widget with a symbol when values are within a range or threshold. With this functionality, you can determine the thresholds for gauge values and dynamically color-code them appropriately. This enables users of the dashboard to quickly look at a widget and determine whether things are good or bad, just based on the color of the value or the annotation added to it. But remember to use common colors that are universally recognized: green for OK, yellow for warning, and red for danger. If you want to add more than these colors, that's fine, but make sure your colors are transitioning through this spectrum.

It can be extremely confusing when these rules are violated. I remember going to a data center once where the hard drive lights had accidentally been wired incorrectly, so all the lights on the drives were red! I went into quite a shock when I thought the entire disk array had failed, only to be told about the mix-up a few minutes later. Everything was fine, and I was able to delete my LinkedIn post about finding a new job before anyone saw it, but that's probably an experience that everyone has when they first visit. Remember to make sure you stick with the boring green/yellow/red pattern. If you need additional colors for whatever reason, make them along the spectrum between those colors (green to yellow, and yellow to red).

4.3.2 Giving context through threshold lines

If I'm looking at a graph, the context of that graph can change greatly based on the time horizon I'm looking at. For example, if the orders per second metric has been bad for four hours, but I'm looking at only the last hour of data, I might not realize that there's been a significant change. The number looks perfectly steady. But if I zoom out, I can quickly see that something significant has happened!

When you design your widget, you're never certain that users will be viewing it within the appropriate time horizon to get the context of previous values. You can solve this by giving the user context via threshold lines. *Threshold lines* are additional lines in the graph that are static, indicating the maximum values for that widget. This way, no matter what your time horizon is when you look at the widget, you can see that you're below whatever limit there should be. Take a look at figure 4.5 and try to determine whether this graph is in a good or bad state.

Without knowing anything about the graph or what a RabbitMQ file descriptor is, you can probably tell that this graph is in a good state. The dotted line represents the threshold for this particular graph. The color-coding of the threshold line is a deliberate choice as well. The threshold is red to indicate that this is a bad threshold or a bad

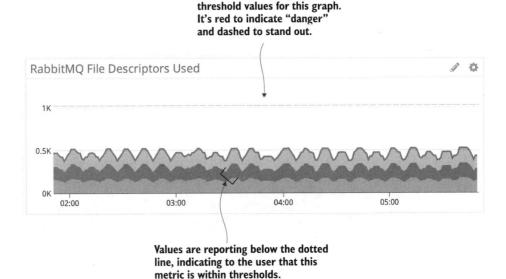

Figure 4.5 A graph that uses threshold lines

line to cross. Now if this were a green line, it might send a different connotation, making you surmise that the metric needs to be above the threshold to be considered healthy. The power of colors!

Another thing you'll notice is that the threshold line is dashed. This is to draw attention to it so that it doesn't blend in with other metric data. If your other metric data is displayed as dashed lines, consider changing the threshold lines to solid. Just be sure that you can easily differentiate them from other metric lines.

4.3.3   *Giving context through time comparisons*

In a lot of workloads, your metric pattern might be variable based on the time of day. This could be due to factors like when your users are online, when certain background processing occurs, or just a general increase in load. Sometimes it's helpful to understand whether the metric data you're seeing is an outlier or is matching up with previous norms. The best way to do this is a time-comparison overlay.

With a time-comparison overlay, you're taking the metrics from the previous 24 hours and applying those datapoints in the same graph, but with slightly different display criteria. In figure 4.6, you can see that database read latency is being compared over a 24-hour period.

Now when looking at a particular spike, you can easily see that it is pretty consistent with historical behavior. But be careful how much value you assign historical performance. Just because something performed this way yesterday doesn't mean it's not a problem. It's just not a new problem, and that's a subtle difference.

If what you've been investigating is something new that's been happening within the last, say, hour, then the historical performance shows that nothing has changed

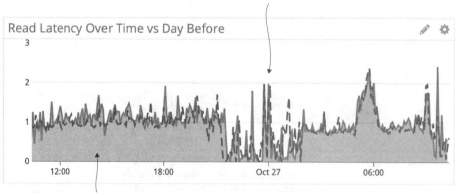

Figure 4.6   Displaying historical metrics on top of the current metrics to give additional context

with the pattern of this metric. Your application is doing just as bad as it was yesterday. But if you were looking for general performance improvements, tuning for this historically high volume could be beneficial. The devil is in the details.

4.4 *Organizing your dashboard*

Now that you have your widgets, you're ready to start logically organizing your dashboard. You should think about the users and the key bits of information they will need when viewing this dashboard. Think of the big two to four items that you think will be the most likely reason your intended users are coming to the dashboard. For checking on things like website performance health, you want to see response-time latency, requests per second, and request error rate as your top three dashboards. When doing investigative research, these three datapoints are probably going to be the things you look at first. If they're performing well and you can find that out quickly, you can then move to the next possible source of the problem in quick fashion.

The organization of your dashboards doesn't need to remain static either. Over time you might find that you've underemphasized some graphs and overemphasized others. Or you might be experiencing a period of instability due to a new problem that's been introduced into the system. In those cases, if you have a leading metric that forecasts problems, it's probably worthwhile to place that metric prominently in the front during the unstable period. The goal of dashboard organization is to provide access to the data you need most often, as quickly as possible.

You might find that different people feel that different metrics should be highlighted. Again, that's likely based on the way different types of users care about different types of data. Don't be afraid to create more dashboards if you need to. Later in this chapter, I'll talk about how to name dashboards to draw the attention of these various groups.

4.4.1 *Working with dashboard rows*

Widgets in your dashboard are aligned in rows. Your widgets should be organized from left to right, top to bottom, in order of importance. In most cases, your widgets will be further grouped into related metrics. All of the disk performance metrics should be located together, the CPU metrics grouped together, and the business key performance indicators grouped together. The one place you should break this rule is the very first row of the dashboard.

The first row of the dashboard should be reserved for your most important metrics. Where they fall in the grouping of metrics is immaterial compared to how quickly you can get access to that data. Since you designed the dashboard with a particular type of user in mind, think of what that user will most likely want access to on a regular basis. What would they check first when they log into the dashboard? These are the items that should go in your first row.

Try to limit that row to no more than five widgets if possible. It's easy to get caught up in the idea that all the metrics are important, but if they're all important, then none of them are. They'll get lost in a sea of widgets, and you'll spend more time researching CPU-level context switches instead of figuring out why revenue is dropping.

Once you've established the first row, think of the various groupings that you might have in your widgets. Which widgets are related and tell different angles of the same story? For example, I would group disk performance metrics together. I'd gather these metrics that surround disk performance so that they were all viewable without much scrolling necessary:

- Disk reads
- Disk writes
- Disk write latency
- Disk queue depth

All of these metrics give me an idea about the overall health of my disk subsystem. Grouping these together allows me to view the disk performance from various aspects to drill down to the source of the problem. If I have a lot more writes than reads and my queue depth is high, I can quickly tell that I'm likely overloading the disk with writes and should start looking for write-heavy processes in my system.

If your dashboarding tool allows it, I also suggest using any grouping functions that the tool has. This will allow you to move the entire group of widgets at the same time if you decide to rearrange your rows at a later date.

4.4.2   *Leading the reader*

Once you have defined your dashboard rows and laid them out in order of importance, you can add the finishing touches to the dashboard. I like to call this *leading the reader.*

You won't know who happens upon your dashboards or their level of familiarity with the system in question. It might be a junior operations engineer troubleshooting a problem, or it might be a senior developer verifying that the last release hasn't had any negative impact on the system. Whoever it is, you should try not to assume too much knowledge on their behalf. The more you can lead them through your dashboard, the better.

You can do this by creating *note widgets.* These are just simple, free-form text areas that allow you to further describe the dashboard, widgets, and widget groupings. You might even want to describe how some metrics relate to each other and how they should be read or interpreted.

Almost all metrics have a sort of known anomaly to them. That's when a metric has a drastic swing under a well-known set of conditions. For example, in our environment, the database memory utilization suddenly drops after a deployment occurs. To someone unfamiliar with this process, this might look a little suspicious. A simple note next to the graph can help guide the reader so that they have a better understanding of that behavior. Figure 4.7 shows an example of such a note.

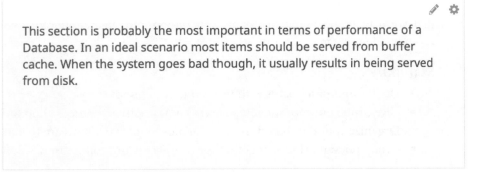

This section is probably the most important in terms of performance of a Database. In an ideal scenario most items should be served from buffer cache. When the system goes bad though, it usually results in being served from disk.

Figure 4.7 A note adds context to a widget.

Notes can also be a great place to leave breadcrumbs for the user. You might tell the reader about another location to look for relevant information with a link to it. Or you might have a deep link to the logging entries for the system being reviewed. Notes are a fantastic way to help people learn about the dashboards and become more self-sufficient in the future.

4.5 *Naming your dashboards*

They say the two hardest things in computer science are cache invalidation and naming things. Dashboards are no exception to this rule. I like to break my dashboards into three sections:

- The intended audience (Marketing, TechOPS, Data Science)
- The system under examination (Database, Platform, Message Bus)
- The view of the system being taken (Web Traffic Reports, System Health Overview, Current Monthly Spending)

By naming your dashboards in this way, you can help people filter out the dashboards that they don't really care about and find the ones that are relevant to their needs. A marketing person doesn't have to spend time clicking through all the TechOps dashboards when their dashboard is named "Marketing – Platform – Web Traffic Reports." They can quickly drill down into what they need and bookmark it.

If you're lucky enough to have a dashboarding tool that supports a folder hierarchy, you can consider making the *intended audience* section a folder, with the *system under examination* section being a subfolder of that, with your dashboards listed in the folder without the long prefix name.

These are not hard-and-fast rules for organizing dashboards. They're merely suggestions on how to think about breaking up your dashboards. You may not even need any deep categorization, based on the number of dashboards you have. If your audience is relatively small, the *intended audience* breakdown might not make sense for you. The goal is to have a systematic naming convention that allows people to find the dashboards they care about. If it makes sense in your organization to rename them after farm animals or famous street names, have at it. Just create some sort of pattern that you can follow and that people can understand. Like your office conference room naming scheme .

Summary

- Design your dashboards with the end user in mind.
- Give context to your widgets so users know whether a value is good or bad.
- Organize your dashboards so that the most important items are first to be seen.
- Group relevant widgets together for easy access and comparison.

Quality as a condiment

This chapter covers

- The testing pyramid
- Continuous deployment versus continuous delivery
- Restoring confidence in your test suite
- How flaky tests contribute to flaky systems
- Feature flags
- Why the operations team should own the testing infrastructure

Imagine you're at one of those quick-serve restaurants where you move from station to station adding ingredients to your final dish. Each part of your meal is a separate ingredient that comes together at the end of the line. Once you get to the end of the line, you might ask for a condiment to enhance the dish. But there is no condiment called "quality." If there were, everyone would order their dish with extra quality at the end. Just drown it in quality! This is exactly what many organizations are doing with their quality strategy.

Lots of companies have a dedicated quality assurance (QA) team that's responsible for ensuring that you're producing a quality product. But the quality of the product can't exist in itself. Overall quality comprises the quality of all the individual ingredients. If you're not checking the quality of the ingredients, the quality of the final product can be only so good. Quality is not a condiment. Not in restaurants, and not in software development.

To consistently deliver a quality product, you have to build quality into every component and ingredient individually, and you have to verify that quality separately before it gets completely absorbed into the final product. Waiting until the end of the development life cycle and tacking on testing can be a recipe for disaster. When you're testing all the ingredients of the product, chances are, you're doing a lot more testing generally. This means the way you structure your testing efforts becomes important. The quality of those test results becomes equally important. You need to be able to trust the outputs of those tests, or people will question their need. But often in the *quality as a condiment* antipattern, you're keeping your eyes on the wrong sorts of metrics around testing.

If you're doing any automated testing, you probably keep a watchful eye on the number of test cases. In fact, you probably thump your chest occasionally, overly proud of just how much automation you have. And despite having 1,500 automated test cases, a full QA team that does regression on every release, you still end up releasing your software with bugs. Not only that, but you sometimes release with embarrassing bugs that highlight the fact that some areas are just not tested at all. You're not alone.

Are there ways to keep from releasing bugs into production? My opinion is no. As long as you're writing software, you'll also be writing bugs that don't get caught and make their way into production. This is your lot in life. This is what you signed up for. I'll give you a minute to digest that.

Now that you've accepted that, I'll tell you it's not the end of the world. You can work on making certain types of bugs much less likely to occur and develop a process whereby when you identify a bug, you know exactly what to do to test for that scenario and ensure that it doesn't happen again. With enough practice, you'll be able to identify classes of errors, perhaps eliminating an entire variety of errors in one swoop. But the process is one of iteration and commitment.

The meat of this chapter focuses on the testing process and how it applies to DevOps. It's not a complete philosophy on how testing should be done, but I will dive into the underpinnings of testing strategies in widespread use today. Once I establish the basics around these ideas, I'll talk about the feedback loop that you get from your test suite and how it builds (or destroys) confidence in what's being deployed. And finally, I'll discuss why testing is important to the deployment process and ensuring that your source code repository is always in a deployable state.

5.1   *The testing pyramid*

Many of today's test suites are centered around the idea of the testing pyramid. The *testing pyramid* is a metaphor for the types of testing that you should be doing for your application. It gives an opinionated view on where the most energy and effort should be expended in the testing life cycle.

The testing pyramid places a heavy emphasis on unit testing being the foundation of your test suite and the largest component of it. *Unit tests* are written to test one specific section of code (known as the *unit*) and ensure that it functions and behaves as intended. *Integration tests* are the next level in the pyramid and focus on combining the various units of the system and testing them in groups. These tests exercise the interactions between the units. Finally, *end-to-end tests* exercise the system from the perspective of an end user.

I'll dive into each of these areas in more detail later in the chapter. Throughout this chapter, I will assume you're doing automated testing in some fashion. This doesn't mean that some manual regression testing isn't also happening, but for the items in this list, I'm assuming a computer is performing these tasks.

> **DEFINITION** The *testing pyramid* is a metaphor to highlight how you should group your tests, along with guidelines for the number of tests that should exist relative to other types of test groups. Most of your tests should be unit tests, followed by integration tests, and lastly, end-to-end tests.

Figure 5.1 shows an example of the testing pyramid. You'll notice three distinct layers: unit testing, integration testing, and end-to-end testing. These groupings are intended to focus the goals of the test suite, with the idea of quick feedback at the base of the pyramid, and tests becoming slower but more extensive as you move up the pyramid stack.

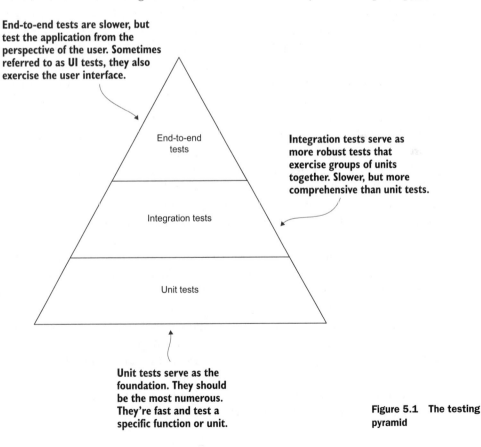

End-to-end tests are slower, but test the application from the perspective of the user. Sometimes referred to as UI tests, they also exercise the user interface.

End-to-end tests

Integration tests serve as more robust tests that exercise groups of units together. Slower, but more comprehensive than unit tests.

Integration tests

Unit tests

Unit tests serve as the foundation. They should be the most numerous. They're fast and test a specific function or unit.

Figure 5.1 The testing pyramid

You may be wondering, what in the name of good software development does the testing pyramid have to do with DevOps? There are two primary reasons it's important.

First, as the DevOps movement pushes for more and more automation, teams like operations might be getting exposed to these concepts for the first time. It's important that they understand the methods and practices currently employed by development teams. Using the same guidelines and practices will help align the teams and create synergies. (Yes, I used the word "synergies." It really does feel like the best word here. Don't judge me.)

The second reason is that as DevOps pushes for more automation, the automation will need to interact with other processes within the software development life cycle. These processes need to be able to emit a signal, which becomes a quantitative metric for a qualitative property. That sentence sounds like I'm going to try to sell you something, so let me give an example.

An automated deployment process would want to know that something is OK to deploy. It needs to know that the code is of good quality. But what does "quality" mean to a computer? It doesn't inherently know the difference between a flaky test that is known to fail regularly and a test that, if it fails, the code should be avoided at all costs. As a developer, you have to design those sorts of qualitative assumptions into your test suites so that automation can make this determination for you. The results of the test suite are as much for machine consumption (automation) as for human consumption. This makes it a topic at least worthy of discussion in the DevOps circle.

The testing pyramid serves as a set of guide rails for structuring your test suite in order to provide maximum speed and quality. If you follow the overall structure proposed by the testing pyramid, you will be able to create accurate feedback quickly to your end user. If your tests are structured so that the majority of them are integration tests, these tests will inherently run slower than their less heavyweight unit tests.

As I'll discuss later in the chapter, as you move up the pyramid, not only does the speed of tests tend to decrease, but also the number of external factors that might influence the tests begin to increase. By using the testing pyramid as a reminder for your test structure, you can ensure that your test suite will be optimized to provide accurate feedback faster than if you placed too much energy higher up the pyramid.

You may be wondering why a DevOps book has a chapter focused on testing. The first point is to highlight that automated testing plays a crucial role in the DevOps approach. The more automation you begin to build into your system, the more important it is to have automated verification that those changes were successful. The second reason is really to speak to the operations staff members who may not be as in tune with the testing process as their developer counterparts. The testing life cycle is so important in DevOps transformations that it's important for operations staff members to understand it just as much as development staff members. Operations staff will need to work on more and more automation, specifically around infrastructure creation and management. Having a foundation for standard approaches to automated testing will serve them well in their DevOps journey.

Hopefully, I've defended why the next 20 or so pages belong in this book, so let's get to it.

5.2 *Testing structure*

The testing pyramid provides a framework for structuring your testing suite. The next section goes into a bit more detail on each hierarchy level in the testing pyramid. The testing pyramid has expanded over the years to encapsulate different methods of testing, such as API tests on top of integration tests as an example. I've shied away from those particular additions and instead consider those part of the integration layer of testing.

5.2.1 *Unit tests*

Unit testing sits at the bottom of the testing pyramid. It's the foundation for all the tests that come after it. If properly designed, any unit test failure should result in tests higher in the stack failing pretty reliably.

So, what is unit testing? In *unit testing*, an individual unit or component of software is tested. This component might be a method, a class, or a function, depending on what exactly is being tested. The key is to ensure that all possible code paths in the unit being tested are exercised and their success evaluated.

> **DEFINITION** *Unit tests* are tests written for individual units, or components, of software. These components are at a granular level in the code, such as a method, function, or class, instead of an entire module of the application.

Unit tests should be written by the developer writing the component or unit under test. The reason is that unit tests should be run regularly by the developer during the creation and subsequent testing of the unit under development! In some circumstances, a unit test will be missed by a developer, in which case it's OK for someone else to write the unit test to ensure thorough testing. But if your organization currently has someone other than the developer writing unit tests, I'm sorry, but you're doing it wrong. Leaving the task to another group means a few things, including the following.

- The developer has the most context for the test case. Because of this, they'll have the best frame of reference for creating the test case.
- The developer will have an automated process for verifying their code. If they ever need to refactor code, they'll be aided by the automated tests they've created around the unit they're working on.
- By ensuring that the developers are writing tests, teams can take advantage of different development practices, like test-driven development, as part of their development workflow.
- If the responsibility is on the developer, it becomes easier to enforce unit testing requirements through processes like code reviews prior to merging the code into the source code repository.

Ensuring that developers are the primary authors of unit tests is a must. If for some reason that doesn't work for your organization, you should look long and hard at the trade-offs. At the very least, you should make sure you have solid answers to how you're dealing with the preceding bullet points.

What is test-driven development?

In the previous section, I mentioned taking advantage of practices like test-driven development (TDD). For those who don't know, TDD is the practice by which a developer turns their code requirements into test cases.

For example, if the function being written must take three numeric values, apply a formula to them, and return the results, the developer could write these requirements as tests before writing any code that implements those requirements. Only after the test cases have been developed does the developer write the underlying implementations for that code. The developer knows when they have functioning code because the test cases should now be passing, as long as they've met the developer's expectation.

This approach encourages developers to keep the units relatively small, which leads to an easier time debugging applications. Also, with the tests being written ahead of the implementation, you can reduce the chance of developers writing tests that concern themselves with implementation details, rather than inputs and outputs.

UNIT TEST STRUCTURE

In terms of structure, unit tests should be isolated as much as possible from interactions with the rest of the system. Anything that isn't part of the unit under test should be mocked or stubbed out. The goal is to ensure that the tests run fast and are not marred by possible failures from other systems.

As an example, suppose you're writing a function that does some calculations to generate a rate of return on an investment. Your function would normally interact with an API to get the original purchase price of the investment. You want that unit test to be able to give you consistent feedback on how *your* code is functioning. But, if inside your unit test you call the actual API, you're introducing new potential failure points that have nothing to do with your code. What if the API is down? What if the API is malfunctioning? This adds noise to your unit test because the failures are outside your control. Faking the API call allows you to keep the test focused on your code. This isn't to say that testing the interaction with the API isn't important; it's just a concern for a different test, higher in the testing pyramid (specifically, the integration tests portion of the pyramid).

Another advantage to faking these types of interactions and keeping things focused is speed. Unit tests should be designed with speed in mind in order to reduce the amount of time a developer needs to wait to get feedback on the change. The faster the feedback, the more likely a developer is to run these tests locally. Keeping the test focused on local interactions also makes it much easier to debug, since you know with certainty it's the function at fault.

DETERMINING WHAT TO UNIT TEST

The hardest part about unit testing is knowing what to write test cases for. To many people's surprise, testing everything can be counterproductive. If you test everything, refactoring is more difficult, not less. This often comes up when developers attempt to write test cases for internal implementations.

If you change the internal implementation of how a problem is solved, all of the corresponding tests against that internal implementation begin to fail. This makes refactoring cumbersome, because you're refactoring not only the code, but also all the tests that exercised that code. This is where it becomes important to understand how your code paths are called.

Let's use the example of the rate calculation. You have a function called `mortgage_calc` that people will invoke to get the total cost of a mortgage with interest. The resulting value should be a dollar amount. The black box of how you go about calculating that may not need to be tested individually if those methods are called only within the `mortgage_calc` function; the detailed implementations of those methods are exercised as a result of testing `mortgage_calc`. This encapsulation allows you to refactor a bit easier. Maybe one day you decide to change the internal implementation of `mortgage_calc`. You can ensure that `mortgage_calc` still exhibits the expected behavior without needing to refactor all the tests for the internal implementation of that function, freeing you up to make code changes with confidence.

The hard part is, I don't have a one-size-fits-all method for solving this problem. The best I can offer is to identify public code paths and private code paths and focus your unit testing around the public code paths, allowing you to change the private paths without spending a ton of time refactoring internal tests. Focus on those code paths that are called from multiple places. Testing internal implementations isn't completely discouraged, but use it sparingly.

Having unit tests at the bottom of the test pyramid reflects that they should also be the lion's share of your test cases. They're usually the fastest, most reliable, and most granular types of tests you can create. The source of failure in a unit test should be pretty obvious, because the unit under test is tightly scoped. Unit tests feature prominently later in the chapter, when I start to discuss the automated execution of tests. This automation is typically done by a continuous integration server such as Jenkins, CircleCI, Harness, and many others.

> **NOTE** Continuous integration servers have become extremely popular as a way to automatically execute a code base's test suite. Continuous integration servers generally have hooks into common code repositories to detect when a change has been merged and to act based on that change. ThoughtWorks (www .thoughtworks.com/continuous-integration) is often credited with inventing continuous integration and has some excellent resources on its website.

5.2.2   *Integration tests*

Integration tests are the next level in the testing pyramid. The goal is to begin to test the connection points between systems and the way the application handles responses to those systems. Whereas in a unit test, you may have mocked out or faked a database connection, in the integration test phase, you'll connect to an actual database server, write data to the database, and then read that data to validate that your operation worked successfully.

Integration tests are important because seldom do two things just seamlessly work together. The two items being integrated might have been built with very different use cases in mind, but when they're brought together, they fail in spectacular ways.

As an example, I once worked for a company that was building a new headquarters. The building and the parking garage attached to the building were being designed separately. When they finally started construction, they realized the parking garage floors didn't line up with the building floors, so additional stairways needed to be added to integrate the two. This is an example in the physical world of a failed integration test!

Integration tests will take longer, considering the interactions that need to happen between components of the test. In addition, each of those components will likely need to go through a setup and teardown process to get them in the correct state for testing. Database records might need to be populated or local files downloaded for processing, just to name a couple of examples. Because of this, integration tests are generally more expensive to run, but they still play a vital part in the testing strategy.

Integration tests should never run their integration points against production instances. This might sound rudimentary, but I feel like it's best to state it clearly. If you need to test against another service, such as a database, you should try to launch that service locally in the test environment. Even read-only testing against production environments could place undue stress on the production servers, creating problems for real users.

Tests that write data are problematic for production as well; when your test environment begins spamming production with bogus test data, you'll probably need to have a pretty stern conversation with your bosses. Testing in production is definitely possible, but it takes a large, orchestrated effort by all members of the technical team.

If launching a local copy of the dependency isn't feasible, you should consider standing up a test environment that's running these services for the test suite to test against. Problems that you run into here, though, might be related to data consistency problems. If you're isolating your dependencies per test case, you can do tests that follow this order:

1   Read the number of rows in the database.
2   Perform an operation on the database, such as an insert.
3   Verify that the number of rows has increased.

This is a common pattern you see in test cases. Not only is it wrong, but it's exceptionally wrong in the case of a shared staging environment. How does your application verify that no one else is writing to that table? What if two tests execute at the same time, and now instead of having $N+1$ records, you have $N+2$ records (where N is the number of records in the database prior to your operation)?

In a shared testing infrastructure scenario, these tests must be much more explicit. Counting rows no longer is sufficient. You need to verify that the exact row you created exists. It's not complicated, but just a little more involved. You'll run into a lot of scenarios like this if you opt to use a shared environment for integration testing. But if you can't have isolated dependencies per test run, this might be your next best option.

> ## Contract testing
>
> Another popular form of testing that's been cropping up is *contract testing*. The idea behind contract testing is to create a way to detect when your underlying assumptions about a stubbed-out service have changed.
>
> If you're going to use a mock or a stub service for your testing purposes, you have to be sure that the service is accepting inputs and producing outputs in the way you expect. If the real service were to change its behavior, but your tests don't reflect that, you'll end up releasing code that doesn't interact with the service correctly. Enter the contract test.
>
> The contract tests are a separate set of tests that run against a service to ensure that the inputs and outputs of the endpoints are still behaving in the way you expect them to. Contract tests are prone to change, so running them at a more infrequent rate isn't uncommon. (Daily will probably suffice.)
>
> By having contract tests, you can detect when another service has changed its expectations and update your stubs and mocks appropriately. If you want more information, see the excellent chapter on contract tests in *Testing Java Microservices* by Alex Soto Bueno, Andy Gumbrecht, and Jason Porter (Manning, 2018).

5.2.3 End-to-end tests

End-to-end tests exercise the system from the perspective of the end user. Sometimes referred to as *UI tests*, they launch or simulate a browser or client-side application and drive change through the same mechanism that an end user would. End-to-end tests usually verify results the same way, by ensuring that data is properly displayed, response times are reasonable, and no pesky UI errors show up. Often end-to-end tests will be launched via a variety of browsers and browser versions to make sure no regression errors are triggered by any browser and version combinations.

End-to-end tests are at the top of the pyramid. They're the most complete test, but also the most time-consuming and often the flakiest. They should be the smallest set of tests in your testing portfolio. If you're overly reliant on end-to-end tests, you'll probably find yourself with a test suite that can be brittle and easily fail between runs.

These failures might be outside your actual test cases. When a test fails because an element in the web page has changed names or locations, that's one thing. But when your test fails because the underlying web driver that powers the test has failed, tracking down and debugging the issue can be a frustrating exercise.

Heavy focus on end-to-end tests

Another common cause of heavy end-to-end tests is that the team responsible for doing the majority of testing is not the development team. Many (but certainly not all) QA teams that are doing programmatic testing lean on UI tests because it's the way they're accustomed to interacting with the application and the underlying data.

A lot of detailed knowledge is required to understand where a value on the page comes from. It might be straight from a field in the database. It might be a calculated value that comes from a database field, with additional context being brought in from application logic. Or it might be computed on the fly. The point, though, is that someone who isn't intimately familiar with the code might not be able to answer the question of where the data comes from. But if you write a UI test, it doesn't always matter. You're checking for a known value to exist on a known record.

In my experience, I've seen testing teams become heavily reliant on production data as part of their regression testing, partly because production will have specific use cases that the testing team can rely on as part of the regression test. The difficulty comes in, however, when production has incorrect data, meaning the bug has already escaped into the wild. Then the end-to-end test ensures that the data matches what's in production instead of what the actual calculated value should be.

As fewer unit tests are employed and more end-to-end tests are used in their place, the situation becomes exacerbated. What can end up happening is that your test suite moves from testing for correctness to testing for conformity, which isn't always the same thing. Instead of testing that 2 + 2 = 4, you test that 2 + 2 = whatever production says. The bad news is, if production says 5, the laws of mathematics get tossed out the window. The good news is that your UI test passes. This just stresses how important it is to make sure the key functions involved are covered in unit tests and that you don't rely on them to be caught higher up in the testing pyramid.

If you've done a lot of work with end-to-end tests, you probably have recognized that they're often brittle. By *brittle*, I mean that they're easily broken, often needing to be handled with kid gloves and an enormous amount of care and feeding. Small, inconsequential changes to the code or the layout of a web page can break an end-to-end test suite.

A lot of that is rooted in the way these sorts of tests are designed. To find a value that you're testing against, the test engineer needs to know and understand the layout of the page. Through that, they can build techniques to parse a page and interpret the value that you're looking for to test against. This is great, until one day the page layout changes. Or the page is slow to load. Or the driver engine responsible for parsing the page runs out of memory. Or a third-party web plugin for ads doesn't load. The list of things that could go wrong is long and distinguished.

The brittleness of testing, combined with the amount of time it takes to execute end-to-end tests, forces these sorts of tests to live at the very top of the hierarchy, and as a result, make up the smallest portion of your testing portfolio. But because of their extensive nature, you end up actually exercising quite a few code paths with a single end-to-end test because the scope of what's under test is so much larger. Instead of testing a single unit or a single integration, you're now testing an entire business concept. That business concept will probably exercise multiple smaller things on its path to success. As an example, say your end-to-end test was going to test the order-generation process. Your end-to-end test might look like the following:

1 Log in to the website.
2 Search the product catalog for unicorn dolls.
3 Add a unicorn doll to your shopping cart.
4 Execute the checkout process (payment).
5 Verify that a confirmation email/receipt was sent.

These five steps are pretty basic from a user-interaction perspective, but from a system perspective, you're testing a lot of functionality in one test. The following are just a handful of things that are being tested at a more granular level with this:

- Database connectivity
- Search functionality
- Product catalog
- Shopping cart functionality
- Payment processing
- Email notification
- UI layout
- Authentication functionality

And this list could arguably be a lot longer if you really wanted to dig into it. But suffice it to say that an end-to-end test exercises quite a bit of functionality in a single go. But it's also longer and more prone to random failures that have nothing to do with the actual system under test. Again, real test failures are valuable feedback, and you need to understand if your system isn't providing correct responses. But if your tests are failing because of hardware limitations, web driver crashes, or other things around the scaffolding of your test suite, then you must consider the value proposition of the test. You might end up playing whack-a-mole as you solve one problem in the testing infrastructure only to create or discover another.

I try to limit the number of end-to-end tests performed to core business functionality. What tasks must absolutely work in the application? In the case of my example, a simple e-commerce site, they might be as follows:

- Order processing
- Product catalog searching
- Authentication
- Shopping cart functionality

The example tested all of those functions with a single end-to-end test. When building end-to-end tests, it's important to understand the key business drivers and to make sure those have good test coverage. But if you get a lot of end-to-end tests, chances are you'll increase your failure rate due to unrelated problems in your test suite. This will create a lack of confidence in your test suite, which generates a lot of other issues on the team. The goal is to make sure each of your end-to-end tests adds more value than it creates additional work and troubleshooting. Your list of things to test may grow and shrink over time.

5.3   *Confidence in your test suite*

Imagine you're in the cockpit of an airplane. The pilot is showing you his preflight checklist. He's running through the routine when something in the routine fails. He turns to you and says, "Don't worry about it; this thing just fails sometimes." He then reruns the steps of the preflight checklist, and magically everything works this time. "See, I told you." How good do you feel about that flight? Probably not very good.

Confidence in your test suite is an asset. When a test suite becomes unpredictable, its value as a confidence-building tool diminishes. And if a test suite doesn't build confidence, what's the point of it? Many organizations lose sight of what a test suite is supposed to provide. Instead, they cargo-cult the idea of automated testing based on nothing more than that's what you're supposed to do. If confidence in the test suite begins to wane, that's something you need to address sooner rather than later.

Gauging confidence in the test suite is more of an art than a science. An easy way to gauge it is the way people react to the test suite failing. A failed test should trigger the engineer to begin investigating their own code, looking at what changed and how that change might have impacted the test suite. But when confidence in a test suite is low, the first thing an engineer will do is rerun the test suite. This is often accompanied with a lack of belief that the change they made could in any way affect the test that is failing.

The next thing that happens when confidence is low is that the build environment begins to be questioned: "Something must have changed with these build servers." That kicks off a series of conversations with whoever supports the build servers burning up their valuable time. My point isn't that these things aren't possible culprits in a failed test scenario. In many situations, they are. But in an environment with low test confidence, these are the first to be blamed, as opposed to the most likely thing that changed in the environment—the code!

You can gauge whether confidence in your test suite is low in various ways. The simplest way is to just ask the engineers. How confident are they in their changes if the test suite passes or fails? They will be able to give you a keen perspective on the quality of the test suite because they're interacting with it daily. But just because confidence in your test suite is low doesn't mean it has to stay there.

5.3.1 *Restoring confidence in your test suite*

Restoring confidence in your test suite isn't a monumental task. It requires identifying the source of bad tests, correcting them, and increasing the speed at which problems are known. You can do that largely by following the testing pyramid to start.

TEST SUITES SHOULD FAIL IMMEDIATELY AFTER THEY ENCOUNTER A FAILURE

When you're running tests, it can be tempting to have your test suite run from beginning to end, reporting all the failures at the end of the run. The problem is, you may end up spending a lot of compute time only to find out the test failed two minutes into the run. What value is gained by the subsequent failures? How many of the integration or end-to-end tests failed because a basic failure in the unit tests has cascaded up the chain?

In addition, the reliability of your test suite generally worsens as you move up the pyramid. If your unit tests are failing, you can be pretty confident that the cause is something wrong with the code. Why continue with the rest of the execution? The first thing I recommend you do to help bolster confidence in the test suite is to divide the suite's execution into phases. Group your tests into levels of confidence, similar to the testing pyramid. You might have several subgroups within the integration tests layer, but if any unit tests fail, continuing on in the test suite carries little value.

The objective is to give developers fast feedback on the acceptability of their code. If you run a set of lower tests that fail, but then continue on with other tests, the feedback gets confusing. Every test failure becomes a murder mystery. As an example, say you have an end-to-end test that failed because the login routine didn't work. You begin your investigation at the top of the failure event (the login page error) and work your way backward. The login page test failed because the renderer action failed, because some required data didn't load, because the database connection failed, because the method for decrypting the password failed and gave a bogus response.

All of that investigation takes time. If you had just failed right at the decryption password method's unit test, you'd have a much clearer understanding of what happened and where to start your investigation. The test suite should try to make it clear and obvious where things failed.

The more time developers spend researching test failures, the lower the *perceived* usefulness of the test suite becomes. I put emphasis on the word "perceived" because confidence and perception are unfortunately intertwined in the human mind. If people waste time troubleshooting the test suite to figure out what went wrong, the idea that the test suite has little value will spread. Making it clear and obvious when something fails will go a long way in helping to combat that perception.

It's also extremely important to have good test case hygiene. If a bug is discovered in production, a test to detect that issue going forward should be created. Finding the same bug slip through the testing process over and over again diminishes confidence not only in the test suite, but also in the product from your end users.

DON'T TOLERATE FLAKY TESTS

The next thing to do is to take stock of which tests are flaky. (Hint: it's probably your end-to-end tests.) Keep a list of those tests and turn them into work items for your team to address. Reserve time in your work cycles to focus on improving the test suite. The improvements can be anything from changing your approach to the test, to finding out the reason for the test's unreliability. Maybe a more efficient way of finding elements in the page would result in less memory consumption.

Understanding why a test is failing is an important part of the upkeep of your test suite. Don't lose sight of that, even if you're improving on just a single flaky test per week. This is valuable work that will pay dividends. But if, after all that work, you find the same test to be failing repeatedly for reasons that exist outside the actual test case, I'm going to suggest something drastic. Delete it. (Or archive it if you don't like to live dangerously.)

If you can't trust it, what value is it really bringing? The amount of time you spend rerunning the test is probably creating a larger cost on the team than the savings of having that test automated. Again, if a test isn't raising confidence, it's not really doing its job. Flaky tests usually stem from a handful of things, including the following:

- The test case isn't well understood. The expected result isn't taking into account certain cases.
- Data collisions are happening. Previous test data is creating a conflict with the expected results.
- With end-to-end tests, variable loading times create "time-outs" when waiting for certain UI components to show in the browser.

There are certainly plenty of other reasons that your tests might randomly fail, but a large batch of them can probably fall under one of these issues or a variation of it. Think about any shared components with other tests that could create a data issue for your test environment. Here are a few questions you can ask yourself that might help improve these collisions:

- How can you isolate those tests?
- Do they need to be run in parallel?
- How do tests clean up data after they've run?
- Do tests assume an empty database before they execute, or are they responsible for cleaning the database themselves? (I feel tests should ensure that the environment is configured as expected.)

ISOLATE YOUR TEST SUITE

Test suite isolation becomes a real problem when your test suite relies heavily on integration and end-to-end tests. Isolating tests is pretty easy for unit tests, because the component under test uses in-memory integrations or entirely mocked-out integrations. But integration tests can be a little trickier, and the problem is commonly at the database integration layer. The easiest thing to do is to run separate database instances for every test. This can be a bit of a resource hog, though, depending on your database system of choice. You may not have the luxury of being able to separate everything completely.

If you can't run separate instances completely, you may want to try running multiple databases on the same instance. Your test suite could create a randomly named database at the start of the test suite, populate the data for the necessary test cases, and then tear down the database after those test cases have completed. For testing purposes, you really don't need a clean, proper name for the database; so as long as it's a legal name from the database engine's perspective, you should be fine. The catch with this scheme, however, is ensuring that your test suites are cleaning up after themselves when they complete.

You also need to understand what you do with the database on a failed test. The database might be an important part of the troubleshooting process, so keeping it around can add a ton of value. But if you remove the automated destruction of the database, you'll absolutely need to contend with humans forgetting to delete the test database after their investigation has completed. You'll need to evaluate the best course for your team based on your organization. Every approach has pros and cons, so you'll need to figure out which set of pros and cons works best for your organization.

There are options for further isolation through dynamic environment creation if your organization is capable of implementing and managing automated environment creation. Spinning up new virtual machines for test cases is an attractive option, but even with automation, the time spent on bootstrapping can be too long to provide the quick feedback engineers crave. Spinning up enough virtual machines at the start of the day to ensure that every test can run in its own isolated machine can save on the spin-up costs, but probably will end up creating actual monetary costs to ensure you have resource capacity.

It also creates a scaling issue as you create a much more linear relationship between your test cases and your supporting infrastructure. Running your test cases in separate Docker containers is a way to reduce this cost, since containers are not only lightweight in terms of resources, but also are very fast to start, allowing you to scale quickly as resource demands rise. Configuring testing infrastructure is beyond the scope of this book, but it's important to highlight those two paths as potential options for further test isolation.

LIMIT THE NUMBER OF END-TO-END TESTS

End-to-end tests in my experience are the flakiest of the bunch. This is mainly due to the very nature of end-to-end tests.

The tests are tightly coupled with the user interface. Small changes in the user interface create havoc on automated tests that depend on a specific layout for the website. The end-to-end test typically must have some understanding of the way the UI is structured, and that knowledge is typically embedded inside the test case in some shape or form. Add to that the pains of executing tests on shared hardware, and you can run into performance issues, which ultimately affects the evaluation criteria of the test suite.

I wish I had an easy answer to solve the woes of end-to-end testing. They're typically unreliable while at the same time being incredibly necessary. The best advice I can give follows:

- *Limit the number of end-to-end tests.* They should be limited to critical path actions for your application, such as sign-in and checkout processes for an e-commerce site.
- *Limit your end-to-end tests to testing functionality and don't consider performance.* Performance will vary greatly in a test environment based on any number of factors outside of just the application. Performance testing should be handled and approached separately.
- *Isolate end-to-end tests as much as possible.* The performance impact of two end-to-end tests running on the same machine can cause what seems to be random issues. The cost of additional hardware is much less than the human cost of troubleshooting these issues (assuming you've done the preceding recommendations first).

I've spent a lot of time talking about the test suite and restoring confidence in it. This may seem off the DevOps path just a tad, but it's important that you have a solid test strategy in place because DevOps' strength comes from the ability to leverage automation. But automation is driven by triggers and signals throughout your environment. Automated testing is one important signal about the quality of code. Having confidence in that signal is a must. In the next section, you'll take those signals coming from your test suite and apply them to the deployment pipeline.

5.3.2   *Avoiding vanity metrics*

When you start to talk about confidence in test suites, people always will reach for metrics to convey quality. This is a good reaction to have, but you need to be wary of the types of metrics you use. Specifically, you'll want to steer clear of vanity metrics.

Vanity metrics are datapoints that you measure in your system, but they're easily manipulated and don't provide a clear picture of the information the user wants. For example, "Number of registered users" is a common vanity metric. It's great that you have three million registered users, but if only five of them log in on a regular basis, the metric can be woefully misleading.

Vanity metrics can be prevalent in test suites. The metric commonly bandied about is test coverage. *Test coverage* is a measurement, usually a percentage, of the number of code paths that are being exercised inside a test suite. This number is usually easily accessed through tooling and can be a rallying call across developers, QA, and product teams. But in reality, test coverage is an example of a vanity metric. Coverage doesn't necessarily speak to the quality of the test or what specifically is being tested.

If I turn on the engine to a car, I'm exercising a great number of components, just by virtue of starting the engine. But that doesn't necessarily mean that all of the components in the car are operating to spec because they didn't immediately blow up when the car started. I call this out now specifically so that when you're designing tests, you're conscious of this vanity metric concept and don't fall victim to its allure.

Test coverage is great, but not having 100% test coverage doesn't mean your testing suite isn't extremely robust. And having 100% test coverage doesn't mean your testing suite is doing anything worthwhile. You must look beyond the numbers and focus on the quality of those tests.

5.4 *Continuous deployment vs. continuous delivery*

Most of you don't need continuous deployment. (Somewhere a thought leader is cringing at the idea that I would mock the holy grail of DevOps, continuous deployment.) For those who don't know, *continuous deployment* is the idea that every commit to your mainline branch (primary/trunk) will trigger a deployment process into production. This means that the latest changes are always rolled out to production. This process is completely automated and hands-off.

In contrast, *continuous delivery* is a practice aimed to ensure that the application is always in a deployable state. This means that you no longer have a broken primary or trunk branch during a release cycle, regardless of how often you do a release.

The two items often get conflated. The main difference is that with continuous deployment, every change that gets committed to the main branch is released through an automated process, with no manual intervention. With continuous delivery, the focus is more on ensuring the capability to deploy code when needed without having to wait for a large release train with a bunch of other changes. Every commit may not be released automatically, but it *could* be released at any time if needed.

For a simple example, imagine a product manager wants to release a small change to fix a problem that a single customer is having. In an environment without continuous delivery, the manager might need to wait until the next release of the system, which could be weeks away. In a continuous delivery environment, the deployment pipelines, infrastructure, and development processes are structured so that a release of an individual piece of the system is possible at any point. The product manager could have development make the change and release that bug fix on a separate timetable than that of the other development teams.

With those definitions laid out, it should be noted that continuous deployment can't really happen without continuous delivery. Continuous delivery is a stop on the journey to continuous deployment. Despite the hype around continuous deployment, I don't feel it's a great goal for all companies. The act of continuous deployment is supposed to force certain behaviors onto the organization. You need rock-solid automated testing if you're going to deploy every commit to production. You need a solid code review process to ensure that multiple sets of eyes have looked at code from whatever review criteria your teams have set up. Continuous deployment forces this behavior because, without it, disaster might ensue. I believe in all these things.

But I also believe that many teams and organizations have a lot of hurdles to overcome before they can realistically begin talking about continuous deployment. When tech teams take weeks to roll out patches for their systems, moving to continuous deployment seems like a pretty big leap. The act of continuous delivery is a better goal for most organizations. The goal of deploying every change as it gets committed is a noble one. But so many organizations are so far away from being able to safely and reliably do that.

Many of their internal processes are structured around the idea of a deliverable unit called a *release*. But when you're doing continuous deployment, even the concept of what a release is has to change within the company. How many internal processes are based on software versions? Sprints, project plans, help documentation, training— all these things are often centered around this ritualistic concept of a release. Considering how far the journey is, targeting the ability to release more frequently will give tremendous benefits without having to create upheaval within the organization regarding how they view, manage, and market their software platform.

But whether you decide on continuous deployment or continuous delivery, the question might come up, how do you know that your code is deployable if you're not deploying it on a regular basis? That brings us back to the testing suite that I started this chapter with. Your testing suite will be one of the signals your teams will use to evaluate whether a change being made breaks the ability to deploy your application. Continuous delivery focuses on this idea of a series of structured, automated steps that application code goes through to prove its viability for deployment. These steps are called *deployment pipelines*.

> **DEFINITION** *Deployment pipelines* are a series of structured, automated steps that exercise a code change, such as unit tests and packaging of the application code. Pipelines are an automated way to prove the code's viability for deployment.

> The result of the pipeline is usually some sort of *build artifact* that contains all of the code necessary to run the application. This includes any third-party libraries, internal libraries, and the actual code itself. The type of artifact that gets produced depends heavily on the system that you're building. In a Java ecosystem, it might be a JAR or a WAR file. In a Python ecosystem, it might be a PIP file or a wheel. The outputted file type will depend heavily on how that artifact is going to be consumed later in the process.

> **DEFINITION** *Artifacts* are a deployable version of your application or a component of the application. It is the final output of your build process. The type of artifact that gets produced will vary depending on your deployment strategy and the language your applications are written in.

With the build artifact being the last portion of your pipeline, the total set of pipeline steps might look like the following:

1 Check out the code.
2 Run static analysis such as a linter or syntax checker on the code.
3 Run unit tests.

4 Run integration tests.

5 Run end-to-end tests.

6 Package the software into a deployable artifact (WAR file, RPM, or a zip file, for example).

The steps are performed on every change that needs to be merged into the primary/trunk branch. This pipeline serves as a signal to the quality and deployment readiness of the change and results in something that can be moved to production (the *deployment artifact*).

This is just an example list. Any number of steps can be added to your pipeline that make sense for your organization. Security scans are a logical addition to this list. Infrastructure testing and configuration management might be another set of items that you would want to add. The takeaway is that your requirements for releasing software can and should be codified as much as possible and placed into a pipeline of some sort.

5.5 *Feature flags*

Whether you're using continuous deployment or continuous delivery, you can protect users from receiving new features and changes with every deployment. It can be unsettling as a user when a company is deploying new functionality multiple times per day. This is a distinct possibility when you move to continuous delivery or deployment. But you can employ several techniques to separate feature delivery from feature deployment—most notably feature flagging.

Feature flagging occurs when code functionality is hidden behind conditional logic tied to some sort of flag or semaphore. This allows code to be deployed to an environment, without necessarily having the code path available to all users. Feature flagging allows you to separate feature delivery from feature deployment. This allows the release of the feature from a marketing or product perspective to be separate and distinct from the technical release.

> **DEFINITION** *Feature flags* are a type of conditional logic that allows you to tie code paths to a flag or a semaphore, which activates the code path. If not activated, the code path is dormant. Feature flags allow you to separate a code path's deployment from the code path's release to the user audience.

The value of a feature flag is often stored in the database as a Boolean value: `true` meaning the flag is enabled, and `false` meaning disabled. In more advanced implementations, the feature flag can be enabled for specific customers or users but not for others.

To give a basic example, say you have a new algorithm to create recommendations for users on the order page. The algorithms for the recommendation engine are encapsulated into two classes. With the feature flag, you can separate when you'll use the new code path from when it gets deployed. In the following listing, you can see the skeleton of such an implementation.

Listing 5.1   Feature flagging a recommendation engine

```
class RecommendationObject(object):
    use_beta_algorithm = True          ⟵      Defines the feature flag.
    def run(customer):                         This value could come
      ┌─▷ if self.use_beta_aglorithm == True:  from a database.
      │     return BetaAlgorithm.run()
      │   else:
      │     return AlphaAlgorithm.run()
class AlphaAlgorithm(object):
    //current implementation details
class BetaAlgorithm(object):
    // previous implementation details
```

Checks the feature flag value and changes execution

This example uses a variable to determine whether the beta version or the alpha version of the algorithm should run. In a real-world scenario, you would probably base this on a database query. You could have a table structured with a feature toggle name and a Boolean value of `true` or `false`. This allows you to change the behavior of the application without needing to deploy new code. Simply updating the database value would have your running applications augment their behavior to start serving the new or old algorithm.

This also has an added benefit: if there's a problem with the new algorithm, rolling back that change doesn't require a deployment, but simply another database update. Over time, once you feel comfortable with the change, you can make it permanent by removing the feature-flagging logic and just making that the default behavior of the application. This prevents code from being littered with tons of conditional logic for feature flags that have surpassed their experimental or testing phase.

In some cases, you might always want feature toggles to exist in order to be able to recover gracefully. Imagine you have a feature flag around code that interacts with a third-party service. If the third-party service is down or having problems, enabling/disabling a feature flag could force your code to not interact with the third party and instead return a generic response. This allows your application to continue functioning but in a slightly degraded mode of performance—far better than being completely down.

Feature toggle libraries exist for just about every programming language imaginable. These libraries give you a more structured way to implement toggles. Many of them also offer added benefits, like providing caching, so that every request doesn't add an additional database query to your system. SAAS solutions are also available for feature flag implementations. A few such examples are LaunchDarkly (https://launchdarkly.com), Split (www.split.io), and Optimizely (www.optimizely.com).

5.6   *Executing pipelines*

The field of pipeline execution is littered with options and poorly used terms. The marketing spin on these tools has led to the misuse of terms like *continuous integration*. This is a pet peeve of mine, and I'll spare you the gory details. Because of this, I'm going to use the term *pipeline executors,* which are a class of tools that allow for the conditional execution of various steps within a workflow.

Figure 5.2 shows an example of a pipeline. Popular tools that fit in this category include Jenkins, CircleCI, Travis CI, and Azure Pipelines.

> **DEFINITION** *Pipeline executors* are a class of tools that allow for conditional execution of various steps within a workflow. They typically have various built-in integrations with code repositories, artifact repositories, and other software build tools.

The dirty secret about pipeline executors is that most of them are the same. They pretty much have feature parity in terms of integrations, hooks, and so on. At the end of the day, though, these pipelines are still running code that your organization wrote. If your test scripts are flaky or inconsistent, it doesn't really matter what build tool you use; it won't make those test scripts suddenly failure-free.

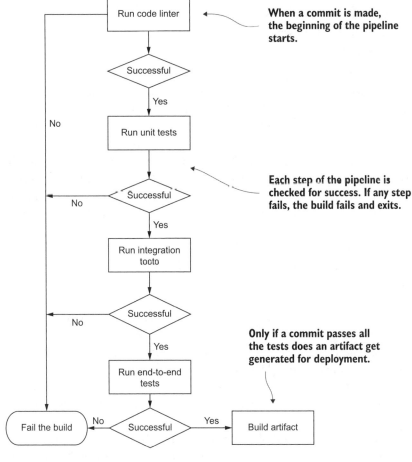

Figure 5.2   The flow of an example build pipeline

If you're going to set up a large committee to discuss and evaluate 10 options, I suggest you scuttle the committee and put that energy into making your build scripts more reliable. Assuming you don't already have a pipeline executor, you should look at your tools from the lens of least organizational resistance. A pipeline executor isn't going to make or break your organization. Having any of the tools is infinitely better than not having them, so if you can get Azure Pipelines into your organization with relative ease, then it's the best choice for you. If Jenkins is an easier sell to your teams, that's the best tool. Don't waste a lot of time evaluating many tools unless you have clear, specific, and unique requirements.

Once you've chosen a tool, it's important to break your pipeline into separate, distinct phases. This is so that you can give your developers rapid feedback on their pipeline execution and assist in pinpointing where the process has broken down. Take, for example, a script that does the following:

1 Runs unit tests
2 Runs integration tests
3 Creates a testing database
4 Loads the database with data
5 Runs end-to-end tests

In a single big-bang script, those steps are all muddled together in a log file that is probably too long, is impossible to read, and forces you to search your way through it, looking for the word "Error." But if this same series of steps were defined as separate phases in the pipeline, you could quickly realize that the error was in loading the test database in step 4, just before the end-to-end tests were going to start.

This is an easy thing to think about when you're talking about test pipelines, because you often think in those terms anyway. But you should remember to make sure that all your pipelines exhibit this behavior; regardless of whether it's a code build, an environment cleanup script, or a repository rebuild, the structure of pipelines remains the same.

Last, regarding pipelines, you should consider what your signal of success looks like for each build. The pipeline, especially in testing, should ensure or confirm that something meets a certain set of criteria or has been executed successfully. Sticking with an example of building code, you want your pipeline to be able to communicate the suitability of a build. A common way to do this is by producing a build artifact as the final step of a pipeline.

A *build artifact* is a packaged version of your software into a single file, usually with a preloaded set of installation instructions in the artifact or binary. With the build artifact as the last step of the build process, its mere existence signifies that it has gone through the necessary steps to become an artifact. That's your signal that the code is suitable for deployment.

If your build doesn't produce an artifact, there has to be a method for tying your version of code to a successful build. The easiest way is to ensure that your code merge process requires a successful build before merging. There are plenty of integrations with pipeline executors that can enforce this behavior. In this way, you can ensure that your primary/trunk branch can be considered a deployable build.

The preceding options are probably the strongest, but there are other alternatives to creating signals if necessary. One option might be a key/value pair that signals a commit hash with a successful build number. This makes it easy for other processes to integrate with this behavior, especially if manual processes must be performed. Another alternative is to integrate with the build server you're using directly as part of the code validation step. Your deployment code (or anything that needs to validate that a build is OK for deployment) can also integrate with the pipeline executor to verify that a successful build was performed for a specific commit. This creates a bit of a tighter coupling to your pipeline executor, making it harder to migrate from it in the future. But it might be worth the payoff if none of the other methods for build signals is worthwhile.

Whatever method you choose, you need to be certain that you have a way to signal quality of code to other downstream processes, most notably deployment. It all starts with a series of structured, quality test cases that can be used as an inference for code quality. Moving those tests into a pipeline executor tool allows you to further automate those processes and potentially provide points of integration.

Continuous integration vs. automated testing

With the explosion in automated testing tools and continuous integration servers like Jenkins, the term *continuous integration* has been muddied. It's important to understand how true continuous integration impacts the development process.

During software development life cycles, engineers would create long-lived branches to develop their specific feature on. These long-lived branches plagued the software development world. When people had a long-lived branch, the responsibility was on the engineer to rebase the primary/trunk branch onto their feature branch. But if developers didn't do that, massive merge conflicts would result that were cumbersome to resolve.

Not only that, but feature development and changes were progressing along in the primary branch, while the feature branch being worked on was static. It wouldn't be uncommon to find that an approach being taken was undone or broken as the result of a change that happened in the primary earlier. Enter continuous integration.

In the continuous integration approach, engineers were required to merge their changes into the primary/trunk on a regular basis, the goal being *at least* daily. This not only eliminated the long-lived branch, but also forced engineers to think about how their code was written so that it could safely be merged into the primary/trunk branch.

Enter the continuous integration server (Jenkins, Circle CI, Bamboo, and others). These applications would run a series of automated tests that were required to pass successfully before the code could be merged to the master. This would ensure that the changes introduced were safe and that potentially unfinished code wouldn't alter the behavior of the system.

(continued)
Over time it became clear, however, that people were conflating the process of continuous integration with the practice of just running automated tests in a continuous integration server. The distinction between the two is all but lost except for the most nuanced conversations. If you'd like to learn more about what continuous integration is really about, I point you to *Continuous Integration* by Paul M. Duvall (Addison-Wesley Professional, 2007), and *Continuous Delivery* by Jez Humble and David Farley (Addison-Wesley Professional, 2010).

5.7   *Managing the testing infrastructure*

The underpinnings of the testing environment often can be overlooked and orphaned in organizations. When you break down the testing environment, you're really looking at a few key components that need to be managed:

- The continuous integration server
- Storage of the produced artifacts from the pipeline
- Testing servers
- Source code being tested
- Test suites being executed
- All the libraries and dependencies that are needed by the test suite

These areas tend to zigzag across lines of responsibility. Quite a bit of hardware is involved. If an artifact is built, it needs to be stored somewhere and accessible to other parts of the deployment pipeline—namely, the servers to which the artifact will be deployed. Separate servers for the test suite to run against are also needed. Finally, the environment will need a continuous integration server, which will need its rights managed as well as network access to the various integration points like the artifact storage location and the source code repositories. It will need its passwords managed and rotated.

Most of these tasks would normally fall inside the realm of the operations staff. But in some organizations, because all of these actions belong squarely in the realm of the development team, the ownership of the testing infrastructure falls into question. I'm putting my stake in the argument and advocating that the operations team own the testing environments. Here's why.

For starters, you need your testing servers to mimic production. Some components are governed by the actual source code being tested—library versions, for example. The test suite should be intelligent enough to install those dependencies as part of the test automation. But there are also more static dependencies that won't change from build to build, such as the database version. The database version is a static dependency that will be heavily influenced by the version that's running in production.

The team that has the best insight into what's running in production is, of course, the operations group. When a patch upgrade goes out to production, that patch should run through the entire testing pipeline. Since the operations team usually dictates when a patch is going to be applied (especially as it relates to security-related patches), it makes sense that they would then trigger the appropriate upgrades throughout the testing infrastructure.

In addition to versions, massive security concerns arise around testing infrastructure, specifically the continuous integration server. Because the CI server requires integrating with key parts of the infrastructure, it becomes a point of sensitivity when it comes to security. Many organizations also use their CI server as an essential component to the deployment process. So, this server will have access to the source code, the build artifact storage location, and the production network. With this level of connectivity, it makes sense to have the operations team own this server so that it can conform to the other security restrictions and processes that exist today. It's too sensitive of a server to have it fall outside the normal security management processes.

Unfortunately, this isn't a slam dunk. The development team will also need some level of control over the environment. Their build tasks will need the necessary permissions to install new libraries within the scope of their tests. Operations surely doesn't want to be involved every time a developer wants to upgrade a dependent library to make sure it's installed. The different libraries used by tests requires an ability for the testing environment to be able to compartmentalize certain operations to restrict them to the current test case. (Many CI servers offer this sort of functionality by default.) Sometimes automated testing will fail, and troubleshooting or debugging might require access to the servers. (Sometimes the issue occurs only on the build servers but can't be reproduced locally.)

All of this is to say that even though operations needs to own the testing infrastructure, a high level of cooperation and coordination will remain between the two teams. Operations staff will need to listen to the needs of software engineers so that they can properly do their jobs. But at the same time, software engineers will have to recognize the outsized power that some testing infrastructure poses and be sensitive to that when not every request can be granted.

5.8 DevSecOps

I want to touch briefly on the subject of a new paradigm that's been emerging in the space: *DevSecOps*. This extension of the DevOps mindset adds security as one of the primary concerns. Many organizations have a security team whose goal is to ensure that the applications and infrastructure that teams use meet some form of minimal safety standard. The *quality as a condiment* antipattern lends itself nicely to discussing DevSecOps because most organizations tack on security toward the end of a project.

During the life cycle of developing a tool, the word "security" may never be mentioned. Then just prior to go-live, a piece of software that wasn't designed from the perspective of security is thrown through a battery of checks, evaluations, and tests that reveal it has no realistic chance of passing.

By including the security team into the DevOps life cycle, you can afford that team the opportunity to be involved in some of the design decisions early in the process and continue the idea of quality *and* security being essential ingredients to the solution. A DevSecOps approach requires the embedding of security scans and tests as part of the pipeline solution, similar to the way testing should operate. Imagine a suite of tests that run with a specific security context against all builds. Imagine a codified remediation process when an application brings in unsafe dependencies. These are some of the successes that DevSecOps can bring, but the road isn't always easy.

The topic is way too vast to cover in this book. If you want a more expansive discussion, I recommend *DevOpsSec* by Jim Bird (O'Reilly, 2016) or *Securing DevOps* by Julian Vehent (Manning, 2018) as great resources.

For starters, you'll need to invest time and energy into basic security-monitoring tools that you can automate and integrate into your build and testing pipelines. This is extremely important because many organizations don't have a formal security program, relying on individual engineers to stay apprised of what's going on in the industry and in the security landscape.

And sure, when there's a large vulnerability in OpenSSL, you'll probably hear about it through your various professional networks. But the organization needs to know about that OpenSSL vulnerability, and it needs a process that is separate and independent from individual actors (and their professional networks) scouring the internet for news of risk.

Automated scanning utilities that are capable of not only scanning your code but also resolving the transitive dependencies in your codebase and scanning those libraries for vulnerabilities are a must. With the web of dependencies that get installed with a simple package, it's unfair to think that any individual could keep track of all those versions, relationships, and vulnerabilities. This is where software shines.

You'll also need to bring your security team into the design process. Most teams view the security team as a sort of "ban hammer." They don't allow you to do anything. But the problem is that most security teams are at the tail end of the relationship; by the time they're engaged, people have *already* done the things they're now asking for permission to do. In reality, the main goal of security is risk management. But you can't evaluate risk without understanding the costs and potential gains. Involving your security team early in the design process allows them to work collaboratively on a solution that balances the needs of the organization both from an execution and a safety standpoint.

As I mentioned earlier, the discussion of DevSecOps is a big one. Start by talking to your security team, assuming you have one. Ask them about how you can work closer together and integrate their processes into the build, test, and deployment processes. Work toward a goal of high-level checks that can be automated and integrated into the various testing pipelines along with the steps to take to engage the security team on future projects.

Summary

- Use the testing pyramid as a guide to logically group tests.
- Restore confidence in testing by focusing on reliability and quick developer feedback.
- Use continuous delivery to ensure that your application is always in a releasable state.
- Choose a pipeline executor tool that offers the least resistance from your organization.

Alert fatigue

This chapter covers

- Using on-call best practices
- Staffing for on-call rotations
- Tracking on-call happiness
- Providing ways to improve the on-call experience

When you launch a system into production, you're often paranoid and completely ill-equipped to understand all of the ways your system might break. You spend a lot of time creating alarms for all the nightmare scenarios you can think of. But the problem with that is you generate a lot of noise in your alerting system that quickly becomes ignored and treated as the normal rhythms of the business. This pattern, called *alert fatigue*, can lead your team to serious burnout.

This chapter focuses on the aspects of on-call life for teams and how best to set them up for success. I detail what a good on-call alert looks like, how to manage documentation on resolving issues, and how to structure daytime duties for team members who are on call for the week. Later in the chapter, I focus on tasks that are more management focused, specifically around tracking on-call load, staffing appropriately for on-call work, and structuring compensation.

Unfortunately, some of the tips here are geared toward leadership. Notice I didn't say "management." Any team member can be the voice and advocate for these practices. And if you're reading this book, you're probably going to be that voice to raise some of these points. Although I prefer to focus on empowering tips that anyone can use, the on-call experience is important enough to break away from that restriction just a bit. Since not all readers may have experience with being on call, a brief introduction to the frustrations might be in order.

6.1 War story

It's 4 a.m., and Raymond receives a phone call from the automated alerting system at his job. Today is the first time Raymond is participating in the on-call shift, so he's sleeping lightly, worried about this very moment. Looking at the alert message, he sees that the database is at 95% CPU utilization. Frantic, he jumps up and logs on to his computer.

He begins looking at database metrics to see if he can see the source of the problem. All the activity on the system appears normal. Some queries seem to be running for a long time, but those queries run every night, so there's nothing new there. He checks the website, and it returns in a reasonable amount of time. He looks for errors in the database logs but finds none.

Raymond is at a bit of a loss. Not reacting seems like the wrong move; he was alerted, after all. That must mean that this issue is abnormal, right? Maybe something is wrong and he's just not seeing it or he's not looking in the right place. After staying awake for an hour or so, watching the CPU graphs, he notices that they're slowly beginning to come back to normal levels.

Breathing a sigh of relief, Raymond crawls back into bed and tries to enjoy his last 30 minutes or so of sleep. He'll need it, because tomorrow he's going to get the same page. And the night after that, and the night after that for his entire on-call shift.

As I discussed in chapter 3, sometimes system metrics alone don't tell the whole story. But they're typically the first thing that comes to mind to build alerting around. That's because whenever you have a system problem, it's not unusual for that problem to be accompanied by high resource utilization. Alerting on high resource utilization is usually the next step.

But the problem with alerting on resource utilization alone is that it's often not actionable. The alert is simply describing a state of the system, without any context around why or how it got into that state. In Raymond's case, he might be experiencing the regular processing flows of the system, with some heavy reporting happening at night as scheduled.

After a while, the alarms and pages for high CPU utilization on the database become more of a nuisance than a call to action. The alarms become background noise and lose their potency as early warning systems. As I said previously, this desensitization to the alarms is known as alert fatigue.

> **DEFINITION**   *Alert fatigue* occurs when an operator is exposed to many frequent alarms, causing the operator to become desensitized to them. This desensitization begins to lower response times as operators become accustomed to false alarms. This reduces the overall effectiveness of the alerting system.

Alert fatigue can be dangerous from both a system response perspective and from an employee's mental health and job satisfaction perspective. I'm sure Raymond didn't enjoy being awakened every morning at 4:00 for no discernable reason. I'm sure his partner was also not pleased with having their sleep disturbed as well.

6.2   *The purpose of on-call rotation*

Before I get too deep in the woods, a basic definition of the on-call process is in order. An *on-call rotation* is a schedule of individuals who are designated as the initial point of contact for a system or process. Many organizations have different definitions of what an on-call person's responsibilities might be, but at a high level, all on-call rotations match this basic definition.

> **DEFINITION**   *On-call rotations* designate a specific individual to be the primary point of contact for a system or process for a period of time.

Notice that the definition doesn't go into any specifics about the responsibilities of the on-call person. That varies by organization. On some teams, the on-call person may serve as just a triage point to determine whether the issue needs to be escalated or can wait until a later time. In other organizations, the on-call person may be responsible for resolving the issue or coordinating the response to whatever triggered the escalation. In this book specifically, I discuss on-call rotation primarily as a means for supporting and troubleshooting systems after hours, when they enter a state the team has deemed abnormal.

With this definition in mind, a typical on-call rotation will last a full week, with each staff member in the rotation taking turns in this one-week assignment. Defining an on-call rotation eliminates a lot of the guesswork for staff members who need assistance after hours, while at the same time helping to set expectations for the staff member who is on call for the week.

If you've detected a problem in the middle of the night and need assistance, the last thing you want to do is wake up four different families to find the person who can help you. The on-call staff member knows that they might be called at odd hours and can take the actions necessary in their personal lives to ensure availability. Without an on-call schedule, I guarantee you that when something goes wrong with the database, anyone who can even spell SQL will be in the woods on a camping trip with absolutely no cell phone coverage. The on-call rotation helps to establish that Raymond needs to sit this trip out in case he's needed.

At the heart of the on-call process from a technology perspective lie your metrics tool, your monitoring tool, and your alerting tools. (They may be one and the same, depending on your stack.) Though your monitoring tool may be able to highlight an abnormal condition in your system, actually getting in touch with the right people to handle that situation is done by your alerting system. Depending on the criticality of your operation, you'll want to ensure that your alerting system can reach engineers via phone calls and email notifications. Some more commercial offerings also include apps for mobile devices that can receive push notifications.

It's important that this notification is automated to improve your response time to outages. Without having automated notification, an on-call rotation doesn't provide the full value of having a problem investigated proactively. Unless you have a full 24/7 network operations center, without an automated notification system, you're probably relying on a customer noticing an issue with the website and then sending communication through your support channels, which probably are also not online in the wee hours of the night.

There's no better way to start the morning than sitting in a meeting explaining to your bosses why the site was down for three hours and nobody noticed. Despite sleep being a biological necessity, it still won't work as an excuse.

This is where your automated notification systems come in. There are several players on the market, as well as at least one open-source solution:

- PagerDuty (www.pagerduty.com)
- VictorOps (www.victorops.com)
- Opsgenie (www.opsgenie.com)
- Oncall (https://oncall.tools/)

These tools not only maintain the on-call schedule for your team, but also integrate with most monitoring and metric systems, allowing you to trigger the notification process when a metric exceeds one of your defined thresholds. Defining these criteria is the focus of the next section.

6.3 *Defining on-call rotations*

On-call rotations can be a difficult thing to reason about. You have a lot of factors to consider, such as the size of the team, the frequency of the rotation, the length of the rotation, and how your company will deal with compensation. It's an unenviable task that, of course, you're going to have to tackle if you're responsible for mission-critical systems.

On-call rotations are touchy because they typically happen organically within an organization, skipping the formality of other employment structures. Without a lot of forethought, your on-call rotation can easily be set up in an inequitable way, putting a heavy burden on staff members.

I've yet to have an interview for an operations engineering role where on-call wasn't discussed, usually with the question, "So, what's the on-call rotation like?" If you don't take special care in designing the rotation, hiring managers have only two choices: lie, or tell the truth and watch your candidate's interest in the role wane in real time. Hopefully, this chapter will help you with a few of those hurdles.

On-call rotations should consist of the following:

- A primary on-call person
- A secondary on-call person
- A manager

The *primary on-call person* is the designated point of contact for the rotation and is the first person to be alerted in the event of an on-call event. The *secondary on-call person* is a fallback if the primary isn't available for some reason.

The escalation to the secondary on-call person might be coordinated via scheduled time, for example, if the primary on-call person knows they'll be unavailable for a brief period of time. Life tends to not adhere to on-call schedules. Bad cell phone service, personal emergencies, and sleeping through alert notifications are all dangers to the on-call process. The secondary on-call role also is designed to protect against this.

Finally, the last line of defense is the manager. Once you've gone through the primary and secondary on-call person, chances are the team manager should be engaged not only for notification purposes, but also to expedite the on-call response.

Moving through these various on-call tiers is called escalation. Knowing when to escalate is going to depend on the team in question, but service-level objectives (SLOs) should be defined for the response time to alert notifications. The SLO should typically be broken into three categories:

- Time to acknowledge
- Time to begin
- Time to resolve

6.3.1   *Time to acknowledge*

Time to acknowledge is defined as the amount of time an engineer has to confirm receipt of an alert notification. This ensures that everyone is aware that the engineer has received the notification and that something needs to be investigated.

If an alert notification isn't acknowledged within the predefined SLO, the alert can be escalated to the secondary person in the on-call rotation, and the timer for the SLO starts again for the new engineer. If the SLO is again violated, another escalation occurs to the manager (or the next person in your escalation path if you've defined it differently).

This continues until someone acknowledges the alert. It's important to point out that once an engineer has acknowledged an alert, they own that alert through the resolution process, regardless of their on-call status. If you acknowledge an alert and cannot work on it for whatever reason, it's your responsibility to get that notification handed off to another engineer who can work on it. This is an important rule designed to avoid a notification being acknowledged, but confusion existing regarding responsibility. If you acknowledge a notification, you own the resolution process for that notification until you can hand it off.

6.3.2 *Time to begin*

Time to begin is the SLO for how long before you begin working on a resolution to the issue. Acknowledging the notification is the signal that the on-call engineer is aware of the issue, but due to circumstances, might not be able to begin working on the issue immediately. In some cases, that could be fine. In others, it could be problematic.

Defining a time-to-begin SLO also helps the on-call engineer schedule their personal life. If the expectation is that an alert gets worked on within 5 minutes of notification, you probably won't travel anywhere without a laptop strapped to your back. If the SLO is 60 minutes, though, you have a bit more flexibility.

This time to begin will vary between services, which could make for a complicated web of exceptions. If the company order-taking platform is down, waiting 60 minutes for work to begin will obviously be unacceptable. But similarly, if even one service has a short SLO (like 5 minutes), the entire on-call experience will be governed by that SLO, because you have no idea what will break or when!

In these situations, planning for the worst-case scenario can lead to burnout of your on-call staff. You're better off planning for the most-likely scenario and using the escalation path to lend an assist when response time is critical. The primary can acknowledge the alert notification, but then immediately begin using the escalation path to find someone who might be in a better position to respond within the SLO.

If this happens repeatedly, you might be tempted to alter your on-call policy for faster response time. Resist that urge and instead alter your priorities so that the system isn't crashing so regularly. I'll talk a bit more about prioritization later in the book.

6.3.3 *Time to resolve*

Time to resolve is a simple measure of how long things can be broken. This SLO can be a little fuzzy because, obviously, you can't create a bucket large enough to encompass every type of conceivable failure.

Time to resolve should serve as a touch point for communication purposes about the issue. If you can resolve the problem within the SLO, congratulations! Go back to sleep and tell everyone about it at stand-up tomorrow. But if you've violated the SLO for time to resolve, this is the point where you should begin notifying additional people about the incident.

Again, in this scenario each service might have a different SLO with differing levels of engagement. Does the alert represent a service being completely down or just in a degraded state? Does the alert impact customers in any way? Understanding the impact to key business indicators or deliverables will influence the time-to-resolve SLO per service.

6.4 *Defining alert criteria*

Now that I've defined what an on-call rotation is, I want to spend a little time talking about what makes the on-call process useful, starting with alert criteria. It can be easy to fall into the trap of sending alerts for all the possible scenarios you can think of that might seem bad. Because you're thinking of these items in a vacuum, you're not attuned to how problematic some alerts can be.

What seems like an abnormal condition on the whiteboard might be a condition that your system enters into and out of rapidly and regularly. You might not fully understand all the necessary contextual components that define a scenario. For example, if you're driving on a long, empty highway, having a quarter of a tank of gas can be a pretty bad scenario. But if you have a quarter of a tank in the city, it's much less of an alarming state. Context matters.

The danger of creating an alert without context is that after an alert is created, it is somehow imbued with a sense of finality. Because of some deep, unknown psychological trauma that afflicts on-call staff members, it can be nearly impossible to convince people to remove a defined alert. People start to recall old stories of "Remember that one time when the alert was right!", and discounting the other 1,500 times it was wrong.

Use the example from earlier in the chapter, where Raymond received a CPU alert. The fact that the CPU was that high for an extended period sounds like something you'd want to alert on when you're designing alerts. But your mileage may vary depending on your workload.

So, let's talk about what makes a good alert. First, an alert should have some sort of associated documentation. It might be details that go directly into the alert or it might be a separate document that explains the steps that should be taken when someone receives the alert. This documentation in all its various forms is collectively known as the *runbook*.

The runbook documents not only how to resolve the issue, but also why the alert is a good alert in the first place. A good alert has the following characteristics:

- *Actionable*—When the alert triggers, it points to the problem and a path for the solution. The solution should be defined in the alert message or in the runbook. Linking directly to the runbook inside the alert notification eliminates the difficulty of finding the correct runbook for a given scenario.
- *Timely*—The alert does as little forecasting on the impact as possible. When the alert fires, you feel confident that you need to investigate it immediately instead of waiting five minutes to see if the alert clears on its own.
- *Properly prioritized*—It's easy to forget that alerts do not always have to wake someone in the middle of the night. For alerts that are needed for awareness, convert those to lower-priority notification methods such as email.

With these three items, you can construct questions for yourself while crafting the alert criteria:

- Can someone do something with this alert? If so, what should I recommend they look at in the system as part of their research?
- Is my alert too sensitive? Will it possibly autocorrect itself, and if so, in what time period?
- Do I need to wake someone up for this alert, or can it wait until morning?

In the next section, I'll begin to discuss crafting the alerts and thresholds that lead you to ask each of these questions and ensure you're making useful alerts.

6.4.1 *Thresholds*

At the center of most alerting strategies are *thresholds*. Defining upper and lower thresholds for a metric is important because in some cases something being underutilized is just as dangerous as something being overutilized. For example, if a web server isn't processing any requests, that could be just as bad as receiving too many requests and becoming saturated.

The hard part about identifying thresholds is, what makes a sane value? If your system is well understood enough to be able to accurately define these values, you're in a better position than most. (In most places, performance testing is always scheduled for next quarter.) But if you're not sure, you'll need to rely on empirical observations and tweak your settings as you go.

Start by observing the historical performance of the metric. This will give you a baseline of understanding where the metric can live in times of good performance. Once the baseline has been established, you should pick a threshold alert that's about 20% higher than these baseline numbers.

With this new threshold set, you'll want to set the alerting mechanism to issue low-priority alerts. No one should be awakened for these metrics alone, but notifications should happen. This allows you to review the metric and evaluate whether the new watermark is problematic. If it's not, you can raise the threshold by another percentage. If there was an incident that happened at this threshold level (or worse, below it) you can adjust the threshold based on the incident surrounding it.

This technique is also useful for becoming aware of growth trends in your infrastructure. I've often set up threshold alerts not as a mechanism to detect problems, but as a checkpoint on growth. Once the alarm starts firing, I realize that the demand on the system has grown X%, and it gives me an opportunity to begin looking at capacity-planning options.

Thresholds will always be a work in progress. As demand grows, capacity will grow, and the capacity will change your thresholds. Sometimes basic thresholds of an individual metric aren't enough. Sometimes you must combine two signals into one to ensure that you are alerting on something meaningful.

New alerts, when there is no baseline

If you're just starting out on your metrics journey, you might be living in a world with no historical performance to really point to. How do you go about creating an accurate threshold when you have no idea about past performance? In this scenario, creating an alert is probably premature. Get the alert out there and creating data. Just having the data puts you in a better place than you were previously.

> *(continued)*
>
> If you're adding this metric because of a recent outage, you may still want to collect at least a day's worth of values before you pick a threshold. After you have some data, pick a threshold alert to start that's above the 75th percentile of your collected set of values.
>
> Let's say we're talking about response time for a database query. If you find that the 75th percentile is 5 seconds, maybe make your initial threshold 15 seconds. This will almost certainly require revising, and I recommend you follow the same iterative approach detailed earlier. But it gives you a starting point to work from and a process for tuning it. If your monitoring tool doesn't allow you to calculate percentiles, try exporting your data and calculating it in Excel by using its PERCENTILE function.

COMPOSITE ALERTING

High CPU utilization on your web tier could be bad. Or it could be you getting your money's worth out of the hardware. (I detest super-large servers running at 10% utilization. You should too.) Now imagine you have another metric of *checkout processing time*. If that metric crosses its threshold and the web tier CPU utilization metric are both alerting, this can help to give the person on call a more robust picture of what's happening. This sort of composite alerting is huge, because it allows you to tie the performance of a system component to a potential customer impact.

Composite alerting can also be useful when you know that a problem manifests itself across multiple axes. For example, while managing a reporting server, I measured several different points. Sometimes because of the way the reporting service worked, a large report would generate a long, blocking HTTP call. This metric would spike the latency on the load balancer. (Because now suddenly an HTTP call was taking more than 45 seconds.) So, I'd get an alert, only to find out that someone ran a long query. But then occasionally, the same latency alert would be a sign that the system was becoming unstable.

To address this, I created a composite alert that would monitor not just for high load-balancer latency, but also for sustained high CPU utilization and signs of memory pressure. These three items individually could indicate a normal system that is just encountering a brief period of load due to a user request. But all three triggering at the same time was almost always a signal of doom for the system. Creating an alert that fired only if all three alerts were in a bad state not only allowed us to cut down on the number of alerting messages, but also gave me confidence that when the composite went off, there was a definite problem that needed to be addressed.

Not all tools support composite alerting, so you'll need to investigate the options at your disposal. You can create composite alerts on many monitoring tools, or you can handle the composite logic on the alerting side with the alerting tools I mentioned previously.

6.4.2 Noisy alerts

If you've ever participated in an on-call rotation, you know that a percentage of alerts probably are completely useless. Although they are well-intentioned, these alerts don't deliver on any of the three criteria that I've defined for a good alert. When you come across a useless alert, you need to put as much energy as possible into either fixing it to be more relevant or just completely deleting it.

I know some of you may be wondering, "But what happens when there's an outage and this alarm could have given us a warning!" It's true that this sometimes occurs. But if you really look at the effectiveness of an alert that has cried wolf one too many times, you must admit that the likelihood of someone reacting critically when it goes off is small. Instead, you roll over and say to yourself, "If it goes off again, then I'll get up and check it."

If you've ever been to a hospital, you'll realize that machines make noises all day long. Nurses aren't running back and forth between rooms in a tizzy, because they've become completely desensitized to the sounds. Everyone reacts to major alarms, but for the most part blips and beeps hum throughout the day without any real reactions from the staff they're intended to keep updated. Meanwhile, as a patient unattuned to those sounds, you're going into a panic every time a machine starts flashing lights.

The same thing happens in technology. I'm sure you have your alarm that says, "The website is down," and that alert triggers an intense triage process. But that low disk space alert that fires every night is usually ignored, because you know that when the log-rotate script runs at 2 a.m., you'll reclaim most of that disk space.

As a rule of thumb, you should be tracking the number of notifications that go out to on-call staff members per on-call shift. Understanding how often team members are being interrupted in their personal lives is a great barometer not only for the happiness of your team (which I'll discuss a bit more later in this chapter), but also for the amount of nonsense alerting that occurs in your organization.

If someone is being alerted 75 times per on-call shift, that's a level of interruption that you should feel throughout the tech organization. With that many notifications per shift, if the pain of system instability isn't felt outside the on-call team, then chances are you're dealing with a noisy alerting system.

NOISY ALERTING PATTERNS

Earlier in this chapter, I discussed three attributes that make a good alert. The alert must be

- Actionable
- Timely
- Properly prioritized

Timeliness of an alert can often help silence noisy alerts while still preserving their value. The catch is, like everything in technology, there's a slight trade-off. Most alerts that are designed by people are designed to alert the moment they detect a bad state. The problem with this approach is that our systems are complex, fluid, and can move through various states relatively quickly. A bad state can be rectified moments later by means of an automated system. Let's go back to the disk space example.

Imagine a system that is being monitored for low disk space. If disk space goes below 5 gigabytes of available storage, the system alerts and pages someone. (1995 me could only imagine having to *worry* about 5 GB free, but I digress.) But imagine a world where this system is backing up to local disk before shipping it to another storage mechanism like Amazon Simple Storage Service (S3) or a Network File System (NFS) backup mount. The disk space would spike temporarily but eventually be cleaned up when the backup script cleaned up after itself or after the `logrotate` command ran and compressed files before rotating them out. When you're paging on the immediate detection of a state, you send a page that isn't timely, because the state is temporary.

Instead, you could extend the detection period of that state. Say you make a check every 15 minutes. Or maybe you send the alert only after four failed checks. The downside is that you could potentially send an alert out 45 minutes later than you normally would have, losing time you could have spent recovering. But at the same time, when you receive the alert, you have confidence that this is something that needs action and resolution, instead of snoozing the alert a couple of times, hoping that it takes care of itself. Depending on the alert, it can be better to get an alert late but know that you need to act.

Of course, this doesn't work for all types of alerts. Nobody wants a "website down" alert 30 minutes late. But the criticality of the alert should also dictate the quality of the signals necessary to detect it. If you have a noisy alert for a critical part of the system, your focus should be on increasing the quality of the signal to detect the condition. You should define custom metrics that are emitted so that you can alert on a strong signal (see chapter 3).

For example, if you're trying to create a system-down alert, you wouldn't want to compare CPU utilization, memory utilization, and network traffic to determine if the system might be having an outage. You would much prefer that some automated system is attempting to log in to the system like an end user and perform a critical action or function. That task might be more intensive to perform, but it's necessary because the criticality of the alert requires a strong, definitive signal (The system is down! Wake everyone up!) versus needing to infer the condition through multiple metrics.

Imagine that your car doesn't have a fuel meter. Instead it tells you how many miles you've driven, how many miles since your last fill-up, and the average number of miles per full tank. You wouldn't want that car! Instead you'd pay a little extra to have a sensor installed that detected the fuel level by measuring it specifically. That's what I mean when I say choose a quality signal for critical functions. The more important the alert, the greater need for a quality metric to base it off.

The other option to dealing with noisy alerts is to simply delete them. Now if you have children or other people who depend on your livelihood, you might be a little concerned with just shutting off alerts. (As of this writing, the job market is pretty hot, so you might be willing to live dangerously.)

Another option is to mute them or lower their priority so they're not waking you up in the middle of the night. Muting the alert is a nice option because a lot of tools will still provide the alert history. If you do encounter a problem, you can look at the muted alert to see if the problem would have been detected and what value the alert could have brought. It also lets you see how many times the alert would have fired erroneously.

If your tool doesn't support that kind of functionality, you can change the alert type from an automated wake-up call to a nice quiet email. The nice thing about this approach is that the email being sent can be used as an easy datapoint for reporting. Every email is an avoided page, an avoided interruption at dinner, an avoided break in family time. But your email client also becomes an easy reporting tool for the paging frequency (assuming your alerting tool doesn't have one).

Group your emails by subject, sender, and date, and you have an instant snapshot into the frequency of alarms. Combine that with the number of times you had an actionable activity around the page, and you can quickly develop a percentage of alert noise. If you received 24 pages and only 1 of them had an actionable activity, you're looking at a noisy alert rate of approximately 96%. Would you follow stock advice that was wrong 96% of the time? Would you trust a car that wouldn't start 96% of the time? Probably not. Of course, if you don't take the next step of examining the effectiveness of these email alerts, you'll instead write an email filter for the alert that automatically files it into a folder and you'll never see it again. Be better than that.

Noisy alerts are a drag on the team and don't add any value. You'll want to focus as much energy as possible on quantifying the value of the alert along with creating actionable activities when the alert fires. Tracking the noise level of an alert over time can be extremely valuable.

Using anomaly detection

Anomaly detection is the practice of identifying outliers in the pattern of data. If you have an HTTP request that consistently takes between 2 and 5 seconds, but then for a period it's taking 10 seconds, that's an anomaly.

Many algorithms for anomaly detection are sophisticated enough to change the range of accepted values based on time of day, week, or even seasonality. A lot of metric tools are starting to shift toward anomaly detection as an alternative to the purely threshold-based alerting that has dominated the space. Anomaly detection can be an extremely useful tool, but it can also devolve into something just as noisy as standard threshold alerting.

First, you'll need to ensure that any alert you create based on anomaly detection will have enough history for the anomaly detection algorithm to do its work. In ephemeral environments where nodes get recycled often, there sometimes isn't enough history on a node for the application to make accurate predictions on what an anomaly is. For example, when looking at the history of disk space usage, a sudden spike in usage might be considered anomalous if the algorithm hasn't seen a full 24-hour cycle for this node. The spike might be perfectly normal this time of day, but because the node has existed for only 12 hours, the algorithm might not be smart enough to recognize that and generate an alert.

> **(continued)**
> When designing anomaly-based alerts, be sure that you think about the various cycles that the metric you're alerting on goes through and that there will be enough data for the algorithm to detect those patterns.

6.5   *Staffing on-call rotations*

One of the most difficult parts of creating an on-call rotation is staffing it appropriately. With a primary and a secondary on-call role, you can quickly create a scenario where people feel they're constantly on call. Knowing how to staff teams to deal with on-call shifts is important to maintaining the team's sanity.

The on-call rotation size cannot be strictly dictated by the size of the team. There are a few items you must consider. For starters, the on-call rotation is like porridge: not too big, not too small. It must be just right.

If your on-call rotation is too small, you'll have staff members quickly burning out. Remember that being on call is a disruption to people's lives, whether they receive an off-hours alert or not. But at the same time, having a team too large means that people are part of the on-call rotation too infrequently. There's a kind of rhythm to the on-call process that requires the ability not only to function at odd hours of the night, but also to understand the trends of the system over time. Staff members need to be able to evaluate whether an alert is problematic or is signaling the beginning of a larger potential problem.

The *minimum* long-term size of an on-call rotation is four staff members. In a pinch or temporarily because of attrition, a team of three can be used for brief periods, but in all honesty, you don't want to go below four staff members for the rotation. When you consider what the on-call rotation entails, you're realistically thinking of a team member being the primary person on call and the secondary person on call during a rotation, usually back-to-back. With a four-person rotation, this means an engineer is on call twice per month. Depending on your organization, the stress of being secondary on-call might be significantly less than being primary, but it still is a potential for disruption in someone's personal life.

The interruptions aren't just personal. On-call duties can strike during business hours as well, stealing away precious time working on the product to deal with firefighting issues. The mental penalty for switching from project work to on-call work and back again is often overlooked. A 15-minute disruption can result in an hour or more of lost productivity as engineers try to mentally shift between these modes of work.

A minimum rotation of four people might be easy for some organizations that have a large department to pull from. But for smaller organizations, coming up with four people to be part of the on-call process might be daunting. In this case, you may have to pull people from various other groups to participate in the rotation.

When you have representation from multiple teams, you run the risk of having someone on call who doesn't have all the necessary access they need to resolve an issue. In an ideal world, you'd want only teams directly responsible for a service in the on-call rotation. But in the exploding world of smaller and more numerous services, that team might have only two engineers on it, a product person and a QA engineer. That's a big responsibility for two people.

The need to potentially expand your support team beyond the immediate service creators is going to put a heavy emphasis on your automation practices. The desire to minimize the number of people with direct production access is in direct conflict with needing to integrate people from other engineering groups into the on-call rotation. The only fix here is automating the most common tasks used in troubleshooting so that the on-call engineer has access to enough information to properly triage the issue.

Note that I used the word "triage" and not "resolve." Sometimes in an on-call scenario, an immediate resolution might not be the answer to a page. There's benefit to be gained just from having a human evaluate the situation and decide whether it's something that needs to be escalated or something that can remain in its present state until the right staff members are available to handle it during working hours.

Being alerted for an issue, but not having the tools or access necessary to fix it, is not an optimal position to be in. The only thing worse than being alerted and not having the access necessary to fix the problem is having the access but being interrupted in the middle of a movie theater right before the big kiss or fight scene or villain monologue or however your favorite type of movie typically resolves itself. If the options are to beat a small group of people into on-call submission by having a short rotation, or to add people who might not be able to fix every problem they're paged for, the lesser of the two evils is clear.

You might find yourself in an exceptionally small organization with only two or three engineers in the entire company! There's a need for on-call rotations, but no staff to hit the minimums. In that case, all I can really say is, "Congratulations, you're probably a startup co-founder!" But seriously, in those situations being scrappy is the name of the game. The best solution is to ensure that you're directly and swiftly addressing the problems that come up as part of on-call through your sprint work. In my experience, with groups this small, not only do they own development and on-call rotations, but they also own prioritization. That allows for rapid fixes to nagging problems.

As I alluded to earlier, teams can also be too big for on-call rotations. If you have a team of 12 engineers rotating on call, that means, assuming a one-week rotation, that you're on call only about three times per year. I can't think of anything that I do only three times a year that I can maintain proficiency at. Being on call is a muscle. Being able to be effective in crunch time is an important skill to have. But if you're on call once a quarter, think of all the small things that you don't do regularly that could become a problem. Are there specific activities that are done only when you're on call? How good are your skills around incident management if you use them only once a quarter? Where is that wiki document that has all the notes for how to solve specific problems? If you think hard, you'll probably come up with a bunch of things that aren't done regularly when you're not on call. All these tasks can add time to your recovery efforts because someone is out of practice.

Another downside to having a large on-call rotation is that the pain of being on call is too dispersed. I know that sounds weird, so just hear me out for a second. When you're on call every four or five weeks, the pain of the on-call process can become familiar. The nagging issues that pop up are frequent enough to you and to all the other members of the on-call rotation that you feel motivated to resolve them. But if the rotation is once per quarter, that pain gets diluted between your on-call rotations and becomes a permanent piece of technical debt. The squeaky wheel gets the grease, unless you use that wheel only four times a year.

Given those concerns, what is the *optimal maximum* size of the on-call rotation? You'll have to take into account just how many interruptions your on-call process generates, but my rule of thumb is that teams have rotations of no larger than eight people, preferably around six.

Once you get more than six people per on-call rotation, I recommend splitting up services and creating multiple on-call rotations around a grouping of services or applications. Depending on how your teams are organized, this split may be logical based on your organizational structure. But if there isn't an obvious breakdown, I recommend reporting on all of the on-call notifications that have been generated and grouping them by application or service. Then spread the services based on alert counts across the teams.

This might cause a bit of an imbalance when you realize that some of your engineers who are the most well versed in a technology are not on the team supporting that technology after hours. Not only is this OK, but I encourage it. You don't want the expertise of a technology to be concentrated in a single engineer.

After-hours on-call support gives an opportunity for other engineers to not only get involved with the technology, but also to be exposed the underbelly of the technology stack through incidents. A dirty little secret about operating production software is that you learn more when it breaks than when it operates normally. Incidents are incredible learning opportunities, so having someone who isn't the expert on a technology participate in the on-call rotation can be a great way to help them level-up their skills. Just have the expert's number on speed dial, just in case, and continue to update your runbooks for each incident.

6.6   *Compensating for being on call*

I have a philosophy around compensation for on-call rotation. If engineers are grumbling about compensation, chances are it's because your on-call process is too onerous. Fairly compensated, salaried professionals seldom gripe about having to work the occasional few hours outside the normal work week. This is a trade-off that gets made in exchange for the flexibility that is often accompanied by being a salaried professional. This isn't to say that compensation isn't deserved by those on call, but if your staff is complaining about it, I would argue that you don't have a compensation problem as much as you have an on-call problem.

Most people I've talked to who have a decent on-call experience are content with the unofficial compensation strategies that their managers employ. That said, it's often beneficial to have some sort of official compensation package for on-call staff members. Just remember that regardless of how little or how much an on-call person is interrupted, if they want official compensation, then they deserve it and should be entitled to it.

I once had to cancel an on-air radio segment because I couldn't find someone to swap on-call duty with. I never got alerted, but I could have been. How would I handle that on the air? Even if people aren't being alerted after hours, it still places demands on their time. I've encountered a few compensation options that seem to work well.

6.6.1   *Monetary compensation*

Cash is king. A monetary compensation policy has a few benefits. For starters, it lets employees know that you truly appreciate the sacrifice that they're making for the organization. The extra cash can also be used to incentivize volunteers for the on-call rotation in the event it's not mandated as part of the employee agreement. (And even if it is mandated, you should still consider and implement a compensation strategy of some sort.) To keep it easy, a flat bonus can be applied to the employee's payroll during on-call weeks. This keeps things simple and predictable.

Sometimes when working with monetary compensation, organizations will add in an additional hourly rate for when you receive a page and must perform after-hours work. This comes with the added benefit of putting a monetary value on the incidents that get generated after hours. As a manager in charge of a budget, I might be content with an application paging out when it's in need of a reboot a few times a week. But when I'm on the hook for the rising on-call expenses, it affords me a new perspective on developing a new, more permanent solution. (It's always about incentives.)

On the same token, some people worry that this disincentivizes workers to solve problems long-term because they lose out on a financial reward. But the truth is, the disruption to living life probably outweighs any sort of financial compensation that comes because of said disruption. In my experience, this is a nonissue, but admittedly, your mileage may vary.

A negative to compensation being tied to hours of work performed after the regular workday is it becomes an enormous accounting problem. Now I must track how many hours I worked during the incident. Do I include the hours when I thought the problem was fixed, but I was on eggshells watching the system and hoping the problem didn't return? Do I include the time I was paged or just the time I was actually working? Maybe I was at an event and had to travel somewhere with my laptop to get to a suitable location to perform work. All this time tracking becomes a bit of a bore and can lead to some resentment from employees.

6.6.2   *Time off*

I've seen a lot of on-call rotations that are compensated with additional time off. This time off can be accrued in different structures, such as receiving an additional day of personal time off (PTO) for every week you're on call (or sometimes only on weeks during which you received a page). This approach can work for a lot of teams, especially because as incomes rise, time becomes a much more precious resource than the monetary stipend you might get from financially compensated on-call teams (depending on how much that compensation is).

Using time off as a monetary compensation tool has a catch, and that's how official it is. A lot of smaller organizations don't have an official on-call policy. It's a technical team necessity but doesn't always get addressed by the organization at large. As a result, these time-off compensation strategies are often done as an unofficial agreement between the on-call staff and their manager.

Assuming a healthy relationship between manager and staff, this might not be an issue. But where does time off get tracked? What happens if your manager leaves? How does that on-call PTO balance get transferred? If you decide to bank two weeks of on-call PTO, how do you submit that into the human resources (HR) reporting system to use as vacation time? If you leave the organization, how do you transfer the value of that saved-up PTO into something that you can take with you? How do you deal with people who pick up an extra on-call shift?

These are common issues that arise when dealing with a time-off compensation strategy for on-call duty. The following are a few strategies that make this a bit easier to manage:

- *Ensure that HR is involved with on-call compensation talks.* This allows the organization to make the compensation an official act as opposed to being handled differently by managers all throughout the organization. It also prevents a new manager from suddenly changing the arrangement without a formal process.
- *Don't allow accrual of on-call PTO.* If your HR team isn't involved with the on-call compensation, just ensure that all staff members plan to use the on-call time as it's earned. This prevents issues with accrued time off, but does create issues for management around resource planning, as the team has lost productivity baked into its schedule. Assuming a day per on-call week, you're looking at 19 working days per team member per month, before any planned time off is considered. It sounds insignificant but adds up to roughly 2.5 working weeks per year. Across a team of four, that's roughly 10 weeks a year lost to on-call compensation. To make matters worse, the staff has probably worked those 10 weeks plus some, but just doing relatively unproductive work (where productivity is measured as new features, capabilities, and value).
- *If you must accrue on-call PTO, log it somewhere.* A shared wiki page or spreadsheet is probably the easiest solution.

6.6.3   *Increased work-from-home flexibility*

Another disruptive portion of being on call is the time period between getting ready to go to work and sitting at your desk. If you've ever had to field an on-call situation while simultaneously trying to get your kids off to school, you can understand the frustration. I've met some teams that have elaborate schedules to stagger the arrival of staff to ensure that they don't have everyone trapped on a commute when the system decides to eat itself. Providing increased work-from-home time during an on-call week is another way of dealing with this.

Allowing a team member to work from home during their on-call week can help solve the commute problem, as well as give the team member back some flexibility that's robbed from them during the on-call week. I've had to cancel personal tasks because I've been interrupted by an important on-call task. I remember times sitting at my kitchen table with my coat still on, working on a "quick fix" problem, only later to realize I'd been at it for over an hour and the place I was going to had closed. When the option to work from home during an on-call week is available, I have the option of running some of those personal errands during my lunch break or taking a quick 15-minute break during the day to handle it. Because my other team members are in the office to handle any issues that arise, it doesn't become a burden on anyone.

If the flexibility of working from home isn't typically an option in your organization, this can be an excellent way to give workers some freedom. But the question arises, is it fair or equitable? With on-call duty causing unscheduled interruptions in a person's life, it seems a little callous to be rewarded by only being able to pick a different office to work from. Some people might find this flexibility a worthy trade-off; others might want that cold, hard cash.

This solution is the most problematic because not everyone values work from home the same. For instance, I personally prefer to be in the office, because I like the socialization aspect. Sometimes folks have different reasons for their need to be in the office, making the work-from-home solution for a given week more problematic than helpful. They could have a lunch date with a friend or an important meeting that will be difficult to do remotely. If you plan to use this option, consider having a conversation with team members before you presume that this is will be a welcomed option by all.

In my experience, making the on-call experience as painless as possible is the best way to help in the on-call compensation conversation. To understand the pain of the on-call process, however, you need to be paying attention to more than just the number of pages, and understand the impact it has on people.

6.7   *Tracking on-call happiness*

Not all on-call interruptions are created equal. Looking at a report of the on-call statistics for a given period, you might learn that there were 35 on-call alerts during a reporting period. But that number doesn't tell the entire story. Were all 35 pages on a single night? Were they primarily during the day? Were they spread across the rotation, or did one person receive a disproportionate number of those alerts?

These are all questions that you should be asking when evaluating your (or your team's) on-call experience. The answers can grant some powerful insights into the on-call process. You'll also get data on increasing efforts to reduce the on-call burden or increasing the level of compensation.

A few pieces of information need to be tracked in order to get a sense of the on-call experience on your teams:

- Who is being alerted?
- What level of urgency is the alert?
- How is the alert being delivered?
- When is the team member being alerted?

Tracking each of these categories will give you a lot of solid insight.

6.7.1 Who is being alerted?

For this, you'll need to be able to report beyond just a team level or service level. You'll want to know specifically which team member is fielding the alert. This is probably the most important piece to identify, because you're attempting to understand the impact on individuals, not just systems.

It's easy to lump alert counts into teams or groups, but the truth is, some systems follow specific patterns. In a four-person rotation, it's not uncommon for team members to always have their on-call duty fall on a particular time of the month. If the billing process always runs the last week of the month, then the fourth person in the on-call rotation might disproportionately see pages related to that business event or cycle.

I'm certain that these signals will show up in one of the other areas that you're reporting on. For example, the number of incidents could jump on the fourth week of the month, prompting some investigation. But the idea is to view this data from the perspective of people. Rolling up that data could erroneously erase the impact it's having on an individual.

6.7.2 What level of urgency is the alert?

An alert might come in that represents signs of far-off impending doom. A database server might be days away from running out of disk space. A trend you've been tracking has crossed a threshold you've defined and warrants investigation. A server might have gone without patching beyond a certain number of days. These are all alerts of things that are wrong in the environment, but they don't require immediate action. The alerts are more informative and as a result can be less disruptive to the on-call team member.

Contrast that with an alert that says, "Database system is unstable." That alert is not only a bit vague, but also alarming enough to warrant looking into immediately. These alerts are of a different urgency and have different response expectations. Letting an unstable database alert sit until morning could have drastic consequences for your company's business and for your continued employment with them. These are the high-urgency alerts that create pain and friction in an employee's life. Keeping track of the number of high-urgency and low-urgency alerts that a team member receives will help you understand the impact of that page.

6.7.3 *How is the alert being delivered?*

A low-urgency alert isn't always delivered in a low-urgency fashion. Depending on your configuration, nonurgent alerts could be delivered in the most disruptive fashion possible. Even if an item is low urgency, the phone call, the text alert, the middle-of-the-night wake-up push notification—all these signals can create stressors for on-call engineers. These stressors lead to more frustrations and lower job satisfaction, and will lead to folks responding to requests on LinkedIn.

I can remember a time when I reviewed my on-call reports to find that one member on the team was getting a disproportionate number of alerts notifying him via phone calls. The metric was a pretty high outlier. I looked at the general number of alerts that went out during his on-call shift and saw that it wasn't any higher than other team members; he just had more interrupting, phone call-based alerts. After a little investigation, I discovered that his personal alerting settings were set to alert via phone call on *all* alerts, regardless of urgency. He was unknowingly making his on-call experience worse than everyone else's. Tracking this metric was the key to helping him achieve a more relaxed on-call experience.

6.7.4 *When is the team member being alerted?*

An alert at 2 p.m. on a Tuesday doesn't bother me as much as an alert at 2 p.m. on a Sunday. When team members are being alerted after hours, it obviously creates a drag on their experience. You don't need to create large elaborate buckets for this because there are only three periods of time that you care about:

- *Working hours*—This is the time period you would normally be in the office. I'll assume 8 a.m. to 5 p.m., Monday through Friday, in this scenario.
- *After hours*—In this period, you would normally be awake but not working. Think of this generically as 5 p.m. to 10 p.m., Monday through Friday; and 8 a.m. to 10 p.m., Saturday and Sunday. Obviously, your personal schedule will alter these timelines.
- *Sleeping hours*—These are defined as the hours of rest, when a phone call has a high likelihood of waking you from a restful state. These are defined as 10 p.m. to 8 a.m. every day of the week.

By grouping interruptions into these buckets, you can get a sense of just how much disruption you're causing. The reports can also be used to trend over time to get a sense of whether on-call rotations are getting better or worse, beyond just a blind "number of alerts" metric.

If you're using any of the major tools I mentioned previously (such as PagerDuty, VictorOps, or Opsgenie), they all have options for this sort of reporting out of the box. If not, I recommend making this data highly visible. If you're doing custom alerting, you might want to consider emitting a metric for every type of page or alert as a custom metric. This will allow you to create dashboarding in your current dashboard tool. Radiating this information in an easily accessible dashboard or report will help draw attention to it.

6.8   *Providing other on-call tasks*

The nature of on-call work makes it difficult to focus on some project work. The amount of context switching that occurs can make it difficult to focus, depending on the alert volume that happens during the day. Instead of fighting the realities of on-call rotations, it's worthwhile to lean into it and structure on-call work beyond just the after-hours support dumping ground and shape it into an opportunity to hopefully make on-call time better.

A common additional task for on-call team members is to play the sacrificial lamb for the rotation and focus on all ad hoc requests that come in for the week. By *ad hoc*, I'm specifically talking about those tickets that come in unscheduled but cannot wait and need to be prioritized before the next work planning session.

An example could be a developer needing elevated access privileges temporarily to troubleshoot a production issue. This type of request could be handled by the on-call staff member. It would create a clear line of responsibility and would streamline communication from the point of the requester, because the requester knows that a dedicated resource is set to perform the task. There is a counterargument, however, that by relegating someone to only support work for the week makes the on-call experience even more unattractive. That's true to a certain extent, but I think you can also sweeten the pot a bit by allowing some self-elected project work.

6.8.1   *On-call support projects*

When you're on-call, you become acutely aware of all the problems that are occurring that wake you up in the middle of the night or interrupt your family dinner. Consider allowing your on-call staff to not partake in the normal prioritized work and instead focus on projects that would make the on-call experience a bit better. Being allowed this focus during the on-call week has its advantages as well, because the problem remains fresh in your memory. Ideas for some on-call projects could be as follows:

- Updating runbooks that are either outdated or don't exist at all
- Working on automation to ease the burden of dealing with specific problems
- Tweaking the alerting system to help guide on-call staffers to the source of potential issues
- Implementing permanent fixes to nagging problems

And you can probably think of a few more options specific to your organization. Finding a permanent solution to nagging problems is probably going to be the most impactful and rewarding. It's also the option that's most overlooked in conventional workflows.

What usually happens is the on-call person fields a few calls that have a specific permanent solution that just needs to be prioritized by the team and worked on. But other firefighting takes place, and as the distance from the issue increases, the likelihood of repairing it also decreases. In a one-week rotation, each staff member has the risk of being exposed to the problem only once per month, assuming a four-person rotation. By giving the current on-call engineer the ability to prioritize their own work, they can address the problem as it's fresh in their memories.

By creating an environment in which the on-call engineers have the power to make their jobs better, you not only reduce some of the burden of the process, but also empower engineers to make it better. This sense of control gives them ownership of the experience.

6.8.2 *Performance reporting*

Being on call gives you a view into a running system that many others never quite see. The reality of a system changes significantly between the time it's being designed and the time it's operating and running in production. The only people who notice this change are the people who are observing the system while it's running. For that reason, I think it's valuable to have the on-call engineer provide a sort of state-of-the-system report.

The state-of-the-system report could be a high-level overview of how the system is behaving week to week. This report might simply review a few key performance indicators and make sure that they're trending in the correct direction. It's a good way to discuss the various on-call scenarios that the engineer faced and to bring other disciplines into the conversation. This allows an opportunity for the production support staff and the engineering staff to discuss the problems that are being faced while supporting production (assuming they're not the same team).

To facilitate this sort of reporting, building a dashboard that highlights all the key performance indicators (KPIs) for the review is a good starting point. The dashboard serves as a set of talking points for the on-call engineer to review. It might just be confirming that things look good, but in some meetings a negative trend or event might warrant further discussion. Overlaying milestones across the dashboard is also beneficial. For example, if a deployment occurred during the on-call week, calling out on the graphs when the deployment occurred could be helpful if any specific step changes appeared in the graphs.

As an example, figure 6.1 is a graph of freeable memory on a database server. The two shaded bars denote a production deployment of the primary application that uses this database server. The obvious jump in memory might warrant a deeper conversation in the reporting meeting. Without this meeting, the memory issue might not have been noticed because memory never dropped low enough to trigger alerting by the monitoring system.

The power of this meeting is to systematically enforce some of the regular reviews and analysis of monitoring that should be happening within your teams, but probably isn't because of understaffing. (Organizations typically discount the type of routine

Amount of Freeable Memory

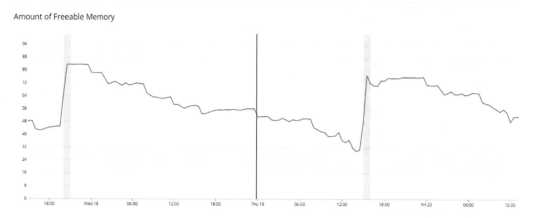

Figure 6.1   Overlaying deployment events on a graph

tasks that should be happening as a matter of good hygiene.) When you build out your reporting dashboard, think of all the things that you feel should be monitored on a regular basis but aren't. Think about the things that you should be doing but don't seem to find the time for.

Imagine if you had to display or report on your system's security patching on a weekly basis, highlighting the last time servers were patched. The regular, public admission of a failing will bring energy to the understanding of why it's failing and what can be done to correct it. If you haven't applied security patches in nine months because you can't find the time to do it, that admission regularly will lead to you getting the time necessary. To quote Louis Brandeis, "Sunlight is said to be the best of disinfectants."

Summary

- Alerts need to be actionable, timely, and properly prioritized.
- Noisy alerts create alert fatigue, rendering the alert useless.
- On-call duty is a disruption to staff members. They should be compensated in some form.
- Track on-call happiness to understand the level of disruption in an engineer's life.
- Structure the on-call rotation so that engineers have time to make permanent fixes.

The empty toolbox

7

The focus on products and features that the organization can sell often dominates our minds as technologists. But what many people fail to realize is that the tools you use to build these products and features are just as important. A carpenter without the right tools will always have a piece of wood too long, a nail protruding out, and a corner that just doesn't look right.

In the world of technology, these imperfections caused by a lack of good tooling are often buried away in a series of small tasks that take too long, are difficult to reproduce, and are error-prone. But no one sees how the sauce is made. No one realizes that the image on the front page of the website has to be resized manually and is prone to being a few pixels off. No one knows that the configuration file reload is done by an engineer connecting to each website and running a command to reload it. And no one knows that out of 50 servers, sometimes a few get missed.

I call this lack of investment *the empty toolbox*. It creates additional drag on teams and their ability to address repeat problems quickly. Instead of reaching for the hammer when a nail is loose, everyone wastes time looking for a suitable hard, portable surface they can use to pound down the nail. It's slower, not as effective, and doesn't produce a result nearly as consistent.

You must think beyond just the product or feature being built when it comes to tooling and automation. You must think of the entire system around the product. People, support systems, database servers, and networks are all part of the solution. How you manage and deal with those systems is equally important.

When entire systems aren't designed with automation in mind, a cascading series of decisions can lead to reinforcing that lack of automation. Imagine that one of the support systems for the platform requires a graphical user interface (GUI) to install software. This leads to a manual installation task. But if the software installation is manual, that becomes an assumption during deployments of the application. If the deployments are manual and the base installation is manual, that supports the idea of the actual server creation being manual. Before long, you have a long chain of manual events. That initial choice of a GUI-based installation leads to a continuing disinvestment in your automation strategy.

One of Gloria's tasks in the morning is to reset the status of orders that failed because of a credit card transaction dispute. One day while performing this typically mundane task, Gloria makes a mistake. While cycling through her command history for her normal query, she inadvertently modifies a variation of the query that she had made while troubleshooting another issue. Instead of her query updating every order in a list of orders, it updates every order that is *not* in the list of orders—a catastrophic error that leads to a pretty big recovery effort to get data back into the correct state.

A manual process, no matter how well-documented, always offers the opportunity for failure. Humans are just not built for these repetitive tasks that computers excel at. This makes it a bit surprising how often organizations fall back onto these solutions, especially in the face of temporary problems. But if you've been in the industry for any length of time, you know that the word "temporary" has a huge range, from hours to years.

Sometimes the decision to rely on a manual process is a conscious decision after weighing the pros and cons of automation. But often the decision is not a decision at all. It's a fallback into old, familiar patterns of solving problems. The implications of choosing a manual process over automation are not weighed or considered. Instead of critically evaluating the options and making a decision with eyes wide open, the inertia of the status quo prevails, and you fall back into the ease of a manual step.

Throughout this chapter, I'm going to discuss automation. Your mind may go specifically to IT operations, but I want to broaden the definition a bit. *Operations* are all the tasks and activities required to build and maintain your product. That might be monitoring servers, maintaining the testing pipeline, or setting up a local development environment. These are all tasks that are required to be performed to add value to the business. When these tasks are often repeated, standardizing the way those tasks are performed is key.

The focus of this chapter is to identify the problems with not investing in automation of tools that support your ability to deliver your product. I'll go through various strategies to approaching automation as well as ways to engage and work with other subject-matter experts within your organization to help jumpstart a culture of automation. But before I do all of that, I'd like to make the case for why everyone should be concerned about operational automation.

> **DEFINITION** *Operational automation* is the development of tools to support and automate the activities necessary to build, maintain, and support the system or product. Operational automation must be designed as a feature of the product.

7.1 Why internal tools and automation matter

Imagine you work at a construction company. The company is working on assembling a new building downtown. You've been assigned to the team, and the first thing they give you is a document with step-by-step instructions for building your hammer, your socket wrench, and your safety harness belt. Chances are that every person on the construction team is working with a slightly different set of tools in terms of quality and accuracy. It also means that a new construction worker is essentially useless for the first week or so after being hired. And as if that wasn't bad enough, you probably don't feel super comfortable about the rest of the process for constructing the building if that's the process for getting the tools that are being used to build it.

Internal tools and automation are the foundation of keeping the day-to-day activities involved with maintaining and building software easy and less time-consuming. The more time you spend doing the basic needs of the craft, the less time you're adding value to the product. Not developing tools and automation is often rationalized as a time-saver, but this is actually costing your teams more time, not less. It's optimizing for the now at the cost of every moment in the future going forward. Manual work balloons into these small, discrete activities that individually may seem like minor time sinks, but collectively account for so much wasted time.

And the ways this time gets wasted can be insidious. People tend to restrict wasted time to the idea of "It took me 15 minutes to do this thing that should have only taken 5." That's one form of waste, but the biggest form of waste doesn't involve working. It involves waiting.

7.1.1 Improvements made by automation

I don't want to assume that automation and tooling is an obvious goal, especially since so many organizations don't have a clear strategy for approaching it. There are four key areas where tooling and automation becomes important, the first being queue time.

QUEUE TIME

If you measure a process that is manual and requires more than one person to perform it, the common enemy that needs to be battled against is queue time. *Queue time* is the amount of time a task or activity spends waiting for someone to perform an action on it. You can almost be certain that anytime a task must pass from one person to another, queue time will be involved.

Think of all the times you had to submit a service desk ticket that should take only five minutes, but you spend two or three days waiting for it to be looked at and addressed. Queue time is the silent killer in many manual processes because it's not wasted effort, but just wasted time, the most precious of resources. Tooling and automation can help you eliminate or reduce queue time by removing the number of handoffs necessary in a process.

TIME TO PERFORM

Computers are just demonstrably better at performing repetitive tasks than any human could ever hope to be. If you must type three commands in succession, the computer will probably complete the entire series of tasks before you finish typing the command for the first. A simple task that takes two minutes begins to add up quickly over the course of a year. A two-minute task you perform five times a week is a little over 8.5 hours a year. An entire working day a year is spent on performing a boring two-minute task.

And not only is that two-minute task faster for the computer to perform, but the problem of automating the task is usually way more interesting and satisfying than performing the task itself. In addition to being more interesting, the work of automating the task demonstrates a capacity for both improvement and use of your automation skill set. Consider which of these sounds better in an interview: "I performed a SQL query successfully 520 times in the past year" or "I automated a task that was being performed 520 times so that no human had to be involved. We used the extra time freed up to automate other tasks so the team could do more valuable work."

FREQUENCY OF PERFORMANCE

Like the preceding example, repeated tasks can be disruptive to an engineer's ability to focus. When a task needs to be performed frequently and there's urgency to the task, it can be difficult for a person to stop what they're doing, move to the new task, perform the new task, and then switch back to what they were doing previously. This act of switching between tasks, referred to as a context switch, can be incredibly burdensome if you have to do it a lot. When a task needs to be executed frequently, that can sometimes lead to an engineer needing to context switch and lose valuable time while they get adjusted to or from the previous task they were working on.

Another issue with frequency of execution is the pure limitation it puts on how often a task can be run if it depends on humans. No matter how important the task, there is just no way you'll have a human run the task every hour, unless it's a critical part of their job. Automation allows you to break free and perform tasks at a much greater frequency if necessary and doesn't create an outsized burden on anyone on the team.

VARIANCE IN PERFORMANCE

If I asked you to draw a square four times, there's a high probability that none of the squares will be identical. As a human, a bit of variance always exists in the things that you do, whether it be drawing a square or following a set of well-documented instructions. It doesn't matter how small the task may be; slight variations will almost always occur in the way things are done. There are all types of small variances that might make a difference one day in the future.

Imagine that you execute a process manually every day at 11 a.m. Or did you start at 11:02 a.m.? Maybe it's 11:10 a.m. today because you had some traffic coming into the office and you're a bit behind schedule. The people who are waiting for the results of the process don't know whether the process is running slower than usual or you forgot to run the script. Is it a problem, and should it be escalated, or should the team just patiently wait? When looking at the logs of the script execution, they notice some days the task takes an extra 15 minutes. Is something wrong with the script on Tuesdays and Thursdays? Or is the human executing it called away to participate in the team morning meeting for a few minutes before returning and finishing things up?

7.1.2 Business impact to automation

These little examples highlight the type of variance that can happen in even the simplest of processes. Figure 7.1 highlights the extra time that is consumed and wasted in these areas by manual tasks.

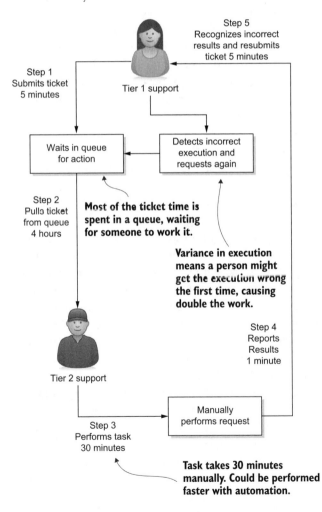

Step 5
Recognizes incorrect
results and resubmits
ticket 5 minutes

Step 1
Submits ticket
5 minutes

Tier 1 support

Waits in queue
for action

Detects incorrect
execution and
requests again

Step 2
Pulls ticket
from queue
4 hours

Most of the ticket time is spent in a queue, waiting for someone to work it.

Variance in execution means a person might get the execution wrong the first time, causing double the work.

Step 4
Reports
Results
1 minute

Tier 2 support

Manually
performs request

Step 3
Performs task
30 minutes

Task takes 30 minutes manually. Could be performed faster with automation.

Figure 7.1 A process flow that's dominated by queue time and repeat work

This doesn't even include things like the steps being followed accurately or data being inputted correctly. But these four areas describe some of the key benefits that automation gives you. If you understand what these areas mean, you can turn them into key business outputs.

Queue time means tasks and activities move through the pipeline faster, resulting in quicker business outcomes. The ability to perform a task quickly, without waiting on handoffs, means the pipeline of tasks moves more fluidly. *Time to perform* means you can do more tasks that were previously being tied up with manual work. That means higher productivity for the engineers involved. *Frequency of execution* means there are some things you can do more often and get the value out of those extra executions. Building on chapter 5, the automation of the test pipeline means you can execute test cases many times per day. Reducing *variance in performance* means you can be certain that the same task is executed the exact same way every time. This is language that auditors love. Your automation and tooling can ensure that it's taking audit-safe inputs and producing audit-ready reporting.

Working on internal tools and automation will drive business efficiencies across these four areas, not to mention empower more staff to perform tasks that previously were saddled with requirements around access and knowledge transfer. I may not know your data model well enough to roll back payment information. But I can be trained to type `rollback_payments.sh -transaction-id 115`. This type of codified expertise allows you as an organization to push down the types of tasks that were previously done by extremely expensive staff members in the organization. If only a developer has the knowledge to perform a task, that's something that is taking away from the developer's time writing code. But if the task becomes automated, it can get pushed further down the line.

Imagine a typical workflow. Someone has an issue with something in the application and creates a support ticket. In many organizations, that ticket gets routed to IT operations. The operations department looks at it but knows it's something wrong with the data, so it gets routed to a developer. The developer figures out the necessary SQL that will put the data into a usable state by all applications. They pass this knowledge down to operations, who then pushes it down to tier 1 customer support. This flow is necessary because of where the knowledge to solve the problem lives.

But once that knowledge has been identified, converting that knowledge into a tool or automation allows the developer to push the fix down to operations. Then once in the hands of operations, figuring out the hurdles of access and security for performing the task might allow them the ability to pass the task back to tier 1 support. Figure 7.2 highlights what the process could look like in an automated world.

Now the customer is being serviced by tier 1 support immediately, instead of waiting for a series of handoffs, queue time delays, and context switches. Automation and tooling empower this process at every phase and highlight why they're such a crucial part of the DevOps journey. Automation encompasses empowerment, speed, and repeatability.

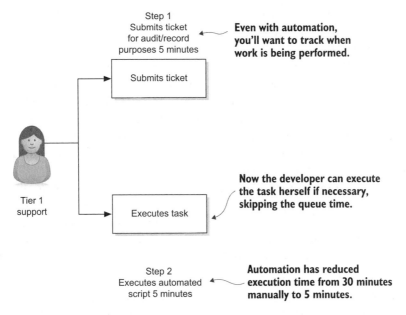

Step 1
Submits ticket
for audit/record
purposes 5 minutes

Even with automation, you'll want to track when work is being performed.

Submits ticket

Tier 1
support

Executes task

Now the developer can execute the task herself if necessary, skipping the queue time.

Step 2
Executes automated
script 5 minutes

Automation has reduced execution time from 30 minutes manually to 5 minutes.

Figure 7.2   Automating the proposed process

7.2　*Why organizations don't automate more*

Considering that automation has such an obvious benefit, it's amazing that more teams don't automate more. The reason is never as simple as a senior leader declaring that the organization isn't going to focus on automation right now. Nobody ever says that. The driving force behind automation is more about having a clear understanding of what your values are and expressing those values through action.

If you asked most people if they think working out and eating healthy is important, they'd say yes. But if you ask them why they don't do it, it's because a bunch of other things have been prioritized ahead of it, which results in poor eating habits and a lack of exercise. I would love to wake up every morning and exercise. But I stay up late helping the kids with homework, then I want to prioritize time with my wife, and then I want to prioritize time for myself. These choices result in me going to bed at 11:45 p.m. and hitting the snooze button repeatedly until 6:30 a.m. Now my time to work out has been missed. Never did I consciously say, "I'm not going to work out this morning," but through my actions, I created an environment where working out just wasn't feasible. I deprioritized working out by prioritizing other things.

Organizations do this all the time with automation and tooling. This failure in prioritization happens in two key areas: organizational culture and hiring.

7.2.1　*Setting automation as a cultural priority*

When you discuss an organization's values, you're describing what the organization has decided is a priority. If automation and tooling aren't in the conversation, it simply will lack the traction necessary to take hold in the organization. The organization builds a culture around what it will and won't tolerate.

In some organizations, drinking a beer at your desk at 3 p.m. on a Friday is a perfectly normal sight. At other organizations, having alcohol in the building at all is grounds for firing. These are two extremes, but they exist, and the organizational culture enforces those norms, not just through rules and policies, but by the behavior of other people in the organization. It's not going to be HR that yells at you for cracking open an ice-cold lager at your desk; it's going to be the people around you. They've been conditioned by what's acceptable in the organization and what isn't. (I'll talk a lot more about this in subsequent chapters.)

Imagine if your organization had the same behavior around automation. Imagine if implementing a manual process was tantamount to smoking a cigar in the change approval board meeting. Building that sort of culture is key to making sure tooling and automation is treated as a priority. Without this mindset, you'll continue to encounter excuses as to why tooling and automation can wait until later.

NOT ENOUGH TIME

There's never enough time to automate something. In many cases, this is because the automation impacts folks at the team level but is solved at the individual level. For an example, imagine that a task gets performed once a week, every week, like clockwork. The task takes about an hour to complete. The team rotates who performs the task. Individually, it's an hour a month; but as a team, it's four hours a month of wasted energy. Automating the task and ensuring that it's working might take a solid eight hours. In the heat of the moment, it's always more advantageous to pay the hour cost, do the task manually, and move on. Investing your personal time and energy is a tough proposition when so many things are competing for your attention.

The lie that you often tell yourself is that "next time" you're going to automate it. Or maybe when things calm down, as if there's ever a time where everything isn't on fire. The job of automating is always on the back burner, waiting for the perfect time when work is quiet, and you have eight contiguous hours to work on a task uninterrupted. This magic time never comes, and even though as an individual this seems like the smarter choice, as a team you could have that eight hours of work pay off in two months' time. This is where the organization can make a huge difference in setting the tone of expectations.

NEVER PRIORITIZED

A sibling of the not-enough-time excuse is the "never prioritized" situation. Automation and tooling never become important enough to be put down on the road map as an organizational priority. Instead, they're always relegated to free time or skunkworks projects. In fact, many times the teams that develop automation and tooling aren't even an official team, but just a small band of engineers who have tired of the current way of doing things.

For automation to become a reality, you need to get it on the list of priorities for the organization or the department. With this recognition come resources, budget, and time, the most critical resource there is. But the prioritization doesn't just occur for fixing old processes. It also has to become a priority in new work as well. Projects should have automation and support tools for the product defined as requirements and deliverables, as part of the project timeline. This sort of prioritization pairs the cultural value of automation with demonstrated action.

URGENCY TRUMPS CORRECTNESS

Stop me if you've heard this one: "Well, what if we do it like this real quick for now and then in V2 we'll fix it all up?" In so many scenarios, our urgency to get a thing done prevents us from doing things the way they should be, with proper automation and tooling. The hardest bad practice to stop is inertia. Once a bad practice is let out in the wild, it becomes harder and harder to stop unless it results in a complete disaster.

Inefficiencies in organizations don't get the share of blame that they probably should. If a task is cumbersome, takes a long time, and wastes human resources—but works—it's often difficult to convince people to pull resources from something that is all of those things *and* doesn't work. The cost of doing it wrong now is often seen as a trade-off that works in favor of the business, but it almost never does.

It's one thing if you're doing it to take ahold of a magical opportunity that has a short time window and a huge payoff. But typically, it's so that someone can meet a date that was randomly picked and then placed in a spreadsheet. The cost of doing it wrong ripples forward through time, saddling future actors with the burden of a bad choice made in a vacuum.

Each of these areas describes how automation is overruled by other priorities. The pressure from other forces can create a change that prevents you from doing what you know is the right thing with regards to automation. But sometimes the lack of automation can be more than just about prioritization.

7.2.2 Staffing for automation and tooling

When a company is initially formed, it usually hires based on its priorities. No company starts with the founder, a manager of HR, and a VP of Legal Affairs. These are all important roles in an organization, but companies grow into those roles as they align with their priorities. If a company is involved with a lot of litigation as part of its business model, a VP of Legal Affairs could make for a smart early hire. But if you're building a new location services platform, a VP of Legal Affairs is probably further down your list of hiring.

The same thing occurs on a smaller scale. Most companies don't start with a dedicated operations team until their support needs grow beyond what is capable for the development staff to handle. Dedicated security teams are often a later hire as well. An incredibly secure product that nobody uses won't be on the market for long. You hire based on your needs and on your priorities. The same is true for automation. You may not necessarily need a dedicated automation expert, but if you're going to make automation and tooling a priority, you need to make sure that your hiring practices reflect this.

TEAMS WITH MONOLITHIC SKILL SETS

When you're hiring a team, you tend to focus on having more of what you already have. After all, those employees are the blueprint for what it takes to succeed in the job. But this thinking leads to a monolith of skills among team members. People tend to hire people who are like them, especially in interviews. If I'm hiring for the skills that I already have, I have the ability to evaluate them more effectively, in my mind.

When an operations team hires a new systems engineer, the team thinks of all the things they do on their current day-to-day basis and evaluate engineers on that criteria. In addition, they have a sort of bias toward the skills that they use, and evaluate candidates under that lens. The result is a team with the same set of skills and the same sets of gaps. This happens on almost all teams.

If automation and tooling is your goal, you'll have to hire for people with that skill set, especially if you don't have that skill in-house. Now the focus on this particular skill set may mean that they lack in other areas that you might be hiring for. If you have a bunch of frontend engineers, your candidate for internal tooling and automation may not have as much frontend experience but will probably have a plethora of backend experience. This needs to be weighed when you evaluate candidates and think about the skills that you need now versus the skill that you've built a ton of expertise around in recent years.

This will probably feel a tad unnatural at first because of the industry's unrealistic expectations around hiring. You're probably not going to find that unicorn developer who has 30 years of iOS experience developing frontend, backend, virtual reality, Docker, Kubernetes, and Windows. You need to diversify the team's skill set so that, as a unit, you can deliver what needs to be delivered.

VICTIMS OF THE ENVIRONMENT

The design of software impacts the ability to support it and automate it. Let's use a simple example. Imagine an application that requires the user to upload a bunch of files to the system via their GUI-based application. An enterprising user might decide that it's more valuable to script this upload and run it from the command line for every file in a given folder. But because the application was designed with only a GUI, the system doesn't expose any other way to upload files.

Now instead of having a simple series of commands to upload files, the user is forced to create an application that simulates the mouse clicks and drags of a regular user. This process is far more brittle than the command-line option, and prone to errors, time-outs, modal windows stealing the focus, and a host of other things that can occur in a GUI-based session.

This mindset of supportability falls into the same product categories as stability, performance, and security. Like these items, supportability is a feature of a system or product and must be handled in the same manner. Without it being treated as another feature of the system, it will consistently be treated as a late add-on that must accommodate the already existing design constraints of the system.

Another by-product of this feeds into the skill-set gap. As the environment continues to grow with tools that don't have the ability to be automated, the skills needed for performing automation begin to atrophy in the organization and the team. If there isn't a lot of room for automation in the environment, the requirement for it begins to fade in the hiring process. People who have had the skill no longer exercise that muscle. Before long, the environment becomes something that enforces the lack of automation among the team.

The slower adoption of automation in Windows-based environments

I had lunch with a hiring manager for a consulting company. The company focused on bringing DevOps principles and practices to large-scale enterprises through consulting services. The problem this hiring manager had was finding Windows engineers with DevOps skill sets. He asked me to lunch to try to figure out why he was seeing this gap in skills between Windows engineers and Linux/UNIX system engineers.

A lot of factors go into this, but as someone who started my career supporting Windows systems, one of the major differences I noticed was the way the systems were designed to support automation. In Linux, everything from a configuration perspective was done either via a simple text file or via a combination of command-line utilities. This created an environment in which automation was not only possible, but straightforward to achieve. A wide variety of tools could help you manipulate text files, and anything that you could execute on the command line could be put into a text file and executed via a script.

In those days, Windows was a different story. With earlier versions of server-based Windows (NT, 2000, 2003), so much of your configuration or automation was wrapped into a pretty GUI interface. Users didn't type commands; they navigated through menus and option trees, and found the right panel that enabled whatever it was they were trying to achieve. This made administration of Windows systems much easier. Instead of memorizing hundreds of commands, with just a vague idea of where a menu option might live, even the most basic administrators could find their way around the system.

The downside to this was that there was no need to build a skill set around automation, because there was no easy, reliable way to automate things. As a result, the automation skill set in the Windows community didn't grow as fast as it did in the Linux/UNIX communities.

Microsoft has made a lot of changes to try to embrace the command line over the years. With the introduction of PowerShell in 2006, more and more management capabilities became accessible via the command line. And as a result, the industry is seeing an increase in the automation skills of Windows administrators. But this is a classic example of how your system design can influence not just the capabilities of supporting the platform, but also the skill set of the team responsible for supporting it.

7.3   *Fixing your cultural automation problems*

To have maintained success in creating tooling and automation in your environment, you must have a plan for changing your culture around automation. No matter how much energy you put into a big automation push, at the end of the day if you haven't changed your culture, your existing tools will rot, and new processes will fall victim to the same issues and excuses that got you to this point in the first place. Like almost everything in DevOps, automation starts with culture.

7.3.1   *No manual tasks allowed*

This is going to sound incredibly obvious, but it's one of the simplest things you can do to begin changing the culture: stop accepting manual solutions on your team. You'd be surprised at how much power the word "no" can have. When someone comes to you with a half-baked process that isn't supportable, say no and then state what you'd like to see as part of the transition process.

You're probably coming up with a thousand reasons as to why saying no is impractical. You might be thinking that some tasks are presented as top-priority requests. You feel like you won't be able to get support or buy-in from your leaders by just saying no. If your leadership has expressed that automation and tooling are a priority, you can highlight that as a reason for refusing a manual task. "I don't think this process is complete, and I'd prefer to refuse incomplete work." Point out to the requesters the areas that you think need to be improved or scripted. You cannot have "no" be the final answer and leave it at that.

7.3.2   *Supporting "no" as an answer*

Be sure to have a ready list of things you'd like to see changed about the process. You can even model your complaints around the impact to the four areas discussed earlier in the chapter: queue time, time to perform, frequency of performance, and variation in performance.

Using these as a guideline, make the case for how your workload will be impacted. When looking at the process, pay special attention to parts of the process with a reasonable degree of uncertainty or chance for error. If you were to make a mistake, what is the impact on the recovery time if you had to run the process again? How many handoffs are required between teams or departments for the process? How frequently will the task need to be performed? What's the driver for the frequency? This is a big one to think about because in some situations growth becomes the driver for frequency. If a task grows in correlation with another metric, like number of active users, you should keep that in mind because it gives you an idea of just how painful the process could end up being.

Also bear in mind the pattern of the task: don't get caught up in the specificity of the task, but rather the generic problem it solves. Running an ad hoc SQL query might be a one-time requirement for that specific SQL query. But before long, running a one-time SQL query becomes the pattern for how certain types of problems are solved. "Oh, if you need to reset that user's login count, just log in to the database and run this SQL query." These patterns become a drain on the team, are error-prone, and usually are evidence of an unspoken nonfunctional requirement. Evaluate the pattern of the task, not just the specific task itself.

Once you understand the overall effort of performing the activity manually, use that to understand the overall effort of automating the same task. Keep in mind that the effort involved with a manual task is usually continual. Seldom do you have a single execution of a task, which means the cost of a manual task is continually paid over time. When you detail all these areas, you have a reason for the "no" response. Later in the chapter, I'll discuss putting an actual dollar value to the manual process versus the effort of automation.

A COMPROMISE BETWEEN MANUAL AND AUTOMATION

Sometimes saying "no" just isn't in the cards. For whatever reason, a task is just too important or the automation too onerous to get it done. This is where I opt to keep a scorecard.

A *scorecard* lists all the manual tasks that you or your team have to perform, but you'd prefer were automated somehow. Each task has a score associated with it: 1, 3, or 9. The score reflects how burdensome the manual task is; the more burdensome the task, the higher the score.

Then the scorecard should be given a maximum value. This might be on an individual basis, a team basis, or an organizational basis. It ultimately depends on which level of the organization you're tracking this.

Now that you have a scorecard, when new manual tasks are being requested of you or your team, score it based on the burden it will place on your team. Once it's scored, see if the additional score will bring your team above the maximum value of the scorecard. If the maximum value on the scorecard has been reached, no new manual tasks can be given to the group without removing some of the tasks via automation.

This is not a per item ratio but a total score—so if your maximum value is 20, and you're at 20 and want to add a task that's been valued at a 3, you can't simply automate a 1 to make room. You'd have to automate three tasks that have a score of 1, or one task with a score of 3 or one task with a score of 9. Table 7.1 shows what a sample scorecard could look like.

Table 7.1 An accounting of all the manual tasks the team must perform, with score rating

Task	Score
Uploading of financial reporting data	1
Export of tier1 customer orders from the data warehouse	9
Cleanup of cancelled orders	9
Creation of feature groups by customer	3
Total—maximum value set at 20	22

This may sound like a basic process, but it creates a simple way for teams to track the amount of manual work they have in the organization and the pressure it's putting on you or the team. If I asked you right now to list all the tasks that you'd like automated, you probably wouldn't be able to do it completely. And even if you did, you probably would have a hard time reasoning about the difficulty of each one. I'm sure the *big* one that you consider a pain will come right off the top of your head. But big problems usually meet resistance to automation because of the effort involved. And that doesn't mean these smaller nuisance issues aren't also a drain on your time. This scorecard approach gives you a means to catalog and track the difficulty of these tasks.

In a lot of organizations, this scorecard will always have items on it. In fact, it will probably be at its maximum value a lot of times. But it's a way to keep your manual processes in check. If you let manual processes run rampant, you won't realize it until everything you do is crippled. Then it can be hard to claw your way back from the brink. With the scorecard approach, you're able to quickly assess where you're at and whether you can make an exception to support an important piece of work. It's also a great place to look to when you have time and want to automate work for yourself or the team.

7.3.3   *The cost of manual work*

Every organization has to deal with money and financials. Even if you're in a nonprofit, how money is spent, and the benefit received from that expenditure, is the lifeblood of every organization. Technologists generally do a poor job of translating the trade-offs that are made into the language of finance. Numbers, whether they are arbitrary scorecards or budgetary dollars, help people make sense of the world.

If you're shopping for a car, comparing comfort, features, and reliability is a lot more difficult than comparing $5,000 versus $20,000. Even if you care about those characteristics (comfort, reliability, features), assigning a dollar value to them gives you a much clearer idea of just how much you value them. All things being equal, I'm sure most people would prefer a fully loaded BMW to an economy KIA. But the minute you start adding dollars to the mix, the choice becomes more nuanced. You need to do the same thing for evaluating manual work versus automation.

UNDERSTANDING THE PROCESS

The first thing to do for both the automated work and the manual work is to decompose the process into the high-level steps that consume time and resources. Once you understand the process, you can begin assigning time estimates to it. Assigning estimates is arguably the hardest portion of this, because you may not have data, depending on whether it's a new or existing process.

For this example, I'm going to assume that you have no data beyond your own experience and intuition. For each step in the process, estimate how long it would take, but instead of giving a single number, give a range. The range should have a lower bound and an upper bound. The range you give should have a 90% chance of containing the correct answer. This is known as a *confidence interval* in statistics, but you'll borrow it here for our purposes. Here you'll use it to represent both the realities of our uncertainty and the variability in task execution.

For example, if I wanted to estimate how much time a ticket spent in the queue, I would estimate that 90% of the time, a ticket is in the queue waiting to be performed between 2 hours and 96 hours (four days). Now you need to be careful about your range for this to be a useful exercise. It's easy to say, "I believe the number will be between five seconds and 365 days." That's not helpful to anyone.

A good way to think of it is like this: if you sample every performance of the task, 90% of the time it will fall within this range. But *only* 90% of the time. If you're right, you win $1,000. If it falls in the range 93% of the time or higher, you will have to pay out $1,000—meaning, if you create the range to be too high, you'll be right more often, which increases your chance of having to pay out. This calibration trick has been popularized by Douglas W. Hubbard and is an easy, quick way to try to keep you honest about your estimates. Figure 7.3 shows the workflow but annotated with time estimates instead of absolute values.

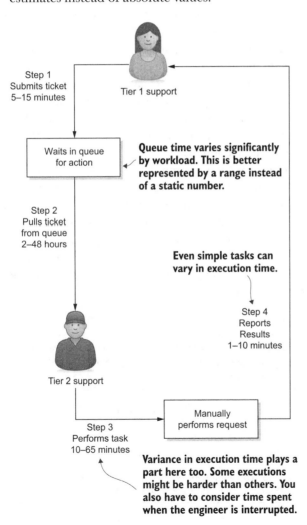

Figure 7.3 The time ranges give a more robust detailing of the variance in the execution.

PUTTING THE ESTIMATES TO WORK

Now that you have a series of time estimates, you can tally up the lower bounds of all the steps and the upper bounds of all the steps to get an idea of what the total process confidence interval can look like. (Again, these are all based on estimates, so there's room for error.)

With this information, you also must think about how often this task will run. The frequency of the task is important because that compounds the amount of time being spent on it. If it runs weekly, that's obviously much worse than if it runs annually. Tally up the number of estimated executions over a given time period.

I like to think of it in chunks of six months. So, you estimate that this will run 3 to 10 times over a six-month period. Multiply that lower and upper bounds by your total lower and upper bound estimate for the task. You've now got roughly the number of hours could be spent on the process every six months. It's a range, so you're admitting that this is variable, but at the same time, the range is way better than the information you had before, which was basically nothing.

You'll need to do the same thing for the automation work, with two major differences. For starters, you'll need to include a maintenance time for the automation. Very seldom do you write code and never have to touch it again. You'll need to estimate how much time you think will need to be spent ensuring that the code performs as expected. If you're not sure, an hour a month is a good rule of thumb. There will be many months when you don't use up your hour, and then some months when you spend four hours supporting it. The second major difference is that you won't multiply the initial automation work. Once you've made that first initial investment, that energy isn't repeated as part of normal operations. This is where the big savings come in.

With these estimates in place, you'll have a range of values for both the manual work and the automated work so you can make comparisons. Now this is simply time spent. It's beneficial to keep the model simple at first. Some folks might argue that it doesn't include how expensive different people's time might be. This is a true concern.

Table 7.2 shows what the calculations might look like. To keep the example simple, I did the calculation based on only three executions.

Table 7.2   Steps to perform a process

Task	90% confidence interval for time spent	Time spent per 6 months (3 executions)
Submit ticket	5–15 minutes	15–45 minutes
Waiting in queue	2–48 hours	6–144 hours
Perform task	10–65 minutes	30–195 minutes
Report results	1–10 minutes	3–30 minutes
Totals	2 hours, 16 minutes to 49 hours 30 minutes	6 hours, 48 minutes to 148 hours 30 minutes

Table 7.3 is a similar table put together for the effort to automate the task.

Table 7.3 Effort required to automate the same process

Task	90% confidence interval for time spent	Time spent per 6 months
Requirements gathering	4–18 hours	4–18 hours
Development effort	2–40 hours	2–40 hours
Testing effort	4–20 hours	4–20 hours
Maintenance effort	1–4 hours	3–12 hours
Total	11–82 hours	13–90 hours

The results for our sample are pretty interesting. With three executions, you see that the time spent executing the task manually and the time spent automating that task overlap each other. Someone might make the case that automating this task might not be worthwhile after all. But here are a few things to keep in mind:

- The estimate is for only 3 executions. If you increase executions to 10, the numbers become much higher for time spent in the manual process.
- The execution time is only six months. If you planned on performing this task for longer than six months, much of the development is a one-time expenditure. Only maintenance continues to occur. This makes automation look even more attractive for the long run.

This is a quick and easy way to start comparing automatic and manual tasks. Some people might complain that it's not robust enough to model all the complexities involved. They'd be right, and if you're willing to put the energy in to do a more formal cost-benefit analysis, it might be worth it. But in most cases, that analysis is never done, and this quick method gives you an idea of whether the automation of the task is even in the ballpark of valuable actions to take.

In the preceding example, I think automation makes a lot of sense, given I modeled only the best-case scenario. And if our imaginary process needs to continue beyond six months, then it's a pretty open-and-shut argument: automation is well worth the effort.

7.4 *Prioritizing automation*

The idea of automation isn't new or particularly novel. It has existed in one fashion or another for as long as computers have been around. The need for automation has grown out of necessity as the number of machines, services, and technologies have exploded as well as the complexity of the services they deliver. Twenty years ago, operations teams were staffed based on a server-to-admin ratio. That strategy in today's world would bankrupt most organizations. Automation is no longer optional. If you're going to be successful, automation must become a priority in your project, your work, and your tools.

7.5   *Defining your automation goals*

Earlier in the chapter, I discussed how automation efforts can center around four areas: queue time, speed of the task, frequency of execution, and variance in execution. These four areas are also great pillars to begin thinking about your goals for automation. By defining these goals, you'll have a better understanding of what automation tools can be at your disposal.

Imagine that your company is excited about a new product with a high potential for positively impacting revenue. But you find out that the API is incredibly limited. Instead of being able to filter out the specific data you need, you'll be forced to download a much larger dataset and to read through thousands of records you don't need to get the handful of records you do need. This isn't an ideal automation scenario, but what are your goals?

If your automation goals are around the frequency of execution, this might not matter so much. The task might take longer than it probably should, but it's still freeing someone up from filtering the data via the user interface and performing whatever transactions are necessary. If the process takes an extra 25 minutes per execution, it still is worth the automation effort. You also get some of the other benefits, like variance of execution, because now you're doing the tasks in a script that executes the same every time. Now let's say that your major driver for this same feature was queue time. If the only way to execute the automation is by being logged into the console of the server, that hinders your ability to integrate it into the ticketing system for self-service execution.

When you start to look at automation, by starting with the four areas of queue time, speed to perform, variance in performance, and frequency of performance, you can begin to understand which of these factors you want to drive down with automation. There might be other reasons you want to automate a task, but often those reasons will roll up to one of these four concerns.

7.5.1   *Automation as a requirement in all your tools*

Seldom does a single tool deliver all the value necessary for your application. Sometimes you'll piece together various components of software. For example, you might have GitHub for a code repository, Jira for ticket and bug tracking, and Jenkins for continuous integration and testing. These collection of applications, scripts, and programming languages in your environment are known as your *tool chain.*

When you're evaluating tools, if automation is a priority, then it must be a feature of the tool chains that you choose. No family of six decides on a Toyota Prius as the family car, because it doesn't meet the family's requirements. If automation is a requirement, choosing tools that make that an impossibility is just as silly. I know that a ton of other constraints go into making a technology decision, and it's easy to blame those constraints on a lack of automation. But how often have you presented the need for automation as a hard requirement? Have you expressed the cost in engineering effort it takes to manage a system that can't be scripted?

When it comes to evaluating the automation capabilities of a tool, the following are a few questions you can ask in order to determine how the capability supports your automation goals:

- Does the application have a software development kit (SDK) that provides API access?
- Does the application have a command-line interface?
- Does the application have an HTTP-based API?
- Does the application have integration with other services?
- Does the GUI provide features that are not accessible programmatically?

When you're evaluating a tool, be sure that you're considering these requirements. Explicitly state your automation needs in your list of requirements. If your evaluation team is giving more weight to some requirements, make sure automation is properly weighted in that evaluation. You don't want automation potentially discounted because other requirements are considered more important. If you don't ensure that the tools you use are up to your automation goals, then no matter how much energy you spend on the next section, you'll never achieve your goals.

7.5.2   *Prioritizing automation in your work*

Prioritizing automation in your work is the only way to build a culture of automation. It can be easy to become overwhelmed by the list of tasks that you need to do on a regular basis. Sometimes it feels more productive to choose the path of least resistance to get a task done.

Sometimes the dopamine hit of checking an item off your to-do list will drive you to make some short-term decisions. But this short-term thinking has long-term implications as the number of manual tasks quickly pile up in the name of the "quick win." When it comes to these quick tasks, they're often the low-hanging fruit of automation. It's in these trenches where automation can make the most difference. It's important that you keep a vigilant mindset around automation as a core value and prioritize these types of tasks when applicable.

Many organizations use a ticket-based workflow. Work is represented by a card in a system, and that card moves through the workflow. In most ticket-based workflows, the amount of time it takes for a ticket to be completed is usually dominated by *queue time*. As I've said earlier, queue time is the amount of time a ticket spends waiting for someone to work on it.

For every minute you're on your lunch break or home sleeping or working on another problem, that's queue time that another ticket is accumulating. If you're the requestor of that ticket, it can be extremely frustrating to be stuck waiting on someone to get around to running a simple command. A task that takes two minutes to complete might spend four hours in a queue. Would you wait on hold for four hours in order to ask a question that will take only two minutes to answer? Probably not.

Everyone loses in this scenario. It's why so many companies are trying to push commonly asked questions to things like automated interactive voice response (IVR) systems or directing customers to a company website where their questions might be answered. The only sustainable way to eliminate queueing time is to reduce the number of items that must enter the queue. This is where automation comes in.

For these sorts of commonly requested tasks, putting some automation in place and creating a method for self-servicing can free your valuable time for your team. But to do this, you must make it a priority. There's no easy way around this. You must forgo doing one thing so that you can do another.

But how do you evaluate when to put the effort into automating a process instead of just doing what's necessary to get the request closed and out the door? This is what usually holds up most automation efforts. A request comes in to execute the same old manual process. A ticket is created to automate the manual process, but it gets forever banished to the backlog with a wishful whisper of "someday..." on the lips of its creator.

The failure is that the ticket needs to be executed while the pain of such a request is still fresh in the minds of its executors. If given too much time, the monotony of the request will fade into memory. Seize the moment and start the work to automate it sooner rather than later!

For starters, don't let the ticket get into the backlog. This advice is especially pertinent for teams that do lots of interruption-driven work, like operations teams. Get it prioritized as soon as possible. Don't wait for it to be evaluated with the rest of the work. Make a case for why it should be prioritized in the current iteration of work or in the very next iteration of work. Once it gets into the sea of other requests, it stands no chance of seeing the light of day again. This is where techniques like letting the on-call staff member prioritize their own work can become a huge win (discussed in more detail in chapter 6).

Once you have the ticket properly prioritized, you should think about how those tickets should be evaluated as good automation candidates or not. The first thing to think about is the frequency with which this request is made. One of the problems with automating tasks that are done infrequently is that the time between executions can be so large that many of the underlying assumptions made by the automation may have changed. For example, if you have a process for maintenance windows that you'd like to automate, that task may run only once or twice a year.

But what in the underlying infrastructure has changed since you made that initial script? Has the type of worker nodes that read from the database changed? Did you remember to update the maintenance script to support the new type of load balancer you're using? Is the method for checking that a service has stopped correctly still valid? A lot of things can change in six months.

If you're in this scenario of infrequent execution, ask yourself how much automated testing you can create around this script. Is it possible that some tests could be run on a regular basis to ensure it's working? In the case of our maintenance script, maybe you can schedule it to run regularly against the staging environment. Maybe you can do it as part of your continuous integration/continuous deployment (CI/CD) pipeline.

Whatever you do, the root of the solution is the same: the script needs to be run more regularly, whether in a testing environment or in real life. If you can't come up with a good solution for scheduling the task more regularly, it might not be a great candidate for automation at this time.

The primary fear is that when it comes time to execute the script, the changes in the environment prevent it from running successfully. This failure breeds a sense of distrust against the automation suite. And when distrust begins to form, it can be incredibly difficult to earn it back, especially for particularly sensitive automation.

7.5.3 *Reflecting automation as a priority with your staff*

An organization that wants to make automation and tooling a priority also needs to distill those priorities into actionable items with regards to staff. Automation isn't lacking just because staff members are lazy. There's more than likely a structural component to how your teams are built and how you manage skill-set improvements in the organization.

7.5.4 *Providing time for training and learning*

Whenever organizations talk about training, it's always assumed that a large expenditure gets you a week's worth of instruction and then magically leaves your staff with all the skills necessary to achieve the goals and tasks at hand. In my experience, paid training seldom pays off the way it was originally intended.

Usually the training is too early, meaning that the training class is far ahead of any practical, day-to-day usage of the skills acquired. You get trained on the new NoSQL database technology, only to have a two-month gap between training and implementation of the technology. You know the old saying: you use it or lose it. The flip side is that the training is too late, and you're stuck with a buffet of bad decisions made in ignorance. It feels like a no-win situation. The fix for that is to build a culture of continual learning.

When you depend too heavily on structured training classes, you're subconsciously treating learning as an event. Learning becomes codified into a structured and rigid practice of consuming knowledge from experts. But with the advent of online training, Safari books, conference talks, and an endless stream of YouTube videos, learning doesn't have to be a completely structured affair. You just have to make time for it.

And in our busy schedules with all of our various projects and goals, seldom do you see time dedicated to this idea of frequent learning. This lack of learning will shackle your team to the current way of doing things without a lens into what's possible. Skill advancement and augmentation is already a fact of life in modern engineering organizations. Some of the top tools in use these days have been on the market for less than 10 years. Whether you're looking at learning a new language to empower staff members to automate their workflows or at a tool that shifts the paradigm and brings automation along with it, you'll need a plan to make sure you and your team members are always learning. All the solutions are a variation on the same concept. You must make time for it.

In my organizations, I treat learning like any other unit of work. I have team members create a ticket that gets tracked in our work management system, and that work gets scheduled and prioritized appropriately. If someone is trying to read a book, they might take the book and break groups of chapters up into tickets. Chapters 1–3 are a ticket, chapters 4–6 another ticket, and so on. This work gets scheduled and put into the work queue, and when the team members get to that ticket, they get up, walk to a quiet corner, and read. That's what investment in these things could look like. If you're saying continual learning is part of the job (and if you're in tech and you're not saying that, you should have your head examined), then it should be done during work hours. Requiring staff members to do all of the necessary learning on their own is not only unfair, but a quick path to burning out your employees.

No matter how you track your work, you need to find a mechanism to include learning in that system. This not only helps you give it the time it needs, but also makes that work visual and known.

BUILDING AUTOMATION INTO YOUR TIME ESTIMATES

Another way to reflect this investment in automation with your staff is to build the time needed for automating tasks into every project, every feature, every initiative. It's common for the automation or tooling of a process to be considered out of scope for the very project that's bringing the work to fruition. As an extension of not accepting manual work, all project estimates should include the time necessary to automate the task.

This is important because it signifies that this automation isn't just nice to have, but is part of the project and the deliverable. If you went online and looked for a recipe to make a cake, you might find that the recipe takes 10 minutes to make, but to your surprise, that doesn't include the time it takes to frost the cake. Would you feel that 10 minutes was an accurate representation? Of course not—because a crucial (and arguably the best) part of the cake-making process wasn't included. This is how you should feel about automation and tooling! If you wouldn't hand a janky, half-baked process to a customer, why is it OK to give it to the people who make and support the product?

When you're building your automation or tooling estimates, consider using the tools from the very beginning of the process. Don't go through the entire project doing the tasks manually and then, when it's complete, build the automation around it. As an example, if you need to run a SQL statement to change the configuration of an application and you intend to automate that, don't wait for the production run to build that automation! When you're doing your initial testing where the task will be needed, build it then. And then continue to iterate on it until it works. Then when you do it in lower environments, you're reusing the tool you've already built and testing it to ensure that it will be solid by the time you move to production. This ensures that the tool gets built and is tested, and also speeds up all the other executions of that task during the testing cycle. You might be eliminating or reducing time spent in those four key areas, meaning that the project is able to move faster.

SCHEDULED TIME FOR AUTOMATION

Many technical organizations have a period where they focus on bad technical decisions and attempt to fix them. This focus on technical debt sometimes doesn't include things like automating old workflows. The focus is on things that don't work at all, so things that are merely inefficient can sometimes get lost in the conversation.

As an organization, you should propose dedicated time within a certain time interval for teams to focus on creating automation around tasks. You'll always have some manual work that falls through the cracks. But if you have a dedicated slice of time for focusing on improvements, it can make a huge difference. Start with a week a quarter for specifically targeting at least one or two work items for automation. Increase the frequency as you start to see the benefits of automating that work. If a week per quarter is too aggressive, find what works best for you. But once you've identified the interval, stick to it and make good use of the time.

7.6 *Filling the skill-set gap*

The plan for automation sounds great, but beyond the hurdle of prioritizing automation, some organizations will have to deal with the reality of a skill-set gap. For many reasons, the teams that need to leverage automation may not necessarily have the skills to create it. This needlessly stalls many automation efforts, mainly because of pride and a lack of optimization through the entire workflow.

Not having the skills to perform a task within a team is not a new concept. In fact, it's the reason entire IT organizations exist. You wouldn't expect human resources staff to roll up their sleeves and launch their text editor every time they need a new bit of data processed in their applicant-tracking software. Instead, they contact the technology department, where those skills and expertise live inside the organization.

That same interaction occurs inside the technical department. The expertise of systems management and support lives within the operations organization. But when an internal technology team has a need for their own day-to-day work, the common logic is that the team should be able to support all those activities themselves. The expertise lives in the department, but not in that specific team unit.

Is there value in having those stark walls in place? Most of the motivation for these walls centers around how the teams are incentivized, which I'll discuss a bit later in the book. Each team is so structured and focused on achieving their own immediate goals that they fail to realize how the poor performance of other teams might impact their own goals. I'll give an example.

The development team needs to deliver a feature by Thursday. Because the deployment process is so cumbersome, the release life cycle requires that the software teams have their work submitted by Monday, so the operations team can perform the deployment in the staging environment by Tuesday. With a production deployment needing to be done on Thursday, that leaves the teams with only Tuesday and Wednesday to perform any testing and break fixes. This might seem like an operations issue (why do deployments take so long?), but it's really an organizational issue because of the impact. The issues may not even be solvable by the operations department alone. Maybe the application isn't packaged in a way that makes a faster deployment possible. Maybe the workflow for the release is broken and puts undue burden on the Ops team.

The cause doesn't matter; the problem is still that the company's deployment process is slowing the cadence of deployments. From this viewpoint, the idea of collaboration between development and operations is a no-brainer. The walls of responsibility are just an organizational detail. You want more effort placed on the problem, not on who owns what. In addition, making the deployments faster would afford the development team more time to test. Now they're not beholden to having the release code ready a day ahead of time to get it deployed. Reducing the cycle time of deploys has benefits for the development team as well.

All this is to say that the skills you need exist in the organization, and engaging the appropriate teams that can help you deliver on your needs isn't just a good idea—it's crucial to the DevOps philosophy. Use the in-house expertise to help you and your team build your own expertise. No one starts with a blank canvas and paints a masterpiece. They study existing works and learn from others. Technology is no different.

When pride gets in the way

If the wins surrounding automation are so obvious, why do so many teams struggle with gaining traction on the automation mindset? Well, a sense of complete ownership exists among teams. The feeling is that production is owned by the operations team. If operations owns it, they want to feel comfortable with all the tooling necessary to support it. A bit of ego is most certainly at play here.

This isn't a judgment or a condemnation. I suffer from the same ego and imposter syndrome issues as the next person. But there's something incredibly humbling about asking someone for help in an area where you're supposed to be the foremost expert.

Take that feeling and bury it. The field of technology is simply too vast for you to know everything about every area. Thanks to the internet, you're constantly bombarded with videos of technical experts showing just how multifaceted and talented they are, leaving you to wonder whether you're even qualified for your job. You are. You may not be a Brendan Gregg or an Aaron Patterson, but few people are. Don't let that discourage you or your confidence. And don't think that asking for help in one specific area diminishes your value as an engineer. *Asking for help is not an admission of incompetence.*

7.6.1   *But if I build it, I own it*

The fear of being perpetually stuck with owning something that you have only tangential involvement in is a real fear. I'm not trying to discount that this reality exists for a lot of people. But in a lot of scenarios, the fear is driven from the idea that your automation scripts aren't considered a true part of the system and the overall solution. As certain changes to the system happen, the automation isn't considered part of the testing strategy, but its breakage becomes a major impact for everyone who uses it.

This turns into an incident that requires the supporting engineer to immediately context switch from their existing work to firefighting mode. And everyone hates firefighting. There's no getting around this risk, but you can minimize it with a few simple tricks.

REDUCING FRICTION AROUND SUPPORT

The first way to reduce this friction is to ensure that the automation being worked on addresses both groups (meaning the group that is asking for help on the automation and the group that's actually performing the automation). If you're asking someone to help you build something that has absolutely nothing to do with their day-to-day activities, human behavior is going to limit that person's willingness to contribute. But if that assistance is going to make both your lives easier, the path becomes a lot easier. This is the *skin-in-the-game concept.*

If both sides have skin in the game, the effort needed to support it is much easier to muster. Because when it breaks, both teams are impacted. Development can't move as fast, and operations will be stuck with using the manual process, taking cycles away from more value-added work. I'll discuss this concept of shared incentives in greater detail later in the book.

Second to the skin-in-the-game concept is the idea of *buy-in from everyone* involved, ensuring that both sides are in active agreement on the approach to the problem and what the solution looks like. For developers, it's key to understand that the other group probably has an idea of what the solution should look like. But they fall on the specific implementation details. Removing them completely from the solution will not only produce a bit of animosity, but also create disinvestment on the side of operations in the overall solution. Similarly, it's important that operations listen to the development team around the scope of possibilities. The development team might take issue with an approach because of its long-term implementation and support implications, poor design, or perhaps not meeting the immediate need.

These are specific examples, but the underlying point is that collaboration is the most important aspect when engaging another group for help. Focus on solving the problem, not advocating for your specific solution. When teams collaboratively come up with a solution, the issue of long-term support suddenly seems to fade into the background.

Leave your baggage at the door

A bit of history from the perspective of operations team members might be in order. Operations groups have historically been the last stop on the release train into production. Unfortunately, in many organizations they're not involved in the process at all until it's time to release the software. In many cases, it's too late for operations to effect change in the way they would like to. This leads to a kind of mental disassociation with the solution, because it's not theirs. They have no fingerprints on them. The solution happened "to them" not "with them," so it gets treated as this sort of other thing.

> **(continued)**
> Likewise, development has had a history of being treated like inept children by operations staff members. The barrier between them and production can feel a little artificial to them, and as a result, residual resentment can build. Their frustration is understandable. They can be trusted to build a system, but when it comes to operating it, they're looked upon as completely incapable and dangerous.
>
> These are broad characterizations, but I've seen it echo true with many engineers. It's important to empathize with your collaborators so that you understand where feelings, objections, and viewpoints are coming from. Even if your organization doesn't match this scenario, I assure you that some underlying hard feelings probably exist among the different engineers in your organization. Some of it might even be baggage from a previous job.

Owning part of the solution is a concern for many, but I challenge you to examine why you're concerned with owning it. It often boils down to a lack of trust in the quality of the solution as well as in the influence that you can exert on it. When a tool adds value and is done well, supportability is rarely a concern.

7.6.2 *Building the new skill set*

Borrowing skills from another team is not a good long-term solution. It should be done only as a stopgap to allow time for the appropriate team to build up the skills necessary to take over support. This usually boils down to a lot of cross-training and mentorship. Once the initial implementation is built, encourage staff members to handle bug fixes and new features, while offering engagement opportunities with the original team members responsible for the initial development.

A series of lunch-and-learns can also go a long way, offering a group setting to allow people to ask questions, walk through the code together, and apply those lessons learned to new problems. Develop small coding challenges for the team to help them build their skill set. The misconception is that everything written needs to be deployed and used in a production environment. But if you can build your skill set by writing little utilities for your personal environment, you can quickly begin to gain confidence and competence in what you're doing.

As an example, at a job I had an engineer who was learning Python read from the Twitter API and produce a list of the most commonly used words ranked in order. The code produced has absolutely no value in the workplace, but the knowledge gained by the engineer is invaluable. The Twitter project gave a specific problem to solve with no risk of real failure, but at the same time built on concepts that will be useful in real work scenarios.

If you're in a leadership position, you might consider making these sorts of assignments part of the body of work that's planned for the week, allowing people to dedicate time during the work week to level up their skills. Learning on nights and weekends is exhausting and sometimes not possible for a lot of people because it competes with the rest of life. But doing it during the work week and reporting on your progress during team meetings drives the importance that you, as a leader, place on this skill.

Another option is to change the way the team is built out in the future. Invert the requirements a bit if your team already has ample talent in one area. For example, if an operations team is already heavily staffed with systems people, maybe you change the focus of the next hire to someone with heavy development experience, but less systems experience, letting them learn that on the job. Diversification of skills is important for any team, so knowing where you're weak and where you're strong will help you fill the gaps.

The skill-set gap is a real problem with the automation portion of a lot of DevOps organizations. But with a little creativity and shared problem solving, your organization has all the talent you need; you just need to tap into it. Once you've tapped into that talent, you need to get that work prioritized by highlighting its importance to the organization. Automation is in fashion now, so it doesn't take the same level of effort to sell leadership on it as in years past. But making the case for why it's important is still worthwhile. You can always highlight the following three points:

- What you'll be able to do faster and how that impacts other teams
- What you'll be able to do more consistently and repeatedly
- What additional work you'll be able to do with the automated task mostly removed from your workload

7.7 Approaching automation

When you talk about *automation*, many people have different and sometimes conflicting ideas about what that means. Automation can range from a series of individual scripted actions to a self-adjusting system that monitors, evaluates, and decides programmatically on each course of action.

> **DEFINITION** *Automation* is the process of taking individual tasks and converting those tasks into a program or script for easier execution. The resultant program can then be used in a standalone fashion or encompassed into a larger piece of automation.

When making a DevOps transformation, you should *always* start thinking about a task with automation in mind. If DevOps is a highway, manual processes are a one-lane tollbooth on that highway. Long-term manual processes should be avoided at all costs. The price is too high and only continues to grow. A case can be made that sometimes a short, time-bound manual process is more effective than an automated process. But be wary of "short-term" fixes. They have a habit of becoming long-term as the necessary work to remove them continues to get reprioritized. If you're considering a short-term manual process, make sure all parties involved have incentives to eliminate it, or you'll end up with a short-term process five years later.

The level of automation that exists in your organization will depend greatly on the technical maturity and capabilities of the team responsible for implementing it. But regardless of your team's skill set, I assure you that every organization can execute and benefit from some level of automation. The automation may not only reduce the amount of work and potential errors that can happen in a system, but also create a sense of safety among the team members who use it if it's designed correctly.

7.7.1 Safety in tasks

Have you ever run a command that has a surprising side effect? Or maybe you've run an `rm -rf *` command in Linux and have to double-check what directory you're in about 20 times before you feel comfortable pressing Enter. Your comfort with running a task is directly related to the potential outcome if things go bad.

Safety in tasks is the idea that the outcome of the task, if done incorrectly, won't produce dangerous results. I'm going to continue using my fear of cooking as an example. I'm always paranoid about baking chicken and not having it cooked thoroughly. The consequence of eating undercooked chicken could be dangerous! On the same note, I have no fear of cooking chicken tenders in the oven. Chicken tenders are typically precooked and frozen, so the consequence of undercooking chicken tenders is much safer than the consequence of undercooking raw chicken. They also have precise instructions with little to no variability. I don't need to perform any modifications based on variables, like the size of the chicken; I just follow the instructions. You attempt to evaluate the risks based on what you know about the task. As you evaluate a task, you're attempting to get a sense of how easy or hard each task is.

Why is safety important, though? Because when you begin automating tasks, you'll need to think about the potential side effects of each task your automation is now executing. To a certain degree, the user has less control over the actions than they did previously.

Imagine you're automating the installation of a program. Previously, the person performing the installation had complete control of every command being performed. They knew what flags were being passed and what specific commands were being performed. In a world where these steps have been wrapped into a single command, they lose that fine-grained control in exchange for simpler execution. Previously, the user owned the responsibility of safety, but now because of automation, that responsibility has passed to you, the developer.

I want you to think about safety as you're automating work and to treat that responsibility with respect, whether the target users for your automation are external clients, internal customers, or even yourself. Good automation does this all the time. Think of something like the command to install packages on a Linux system. If you type in `yum install httpd`, the command doesn't just automatically install the package. It confirms with you what package it found and is going to install, along with all the dependencies that will come with that. If your package conflicts with another package, instead of saying, "Well, the user said install it, so let's just break everything," it instead errors out with a failure warning. There are command-line flags you can specify to force the installation if you really mean it, but forcing you to specify that additional flag acts as a safety feature to ensure that you know what you're really asking for.

You can create various levels of safety around a task. The amount of effort you put into safety is usually directly proportional to the amount of risk if things go wrong and the likelihood that they will go wrong. With a mental simulation of the tasks to be performed and some understanding of how complexity works, you can begin looking at your processes and thinking about where safety can be improved. You should start with looking at the automation of tasks.

7.7.2 Designing for safety

When you're developing applications, a lot of energy is put into ensuring that the end user is well understood. Entire disciplines have been created around the user experience and the user-interface design to ensure that as part of the application's design, you have an accurate understanding of who the most likely user is, what their experience and expectations are, and the type of behaviors they exhibit and ultimately inflict on the system. The thought process is that if it's dangerous and the system allows the user to do it, then it is the fault of the system, not the user. For end users, this is a great proposition, and applications from Facebook to Microsoft Word are stronger because of this discipline.

But you don't take a lot of these things into account when you're developing systems to be run in production. Tooling to support the application is usually bare or nonexistent. Critical tasks that must be performed are often left to the lowest level of technology possible. It's not uncommon for something as simple as a password reset for an admin account to be relegated to a handcrafted SQL query that everyone stores in their notes app with all the other esoteric commands that are needed to keep the system functional.

This is not only undesirable, but also dangerous when common tasks require steps to be taken outside the defined parameters of the application. Using the password as an example, someone might easily execute the command `UPDATE users SET PASSWORD = 'secret_value' where email = 'admin@company.net'`. The code looks pretty straightforward, and it's easy to reason that this SQL should work. That is, until you realize the security implications: the password fields in the database are *hashed*.

> **NOTE** Hash functions allow a user to map any sized data value to another data value of fixed size. Cryptographic hash functions are often used to map a user's password to a hashed value for storage. Because hashing functions are one-way, knowing the hashed value isn't useful for determining what input created that hashed value. Most password systems will take the user's submitted password, hash it, and then compare the hashed value it computed with the hashed value that's stored for the user.

After running the SQL statement, the password still doesn't work. You could hash the password yourself, but now you'd need to know what hashing algorithm was used, among other things. In addition, many applications keep track of audit changes inside the database. But because this is an application function, the changes that you're making via SQL probably aren't being logged. As a result, the audit trail doesn't show who changed the password or when they changed it. You also can't tell whether the password change was nefarious in purpose or not. If the password changes are typically done in this fashion, a legitimate change and a criminal change look exactly the same. If the change was done through the application, you would expect to see an audit trail leading you to the person who performed the action. If you don't see the audit trail, yet you confirm that the password was changed, it leads you down a different path of investigation.

The process for creating safe support actions for operators of the system isn't radically different from what you would do in soliciting requirements and expectations from an end user. The person who runs the system is really just an end user with a different perspective on the system.

NEVER ASSUME THE USER'S KNOWLEDGE

It's easy to assume that the person operating the system will have as complete and comprehensive knowledge as the person who is designing or developing it. This is almost never the case. As systems grow and become more complex, you must presume that the operator is working with a limited set of knowledge about the system. Assuming the user doesn't have complete information will influence how you alert, inform, and interact with the user.

Probably most important, you shouldn't anticipate that when presented with a decision point, the user will choose the most logical course of action for the situation. This holds true for written documentation or for complex self-regulating automation systems. This isn't to say that your system should be designed so that anyone in the company can operate it, but the minimum expectations of the user should be well understood when the process is being created.

ACQUIRE THE OPERATOR'S PERSPECTIVE

UX engineers spend a lot of time with potential users of the system. One of the reasons is to gain insight from the user's perspective into how they see and view the application they're interacting with.

The same is true of operators of the system. Your perspective shapes how you view and interpret all the data that's coming from the system. A log message that might be incredibly useful to a developer who is testing the software on their local workstation might be totally irrelevant and dismissed by an operator of the system in a production environment. The best way to get that insight is by sitting with operators and talking about the design of your process or automation. Get their feedback on how things should be handled. I assure you that their perspective will be valuable, and the way they view the same problem you've been staring at for weeks will surprise you.

ALWAYS CONFIRM RISKY ACTIONS

The greatest fear I have in life is accidentally deleting my entire Linux system. The operating system allows you to make fatal mistakes without the benefit of a confirmation prompt. Want to delete every file on the system, including important system files? The system will let you do it!

Don't let your processes do that. Whenever possible, if a step requires you to take some sort of destructive action, you should confirm with the user that they should do it. If it's automation, a simple TYPE YES TO CONTINUE prompt should be sufficient. If it's a manual process that's being done via checklist, be sure to highlight on the checklist that the user is about to perform a dangerous step and to double-check the inputs before continuing.

AVOID UNEXPECTED SIDE EFFECTS

When designing automation, you want to try to avoid performing actions that are perhaps outside the immediate scope of what an operator might expect from the system. For example, say a user is executing a backup script for the application server, but the script requires the application to be shut down first. It might seem intuitive to just have the script perform the application shutdown, but ask yourself whether this requirement is something that the average operator would know and be aware of. Informing the user that the application must be shut down first, before exiting, goes a long way toward preventing a surprise for the user.

Now that you have an eye out for ensuring that you don't surprise the user with unintended behavior, you can begin to look at how complexity in the tasks you're automating lead to different approaches and different sets of problems.

7.7.3 Complexity in tasks

All problems and their subsequent tasks have varying levels of complexity. Cooking is a perfect example. I'm a lousy cook. But depending on what I'm cooking, various levels of complexity may exist. Cooking chicken tenders is much simpler than cooking raw chicken.

Being able to order and categorize the complexity of a task has value because it gives us a starting point to think about how the task is approached. You don't need a ton of prep work to cook chicken tenders, but you might add a little extra time when cooking raw chicken for the first time.

To understand these issues a bit better, it often helps to use a framework of some sort to understand and give language to concepts. For this case, I'll borrow from David Snowden's *Cynefin framework*.[1]

> **NOTE** The *Cynefin framework*, used as a decision-making tool, offers various domains. The definitions for his domains apply to this complexity conversation.

---

[1]For more information on the Cynefin framework, see David J. Snowden and Mary E. Boone (2007), "A Leader's Framework for Decision Making," *Harvard Business Review* (https://hbr.org/2007/11/a-leaders-framework-for-decision-making).

The Cynefin framework allows you to place the complexity of the problem into one of four contexts. The names for these contexts are *simple, complicated, complex,* and *chaotic.* For teaching purposes, I'm going to limit my usage to the first three contexts because addressing the chaotic is probably worth its own book and not something that general automation tips could reliably reason about.

SIMPLE TASKS

Simple tasks are those that have a handful of variables, but those variables are well-known and well understood. The way the values of the variables impact the necessary steps is also well understood.

An example might be installing a new piece of software. The variables might be your operating system type and the version of the operating system you're running. Both variables, when changed, might impact the steps that you need to take to get the software installed. But because these values and their impact are well understood, they can be enumerated and documented ahead of time to help someone install the software for all supported operating system types.

As an example, the steps to download database software differ based on your operating system. If you're using the RedHat-based operating system, you might need to download and install the software via an RPM package. If you're using Windows Server, you might download an MSI installer. Despite these being two different methods to get the software installed, their steps are still well understood and can be detailed ahead of time.

COMPLICATED TASKS

Complicated tasks have numerous steps that are not easy or straightforward. They require various levels of expertise, but once you've done it, the task is often repeatable. An example might be manually promoting a database server from a secondary to the primary. Several steps require gathering more information as input to later tasks, so distilling the steps into simple tasks can be somewhat difficult.

Using the database server promotion example, you might have several decision points. If the slave database server you intend to promote is not fully in sync with the master, you might need to take a series of actions that then alter the steps necessary to perform the database promotion. With the appropriate level of expertise, you might be able to break these complicated tasks into a series of simple subtasks, but the execution of subtasks will most likely be done based on different decision points throughout the process. For example, if the slave database server is in sync, begin subtask X, but if it is not, begin subtask Y.

COMPLEX TASKS

Complex tasks typically involve many variables, with each variable potentially impacting the effects of the other variables. Fine-tuning a database is a perfect example of a complex task.

You cannot just set up a series of generic options and expect great performance. You have to consider your database workload, available resources on the server, traffic patterns, and trade-offs between speed and recoverability. If you've ever been on Stack Overflow, you've probably seen questions that are answered with, "Well, it depends." That simple phrase is a signal that the forthcoming answer requires some expertise and some nuance in understanding. Complex tasks require a level of expertise in order to understand how different aspects of the task relate to and affect each other.

7.7.4 How to rank tasks

Something I've learned about over the years is "the curse of the expert." It can be difficult to separate what you know from what the intended performer of the task knows. An important thing to keep in mind when you're ranking these tasks is that the complexity of the task should be considered from the person who is executing the task, not from the perspective of your own expertise.

This can get tricky and might require cross-functional collaboration. If you were writing instructions for how to deploy software, the level of detail you use should change based on your target audience. If the instructions are for the operations group that has experience deploying similar code, your level of detail would differ than if you were writing it for someone with no context of the environment. Similarly, when you're implementing a task to restore the database, the complexity from the perspective of implementing the task is different from the complexity of the person executing it.

Understanding the complexity level of a task allows you to think about how to approach executing the task through the viewpoint of safety. The complexity of the task doesn't map directly to its potential negative impact. If you were making a cake, you would consider the task of "preheat the oven to 350 degrees" a simple task. But accidentally setting the oven to 450 degrees could be disastrous for the outcome. (As stated previously, I'm a horrible cook, so this might not be true at all.)

When you evaluate a task for automation purposes, you might instantly judge your ability to automate it based on the complexity of the task. But don't be afraid to take on complex tasks that have low risk if they fail or are incorrect. If the outcome of the automation is low risk, learning about the complexity of the task through trial and error might not be that bad. Think of an unintended installation. The worst thing that could happen is that you must start the installation over again. Tackling this task, which on its face might seem complicated, is pretty risk free. You can iterate on it over time and get the process just right. Automation that deletes data in the database, however, should probably have a much higher degree of certainty.

You want the operator to be able to execute a task, knowing that different levels of safety are built into the task to protect against disastrous consequences if they make an error. Think about the anxiety level you might have if I gave you a complex task but told you that if you got it wrong, you'd get an error message and could try again. Now imagine that exact same task, but now I tell you that if you get the command wrong, you could shut down the entire system. That shift in user anxiety is why you want to consider levels of safety in your task creation.

Do you rank the task or the overall problem?

When looking to automate a task, you might be confused about whether you should be attempting to rank the complexity of the individual, discrete tasks or the complexity of the overall problem itself. For example, do I rank the task of cooking chicken? Or do I rank the four individual tasks that result in my overall solution of cooking chicken?

I would focus on ranking the individual tasks. Generally, the problem will be categorized based on the most complex task within it. As an example, if you have a problem that has four underlying tasks, and you ranked three of the tasks as simple and the final task as complex, the overall problem would be considered complex.

7.7.5 *Automating simple tasks*

Automating simple tasks is a great place to start to introduce safety into your processes and systems. Simple tasks are typically orderly and easy to codify into a scripting language. If this is your first attempt at automating a task, the advice is to always start small and simple. Also focus on tasks that are executed frequently; this way, you can continue to get feedback on your automation. Having your first piece of automation be something you run once a quarter doesn't give you a lot of opportunity to learn and tweak the process.

The simplest way to start is to focus on small objectives of the automation and to slowly build on them. If you look at the final vision for your automation to start, you could quickly become overwhelmed with potential problems and hurdles. A simple goal might be just getting a multistep task executed via a single command-line utility. For an example, going back to Gloria from the beginning of the chapter, let's say her process looks something like the following:

1 Get a list of all orders in the failed state.
2 Verify that the orders are both failed orders and orders that have been cancelled by the payment processor.
3 Update the orders to the new state.
4 Verify that those orders have moved to the new state.
5 Display the results to the user.

These steps seem easy and straightforward, but they can still cause issues if a step is missed. What if the operator issues the wrong SQL command in step 1? What if the operator updates the wrong orders to the new state? These steps can easily be codified into a simple shell script as a first attempt at automation. Take a look at the following code I'll call `update-orders.sh`:

```
#!/bin/bash
echo "INFO: Querying for failed orders"
psql -c 'select * from orders
    where state= "failed"
    and payment_state = "cancelled"'
echo "INFO: Updating orders"
```

The query shows how many orders are currently in the failed state and lists them.

```
psql -c 'update orders set state = "cancelled"
    where order_id in
       (SELECT * from orders
            where state = "failed"
            and payment_state = "cancelled")'
echo "Orders updated. There should be no more orders in this state"
psql -c 'select count(*) from orders
    where state= "failed"
    and payment_state = "cancelled"'
```

Updates the orders in the failed state

Redisplays those orders to the user

This seems incredibly simplistic, but it provides a level of consistency that allows for an operator to feel comfortable and safe in its execution. It also gives you repeatability. Every time someone executes this process, you can feel confident of the steps taken and the outcome. Even with a simple task such as this, executing a single line of update-orders.sh seems easier and preferable to the five-step process detailed previously.

Astute readers may ask themselves, "How do I know one of these steps doesn't fail?" It's a fair question, but what if the step failed when you were executing it manually? You'd probably have the operator stop and perform some sort of initial troubleshooting. You can do the same with your automation, prompting the user whether to continue after each step.

The modified script follows. It's a bit longer now, but it gives you an opportunity at key parts of the script to exit if the operator sees something that doesn't seem correct in one of the previous command outputs. Again, remember that you're focused on getting started, not on the automation winning a hackathon contest.

```
#!/bin/bash
echo "INFO: Querying for failed orders"
psql -c 'select * from orders
where state= "failed"
and payment_state = "cancelled"'
response=""
while [ $response != "Y" || $response != "N" ]; do
    echo "Does this order count look correct? (Y or N)"
    read response
done
if [ $response == 'Y' ];then
    echo "INFO: Updating orders"
    psql -c 'update orders set state = "cancelled"
            where order_id in
                (SELECT * from orders where state = "failed"
                and payment_state = "cancelled")'
echo "Orders updated. There should be no more orders in this state"
psql -c 'select count(*) from orders
    where state= "failed"
    and payment_state = "cancelled"'
else


fi
echo "Aborting command"
exit 1 #
```

This section gives the user context for an action taking place and gives them the opportunity to abort.

In a more advanced script, you might try to do some additional error handling to get a sense of how you might be able to recover from a condition. But for your first take at automation, this is more than enough. It gives the operator the safety to do the job with a consistency that makes the script's execution more predictable than if you left it to the operator. The message is consistent, the length of time to log off is consistent, and the order of execution is consistent.

As you become more comfortable with the possible points of deviation, you can begin to introduce more error handling and less user confirmation. If the script runs 500 times without any failure in the `broadcastmessage.sh` portion of the script, you might decide that the extra handler isn't providing much value in comparison with how much it's costing you to verify each step. The key is to not assume that your automation software is static, no matter the level of sophistication. You can continue to iterate to make it better, more robust, less user-dependent, and generally more helpful. Next steps in this automation life might be as follows:

- Recording the start and stop time of the entire
- Logging how many records were updated to an audit system
- Logging the dollar value of failed orders for accounting purposes

You can continue to improve your automation as you become more comfortable with the task and its possible outcomes. Don't let perfect be the enemy of good. Automate the steps that you feel comfortable with, and as you gain more expertise in the task, let the automation evolve. Continued maintenance is something that you must consider, because your environment and process will be constantly evolving.

7.7.6   *Automating complicated tasks*

Simple tasks have a straightforward path and are easy to get started. But complicated tasks can be a bit more cumbersome because often they must retrieve information from one source to use as input for another. These tasks may have unknowns at the time of execution that makes determining responses or input values not quite as straightforward as they would normally be, but the value of these responses is still knowable with a limited set of variables.

For example, if you operate in a cloud infrastructure, simple tasks such as restarting a service can become complicated. Because of the dynamic nature of the cloud, you may not know at design time which servers are running the service you need to restart. There might be one; there might be a hundred. Before you can even begin the task of automating the restart, you must be able to identify where the work needs to happen.

This is another example of how developing and iterating over time might be a beneficial approach to reaping safety benefits, while at the same time moving the team forward. Maybe you leave the discovery of where to run the restarts to human effort, with your script merely prompting for a list of IP addresses to execute the script against. As you become more skilled and more comfortable with your automation, you may move to having your script query the cloud provider's API to find the list of IP addresses.

When you're working with complicated tasks for automation, you want to take a basic approach to dealing with the task. Always keep in the back of your mind that when it comes to automation, the safety of execution is always something to design for. You should evaluate two areas: the negative impact or consequence of getting a step wrong, and the ease of performing the success or failure of the step.

As an example, imagine you're looking at restarting a process from a last known good position. Once you restart the process, it will begin processing data from the position you specify. If you get the position wrong, you could end up either skipping data by moving too far in the log sequence, or duplicating data by moving too early in the sequence and reprocessing data. You'll mark as *high* the consequences of getting this step wrong. Next, you must get the log sequence number. If you're lucky, there might be a system command that gives you the log sequence number. Figure 7.4 shows how easy it is to retrieve the log sequence number.

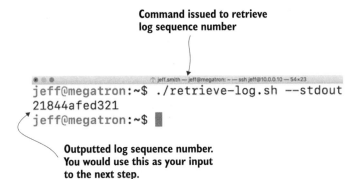

Command issued to retrieve log sequence number

```
jeff@megatron:~$ ./retrieve-log.sh --stdout
21844afed321
jeff@megatron:~$ ▌
```

Outputted log sequence number. You would use this as your input to the next step.

Figure 7.4   Output from the log sequence retrieve script

The likelihood of you getting this wrong is low. This looks like a good candidate to automate in its entirety. Now if this output was buried within a bunch of other output requiring you to do some arcane, unreadable regular expression-matching, that might change your position on the task's difficulty, moving it to medium. The accuracy of the task being a medium, in combination with the high consequence of getting it wrong, might push you outside your comfort zone for automation to start with. You could rely on an operator to get the log sequence number manually and feed that step into your automation task.

The process for identifying potential automation levels follows:

1 Break the complicated tasks into a series of simple tasks.
2 Evaluate each simple task to understand the negative consequences of getting that task wrong. Rank it from 1 to 10.
3 Rank the difficulty of performing that task with certainty via automation or scripts. Rank the confidence on retrieving an accurate value from 1 to 10.

4 Plot these two lines in a quadrant to evaluate the overall level of difficulty.

5 Decide whether the task should be performed manually (prompted) or rolled into the automation based on your comfort level of where it falls in the quadrant.

These steps will become overkill as you can quickly intuit whether a task has particular risks or not. But if you're just getting started, this can give you some guidelines on how to proceed with regards to your automation. Until you get comfortable, you can use the quadrant graph shown in figure 7.5 to plot your rankings. Based on the quadrant that the simple task ends up in should help you in deciding on how difficult or easy it will be to automate and the type of automation interaction you should use.

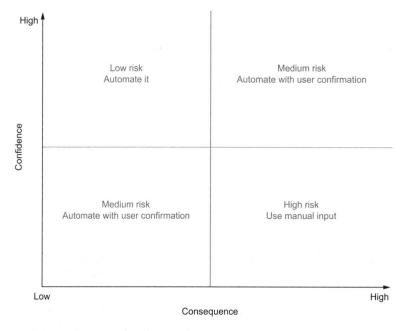

Figure 7.5   Plotting the risk involved with automation

7.7.7 *Automating complex tasks*

The automation of complex tasks is no small feat. It takes an experienced team that is dedicated to the automation systems being created. Though automating complex tasks is possible, I'll reserve this conversation for later in the book, once you've gone through a few other topics. Depending on the size and experience level of the team, this could lead to creating silos of knowledge, where only a select few are anointed with the privilege of certain tasks.

Summary

- Operational automation is a feature of the system and should be considered as early in the design process as possible.
- Prioritize automation not just in the work you do, but also in the tools you choose.
- Identify good candidates for automation by examining the task's complexity and basing the automation approach on that complexity level.
- Address skill-set gaps by leveraging other parts of the organization for assistance.

Off-hour deployments

This chapter covers

- Longer release cycles and their impact to the team's deployment confidence
- Automation techniques for deployments
- The value of code deployment artifacts
- Feature flags for releasing incomplete code

Deployments are sometimes big, scary events. Sometimes the ritual around these deployments can be justified. But it's much more common that the eventfulness of your deployments is a symptom of something deeper going on with your deployment strategies. *Off-hour deployments* are an antipattern that feels justified in protecting your organization. But in reality, you're treating the symptom instead of the problem. If you get calendar invites for routine deployments, there might be a better way.

8.1 War story

Patrick runs the product organization at the FunCo company. One day his phone rings, and it's Jaheim from the sales department. Jaheim has been working his way into a sales meeting with Quantisys, a large player in the market. He finally got a

154

chance to demo the software in front of the Quantisys senior leadership team, and they absolutely fell in love with it.

But like all dream deals, there's a catch. The software needs to integrate with Quantisys's current billing system. Jaheim knows that billing integrations are high on the list of features the development team is working on. He hopes that if he can get the integration Quantisys needs prioritized and implemented quickly, it might be enough to salvage the deal.

Patrick listens to Jaheim's story and agrees that it's a tremendous opportunity. He can rearrange priorities to land such a large customer, but there's another catch. Even if the feature could be completed in two weeks' time, the product operates on a quarterly release cycle. It is February, and the next release cycle isn't until mid-April. Patrick goes back and works with the development team to see if they can figure out a way to do a targeted release with just this feature set. Unfortunately, there are a slew of commits to the codebase that will be difficult to untangle with any level of safety.

Jaheim takes the April date back to the customer, but they simply can't wait that long to make a decision on their software, especially considering that even in April the feature would be brand new and might suffer from any number of bugs, delivery delays, and just general compatibility issues. The customer opts for another solution, Jaheim misses out on closing a great deal, and FunCo loses what surely would have been a significant contributor to revenue.

Sometimes you can draw a direct line between technical operations and potential revenue and sales opportunities. When you think about the business of software, new features basically function like inventory. In a non-software business, a company deals with inventory on its shelves. Every moment that inventory is sitting represents unrealized revenue to the organization. The company had to pay to acquire the inventory, and has to pay to store it and track it.

That inventory also represents potential risk. What if you never sell the excess inventory? Does the inventory lose value over time? For example, let's say your warehouse stocks the hottest Christmas gift this season. If you don't sell that stock, there's very little chance that it will fetch the same price next season, when a hot new toy dominates children's imaginations.

A similar situation occurs when it comes to features in software. To acquire these features, software developers must pour time and energy into bringing them to reality. Those developer hours cost, not just in hours worked, but also in the form of lost opportunities. A developer focused on one feature may not be working on another. This is often referred to as the *opportunity cost*.

But a feature doesn't begin to create value for the organization when it's complete. It begins to build value for the company only after it's been deployed and released to users, whether to all users or to just a specific subset. If the new features can't be delivered to a customer in a timely fashion, that's all value that was created but couldn't be captured by the company. The longer the software sits unused in a repository, the greater chance it has not only to become waste, but also to potentially miss the market it was originally intended for.

Think of it like this: if my software has a feature that integrates with Google Reader, that might be value that my customers want to get their hands on. In fact, it might be the feature that causes people to sign up for my product. But because of issues with the release cycle, even though the software feature is finished in January, I can't release it until April. In a shocking turn, Google announces that it will be shutting down Google Reader in early July.

Your knee-jerk reaction might be that the development team can't predict the future! Google Reader shutting down is an unforeseen event that's beyond the scope of the delivery team. That's true, but the event reduces the amount of time that the feature can provide value for the team. If the team could have released the feature when it was ready, it would have had seven months to attract customers to the platform based on that feature. Instead, they were reduced to offering the feature for only three months before it became completely irrelevant.

This example has plenty of room for "whataboutism" (what about X, what about Y?) You can argue about whether the idea for the feature was a good one to begin with, but that's not the point. The point is that the feature was complete but couldn't begin generating value for the organization until it was practically too late. Besides this business risk of wasting code value, a slow release process has other negative effects:

- *Release cramming*—The release process is so painful that teams avoid doing it regularly. This leads to larger and larger releases, making the release riskier.
- *Rushed features*—Larger releases means less frequent releases. Teams might find themselves rushing a feature to ensure they can make it for the next release cycle.
- *Crushing change control*—When you have larger releases, they become riskier. The more risk, the bigger the impact of failure. The larger the impact of failure, the tighter the process becomes with additional layers of approvals and change control heaped on top.

This chapter focuses on the deployment process and how you can help reduce the fear and risk of deployment inside your teams. Like most things in DevOps, one of the key solutions to help you do this is to include as much automation as the process can stand.

8.2   The layers of a deployment

When I think of a deployment, I think of it in layers. Deployments have multiple pieces, and once you start looking at it in those terms, you can begin to see that there are multiple places to make a deployment and a rollback just a bit easier.

In many organizations, especially large ones, a series of separate deployments seem to happen. But these are all part of the same deployment! A deployment of code does you no good if the database change hasn't been applied. As illustrated in figure 8.1, a deployment can be depicted in layers:

- *Feature deployment* is the process of enabling new features across the application.
- *Fleet deployment* is the process of getting the artifact deployment done across many servers.
- *Artifact deployment* is the process of getting new code installed on a single server.
- *Database deployment* is the process of any changes that need to happen to the database as part of the new code deployment.

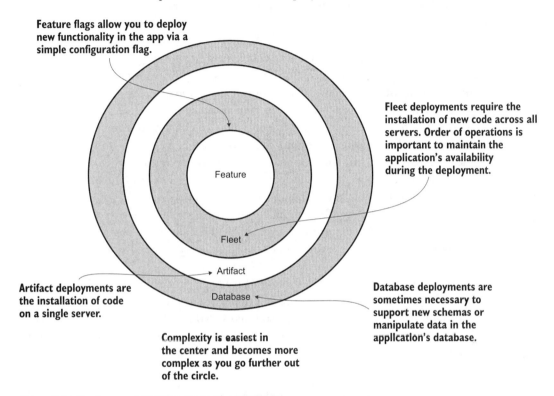

Feature flags allow you to deploy new functionality in the app via a simple configuration flag.

Fleet deployments require the installation of new code across all servers. Order of operations is important to maintain the application's availability during the deployment.

Artifact deployments are the installation of code on a single server.

Database deployments are sometimes necessary to support new schemas or manipulate data in the application's database.

Complexity is easiest in the center and becomes more complex as you go further out of the circle.

Feature
Fleet
Artifact
Database

Figure 8.1 The layers of deployments in an application

It's also valuable to think of these as separate concepts, because in a lot of instances deployment processes have blended the steps together. If you haven't thought about how you can roll back a single feature, that just means the feature deployment and rollback are part of the artifact or fleet rollback. And if you don't think of these as all part of supporting the same deployment, you create a world in which the release process has to cross many teams, with coordinated actions that don't take into account the details of the other processes.

With the mindset of these being parts of a whole, I tend to look at the datastore deployment as the first part of the deployment process. This is due to the sensitivity of the database, as well as the fact that it's a shared piece of infrastructure. Every application server in the pool will use the same database, so ensuring that its deployment goes well should be a top concern. It's also possible that your new version of code is dependent on database changes being performed prior to the code starting up. Imagine if your new code is expecting a table, but that table doesn't exist yet.

Second, you have your artifact deployment. The deployment artifact is the logical unit of the deployment that concerns itself with getting new code onto a running server. The artifact deployment doesn't concern itself with coordinating with other nodes or handling end-user traffic gracefully. Its primary focus is getting new code onto a server.

Third, you have the fleet deployment. This is where you concern yourself with performing the artifact deployment across your entire fleet of target servers. At this layer, you begin to concern yourself with things like user traffic and load-balancer routing. At this layer, a lot more coordination needs to happen across servers because you need to ensure that enough available capacity remains to continue to serve users.

Last is the feature deployment. It's common to think that a feature deployment and a code deployment are one and the same, but as discussed previously, a bit of nuance exists. A feature might not be deployed to users at the exact same time as the code that provides it is deployed. A feature that's hidden behind a feature flag allows us to separate those two ideas, as one must happen before the other. (The code deployment containing the feature has to go first, or there's no feature to enable.) But if you think of the feature deployment as separate, it means you can begin to think about a rollback of a feature that doesn't necessarily involve the rollback of the code that provides it.

As you think about the deployment and rollback process, you should be thinking about it in the context of these phases of a deployment. This will help you create isolation for failure and recovery purposes, so that everything doesn't instantly resort to an entire rollback of the fleet. Sometimes a more localized solution is available. I'll talk about that later in this chapter.

The IOTech deployments: Approaching the deployment

IOTech is a fictious company that makes monitoring software. Marcus is working on a new feature that is going to need to be rolled out and iterated on over a few weeks. The project could have significant negative performance impact, but unfortunately, because of the nature of the data, it is incredibly difficult to replicate it and the transaction rate in a lower environment. Therefore, Marcus is going to need to think carefully about how the deployments are structured.

Several database changes will be necessary, so he'll need to think about how to structure the code not only so that the database schema can support different versions of the code, but also so that data integrity is maintained if he needs to roll back the database layer of the deployment. Because of the potential performance impact, he'll also want to be able to roll back his change without forcing a rollback of the entire application. For that, he'll think about having the capability to turn his new functionality on and off without the need for an entire rollback.

8.3 *Making deployments routine affairs*

The deployment process details the steps necessary to get your code into a state that's usable by your customer. This involves moving code from a development or staging environment to the production servers where customers interact with it. It can also include database-level activities to ensure that the code and the database schema are compatible with each other.

Up until now, I've described the code and the features they provide as one and the same. Deploying new code means deploying new features. But in this and subsequent chapters, I'll make the case that the delivery of new code can be decoupled from the delivery of new features—the same way a database schema change can be performed in phases instead of in a single big-bang approach.

One of the ways you make an activity routine is to do it in a controlled environment beforehand. The more you can make the environment like the real thing, the better and more comfortable you become. This all starts with our preproduction environments.

8.3.1 *Accurate preproduction environments*

Accuracy in preproduction environments is key to the confidence they inspire in subsequent steps throughout the process. Let me start by stating my definition of a *preproduction environment*. It's any application environment that isn't production.

Not all preproduction environments are created equal, however. You might have a preproduction environment in which the nodes are extremely small, and the database is a smaller subset of production data. But the way the environment is configured should be the same, minus any performance-specific tuning. Factors that might differ include the number of database connection threads between production and preproduction, because the size of your database servers will likely be radically different. But if you're running Apache HTTPD 2.4.3 in production, you should be running that in preproduction as well. If you're forcing all traffic to be Transport Layer Security (TLS) based in production, you should force all traffic to be TLS-based in preproduction.

The more confidence you have that an environment mimics production, the more confidence you'll have in the deployment process. Unfortunately, staging environments are often targets for cost-cutting measures. Reproducing an entire production environment can become prohibitively expensive, so people begin to ask, "What's the minimum we can do and still get value?" The staging environment becomes a shell of what's in production and not just with regards to hardware performance.

The staging environment might be a shrunken version of the current production infrastructure; you might have eight or nine distinct application servers in production, but these services get boiled down to a single server, running eight or nine applications as separate processes. It's better than nothing, for sure, but doesn't even remotely reflect the realities of production.

The focus should be on ensuring that the environments are *architecturally* the same. The patterns for the way services are delivered should be replicated in preproduction environments, even if the size and count of servers differs. The closer you get to production in your development process, the more similar these environments should become.

The minor differences in environments can quickly begin to add up. How do you test a rolling deployment in this environment? What if there's an accidental assumption on the part of development that a file will be accessible by two different applications? For example, let's say your product has an application server for processing web requests and then a background processing server. During the development process, someone makes the mistake of creating a file that needs to be accessible by both the application server and the background processing server. This passes through local development without any alarms because all the processes exist on a user's workstation. It moves to the staging environment, where again, different application processes exist on the same physical machine. Finally, you make the move to production, and suddenly everything falls apart because the application server can access the file, but the background processing server can't because the file is on a separate physical host!

As another example, assumptions could be made about network boundaries. Say you have a process that normally doesn't connect to the database server, but for this new feature, it must establish a connection. Again, you fly through local development. Staging isn't a problem because, again, all the application components live on the same machine. There's no chance of encountering any sort of network or firewall rule. You don't find out the impact of this environmental difference until you've hit production, and suddenly everyone is confused when this background processing job won't start after the new deployment because it can't connect to the database server.

The key to solving this problem is to make the staging environment mimic production as closely as possible, in terms of architecture and topology. If there are multiple instances of an application service, on separate machines in production, the same pattern should be replicated in the staging environment, albeit on a smaller scale in terms of the number and power of the hosts. This allows you to create a more accurate reflection of what the application will encounter and behave like in the production environment.

Notice I said "more" accurate, and not "completely" accurate. Even if you size your environment and match it to be the exact same specs as production, it will never truly mimic production. Knowing that is also a major part of making deployments routine affairs.

Docker and Kubernetes: New tech, same problems

You've probably at least heard of Docker and Kubernetes by now. *Docker* is the most popular container technology in use today. But that begs the question, "what are containers?" *Containers* allow developers to package all the necessary components of an application into a single artifact (the container). Inside the container are all the libraries, files, applications, and other dependencies necessary to run the application. Containers use two key features of the Linux kernel: cgroups and namespaces. These features allow you to completely isolate a container running on a host machine from other containers.

Compared to virtual machines, containers are much lighter from a resource perspective because they share the kernel of the host operating system. This eliminates a lot of duplication of resources that exist in virtual machines. Containers also launch a lot faster than virtual machines, making them attractive for large deployments as well as local development environments.

Kubernetes is a tool that manages the deployment, configuration, and management of Docker containers. Originally written by Google, it has become the leader in Docker deployment management tools. Kubernetes (sometimes referred to as *K8s*) has facilities to support many of the hurdles people encounter when managing containers in production, such as making containers publicly accessible to other services, managing disk volumes for the containers, logging, communicating between containers, and providing network access controls, just to name a few. Kubernetes is a *big* piece of software that and requires a fair bit of focus to manage effectively.

These technologies are the flavor of the day, and I don't want to knock their value. They are so incredibly transformative that it's difficult to resist using them. If you're using them in local development environments, you can save yourself a lot of time and energy in managing your local development environment with containers.

The problems can occur after you move from your local development environment to some other nonlocal testing environment. While developers might be eager to do more of their work in a Docker/Kubernetes ecosystem, production support teams are sometimes reluctant to revolutionize the way they handle everything they do today. This creates the rather backward situation of having your staging environments being more technically capable than your production environment. For some people, this is somehow more acceptable than it should be. Now your application is being tested in an environment that is cooler for your résumé, but still bears little to no resemblance to what will happen in the production environment.

This isn't to say that I'm against Docker and or Kubernetes. I'm a big fan of both technologies. But if you're going to use them in your staging environment, I *strongly* suggest that you use them in production as well.

For starters, if you're doing testing right, you're going to need to solve all the hairy problems that people who operate these systems complain about. If you've solved the problems in staging, only a minimal amount of additional effort is required to solve them in production as well. Ironically, most people stop at the staging environment because they have a fear of deployments. They've done some magical incantation to get Docker/Kubernetes working in staging and seem content with leaving it as is. If it breaks, eh, it's just staging.

That attitude is going to lead to many issues not being caught in testing and being released into production. Not to mention, you now have the cognitive burden of ensuring that your software functions in both a containerized mode and in virtual machine mode, leading to multiple ways to do everything regarding its life cycles. Deployments are different, patches are different, configuration management is different, restarts are different—and each of these differences requires a solution for both platforms.

> **(continued)**
> Docker and Kubernetes can be great tools for local development. If they leave the developer's laptop, though, you should consider what the path to production looks like. To use them in production often requires buy-in from all the people who will be involved in supporting the environment. If you're going to develop, manage, and deploy K8s yourself, then go forth! But if you need the assistance of another team, get their buy-in early so that your deployment doesn't stop at the gates to production.

8.3.2   *Staging will never be exactly like production*

In a lot of organizations, a ton of energy and effort is put into making the staging environment behave exactly like production. But the unspoken truth is that production and staging will almost *never* be alike. The biggest elements that are missing from staging environments are the elements that often cause the most problems in a system: users and concurrency.

Users are finicky creatures. They always do something unexpected by the system's designers. The gamut ranges from using a feature in an unexpected way to deliberately malicious behavior. I've seen users trying to automate their own workflows, resulting in completely nonsensical behavior at a nonhuman pace and frequency. I've seen users trying to upload massive movie files to an application that's expecting Word documents.

Users are always going to try to accomplish something unique and interesting in your system, and if you don't have real users in your staging environment, you have to be prepared for a plethora of scenarios that your system wasn't tested against. Once you encounter one of those scenarios, you can add test cases to your regression suite, but know that this discover, repair, verify cycle is something that you will constantly experience in your platform. Leaning into that reality instead of constantly fighting it is the only way you're going to make sense of why your staging environment doesn't reveal failures in the test cycle.

Many companies try to solve this by using *synthetic transactions* to generate user activity.

> **DEFINITION**   *Synthetic transactions* are scripts or tools that are created to simulate activities that would normally be performed by a user. They're often used as a method for monitoring an application from the user's perspective or for simulating user activity on systems that don't have the desired amount of organic user traffic.

Synthetic transactions are a great option and strive to make the environment more like production. But don't be fooled into thinking that this is a panacea for your testing woes. The same problems exist, in that you can't possibly brainstorm all the things that an end user might do. You can make a best effort to catch all the cases and continuously add to the list of synthetic tests, but you'll always be chasing user behavior. Couple this with the fact that applications are seldom finished, and you'll constantly be adding new functionality to an application—functionality that is ripe to be disrupted and or abused by your end user population. I'm not suggesting that synthetic transactions aren't worth the effort, but merely preparing you for the reality of their limitations.

Concurrency is another issue that can be difficult to simulate in staging environments. By *concurrency*, I mean the collection of multiple activities taking place at the same time on a system. You might have an ad hoc report executing at the same time as a large data import. Or you might face the combination of hundreds of users all attempting to access a dashboard whose response time has increased by a single second.

It's easy to make the mistake of testing in isolation. Testing the performance of an endpoint with a single user may yield very different results as compared to having tens, hundreds, or thousands of users competing for that same resource. Resource contention, database locking, semaphore access, cache invalidation rates—all these things compound to create a different performance profile than the one that you might have seen in testing.

I can't count the number of times I've encountered a database query that runs relatively quickly in the staging environment, but then the minute I run the same query in production, it's competing with other queries that are hell-bent on monopolizing the database cache. The query that in staging was being served from memory must then go to disk in production. My 2 ms query balloons to 50 ms, which can have a rippling impact throughout the system, depending on resource demands.

You can try to mimic concurrency in your staging environments by doing synthetic transactions and ensuring that your staging environment is doing all the same background processing, scheduled tasks, and so on, but it will always be an imperfect process. There is almost always a time when another third-party system accesses your application haphazardly. Or background processing might be difficult to replicate because of its interaction with an external system. (Check chapter 5 for ways to handle third-party interactions.)

Despite our best efforts, generating concurrency will run into similar hurdles as simulating users. It'll be a constant fight as the platform evolves. This is work that is never done. Despite that reality, it's still a worthwhile effort, but it will never answer the question "How do we make sure this never happens again?" That question is a symptom of not understanding the complexity in the systems that are being built and the endless number of possible scenarios that can be combined to create an incident. In the next chapter, a section on conducting a postmortem of incidents will deal directly with that question and its toxicity.

In many organizations, deployments are large productions. Communication is sent out weeks ahead of time; staff members are alerted and are on-the-ready in case something goes bad. The team might even create a maintenance window for the release so that they can work without the prying eyes of customers looking to access the system. Sometimes a deployment process is detailed in pages upon pages of Microsoft Word documents, with screenshots highlighting all the necessary steps that need to be taken. If you're lucky, the document might even highlight steps that can be taken in the event something goes wrong, but those documents are rarely of any use because of the multiple ways that a deployment process can break down.

Why is the deployment process so fragile and so feared? In a word, *variability*.

When you deal with software and computers, one of the silent partners in everything you do is predictability. If you can predict how a system is going to behave, you have much higher confidence in having that system perform more and more tasks. The predictability builds confidence, and confidence leads to a faster cadence.

But where does this variability come from? For starters, it comes from our feeling of how rehearsed the process is. For example, the reason many of us have staging environments is not just for testing, but for a sort of dry-run rehearsal prior to the real thing. Just like a stage play, repetition builds confidence. A theater group that has rehearsed a show many times will feel much more comfortable on opening night than a theater group that practiced the show one time in a rough mockup of what the stage will look like for the final show. In case you missed it, this is a metaphor for many lower environments and their management.

8.4   *Frequency reduces fear*

I used to be terrified of flying. I always had these scary thoughts running through my head about what might happen during the flight. Whenever the plane banked in one direction or another, I assumed it was the pilot losing control of the plane and beginning our descent into oblivion. Turbulence was also the stuff of my nightmares. Sitting in this metal tube 20,000 feet in the air and feeling it start shaking violently was not my idea of relaxing travel.

But over time, I flew more and more. Before long, the rituals and the bumps and shakes of airplane travel became routine. Turbulence was a normal occurrence. The plane had to bank after takeoff to make sure the flight was headed in the right direction. Even though I wasn't intimately familiar with every flight plan, the rhythms of the flight felt familiar to me. Familiarity reduced fear.

Familiarity with the deployment process can also reduce your fear of performing it. There are several reasons that frequently deploying is a good thing.

The first is practice. The more often you do a task, the better you get at it. A cook could never function if every time he got an order for pancakes, he was consumed with uncertainty because cooking instructions had updated. By performing a deployment infrequently, each deployment occurs under different circumstances. Are there database changes in this deployment? Are the people performing the deployment the same as the people who performed the last deployment? Are the applications so tightly coupled that several applications must be deployed at the same time? If so, are the same mixture of applications being deployed as the last time?

Even with that relatively modest list of options, you can see that the number of ways that a deployment can differ grows quite quickly. If you're deploying once a quarter, that's only four times a year that someone on the team has the chance to be exposed to the deployment process. (I'll say eight times per year, considering you'll probably deploy into the staging environment prior.) That's not a lot of opportunities in the grand scheme of things, especially if the deployment process is saddled with a bunch of manual tasks.

In conjunction with practice is the sheer number of changes that might go out with every release. The more you pack into a release, the larger your risk of something going wrong. This is inherent in just about anything humans do. The larger the change, the bigger the risk. But this means that as you delay the process of releasing, not only does the number of changes build up, but so does the fear around the release.

Imagine if fear was a reservoir, something you could measure. Fear would tend to build in this reservoir as more time passes between releases. As the number of changes build up in the release, more fear builds. Sometimes the types of changes in a release might also increase fear. If your release is changing a bunch of graphics for the website, that's very different than if your change is releasing five new database schema changes.

So, if these things increase fear, what reduces fear? The inverse of all these things. Fewer components changing per release reduces fear. Knowing that a release is isolated to one system, and one specific component of the system, creates a lot less fear around the release. That's because it's scoped small enough that you can rationalize the potential impact caused by the change. Release cadence is another thing that reduces fear. The more often you release, the more in touch you feel with the system. Assuming these releases are successful, you begin to build up confidence in the release process itself. The anxiety around the process begins to dissipate.

But when fear of deployments continues to rise, the resistance to deployments becomes larger and larger. The resistance largely comes from the operations team, which is traditionally responsible for the uptime of the system. But the resistance can come from anywhere in the organization, especially management.

Automation will also feed into this cycle of fear reduction. The more you automate, the more reliable the process becomes. Once that fear has reached a low threshold, the barriers around deployments begin to open. You move from a strict "after 8 p.m. only" deployment window to the occasional daytime deployment, to the frequent daytime deployment, to the "why on earth would we not just deploy right now?" deployment.

I've documented some of these relationships in figure 8.2, using a system diagraming approach, which I'll use a bit more frequently in the coming chapters.

You can see in the top image that if you were to measure the fear of the deployment, it would increase based on the number of changes going into the release. This leads into the "Fear of deployment" bucket. The only way to reduce that risk is by performing a deployment. But every deployment runs the risk of failure. Failed deployments increase people's resistance to deployments. This resistance means fewer deployments, which results in more changes per deployment. This is what they call in systems speak a *feedback loop*. The very act of protecting the system is leading to the state that helps to cause it. Slowing down deployments is, in fact, feeding into the reasons that

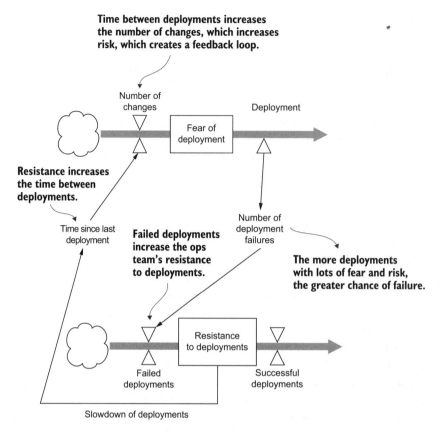

Figure 8.2   The impact of delayed and failed deployments on the fear surrounding the deployment

deployments are dangerous. I'll continue to use this type of systems diagramming later in the book.

The IOTech deployments: Switching the deployment cadence

Typically, Marcus's application gets deployed once a quarter. But the impact of his change is too large to risk releasing the changes with such a large collection of others. He'll never be able to tell whether the other changes are impacting his.

Through some negotiations, Marcus has figured out a path that will allow him to release his code in small bits once every two weeks over the next two months. This frequency, along with a smaller change set, gives him the confidence that he can iterate quickly while minimizing risk to the current production implementation. But this frequency is going to require him to help the other support teams get over their fear of the deployment process.

8.5   *Reducing fear by reducing risk*

Now that you know the value of more frequent deployments, the logical question is how to get there. It starts with automated testing. Getting more automated testing into the pipeline is going to be the baseline for any sort of automated deployment pipeline.

I talked at length in chapter 5 about defining test pipelines. Make sure that your development team is developing a good number of unit tests. If you have little to no tests, then it could be worthwhile to suggest a hack day, where people do nothing but focus on making good unit tests. You can assign different areas of the code to different teams and have a goal of generating X many solid unit tests per hack day. If you do this a couple of times a month, it won't be long before you're building up a great battery of tests.

The next thing you'll need to do is make testing part of the culture of the organization. Enforce the idea that merge requests without test cases are incomplete merge requests. Make it part of the code review process, or even better, make it part of your build pipeline!

Remember how I talked earlier in chapter 5 about using linters? Linters allow you to codify style guidelines for developers. If you want variables to be named with underscores, you can define this in your linter. You can also use linters to ensure that certain behaviors exist. Part of the linter test can be to verify the existence of tests. This is sort of a qualitative test, since your linter will probably not be capable of discerning the quality of those tests, but it's a solid first step to get developers accustomed to the idea that this is a new cultural requirement in the organization. Over time, you can make your linters more robust to catch a variety of formatting conventions, existence of code standards, and more. Now, when someone tries to run a build with no unit tests that surround their new code, they can get feedback from the test suite that they haven't met the requirements of a merge request. Start small and build from there.

This approach won't be without its detractors. Change scares people, and it will certainly drive folks to question whether automation will catch everything. To prepare for these conversations, you should be as candid as possible. It won't catch everything. But neither does your manual testing, because if it did, you probably wouldn't have an issue with the frequency of your deployments.

Automated testing is often held to the unfair silent standard that if it doesn't catch everything, it isn't worth anything. People don't openly say that, but they treat it that way in their behaviors and their approach. Teams will stall on automation because of all these esoteric edge cases that might be difficult to catch. The automation must be flawless. That's a false dichotomy, and you should fight that at every level of the organization.

Automated testing will continue to build value over time as you continuously add to the list of cases and scenarios that you test for. Automation isn't about eliminating uncertainty about a release entirely. It's about reducing that uncertainty to a value that you and the organization can tolerate. If you're going to increase the frequency of your deployments, you must start with the frequency of your test cases.

8.6   *Handling failure in the layers of the deployment process*

The fear of deploying is also related to the effort it takes to roll the change backward in the event of a failed deployment. If I promise to never tell anyone, I want you to think of how many times you've made a change on a live system without extensive testing because you knew that getting the system back to its original state was easy. Remember the days of hot editing a configuration file on a node and reloading the config? (I'm sure you never did this.) You felt empowered to do this for two main reasons:

- The risk and potential exposure of the failure was incredibly low.
- The ability to detect the failure and roll back was incredibly high.

That's it. That's why you were willing to circumvent change management and proper deployments. You were conducting an experiment, the experiment would impact a small number of people for a short period of time, and getting things back to normal operating conditions was incredibly easy and well understood.

When you think of the example in your mind that I'm talking about, you'll probably make any number of excuses as to why that case was different. But the two characteristics that empowered you were the same. You'd never "upgrade the database server really quick" when troubleshooting an issue. The risk is too high, and the rollback too muddied. But you'll gladly hack up a text file on a running server and reload the web server process. By understanding these two fundamental enablers for fast change, you can begin to identify ways to replicate them in your deployment process.

With automated testing and your pipeline in place, you must consider how you go about rolling back from failure. Those options can occur at many layers of the deployment onion. Do you need to roll back just a feature? Or do you need to roll back the entire release? Do you roll back the software on each node, or can you flip back to a set of older nodes running the previous version of the application code? This section covers the layers of the onion and what the deployment and rollback scenarios can look like in each of them.

8.6.1   *Feature flags*

A popular option that was also discussed in chapter 5 is a feature flag. You place new functionality behind a feature flag. If the feature flag is off, the original code paths are executed. But if the feature flag is switched on, the code executes a different, typically new, code path. The flags should be set to a default setting of OFF.

When you make your deployment, from a functionality perspective, a lot of the code might be the exact same execution path as was being run in the previous version of the software. The difference is the capability to enable that flag to turn on new functionality and new code paths. Once a deployment has been completed, after a brief period to confirm that no other unrelated issues exist with the deployment, you can enable feature flags.

Another added benefit to this is that now you can separate the marketing launch of a new feature from the actual deployment of the new feature. Having a bit of slack time between when the application code is ready and deployed and when all of the promotional material for it needs to go out relieves a lot of pressure off the team, as they don't have to be completely bound to this sort of arbitrary date that's driving development efforts. You can deploy the code, get all the marketing efforts together, and then when the business is ready, launch the code.

Once your code is in the wild and working as expected, in a future release you can remove the feature flag logic, making it a permanent part of the code path. In some cases, you might want to leave the feature flag functionality for failure-handling purposes. For example, if your site has some sort of affiliates integration, you might want a permanent feature flag around that functionality. This way, if the affiliate is having problems, you can disable the feature flag to avoid long page-load times. The decision on whether to remove or keep a feature flag will depend heavily on its use case.

8.6.2 *When to toggle off your feature flag*

Feature flag deployments carry a small caveat, however. How do you know if a feature or function is working? I wish I could tell you exactly what to check. But I did hint toward a strategy around this in an earlier chapter: metrics.

When you're thinking of a new feature, you must also think of the surrounding ways to measure the feature's efficacy. How do you confirm that the feature is doing the things that it's supposed to do? Say, for example, the new feature enables users to use a new recommendation engine. How might you verify that the feature is functioning?

To start, you must be able to clearly state the intended outcome of the new feature. For our example, your outcome statement might be, "The recommendation engine feature enables the new BetaAlgorithm. The BetaAlgorithm has been optimized to leverage input about a user from multiple sources, combining them to create a more complete picture of the user's preferences. The new algorithm should be faster and more thorough in its recommendations, and provide higher relevancy to the user than the AlphaAlgorithm."

This is a lot for us to unpack and build metrics around! When I read that statement, I can think of a few metrics that I'd want to build into this feature to verify that it's working appropriately:

- The time it takes to generate a recommendation
- The number of recommendations generated per user
- The click-through rate of the recommendations

These three metrics will go a long way in helping you understand whether the new engine is performing as it should. Embedding these metrics emissions into the algorithm will allow you to build dashboards displaying the relevant information to the feature flag owner. Most of these metrics are easy to grab or to create. For example, a simple timer will go a long way in providing information on the speed of your algorithms. It's simple to do and won't add much to your algorithm. The following listing highlights a simple implementation.

Listing 8.1   A quick example of timing the method

Standard time library in Python. There are many to choose from.

```
import time
class BetaAlgorithm(object):
    start_time = time.time()
    // Recommendation implementation details
    end_time = time.time()
    total_time = end_time - start_time
```

Records the start time and end time

Calculates the total time spent and then emits this metric to your monitoring system

Several programming libraries and modules offer way more sophisticated options for timing code. My point in using this rudimentary version is to highlight that regardless of your language or tools, you can make these sorts of measurements right now. The number of recommendations that gets generated could also be easily calculated. It might be as simple as counting the number of recommendations in the array and emitting that metric. The click-through rate can probably be inferred by HTTP logs that you're already generating. Now with these three items, you can begin to get an understanding of how the recommendation engine is performing, which leads directly into your decision on whether the feature flag should be turned off or left on.

I might have left out one piece of information. Did you notice? I'll state it in case you missed it: if you're implementing these metrics to ensure that a feature works, the metrics are of value only if you have something to compare them to—so you need to get these exact same metrics for the existing recommendation engine.

This need for comparison between future state and current state will have to be embedded into your feature-planning process. When you have a new feature, you have to not only brainstorm the metrics and criteria for determining that it's a success, but also make sure that you have data for comparison to the current way things are done. Obtaining that data is easy, but you must think about and implement this step much earlier in the feature development process.

Doing this as part of another, separate release is prudent because it gives you the ability to begin collecting data on the current state of things while you're building the new future state. You might also end up discovering something about the feature that you hadn't previously known. Maybe you find out that the recommendation referrals are a smaller part of your business than you had originally assumed. Or maybe you learn something about the types of products that are being referred. The point is that the act of measuring today's state so that you have something to compare to the future state is the only way to tell whether your changes are actually an improvement.

The imperfect measurement

Sometimes people struggle with measuring something because they're concerned that the measurement will be imperfect or imprecise. This is a silly concern that so many people, including myself, have had. Almost *all* measurements are imperfect. Sometimes, the very act of measuring something changes the behavior of it. This is one of the cognitive biases known as the *observer bias*.

The point to remember is that you measure something in order to remove or reduce your uncertainty about it. If you're travelling somewhere that you've never been, you might ask what the weather is like there. Your friend might give you a range, between 10 degrees and 30 degrees Fahrenheit. Now that's a pretty imperfect response, but it doesn't have to be perfect to be useful. You now know that shorts are out of the question and that you should look at pants, long sleeves, and maybe a few sweaters. Even that range reduced your uncertainty about the temperature in order to make a useful decision.

That's all you're attempting to do with measurements for comparative purposes, as in our example about the recommendation engines. Even if the numbers are wrong, they're correct in comparison to each other. Whether the number of recommendations is 5 versus 50, or 1,000 versus 10,000, it doesn't matter. We know that one engine is giving out roughly 10 times the number of recommendations when compared to the other. It gives us greater clarity about how the function is performing relative to the previous implementation and is therefore good enough for our purposes.

Don't get caught up in the perfection of measurements. Often just a little bit of information can shed a lot of light when you know absolutely nothing about what you're measuring. If you want to learn more about various ways to think about and carry out measurements, check out *How to Measure Anything* by Douglas W. Hubbard (Wiley, 2014).

8.6.3 Fleet rollbacks

Let's assume for now that the feature flag approach to rollbacks wasn't taken or isn't an option. But you still need to be able to revert to the previous version of code in its entirety. You can handle this in a couple of ways.

The first and preferred method, if you're capable of it, is the fleet rollback, also known as blue/green deployments. The second method is a rolling deployment of artifacts. Both are detailed in this section.

BLUE/GREEN DEPLOYMENTS

The *blue/green deployment* is, of course, the holy grail of public/private cloud infrastructure. Instead of deploying code to existing servers, you simply create new servers that are running the new code. By grouping the servers behind load balancers, you can modify which set of servers (or fleet) are receiving traffic. In a typical scenario, you have an infrastructure setup like figure 8.3: you have a load balancer in front of the application, pointing to a stack of servers.

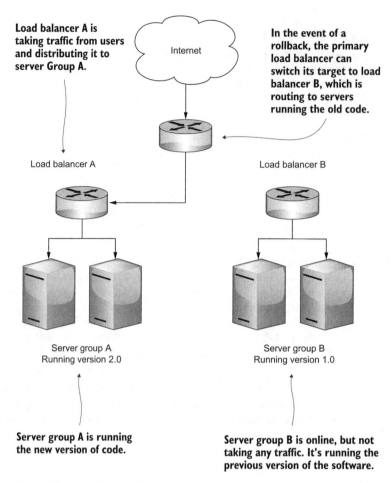

Load balancer A is taking traffic from users and distributing it to server Group A.

Internet

In the event of a rollback, the primary load balancer can switch its target to load balancer B, which is routing to servers running the old code.

Load balancer A

Load balancer B

Server group A
Running version 2.0

Server group B
Running version 1.0

Server group A is running the new version of code.

Server group B is online, but not taking any traffic. It's running the previous version of the software.

Figure 8.3   A common load balancer pattern for managing two sets of servers running different codebases

In this example, when you deploy your code, you're creating brand-new servers. Once they're up and running, you promote those nodes to start handling traffic. Your load balancer switches from one set of servers to another set of servers. You can even do this in stages. Instead of sending all your traffic to the new nodes at once, send it in incremental chunks. You start with 10% then move to 20% in as many steps as you feel comfortable, ultimately ending with 100% traffic on the new nodes. This pattern, common in cloud architecture, is incredibly powerful because the rollback method is as easy as pointing the main load balancer back to the old set of nodes. You can leave that old set of servers running idle for as long as you need that recovery window to be. Once you feel comfortable with the new code, you can spin them down. It makes for a clean process in the cloud, but it does come with a few caveats.

The first caveat in this design is that you'll need to make sure that your database schemas are compatible between versions of the application. Having two sets of servers does you no good if the new code modifies the database in a way that is incompatible with the old version of the application. I'll go into detail in the subsequent section about how to manage database schemas in order to manage compatibility between application versions.

The second caveat to this process is background processing. It's not uncommon for an application to make data changes as part of background processing that isn't directly tied to user interactions. You might have a web server that listens to a queue to send email notifications to users in the background after successful password resets. Even if that server isn't receiving web-based traffic, it might still be performing these types of background activities, in which case you have two versions of the application performing the same actions. This might be fine, depending on how your application is designed, but it's something that you must consider when you roll this out.

One way to handle this situation is by ensuring that all background processes on new application deployments start in the Off state. Then only as part of the promotion process do the background processing services become active and enabled. You can implement this in several ways. One of my go-to solutions has been to have a configuration parameter set in my configuration management tool.

> **DEFINITION** *Configuration management* is the process used by your organization to establish and maintain conformity across your various applications. Configuration management tools assist in this by providing you with a language for defining a specific configuration and a processing engine for applying and enforcing that configuration. Popular tools are SaltStack (www.saltstack.com), Chef (www.chef.io), Puppet (https://puppet.com), and Ansible (www.ansible.com).

The configuration parameter acts as a signal to the application or to configuration management software that the application should be in a specific mode. Flipping that configuration bit tells my software to behave a different way. All configuration management software has attributes about the node that you can use for this. In Puppet it's called a *fact*, in SaltStack it's called a *grain*, and in Chef it's called an *attribute*. Whatever your tool-du-jour is, rest assured that you can specify a value like this in your configuration and then have your configuration management tool enable or disable services accordingly.

Having ways to be able to distinguish whether a node should be actively working and taking traffic will be valuable for any other number of reasons. It's nice to be able to identify non-traffic-taking nodes so that they're candidates for deletion, removal, or shutdown. It's also helpful to understand why half your web nodes are only at 5% CPU utilization. Being able to quickly identify which nodes are active and which are inactive helps to solve this.

A third caveat is ensuring that your application servers don't store any state on their local disk. This is a huge no-no for various reasons, but it further complicates the rollback process when you must concern yourself with state existing on a set of boxes that will no longer be serving traffic. A common piece of state stored locally on boxes is session data. When a user's session is created, it's sometimes stored locally to the machine that the user is connected to at the time. This creates a dependency that the user always be routed to that specific instance or risk losing their session. Sometimes the session is only holding their authorization token, but sometimes it's also responsible for tracking some work that's currently in progress.

Isolate background processing

It's not uncommon for a process that is responsible for user-based request handling to do some background request processing as well. I try to avoid this design whenever possible, mainly because of scaling concerns.

The way a user-facing web server needs to scale could differ drastically from the way a background engine needs to scale. If you combine these actions into a single process, scaling one will typically mean scaling the other. Isolating background processing into its own process separates these concerns.

I've experienced situations where background processing was extremely heavy on the database. Because of this, regardless of load, I wanted only X many background processes working at any given time. The tasks being processed had no real-time requirement, so a delay due to traffic volume was acceptable. But I was trapped because scaling my web traffic meant scaling my background processors unless I did some special configuration magic to disable it on a scale event.

When you couple two different operations, always be wary of how these operations will need to scale. If they have different scaling concerns, it might be worth the effort of separating the two.

8.6.4   *Deployment artifact rollbacks*

If you're not in some sort of public/private cloud, rolling out new servers as part of the deployment is going to make your deployments take a lot longer if you have to order the servers ahead of the deployment. The other option is to have two sets of servers that you flip back and forth between on releases. The problem there, however, is that you must concern yourself with cruft from the various releases beginning to build up over time.

Unless you're *extremely* disciplined, you could create a world where the two sets of servers begin to drift over time as a result of their deployment patterns. Maybe server set X received a package that brought in dependencies, but after a rollback, server set Y never received that package and therefore never received those extra packages. If that happens over the course of 30 or so deployments, suddenly your two servers are brothers, but they're not identical twins. Think more like the Danny DeVito and Arnold Schwarzenegger kind of twins (*Twins*, 1988). (Apologies for those reading this in the year 2030. For many reasons.)

The better way to handle this will be via your operating system's package management system. *Package management systems* provide a standardized method for defining software installations for a given operating system. Package management tools provide an ecosystem that helps administrators manage package retrieval, installation, uninstallation, and dependency management. With the package management system, you can easily handle the rollback of a new piece of software because the system is designed to track all of the changes that were made to get the system installed in the first place.

By being able to uninstall all the changes cleanly with a single command, rolling back the application becomes much easier. And if you do it a server at a time, you can most likely complete the rollback without ever having to take down the application. There will be a period when some users get the new application and others get the old, but the trade-off is worth it and relatively low risk. But the requirement here is that your application is being packaged via your operating system's package management system.

8.6.5 *Database-level rollbacks*

The datastore in an application is always the dicey part of a deployment. If you need to make changes to the database, there's always the distinct possibility that the change is a breaking change for your code.

A classic example is that you have a table for which you need to change the data type. Maybe before it was a VARCHAR(10) and now you realize it needs to just be a TEXT field. When you execute your deployment, your new code will have a model for the table that is going to want to see that new field be a TEXT instead of a VARCHAR(10). Chances are, before you start your application server, you'll run a database migration that has an ALTER TABLE statement in it to make the change. But lo and behold, when you release, you realize that there's some other issue that's going to force a rollback. Your options at this point are as follows:

- Fail forward. Fix the issue and deploy again.
- Execute the reverse ALTER TABLE statement to revert it back to the previous value, and then roll the code back.

Neither of these options sounds particularly appealing. But with a little forethought, you can prevent this situation from happening altogether.

RULES FOR DATABASE CHANGES

The primary rule for database changes is this: always try to make additive changes to the database. Avoid changing things that are already in place, because somewhere there's probably a dependency on it that will be impacted by your change. Instead, always try to move the database schema forward by making additions to it. Let's take our TEXT column change from the preceding example. Instead of changing the existing column, what if we were to make a brand-new column with a new name that was a data type of TEXT. Now if you need to roll back, the column that you originally needed is there and you can roll back safely.

This sounds wonderful, but you're probably thinking, "But now I've got a completely empty TEXT column, though!" You're not wrong. Your new column is completely empty, and there are two ways to handle this. Depending on the size of your table, you might do a big data load. Copy all the data from the old column into the new column. Your mileage on this will vary based on the table size. You'll be generating a *lot* of write activity all in one bang on very large tables, so it might not be the best way to handle it.

Another option would be to have a background job that populates the new field slowly over time. It could be something that reads rows in predefined chunks and copies all the data over. This allows you to populate the field in a much more relaxed fashion rather than a big-bang approach. Also, because the column is additive, you can separate the database migration from the code release that will actually leverage it. There's no reason you can't make the database schema change weeks before the actual release that will use it. The caveat with this approach is that you'll need to run this background job continuously until you deploy the new code that will leverage it. Even if you populate the column with all the historical records, new records are likely being generated all the time. Until you deploy the new code that populates the new field, your two fields will continue to drift apart. Because of this, runs of this background population task will be necessary as you work your way up to the final production release to ensure the new field is populated in its entirety.

The third option is really the best of both worlds. You can make the database schema change, paired with a release of code that still looks at the old column. But your new code does some extra work. Instead of reading from the old column, it starts to use the new column. When it needs to look up a record, first it checks the new TEXT column. If that column is NULL, the application logic tells it to check the old column and read it for a value. Now that your code has the value, it inserts that value into the TEXT column field and continues on with its normal operation. I've outlined a flow of it in figure 8.4..

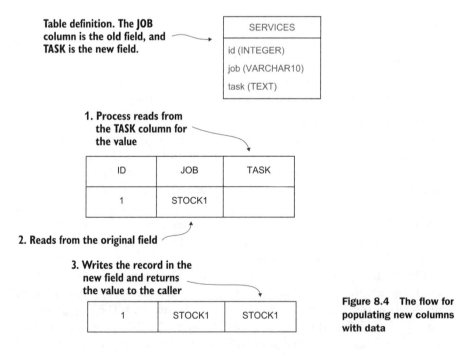

Figure 8.4   The flow for populating new columns with data

This pattern allows you to populate the records as they're read. It adds a little bit of latency to the request, because now you might have to experience an extra read and a write. But the pattern also allows you to maintain both versions of the database schema while at the same time being able to slow the number of writes to the table instead of just having a single big bang. Again, this is helpful with extremely large tables.

Now you have the new column populated, and the code that uses the new column has been battle-tested and is now part of everyday life for the application. Now that you know you won't need the old column anymore, you can schedule a DROP of the column in an upcoming release. As a final sanity check, you can ensure that the new TEXT column has been populated for all records. If not, you can run a background job or a big-bang SELECT/INSERT statement to get the last few straggling records. Once that's done, a database migration with the DROP COLUMN statement can be run, and you can consider the migration complete while ensuring you have the capability to roll back.

This does add steps to your release process. As shown in figure 8.5, you're now talking about a data schema change taking at least two releases—the first to introduce the new column and the second to remove the old column. While it may sound cumbersome at first, it really isn't. And the effort spent is well worth the comfort of knowing that you can roll back your application without fear of losing data or suddenly having your data become incompatible with the old version of your application server.

Thinking about how you roll back your application deployments and ensuring that those rollbacks are safe, fast, and reliable can go a long way toward taking the fear out of your deployment process. I've given you a few high-level examples of what can be

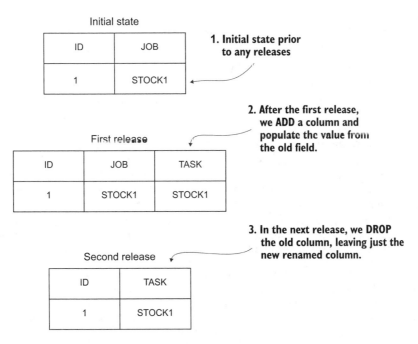

Figure 8.5   The flow of the release process for database changes

done to make this a reality, but it's by no means the only way that this can be accomplished. No matter what approach you use, the goal remains the same. Reduce the risk of deploying by using options like feature flags. Make the ability to roll back easy and fast.

VERSIONING YOUR DATABASE

A common idea that I see getting missed is that your database also has a version associated with it, like any other artifact you create. The versioning is implicit, meaning it happens whether you actively track it or not. If you don't believe me, try running a database and its corresponding application software with two different schema expectations. If the database isn't at the version that your software is expecting, you're going to encounter problems.

The key to database versioning is to know all the SQL statements that were executed to get your database to the point that it's currently at. Any engineer should be able to run a series of commands to bring the database to a specific version, where the table schema matches as expected. Being able to re-create your database from scratch gives you a lot of flexibility around testing, generating smaller data sets for experiments, and having a well-known path for modifying the schema. Tools like Flyway (https://flywaydb.org) allow you to manage your database, as well as provide a structure for performing rollbacks of schema changes. And because your SQL statements are specified as code, it makes for an easy interface to loop schema changes into your development review process. With database migrations, you know that your database remains consistent through the entire software life cycle, from local development all the way to the rollout of production. Because it's done via automation instead of production copy and paste, you can be confident that it's being performed consistently.

Flyway isn't the only option. Most popular web frameworks like Django and Ruby on Rails already have a built-in mechanism for handling database migrations. Regardless of the tool you use, try to avoid database schema changes performed by hand. This will also help to simplify the deployment process. Your database schemas now are performed and rolled back in a uniform fashion, regardless of what statements are being run.

The IOTech deployments: Feature flag and database changes

Marcus knows that his code might need to be rolled back in the event the performance metrics are bad. The problem is that his new code requires a new data column as well as an index on that column. The new column replaces an existing column, but with a different data type. Deleting the old column right away would mean that if the feature flag got toggled off, the old code wouldn't work any longer. Marcus will need to maintain both the new column and the old column until he feels comfortable making the new feature the permanent execution path going forward for the codebase.

The feature flag will allow him to toggle the application's behavior. When the feature flag is on, the code will check to see whether the value is already stored in the new field. If so, the code retrieves the value and uses it. If not, the code reads the necessary input data from the old field, transforms it to the new data type, and stores it. This allows Marcus to support both versions.

8.7 Creating deployment artifacts

In many organizations, a deployment requires copying a bunch of files from one location to the other. Each grouping of files might need to go to a different directory. Instructions read like the following:

1 Copy `./java/classes/*` to `/opt/app_data/libs`.
2 Update `/etc/init.d/start_worker_app.sh` and add `/opt/app_data/libs` to the `CLASSPATH` variable.
3 Restart the application server.

If any one of these tasks gets missed, the deployment might fail. In addition, it might be hard to know that each of these tasks was performed in order. Copying a large folder to another server could be error-prone. This is where deployment artifacts can come into play. This section discusses the value of creating an artifact that represents the code you're deploying, as well as some of the reasons and benefits behind doing so.

When you merge code and put it through all your automated tests and checks, at the end of that process comes some sort of artifact. That artifact is usually a deployable piece of code, a WAR file being a common example. But even with a WAR file, components still need to be installed; a WAR file needs an application server as part of the deployment, because that's what runs the code. Once you deploy the WAR file, you'll probably need to reload or restart Tomcat, maybe even clear some caches. And this is the best-case scenario, when you have something like Java that produces an artifact. But what about interpreted languages like Ruby or Python? What do those processes look like? How are they packaged for deployment purposes? That's what I'd like to focus on in this next section.

I try to keep as much of the application packaged together as I can. If I can bundle the installation scripts and the code together, that's a world of awesomeness for me. You could do something as simple as zipping up the installation code along with all the source code into a single file and shipping that as your deployable artifact. Now, even if you have little knowledge of the deployment process, you can copy the zip file to a server, unzip and run the `install.sh` script or whatever it might be. This is an improvement over many deployment processes that have lengthy Microsoft Word documents detailing the arcane art of the deployment. But I prefer to go one step further and use the package management system of the operating system.

8.7.1 Leveraging package management

For all the custom ways people package software for deployment, it's always surprising to me that the package management approach is so often overlooked. Every operating system has some way of managing the various pieces of software installed on them. RedHat-based Linux systems have RPM (https://rpm.org), Debian-based systems have DEB (https://wiki.debian.org/PackageManagement), Windows-based systems have NuGet (https://docs.microsoft.com/en-us/nuget/what-is-nuget), and macOS has Homebrew (https://brew.sh). All these package managers share a few things in common:

- They combine package installation scripts with the actual source code to be deployed.
- They have specifications for how to define dependencies on other packages.
- They handle the installation of dependent packages.
- They provide administrators with a mechanism to query which packages have been installed.
- They handle the removal of software that they've installed.

These features are underrated by people who are attempting to package their application software. Let's break down what an application installation is doing. It basically needs to perform the following actions in some order-dependent fashion based on the application:

- Remove unnecessary or conflicting files.
- Install any software that the application will be dependent on, but doesn't directly provide.
- Perform any preinstallation tasks, such as creating users or directories.
- Copy all the files to the appropriate file locations.
- Perform any post-installation tasks such as starting/restarting any dependent services.

Operating system package management tools allow you to take all these tasks and combine them into a single file. On top of this, if you're running your own repository server, the package management system will also have tools for fetching the appropriate version of software. When packaged appropriately, your deployment process can look as simple as this:

```
yum install -y funco-website-1.0.15.centos.x86_64
```

That single command can handle all your dependencies, post-install scripts, and restarts. It also ensures that your deployment process is uniform, as it will perform the exact same steps on every installation. The other benefit is that if your code depends on third-party libraries, you're no longer dependent on the whims of the internet to ensure that those packages are available. They can be stored in your RPM as part of the package without being worried about changes to the compilation process or transitive dependencies being satisfied slightly differently. You're getting the exact same code and deployment across all of your environments. I'll walk through a brief example.

THE FUNCO WEBSITE DEPLOYMENT

For this example, I'm going to use a Linux website. I chose Linux so that I could specifically use a tool called FPM, which stands for *Effing Package Management* (https://github .com/jordansissel/fpm). The tool is designed to provide a single interface for producing multiple package format types. DEBs, RPMs, and Brew packages all have their own format for defining the build process of a package. FPM creates a generic format and then allows you through command-line flags to generate packages for the following:

- RPM
- DEB
- Solaris
- FreeBSD
- TAR
- Directory expansion
- Mac OS X .pkg files
- Pacman (Arch Linux)

Now most of us don't have the problem of running all these operating systems in a single environment. Personally, I find the power of FPM is more that I need to learn a single interface. If my next job is a Debian shop, I don't need to learn the Debian syntax for creating DEBs. I can just use FPM and then output Debian files. But I digress.

You'll want to set up the package-building process on some sort of dedicated build server—preferably, connected to your continuous integration (CI) server, whichever one you might use. This allows you to treat the deployment package creation process as part of your normal development and testing workflow. Also, many CI servers have a plugin architecture, which allows you to extend the functionality of the CI server. A common plugin that a CI server's community creates is for various artifact repositories. These plugins automate the management of the artifact file, copying it to the repository server upon successful build of the software. This feature is heavily used in most CI server pipelines.

When creating a package with FPM, I like to structure my project into five files:

- Preinstall script
- Post-install script
- Pre-uninstall script
- Post-uninstall script
- Package build script

The preinstall/post-install/uninstall scripts are the different commands you'd want performed at that portion of the installation. This allows you to set up and tear down any files, directories, or configurations you need prior to installation. For example, in one of my own FPM projects, I have a preinstall script that sets up whatever user is necessary for the application. The following listing highlights that script.

Listing 8.2   Preinstall script for web application

```
#!/bin/bash

#Check if the application user exists
/bin/getent passwd webhost > /dev/null          If the user doesn't
if [[ $? -ne 0 ]]; then                      ◄─── exist, create it.
    #Create the user
    /sbin/useradd -d /home/webhost -m -s /bin/bash webhost
```

```
fi
#Recheck if user application user exists         Make sure the user
/bin/getent passwd webhost > /dev/null    ◁──┘   got created or fail.
exit $?
```

This is a pretty simple example, but it allows us to codify all the setup that needs to happen prior to the package being installed. The installation of our software might be critically dependent on that user existing. Maybe it got deleted, maybe it's a new server, or maybe it's a new application that lives alongside many other applications. This logic here removes the dependency for the user creation to happen outside the package installation by another process or tool. You can do this across the four files I mentioned previously, to ensure that preparation and cleanup are properly handled during installation and uninstallation.

Configuration management vs. deployment artifact

A conflict arises for companies that use configuration management. When do you let the deployment artifact handle things like user creation or directory creation, and when do you let your deployment artifact handle it? It largely depends on your configuration management strategy.

In many organizations, companies opt for more generic implementation servers with configuration management. Configuration management doesn't build a billing application server; it just builds a generic application server running Tomcat, Spring Boot, WebLogic, or whatever tool you're using. In this case, it makes sense for the package management software to handle those little detailed bits of user and directory creation, because the configuration management strategy is attempting to absolve itself of being a "billing" server. Instead, it's a basic Tomcat server that could be running any number of applications, so the configuration management software can't be concerned with the details of the billing application. This is a perfect use case for baking more of that responsibility into the deployment artifact.

But if your configuration management strategy is more focused on creating distinct implementations of servers, you might prefer all of the application setup in configuration management. Maybe it's incredibly important that file directory permissions are constantly enforced for the billing application server. Having your configuration management software be aware that this is a billing server allows it to enforce the necessary directory permissions. Using configuration management allows for a much tighter and regularly enforced configuration of the application server. If configuration management is handling all the configuration, you're protected against manual configuration changes creating drift among your application servers, because the correct configuration gets reapplied regularly. This, of course, puts more pressure on your configuration management tool, as it now must manage more resources on the agent nodes.

There's no right or wrong answer, but I'd let your configuration management strategy dictate where this sort of application setup logic should exist.

With the preinstall and post-install scripts done, you can look at the actual build scripts. That's the process of getting all the files you need onto the server in the locations you need to make your package. You might have WAR files that need to go in specific locations, or Python code that needs to be fetched from your code repository.

What I prefer to do is set up a temporary file location for my build; let's say, for example, in /home/build/temp

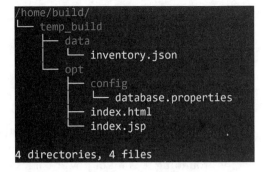

Figure 8.6 An example directory structure for the build artifact

_build. If you're using a CI server, that temporary directory might be a special directory created for you by the CI server to isolate you from other builds. I'll then treat the directory /home/build/temp_build as if it were the root directory on my target system. This allows me to build my package in a way to mimic my output. Figure 8.6 shows an example of what the directory might look like on your system after getting all the necessary files onto the build server.

Now you might be concerned about the location of these directories, because when you install the package on an actual running system, you don't want them to live under /home/build/temp_build. With the FPM command, you can specify a prefix to all installation paths. This means that the paths in the /home/build/temp_build folder will be treated as relative paths. When you build the package and you specify the flag –prefix=/, the package system will ignore the full path and install everything starting at the root directory. So /home/build/temp_build/opt gets installed as /opt on the target system where the package is installed.

After you've downloaded all your files and packages, you can also use the FPM command-line utility to add package dependencies. You can use the –depends flag multiple times to specify different packages to install. The great thing about this is that when you install the package, if the dependencies don't exist, they'll be fetched from your configured package repositories and installed on the system prior to your package being installed. Your final FPM command might look something like the following listing.

Listing 8.3 A sample FPM command

Output-type specifies the resulting package type

What you want the package to be named

```
fpm –input-type dir –output-type rpm \
  --name funco-webapp                 \
  --version 1                         \
  --depends "openssl"                 \
  --depends "openssl-devel" \
  --pre-install pre_install_script.sh \
```

Version number to handle updates and rollbacks

Defines a dependent package by its package name

The preinstall script created by you

```
--post-install post_install_script.sh\
-C /home/build/temp_build           \
--prefix /                          \
                                    \
  .
```

The post-install script created by you

Changes to the directory where the contents of the package live

The starting path you want all the files in the package to assume

Tells FPM to package all the files in the project directory

The command is a bit lengthy, but the resulting file will be worth the effort. Now your application has been codified into a single file, with a rich, robust ecosystem surrounding it. A lot of power comes with using the operating system packaging system. You also have an artifact that doesn't change from environment to environment. Speaking of which, there is one additional piece I should talk about: configuration files.

The IOTech deployments: Packaging software

Marcus knows that the next couple months are going to see multiple deployments. This is a lot of strain for the Ops team, which typically follows a series of written instructions for how to deploy software. It's error-prone, tedious to write, worse to maintain, and you might get a different result every time.

Marcus decides to use the Linux system's package management utility instead. It allows him to embed a lot of pre- and post-processing steps inside the package. The operations team is already intimately familiar with it because they use the package management software to install the many other dependencies that Marcus's code depends on.

Even though the team doesn't have a lot of fancy orchestration software to manage the deployment process, converting it to an RPM allows Marcus to trim the deployment documentation from seven pages of commands and screenshots, down to about one page. The operations team still needs to perform the package installation manually, as well as coordinate doing the installation per server, but it's a welcome improvement! They would normally perform that seven-page document for each server. It's not perfect, but the package approach has reduced the number of steps significantly, making it less error-prone and incredibly faster to do both a deployment and a rollback if necessary.

8.7.2   Configuration files in packages

This idea of packaging might sound intriguing to you, but what do you do about configuration files that change from one environment to the next? These are usually things like database connection strings, caching server locations, or even other servers in the environment. This isn't something you necessarily want to package together, because you'd have to package it for every environment configuration you have. Yuck! There are a few options available to handle this:

- Dynamic configuration through key/value stores
- Configuration management modification
- Configuration file linking

More solutions might exist, but these are the most common patterns I've seen and used.

DYNAMIC CONFIGURATION THROUGH KEY/VALUE STORES

A slew of key/value stores have come onto the scene lately. *Key/value stores* are databases that store an array of keys, with each key corresponding to a single value. The value might have data represented in any number of ways, but the data is treated as a single unit. The key will map to a value, regardless of how complex that value might be. Many key/value stores are accessible via an HTTP interface, making them great tools for storing configuration information because of their ease of access. Popular key/value stores are Consul by HashiCorp (www.consul.io), the open source etcd (https://github.com/etcd-io/etcd), and Amazon's DynamoDB (https://aws.amazon.com/dynamodb/).

A pattern that I've seen is that an application is designed in such a way that it can determine minimal bits of information about itself—just enough to know where to find its key/value store and what configuration from the key/value store it should be asking for. Figure 8.7 illustrates the process.

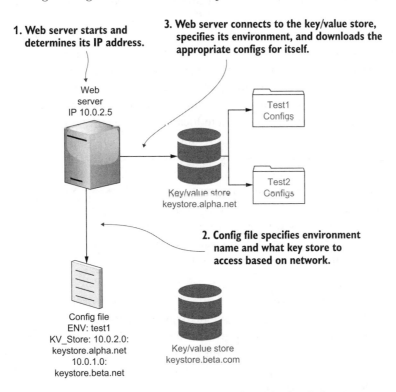

Figure 8.7 An example workflow of the interaction with a key/value store

This allows the server to load those values and bootstrap itself to begin serving traffic. This might be anything from database configuration options, to thread-pooling settings for the application. Just be cautious about storing sensitive information in plain text in the key/value store.

The downside to this approach is that your key/value store enters the critical path of your application process. If it's down for any reason, you can't get the configuration you need to start your application. It also creates an extra dependency for local development that can lead to either requiring the key/value store on local setups or having differing code paths, one for local development and one for other running configurations. The next option, however, can give you a bit of both worlds.

CONFIGURATION MANAGEMENT MODIFICATION

If you're using configuration management in your environment—which you should be—you have another option of having configuration management replace the necessary configuration files that are being installed by the RPM package. In fact, you could have your configuration management commands executed as part of the post-install script to ensure that your config files match the appropriate settings necessary. This allows software engineers to specify sane defaults for their local development process and have those files checked into source code, but still offers the operations support engineers the ability to replace those files with production-appropriate configurations or settings.

If you're interested in still using the key/value store approach, another method I've used is to have configuration management replace the configuration files for the application based on values in the key/value store. Instead of the application reading from the key/value store, it continues reading from local configuration files. Your configuration management reads the configuration settings from the key/value store and inserts the values into the appropriate location in the configuration file. If your configuration management runs in continual enforcement mode, this allows you to make changes to configuration files across your fleet by updating the key/value store and having your application restart or reload its configuration files.

This is a great alternative if you don't have the bandwidth or desire to modify your application to support the key/value store configuration approach. It also has the added benefit of allowing you to specify defaults inside your configuration management tool, so if the key/value store is unavailable, the configuration files on the application server can remain in place, powering the application.

CONFIGURATION FILE LINKING

And yet another option is to link the configuration files as part of the package installation process. This puts the operations engineers in the driver's seat for supplying the configuration files for a server outside the installation path of the package. If a package is installed in /opt/apps, the configuration files should live in /opt/configs or somewhere else outside /opt/apps. Wherever the files are stored, they should be well-known and well-defined locations and paths.

Now when your package is installed, as part of the post-install script, it should create symlinks between the files inside the package and the files outside the package. This allows you to manage the configuration separately, but again doesn't change the development process because the application is still reading configuration from the same location. The operating system handles the symlink transparently to the application. The operations engineering staff can update the configuration files based on the environment that the server is part of. You can even use configuration management again to create these files outside the installation directories.

These aren't the only three options available to managing configuration files, but hopefully they give you enough of an idea on the possibilities to choose an approach that works best for you and your applications.

Why you should be using configuration management

Configuration management is becoming more widespread in organizations, but it still has a way to go before it is considered ubiquitous. With that in mind, I want to highlight some of the reasons you might want to focus on configuration management.

For starters, it is one of a few ways that you can maintain the type of consistency of configuration throughout your environment. Using configuration management takes the manual configuration portion out of maintaining servers. Every configuration management tool provides a facility for data lookup when needing to provide values. This means you can easily set different values based on criteria. You can decide how much memory to assign to a JVM based on the available memory on the server. Or you can classify servers into categories and assign values based on that category.

Configuration management also allows you to commit these configurations to a source code repository. This gives your infrastructure access to all the development workflows that are happening to your source code. Peer reviews, managed approvals, and an auditable history are just some of the things that managing your configuration via source control gives you.

One of my favorite features of configuration management is remote command execution. Some tools handle this better than others, but remote execution offers you the power of consistency when needing to execute a command across a range of servers. These tools offer powerful targeting syntax so that you can specify which nodes specifically you want to execute the command, along with batching and timing requirements. You can specify you want a service restarted across all the job processing nodes, but you want the server restarts to happen in batches of 5 with a 15-minute wait between each batch.

If you want to move to a DevOps workflow, managing your servers via some form of configuration management is table stakes.

8.8   *Automating your deployment pipeline*

Now that you have a deployment artifact of some kind, you can begin tying all these pieces together to form your deployment pipeline. You should have a set of automated tests that have been built out as part of your testing workflow, as discussed in chapter 5. At the end of that, you should be producing some sort of build artifact. Now, with that build artifact complete, you can take it and package it as part of a deployment artifact. The deployment artifact will wrap up your build artifact with whatever setup instructions are necessary to deliver your code to your customers. You can tie these things together to produce the final delivery mechanism, getting the deployment artifact deployed across your fleet. As I continue to stress, this all needs to be automated as much as possible.

Your architecture has a massive influence on how you go about automating the workflow, but the basic steps are almost always the same:

1 Perform prerequisite steps such as database schema changes.
2 Place a node out of service so it is no longer performing work.
3 Deploy the software package to the node.
4 Verify that the deployment completed successfully.
5 Return the node back to service.
6 Move to the next node.

This might vary slightly depending on your deployment capabilities. For example, if you're bringing up all new servers, you might perform these steps on all of the new servers and then bring the entire collection of new servers online at the same time, as opposed to individually. I've talked earlier in this chapter about fleet rollbacks, so I won't reiterate here. If you don't have the advantage of doing a fleet rollback, you'll want to look at these six steps.

8.8.1   *Safely installing the new application*

Let's assume you have a basic web application with a load balancer on the frontend and a collection of web servers on the backend, a common setup. The first thing you need to do is remove the node from the load balancer pool. There are a few ways to accomplish this. With any luck, you have API access to the load balancer and can make a call directly to it to remove the node from the pool.

Another option is to simply install a host-based firewall rule to block traffic from the load balancer during the deployment. You might block all traffic on port 443 from accessing the node, with a few noted exceptions. This will create a similar failure condition on the load balancer to remove the node from the pool. There are probably a ton of other ways that you can do this, but remember, just because you don't have API access doesn't mean you still can't achieve your goal. Think outside the box!

Now that your node is removed from the load balancer, you can begin to deploy to the nodes. If you're using a package manager, this might be as simple as using the update command of your package management system, like `yum update funco-webserver`.

This will be handled by the YUM package management system and will be responsible for uninstalling the previous version of the code, installing the new version of the code, and doing any of the predefined uninstall and install commands specified within the package.

Once the package is installed, you can run your verification process. I prefer to try to fetch the site from the node somehow. This might be as simple as a `curl` command directly to the node or node group in question, bypassing the load balancer. At this point, you're simply verifying that the deployment completed successfully, not necessarily verifying that the release is good. You just want to make sure that when you add the node back to the load balancer pool, it will be able to service the request. I typically rely on a task that's as simple as verifying that the login page loads. You can get more sophisticated as time goes on, but know that even a simple check is infinitely better than no check at all. Embracing incremental improvements will allow you to move fast, while still leaving room for getting better as you get more information about the types of failures you'll run into.

Now that you've verified the installation of the package and that the service is running, you can undo whatever step you took to remove the node from the pool. Verify that your application is added back to the pool and taking traffic before moving to the next node in the pool. You can do this by checking the web logs of the application server or by accessing the API of the load balancer, if it has one and is accessible to you. Once it's added, you move on to the next one. Regardless of how you verify that a server is live, it should be automated and baked into the deployment process. If the automation can't determine the status of a deployment, then in most cases it's probably wise to stop the process. Whether or not the automation should perform a rollback immediately will depend heavily on your environment and rollback process. Ideally, you'd never want your automaton to leave your application in a broken state if it can be avoided.

The deployment is the last piece of the automation puzzle for this process. Now with feature flags, you can enable functionality and disable functionality based on the validation of the release process, whether that be manual regression testing or part of an automated test suite. But with feature flags, you can disable new functionality without having to roll back the application in its entirety. If you do have to roll back, the package management process has made that just a little bit easier. You can use the `yum downgrade` command to manage rolling your application installation back to a previous version. Depending on the dependencies you specify, you might need to downgrade your dependencies as well if you have specific version requirements, but in a lot of cases, simply downgrading your application package will suffice. This combination of activities gives you the safety you need to reduce the fear of your deployment process. Fear is often a major contributor to your release cadence being slower than you might normally want.

Another important note is that these steps and phases are encapsulated in such a way that they don't need to be performed at the same time. You can make progress on your pipeline by doing automated testing first. Then make improvements by packaging your deployment artifacts. Then move to automating the deployment process. It doesn't have to be all at once! Move in slow steps to continuously improve on what you're doing today. Over time, you'll get there. Just never settle for where things are today; always look for where you can make life just a little bit better tomorrow.

Summary

- Fear is a major driver for a slower release cadence.
- Fear is reduced when risk is lowered and when getting back to a good state is fast and well understood.
- Staging will never be exactly like production. You must plan accordingly.
- Using the operating system's package management is a great way to create deployment artifacts.
- Database changes should always be additive and take two releases. Add a new column in the first release and delete the old column in the second release.
- Take an incremental approach to automating your deployment pipeline.

Wasting a
perfectly good incident

9

This chapter covers

- Conducting blameless postmortems
- Addressing the mental models people have during an incident
- Generating action items that further the improvement of the system

When something unexpected or unplanned occurs that creates an adverse effect on the system, I define that action as an *incident*. Some companies reserve the term for large catastrophic events, but with this broader definition, you get to increase the learning opportunities on your team when an incident occurs.

As mentioned previously, at the center of DevOps is the idea of continuous improvement. Incremental change is a win in a DevOps organization. But the fuel that powers that continuous improvement is continual learning—learning about new technologies, existing technologies, how teams operate, how teams communicate, and how all these things interrelate to form the human-technical systems that are engineering departments.

One of the best sources for learning isn't when things go right, but when they go wrong. When things are working, what you think you know about the system and what is actually true in the system aren't necessarily in conflict. Imagine you have a car with a 15-gallon gas tank. For some reason, you think the gas tank is 30 gallons, but you have this habit of filling your gas tank after you burn through about 10 gallons. If you do this religiously, your understanding of the size of the gas tank never comes into conflict with the reality of the gas tank being only 15 gallons. You might make hundreds of trips in your car without ever learning a thing. But the minute you decide to take that long drive, you run into problems at 16 gallons. Before long, you realize the folly of your ways and start taking the appropriate precautions now that you have this newfound information.

Now there are a few things you can do with this information. You can dig deep to understand why your car ran out of gas at gallon 15 or you can just say, "Welp, I better start filling up every five gallons now, just to be safe." You'd be amazed how many organizations opt to do the latter.

Many organizations don't go through the mental exercise of understanding why the system performed the way it did and how it can improve. Incidents are a definitive way to prove whether your understanding of the system matches the reality. By not doing this exercise, you're wasting the best parts of the incident. The failure to learn from such an event can be a disservice to future efforts.

The lessons from system failures don't always come naturally. They often need to be coaxed out of the system and team members in an organized, structured fashion. This process is called by many names; *after-action reports*, *incident reports*, and *retrospectives* are just a few terms. But I use the term *postmortem*.

> **DEFINITION**   A *postmortem* is the process by which a team assesses the events that led up to an incident. The postmortem typically takes the format of a meeting with all of relevant stakeholders and participants of the incident handling.

In this chapter, I will discuss the process and structure of the postmortem, as well as how to get a deeper understanding of your systems by asking deeper, more probing questions about why engineers decided to take the action that they did.

9.1   The components of a good postmortem

Whenever there's an incident of enough size, people begin to play the blame game. People try to distance themselves from the problem, erect barriers to information, and generally become helpful only to the point of absolving themselves of fault. If you see this happening in your organization, you likely live in a culture of blame and retribution: the response to an incident is to find those responsible for "the mistake" and to make sure that they're punished, shamed, and sidelined appropriately.

Afterward, you'll heap on a little extra process to make sure that someone must approve the type of work that created the incident. With a feeling of satisfaction, everyone will walk away from the incident knowing that this particular problem won't happen again. But it always does.

The reason the blame game doesn't work is that it attacks the people as the problem. If people had just been better trained. If more people were aware of the change. If someone had followed the protocol. If someone hadn't mistyped that command. And to be clear, these are all valid reasons things might go wrong, but they don't get to the heart of *why* that activity (or lack of) created such a catastrophic failure.

Let's take the training failure as an example. If the engineer wasn't trained appropriately and made a mistake, you should ask yourself, "Why wasn't he trained?" Where would the engineer have gotten that training? Was the lack of training due to an engineer not having enough time? If they weren't trained, why were they given access to the system to perform something they weren't ready to perform?

The pattern with this other line of thinking is that you're discussing problems in the *system* versus problems in the *individual*. If your training program is poorly constructed, blaming this engineer doesn't solve the problem, because the next wave of hires might experience the same problem. Allowing someone who might not be qualified to perform a dangerous action might highlight a lack of systems and security controls in your organization. Left unchecked, your system will continue to produce employees who are in a position to make this same mistake.

To move away from the blame game, you must begin thinking about how your systems, processes, documentation, and understanding of the system all contribute to the incident state. If your postmortems turn into exercises of retribution, no one will participate, and you'll lose an opportunity for continued learning and growth.

Another side effect of a blameful culture is a lack of transparency. Nobody wants to volunteer to get punished for a mistake they made. Chances are, they're already beating themselves up about it, but now you combine that with the public shaming that so often accompanies blameful postmortems and you've now built in incentives for people to hide information about incidents or specific details about an incident.

Imagine an incident that was created by an operator making a mistake entering a command. The operator knows that if he admits to this error, some type of punishment will be waiting for him. If he has the ability to sit silently on this information, knowing that there's punishment for the mistake, he's much more likely to sit silently while the group spends a large amount of time attempting to troubleshoot what happened.

A culture of retribution and blamefulness creates incentives for employees to be less truthful. The lack of candidness hinders your ability to learn from the incident while also obfuscating the facts of the incident. A blameless culture, whereby employees are free from retribution, creates an environment much more conducive to collaboration and learning. With a blameless culture, the attention shifts from everyone attempting to deflect blame, to solving the problems and gaps in knowledge that led to the incident.

Blameless cultures don't happen overnight. It takes quite a bit of energy from coworkers and leaders in the organization to create an environment in which people feel safe from reprisal and can begin having open and honest discussions about mistakes that were made and the environment in which they were made. You, the reader, can facilitate this transformation by being vulnerable and being the first to share their own mistakes with the team and the organization. Someone must always go first, and since you're reading this book, that person is probably going to be you.

9.1.1 *Creating mental models*

Understanding how people look at systems and processes is key to understanding how failure happens. When you work with or are a part of a system, you create a *mental model* of it. The model reflects how you think the system behaves and operates.

> **DEFINITION** A *mental model* is an explanation of someone's thought process about how something works. The mental model might detail someone's perception of the relationship and interaction between components, as well as how the behavior of one component might influence other components. A person's mental models can often be incorrect or incomplete.

Unless you're a total expert on that system, however, it's reasonable to assume that your model has gaps in it. An example is that of a software engineer and their assumptions of what the production environment might look like. The engineer is aware that there's a farm of web servers and a database server and a caching server. They're aware of these things because those are the components that they touch and interact with on a regular basis, both in code and in their local development environments.

What they're probably unaware of is all the infrastructure components that go into making this application capable of handling production-grade traffic. Database servers might have read replicas, and web servers probably have a load balancer in front of them and a firewall in front of that. Figure 9.1 shows an engineer's model versus the reality of the system.

It's important to acknowledge this discrepancy not just in computer systems, but in processes as well. The gap between expectations and reality is a nesting ground for incidents and failures. Use the postmortem as an opportunity to update everyone's mental model of the systems involved in the failure.

Engineer's understanding of the system

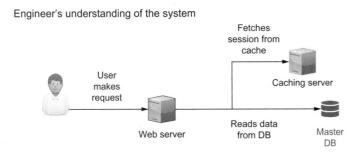

The actual system

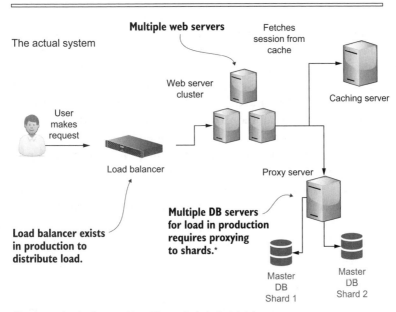

*Database shards allow you to partition a single logical database
into multiple servers; useful for databases under heavy load.

Figure 9.1   The engineer's mental model (top) versus reality (bottom)

9.1.2   *Following the 24-hour rule*

The *24-hour rule* is simple: if you have an incident in your environment, you should have
a postmortem about that incident within 24 hours. The reasons for this are twofold.

For starters, the details of the situation begin to evaporate as more time passes
between when the incident occurs and when the incident is documented. Memories
fade, and nuance gets lost. When it comes to incidents, nuance makes all the difference. Did you restart that service before this error occurred or after? Did Sandra
implement her fix first or was it Brian's fix first? Did you forget that the service
crashed the first time Frank started it back up? What could that mean? All of these little details may not mean much when you're attempting to figure out what solved the

issue, but they definitely matter in terms of understanding how the incident unfolded and what you can learn from it.

Another reason to do the postmortem within 24 hours is to be sure that you're leveraging the emotion and the energy behind the failure. If you've ever had a near-miss car accident, you become super alert following it. And that level of alertness and intensity will stick around for a certain amount of time. But sooner or later, you begin to fall back into your old habits. Before long, the sense of urgency has faded, and you're back to driving without a hands-free unit and responding to text messages while you're at stoplights.

Now imagine if you could instead use that short period of heightened awareness to put real controls in your car that prevent you from doing those poor or destructive actions in the first place. That's what you're trying to do with the 24-hour rule: seize the momentum of the incident and use it for something good.

When you have an incident, a lot of pent-up energy arises because it's an event that's out of the ordinary, and typically someone is facing pressure or repercussions from the failure. But the more time that passes, the more the sense of urgency begins to fade. Get the ball rolling on follow-up items to the incident within the first 24 hours while it's still something of note to your team members.

Lastly, having the postmortem within 24 hours helps to ensure that a postmortem document gets created. Once the documents are created, they can be widely circulated for others to learn about the failure and can serve as a teaching tool for engineers of the future. Again, incidents have mounds of information in them, so being able to document a failure in enough detail could go a long way to training engineers in the future (or to use the incident as an interesting interview question for future engineers).

9.1.3   *Setting the rules of the postmortem*

As for any meeting, certain guidelines need to be set forth in order to have a successful postmortem. It's important that you walk through these rules, in detail, prior to any postmortem meeting. The rules are designed to create an atmosphere of collaboration and openness.

Participants need to feel at ease admitting to gaps in their knowledge or their understanding of the system. There are plenty of reasons that team members might not feel comfortable sharing this lack of expertise. The company culture might shun those who display even the slightest hint of lacking complete expertise. The company culture might demand a level of perfection that's unrealistic, leading to team members who make mistakes or who aren't complete experts on a topic feeling inadequate.

It's also not uncommon for team members, for reasons of their own, to have this feeling of inadequacy. These negative emotions and experiences are blockers to total learning and understanding. You need to do your best to try to put those emotions to rest. That's the goal of these rules and guidelines:

- Never criticize a person directly. Focus on actions and behaviors.
- Assume that everyone did the best job they could with the information that was available to them at the time.
- Be aware that facts may look obvious now but could have been obfuscated in the moment.
- Blame systems, not people.
- Remember that the ultimate goal is understanding all the pieces that went into the incident.

These rules will help focus the conversation on where it belongs—improving the system—and will hopefully keep you out of the finger-pointing blame game. It'll be up to the meeting facilitator to ensure that these rules are always followed. If someone breaks the rule, even once, it can serve as a signal to the other participants that this is just like any other meeting where management is looking for a "throat to choke."

9.2 *The incident*

It's 1:29 a.m. The monitoring system has detected that one of the background-work queues has exceeded its configured threshold. Shawn, the operations on-call engineer, is sound asleep when he receives a page around 1:30 a.m. The alert reads, "Worker processing queues are unusually high." When Shawn reads the page, it sounds more like a status than an actual problem. Based on what the alert says, he doesn't feel there's any risk in waiting for the alert to clear. He acknowledges the alert and snoozes it for 30 minutes, hoping that will be the end of it.

After 30 minutes, the alert pages again, only now the queue has grown even larger in size. Shawn isn't really sure what the queue that is alerting is used for. He's aware that several background processing jobs operate off these worker queues, but each job handles from a different queue. He opts to restart the report queue jobs he is aware of and see if that clears the problem. It doesn't. Two queues are still reporting an extraordinarily large queue size. He confirms that these numbers are excessive by comparing the queue size to historical graphs of the same queue.

At this point, Shawn decides he needs to page an on-call development engineer. He navigates to the confluence page where the on-call information saved. To his dismay, the on-call engineer doesn't have a phone number listed, just an email address. The on-call page doesn't list who should be contacted in the event the primary on-call person isn't available. Rather than start randomly dialing the phone numbers on the list, Shawn opts to just escalate to his own manager for guidance. His manager logs in and assists with troubleshooting, but quickly exhausts his understanding of the system as well. The manager decides to escalate to the principal engineer.

The principal engineer receives the call and hops online to begin investigating. The `consumer_daemon` is a background processor responsible for processing one of the two queues identified earlier by Shawn. The principle engineer discovers that the `consumer_daemon` has not been running for a couple of hours. The queues continued to grow as other workers added to the queue, but with the `consumer_daemon` not running, nothing was taking messages off the queue and processing them. The engineer restarts the `consumer_daemon`, and processing begins to pick up. Within 45 minutes, the system is back to normal.

9.3   *Running the postmortem*

Running the postmortem meeting can be a bit of a grueling experience. It usually takes a mix of skills to get the most out of a postmortem. You don't need full representation for it to be useful, but you'll find that there's way more value in expanding the team pool in order to increase diverse perspectives.

9.3.1   *Choosing whom to invite to the postmortem*

I'm going to start this section with some of the technical roles that should be in attendance. But whatever you do, please don't think of the postmortem as a purely technical affair. A lot of context goes into some of the decision-making problems that occur during an incident. Even if people don't contribute directly to the incident, stakeholders often have an interest in understanding what happened and the age-old, inappropriate question of "How do we prevent this from ever happening again?"

The start of your invite list should be all of the people immediately involved with the incident recovery process. If they were involved in the recovery effort at all, I recommend they be in attendance. But in addition, other people could benefit from the postmortem who are typically overlooked.

PROJECT MANAGERS

It's not uncommon for project managers to have a vested interest in the incidents that are occurring in the environment. For starters, they almost always are sharing technical resources with the day-to-day responsibilities of running a production environment. Understanding the underlying technical issues while also having a firsthand account to assess the impact to other projects can be beneficial.

Project managers can also communicate the impact that the incident had on existing projects and resources. Understanding the impact to other work helps you understand the ripple effects of an incident. It's also not uncommon for a project manager's timeline to have created some urgency around solving a problem. That sense of urgency could have led to a feature, product, or task being performed in extreme haste, opening the door to create the failure conditions that lead to the incident.

BUSINESS STAKEHOLDERS

Business stakeholders may not fully understand all the technical jargon that gets thrown around during a postmortem, but they will home in on specific details that could shed some light on how incidents should be run in the future. Business stakeholders can translate what the technical details mean for the business and help put the incident into a business outcomes view.

An incident at 9 p.m. on a Tuesday, when user activity is relatively low, might seem like a low-impact incident. But the business can tell you that this particular Tuesday was the month-end closing process. Because of the outage, analysts couldn't complete their work for the closing process, so bills will go out late, which means accounts receivable will be delayed, which can lead to a cash flow problem. This is a bit of an exaggeration, but it's not too far from the realities that ill-timed incidents can create. Having the business stakeholder in the room can help to give context as well as transparency to the incident management process.

HUMAN RESOURCES

This category is an interesting one based on previous experiences. I don't recommend inviting HR to all your postmortems, but I've definitely done this when I knew one of the contributing factors was resources and staffing.

Having an HR representative listen to an incident unfold and all of the pain points that happen because you simply don't have enough staff can be eye-opening. Choose your battles wisely, but I have definitely received additional headcount in the past after having an HR staff member listen to our inability to resolve an issue because the on-call rotation was too small and a key staff member was sleeping because of a long-running migration project the night before.

9.3.2 *Running through the timeline*

The *timeline* of the incident is a documented series of events that occurred during the incident. The postmortem will run much smoother if everyone can agree on the series of events that occurred, as well as the order and the time at which they occurred.

Whoever is running the postmortem should attempt to assemble a rough timeline prior to the meeting as a starting point. If you must construct the timeline from scratch in the meeting, you'll spend an inordinate amount of time as everyone attempts to rack their brains remembering what happened. If the postmortem organizer creates a starting point, it serves as a prompt for all the participants in the incident. With those prompts being called out, smaller, more intricate details tend to rise to people's memory a bit easier.

DETAILING EACH EVENT IN THE TIMELINE

As the postmortem organizer, each event on your timeline should have a few bits of information:

- What action or event was performed?
- Who performed it?
- What time was it performed?

The description of the action or event that was performed should be a clear, concise statement about what transpired. The details of the action or event should be devoid of any color, commentary, or motivations at this point. It should be purely factual—for example, "The payment service was restarted via the services control panel." This is a clear statement of fact.

A poor example would be "The payment service was restarted incorrectly and unintentionally." This adds arguable aspects to the action. Incorrect by whose standards? Where were those standards communicated? Was the person who performed the restart trained incorrectly? By removing these words of judgments, you can keep the conversation on track instead of derailing into a pedantic discussion on how the action has been categorized. That's not to say that this color isn't important; it is, and I'll get to it momentarily. It's just not beneficial for this part of the process.

Who performed the action is another fact to document. In some cases, the event might have been performed by the system itself and not by a user. For example, if the action or event is "The web server ran out of memory and crashed," the person who performed the action would just be the name of the server.

How granular you get with that can be up to you. I normally just describe the *who* as the application and the component of the application that it belongs to. The who might be "payments web server." In some cases, you might want to be even more specific, such as "payments web server host 10.0.2.55" in order to call out the node in detail, especially if multiple nodes of the same type are behaving in different ways that are contributing to the problem at hand. The detail will ultimately depend on the nature of the issue you're dealing with.

If the *who* in this case is a person, you can note either the person's name or that person's role. For example, you might say "Norman Chan," or you might simply say "systems engineer 1." The value of using a role is that it prevents someone from feeling blamed in the postmortem document. If someone made an honest mistake, it feels a little punitive to repeat that person's name over and over again in a document detailing that mistake and the problems it created.

Another reason for using a role or title is that the entry will maintain its usefulness over time. These documents become a matter of record that future engineers will hopefully use. An engineer three years from now may have no idea who Norman is or what his job role or function was. But knowing that a system engineer performed the actions specified sets the context around the change more clearly. Whereas I might ask if Norman was authorized to perform the action he took that's detailed in the postmortem, I'm well aware that "systems engineer 1" was authorized to do it, because I'm aware of that role, its permissions, and its scope and responsibilities.

Lastly, detailing the time of the event is necessary for purposes of establishing *when* the events occurred and ensuring that the order of actions is well understood across the team.

With each event detailed in this manner, walk through the timeline, soliciting confirmation from the team on the specifics, as well as confirming that no other activity occurred in between that might have been missed. Circulating the timeline ahead of the meeting, giving people a chance to review it, helps to speed up this process a bit, allowing the timeline to be updated offline, but if you have to do it in the meeting, so be it. Now that the timeline has been established, you can begin to walk through specific items to gain clarity.

Here's an example of how you would document the example incident from section 9.3:

- At 1:29 a.m., the monitoring system detected that the background work queue was above configured thresholds.
- At 1:30 a.m., the system paged the on-call operations engineer with an alert that read "Worker processing queues are unusually high."
- At 1:30 a.m., the on-call engineer acknowledged the alert and snoozed it for 30 minutes.

ADDING CONTEXT TO THE EVENTS

With the timeline established, you can begin adding a bit of context to the events. Context provides additional details and motivations behind each of the events that occurred. Typically, you'll need to add context only to events or actions that were performed by a human, but sometimes the system makes a choice, and that choice needs to be given clarity. For example, if a system has an emergency shutdown mode, explaining the context for why the system went into an emergency shutdown might be beneficial, especially when it's not clear why such a drastic action had to be taken.

Context around events should be given with the motivation of understanding a person's mental model of the situation at hand. Understanding the mental model will help explain why a decision was made and the underlying assumptions that went into that decision. Remember to respect the rules of the postmortem and avoid passing judgment on someone's understanding or interpretation of how the system operates. Your goal is to learn, because chances are, if one person has a misunderstanding about it, then many people have a misunderstanding.

Take a look at each event and ask probing questions about the motivation behind that decision. Some ideas around probing questions are as follows:

- Why did that feel like the right course of action?
- What gave you that interpretation of what was happening in the system?
- Did you consider any other actions, and if so, why did you rule them out?
- If someone else were to perform the action, how would they have had the same knowledge you had at the moment?

When forming questions like this, you might notice something interesting: they don't presume that the person's action was right or wrong.

Sometimes in a postmortem you can learn just as much from someone performing the right action as the wrong action. For example, if someone decided to restart a service and that is the action that resolved the incident, it's worthwhile to understand what the engineer knew that led them to that course of action. Maybe they knew that the failing tasks were controlled by this one service. Maybe they also knew that this service is prone to flakiness and sometimes just needs to be restarted.

That's great, but then the question becomes, how do other engineers get that knowledge? If they did have that suspicion, how could they confirm it? Is it purely just experience, or is there a way to expose that experience in a metric or dashboard that might allow someone to verify their suggestion? Or better, maybe there's a way to create an alerting mechanism to detect that failed state and inform the engineer? Even when someone takes a correct action, understanding how they came to that correct action can be valuable.

Another example from a real-world incident occurred when a database statement as part of a deployment was running long. The engineer performing the deployment recognized that it was running long and started the troubleshooting process. But how did he know the command was running long? What was "long" in this context? When asked about that, it was because he had run the same statements as part of the staging environment deployment and had a rough idea of how long that took in the previous iteration. But what if he wasn't the engineer to perform the production deployment? That context would be lost, and the troubleshooting effort might not have started for a great deal longer.

Getting to these sorts of assumptions is the heart of the postmortem process. How do you make improvements on sharing this expertise that people collect over the years and rely on heavily in their troubleshooting process? In the preceding example, the team decided that whenever a database statement for a deployment was run in staging, it would be timed and recorded in a database. Then when the same deployment ran in production, prior to executing the statement, the system would inform the deployment engineer of the previous timed runs in staging, giving this engineer some context for how long things should take. This is an example of taking something that was successful during an incident, understanding why it was successful, and making sure that the success can be repeated in the future.

An example from our incident might be asking the principal developer why he opted to restart the `consumer_daemon`. Here's what a sample conversation might look like in this scenario:

> *Facilitator: "Why did you decide to restart the* `consumer_daemon`*?"*
>
> *Principle engineer (PE): "Well, when I logged on to the system, I recognized that one of the queues in question had a naming convention that corresponded to the* `consumer_daemon`*."*
>
> *Facilitator: "So all of the queues follow a naming convention?"*
>
> *PE: "Yes, the queues are named in a structured format so you have an idea of who the expected consumer of that queue is. I noticed that the format suggested the* `consumer_daemon`*. I then looked for logs from the* `consumer_daemon` *and noticed there were none, which was another hint."*
>
> *Facilitator: "Oh. So, if the Ops engineer had known to look at the* `consumer_daemon` *logs, that would have been a sign when it came up empty?"*
>
> *PE: "Well, not quite. The* `consumerdaemon` *was logging things, but there's a particular log message I'd expect to see if it was performing work. The problem is, the log message is kind of cryptic. Whenever it processes a message, it reports about the update to an internal structure called a* `MappableEntityUpdateConsumer`*. I don't think anyone but a developer would have made that connection."*

You can see from this conversation that specific knowledge exists inside the developer's mind that was crucial to solving this problem. This information wasn't generally available or well-known to the engineer or to the facilitator. This sort of back-and-forth about an action that the developer took correctly goes to the value of conducting these postmortems.

In the same light, understanding why someone made the wrong decision can also be valuable. The goal is to understand how they viewed the problem from their perspective. Understanding the perspective gives necessary context around an issue.

One year, I went to a Halloween party dressed as The Beast, from the popular story *Beauty and the Beast.* But when my wife wasn't standing next to me in her outfit as Belle, people didn't have the context, so they assumed I was a werewolf. But the moment my wife stood next to me, they instantly were given the missing context, and their perspective on my costume changed completely. Let's look at what the conversation between the operations on-call engineer and the facilitator of the postmortem says about the context of his decision to acknowledge the alarm and not take action:

> *Facilitator: "You decided to acknowledge and snooze the alert when you first received it. What went into that decision?"*
>
> *Ops engineer: "Well, the alert didn't indicate an actual problem. It just said that the queues were backed up. But that can happen for any number of reasons. Plus, it was late at night, and I know that we do a lot of background processing at night. That work gets dumped into various queues and processed. I figured it might have just been a heavier night than usual."*

This conversation sheds some context on the Ops engineer's perspective. Without that context, we might assume that the engineer was too tired to deal with the problem or was just generally trying to avoid it. But in the conversation, it's clear that the engineer had a perfectly viable reason for snoozing the alert. Maybe the alert message should have been better crafted, indicating the potential impact in business terms instead of communicating just the general state of the system. This miscue lead to an additional 30 minutes of troubleshooting time wasted, as well as a further buildup of items that needed to be processed, potentially increasing the recovery time.

It's not uncommon for people to have a flawed view of the way they think a system behaves as compared to the way it actually behaves. This goes back to the concept of mental models introduced earlier. Let's add a bit more context from the conversation:

> *Facilitator: "Did restarting* consumer_daemon *ever occur to you?"*
>
> *Ops engineer: "Yes and no. Restarting* consumer_daemon *specifically didn't occur to me, but I thought I had restarted everything."*
>
> *Facilitator: "Can you explain that in a bit more detail?"*
>
> *Ops engineer: "The command I used to restart the services gives you a list of Sidekiq services that you can restart. It lists them by queue.* consumer_daemon *is one of the queues. What I didn't know was that* consumer_daemon *is not specifically a Sidekiq process. So, when I restarted all the Sidekiq processes, the* consumer_daemon *was omitted from that, because it doesn't run in Sidekiq with all the other background processing. Additionally, I didn't realize that* consumer_daemon *was not just a queue, but also the name of the process responsible for processing that queue."*

This context highlights how the Ops engineer had a flawed mental model of the system. It also highlights how the wording on the command he uses to restart the service was also at fault for extending the outage.

Figure 9.2 highlights his expectations of the system versus the reality. You'll notice that in the engineer's mental model, the consumer_daemon processes from the p2_queue, when in reality it processes from the cd_queue. Another flaw in the mental model is the engineer presumes that the generic restart command will also restart the consumer_daemon, but in the actual model, you can see that there is a specific consumer_daemon restart command.

Because of the way the commands were grouped, the engineer inferred something that wasn't true—but had no way of knowing that those assumptions were wrong. This might lead us to an action item to fix the wording of the restart service help documentation.

The way you name things will inform people's mental models. If you have a light switch and above the light switch the words "Fire Alarm" are written in bold red letters,

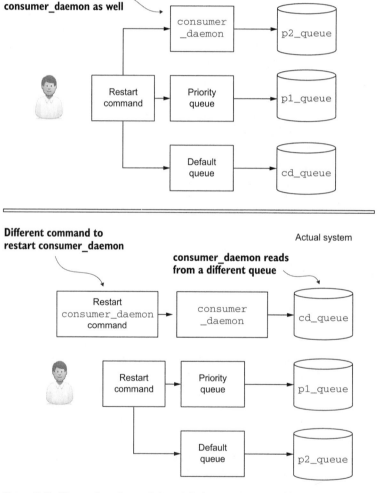

Figure 9.2   The engineer's mental model of `consumer_daemon`

that might change your understanding of what the light switch does. When someone asks you to "turn off all the lights," you would most likely skip this light switch because its label has altered your understanding of what it does. Mental models of systems are affected much the same way. Identifying these mistakes and correcting them is a key area of focus during the postmortem process.

9.3.3 Defining action items and following up

A postmortem is great for creating additional context and knowledge around an incident. But most postmortems should result in a series of action items that need to be performed. If an engineer made a poor decision because they lacked visibility into a part of the system, then creating that visibility would be a useful action item coming out of the postmortem.

Another bonus of action items in a postmortem is that they can demonstrate an attempt at getting better and improving the reliability of the system. A postmortem that is just a readout of what occurred doesn't show any proactive measures on getting better at handling issues in the future.

Action items should clearly define and be structured in the format of "*who* will do *what* by *when*." An action item is incomplete if it doesn't have these three crucial components. I've seen many organizations fail at making concrete progress on follow-up items because the task gets defined way too loosely. For example: "We will implement additional metrics for order processing." That doesn't sound like anything actionable to me. "We" is not really defined, and while additional metrics for order processing sounds like a noble goal, the fact that the task has no date means that it has no priority. And when it comes to action items coming out of a postmortem, the urgency of the task fades as time goes on.

OWNERSHIP OF ACTION ITEMS

Getting commitment from the team on action items can be a difficult task. Most people aren't sitting around looking for additional work to do. When an incident comes about, it can be a challenge to get individuals to commit to having a piece of work done, especially if the work is nontrivial. Asking someone to create a new dashboard is one thing, but asking someone to rearchitect how a work queue system functions is a heavy ask.

Your best path to making progress on these items is to treat them as the different asks that they are. Action items should be separated into short-term and long-term objectives. *Short-term objectives* should be those tasks that can be performed in a reasonable amount of time and should be prioritized first. *Reasonable* is obviously going to be a moving target based on the workloads of different teams, but the team representatives should be able to give some idea on what's realistic and what's not. *Long-term objectives* are those items that will take a significant effort and will require some form of prioritization by leadership. Long-term objectives should be detailed enough that their scope and time commitment can be discussed with leadership. You'll want to be sure to capture the following in your notes:

- Detailed description of the work that needs to be performed
- Rough time estimate of how long the team thinks the work will take to be performed.
- The decision-maker responsible for prioritizing the work

Once your list has been separated into short-term and long-term objectives, it's time to get commitment on the short-term items first. As discussed previously, each item should have a concrete owner, the person who is going to perform the task and negotiate a due date for that action item. Remember to take into account that this is new, unplanned work being added to someone's already existing workload. Having a date a bit into the future is better than not having a date at all. Offer some flexibility and understanding when team members commit to dates. Everyone's assumption will be that these things need to be done immediately, and although that's the preferred outcome, having the work done in five weeks is better than leaving the meeting in a stalemate, with no dates committed.

After your short-term list of action items has been filled out, move to the long-term objectives. Whereas short-term objectives are translated directly into action items, long-term objectives have more of an intermediate step. It isn't possible to assign ownership and due dates directly to a long-term action item because of its scope. But if you leave it as is, the item won't go anywhere.

Instead of having an action item for completing the work, the action item owner becomes responsible for advocating for the work to be complete. Who is going to submit the request through the prioritization process, by when? That action item owner will handle the follow-up of the request through the prioritization process until it's scheduled and in progress by the team to ultimately resolve it.

Now you should have a complete list of action items along with detailed information about long-term objectives. Table 9.1 shows an example readout of the information.

Table 9.1   A list of action items from the postmortem

Action item	Owner	Due date
Update the restart script to include `consumer_daemon`.	Jeff Smith	EOD—Friday April 3, 2021
Submit request for detailed logging in `consumer_daemon`.	Jeff Smith	EOD—Wednesday April 1, 2021
Long-term objective	**Estimated time commitment**	**Decision-maker**
The logging for `consumer_daemon` is inadequate. It requires a rewrite of the logging module.	2–3 weeks	Blue team's management

FOLLOW UP ON ACTION ITEMS

Putting someone's name to an action item doesn't guarantee that the owner of the item will get it done in a timely fashion. There are a ton of competing forces on a person's time, and items get dropped all the time. As the organizer of the postmortem, however, it's up to you to keep the momentum going toward completion.

During the postmortem, the team should agree to a cadence of updates from the group at large. Assigning each action item a ticket in any work-tracking system you use can work well. This system helps make the work of the action items visible to everyone as well as provide a method for people to check the status on their own.

The postmortem facilitator should then be sending out updates at the agreed-upon frequency to the postmortem team. The facilitator should also reach out to team members who have missed agreed-upon deliverable dates to negotiate new dates.

You should never let an item continue to remain on the list of incomplete action items if it has an expired due date. If an action item is not complete by the agreed-upon date, the facilitator and the action item owner should negotiate a new due date for the task. Keeping task due dates current helps give them a sense of importance, at least relative to other items in a person's to-do list.

I can't understate the importance of following up on completing postmortem action items. These types of action items always get caught up in the whirlwind of day-to-day activity and quickly fall in the priority hierarchy. The follow-ups help keep these action items afloat, sometimes just for the sake of not receiving these nagging emails!

If you fail to make progress on an item, it might be worthwhile to document the risk that not completing the item creates. For example, if an action item to fix a poorly performing query never seems to get prioritized and or make progress, you can document that as an accepted risk as part of the incident. This way, you can at least propose to the group that the issue isn't deemed important enough (or has a low likelihood of being repeated) and isn't worth the effort of completing when compared to other demands on the team's time. But it's important that this be documented in the incident so that everyone is agreeing and acknowledging that the risk is one the team is willing to accept.

This isn't always a failure! Sometimes accepting a risk is the correct business decision. If a failure has a 1% chance of occurring, but is going to require an outsized effort by the team, accepting that risk is a perfectly reasonable alternative. But teams often get hung up is on *who* gets to decide that a risk should be accepted. Proper communication and a group consensus must be part of that risk acceptance.

9.3.4 Documenting your postmortem

Writing down your findings from a postmortem carries tremendous value. They serve as a written record for communication to people outside the immediate postmortem team, as well as a historical record for future engineers who encounter similar problems. You should expect the audience of your postmortem to have a mix of skill sets in the organization. You should write it with other engineers in mind, so be prepared to provide low-level details. But if you structure the document appropriately, there are ways to provide high-level overviews for people who aren't as technically savvy as engineers.

Keeping the structure of postmortem documentation consistent helps to maintain the quality of the postmortems. If documentation follows a template, the template can serve as a prompt for the information you need to provide. As you move through the postmortem document, the information within in should get more detailed as you progress through it.

INCIDENT DETAILS

The first section of the postmortem document should contain the *incident details*. Here you should outline these key items:

- Date and time the incident started
- Date and time the incident was resolved
- Total duration of the incident
- Systems that were impacted

This list doesn't need to be written in any sort of prose format. It can be presented as a bullet list at the top of the page. Having this information at the very top enables you to easily locate it when you're looking for help regarding incidents generally. Once you're no longer thinking of the specific details of an incident, you may want to search this documentation as you're looking for information in the aggregate.

An even better solution would be to also add this information to some sort of tool or database that is reportable. Something as simple as an Excel document could make summarizing a lot of this data easier. A database would offer the most flexibility, but for this section, I focus on basic paper-based documentation.

INCIDENT SUMMARY

The *incident summary* is the section where a formal, structured writing of the incident should live. This section should provide high-level details of the event with context that doesn't get too deep into the specifics. Think of this as an executive summary: people who are not technical can still follow the reading and understand the overall impact of the incident, what the user experience was like during the incident (if applicable), and how the incident was ultimately resolved. The goal is to keep the incident summary under two or three paragraphs if possible.

INCIDENT WALK-THROUGH

The *incident walk-through* is the most detailed section of the postmortem report. Your target audience in this section is specifically other engineers. It should provide a detailed walk-through of the incident timeline that was created during the postmortem meeting. The detailed report should not only walk through the decision process behind taking a particular action, but also provide any supporting documentation such as graphs, charts, alerts, or screenshots. This helps give the reader the context of what the engineers participating in the incident resolution experienced and saw. Providing

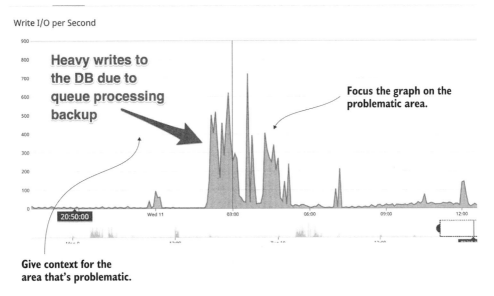

Write I/O per Second

Heavy writes to the DB due to queue processing backup

Focus the graph on the problematic area.

Give context for the area that's problematic.

Figure 9.3   Share and annotate graphics in your postmortem.

annotations in screenshots is extremely helpful too. In figure 9.3, you can see with the big red arrow how pointing out problems in the graph gives context to the data as it relates to the incident.

Even though the walk-through section is intended for other engineers, it shouldn't presume the experience level or knowledge of an engineer. When explaining key technical aspects of the incident, it's worthwhile to give a primer on the underlying technology that is leading or contributing to the problem. This doesn't have to be exhaustive, but it should be enough for the engineer to understand at a high level what's occurring or, at the very least, provide enough context so that they can begin to research it on their own.

As an example, if the incident being reported on was related to an excessive number of database locks, a brief explanation of how database locking works might be in order for the postmortem document to be a bit clearer to readers. The following is an example from an actual postmortem report of how you might segue into the details of an issue:

> *In production, a number of queries were executing that are not typically running around the time of the deployment. One query in particular was a long-running transaction that had been around for a while. This long-running transaction was holding a* READ LOCK *on the* auth_users *table. (Unfortunately, we were not able to capture the query during the troubleshooting phase of the incident. We did confirm that it was coming from a Sidekiq node.)*
>
> *Transactions and Locking*
>
> *When a transaction is running, the database will acquire locks on tables as those tables are accessed. All queries will generate some kind of lock. A simple* SELECT *query will generate a*

READ lock during the lifetime of that query. This, however, changes when a query is executed inside a transaction. When a query is made inside a transaction, the lock it acquires is maintained for the lifetime of the transaction. Using this nonsensical transaction below as an example:

```
BEGIN TRANSACTION
SELECT COUNT(*) from auth_users;
SELECT COUNT(*) from direct_delivery_items;


COMMIT
```

The auth_users *table would have a* READ LOCK *for the entire time that the* direct _delivery_items *query was executing. Considering the size of* direct_delivery _items, *this could be a lock for more than 10 minutes, even though the lock is not needed from an application perspective. This is basically what was transpiring the day of the outage. A long-running query had a* READ LOCK *on* auth_users, *which prevented the* ALTER TABLE *statement from acquiring a lock.*

COGNITIVE AND PROCESS ISSUES

This section for *cognitive and process issues* should highlight the things that the group has identified as areas for improvement. Consider all of the areas where people's mental models were not correct. Maybe the documented process for handling the incident missed a step. Or maybe the process didn't take into account this particular failure scenario. It could be something as simple as how the incident was managed or something more specifically technical, like how the database failover was performed.

This section isn't about creating and assigning blame, but about identifying the key areas that helped contribute to the failure. Pointing out these items in a bulleted list is enough, with a bit of detail around it as well.

ACTION ITEMS

The final section should be nothing more than a bulleted list of the open *action items* that have come out of the postmortem meeting. The bulleted list should detail the components of all the action items: *who* will do *what* by *when*.

9.3.5   *Sharing the postmortem*

Once the postmortem has been completed, the last thing to do is to share it with the rest of the engineering organization. You must have a single location where all postmortems are stored. You can categorize those postmortems into groupings that make sense for your organization, but there should be a single location where all postmortems and the subsequent categories can be found. It can be difficult to categorize postmortems to some degree, because system failures are seldom isolated. They can have rippling effects across a platform, so a failure in one subsystem could cause failures in additional subsystems.

Many documentation systems use metadata or labels to help aid in categorizing information. The labels serve as pieces of additional information that are typically used in search engines. But with labels, you're able to find different document types that might relate to the same subject, regardless of the document's name or title. If the documentation system you're using allows for labels or other forms of metadata to add to the document, you might be better off not creating a category or hierarchy at all and instead using the metadata options to detail documents. This allows you to have a document labeled with many keywords, so that if it does relate to multiple systems or departments, you can just add a label for each of the areas that's impacted.

It's also preferable that your documents follow a naming convention. The convention can vary based on your organization, but I strongly recommend that the first component of the document name be the date that the incident occurred. So, for example you'd name a postmortem "01-01-2019 – Excessive DB locking during deployment." This gives a brief summary of the event, but at the same time, the date allows people looking for a particular incident to home in on the correct document with relative ease.

Lastly, when it comes to sharing postmortems, try to avoid restricting access to the documents if possible. You want that information to be widely read for communication purposes, and so that everyone understands the expectations for conducting these postmortems. Making the documents available to only a select group of people might send the wrong signal that only those select people are responsible for writing postmortems.

Summary

- Blameful postmortems are not effective.
- Understand the engineer's mental model of the system to better understand decision-making.
- Action items should be defined as *who* will do *what* by *when*.
- Document the postmortem with different audiences intended for different sections.
- Have a central location for sharing all postmortems with the team.

Information hoarding:
Only Brent knows

This chapter covers

- Recognizing information hoarding
- Using lightning talks as a way to stay engaged
- Structuring lunch-and-learns
- Blogging and writing as a means of communicating
- Using external events and groups to increase knowledge-sharing practices

Unless purposeful action is taken, information tends to coalesce around key individuals. It makes those individuals incredibly valued but also equally burdened. Processes and projects can come grinding to a halt when that key person is out of the office or otherwise unavailable. I call this the *only Brent knows* antipattern, a nod to the character from *The Phoenix Project* by Gene Kim, Kevin Behr, and George Spafford (IT Revolution Press, 2018). It happens when information sharing isn't fostered throughout the organization, and team members begin to disengage from topics that are the realm of key personnel.

Throughout this book, I've been discussing the value of collaboration among staff members and empowering those staff members with the capabilities they need to succeed. But one facet about empowerment goes beyond access restrictions and permissions. It goes deeper into the practice of empowering through knowledge and awareness.

Many people take knowledge inside their organization for granted, but the more knowledge you gain about a topic, the more painfully obvious it becomes just how complex and nuanced it can be. From the outside looking in, a deployment sounds like an easy, core activity. But the deeper you get into the deployment process, you begin to realize all the little steps that were obfuscated from you as a layperson.

The act of sharing information isn't much different. From the outside, making information available seems to be the only thing that's needed to awaken people and engage them in areas outside their own. Unfortunately, that's not true, and the realities of knowledge sharing go way beyond just putting information into a wiki page.

Information hoarding is a popular affliction that companies face. It happens when information is siloed into a specific area of the organization. And while the concentration of knowledge isn't necessarily bad, teams can build artificial barriers around that knowledge.

Many times, it's not a conscious choice, but the result of seemingly disconnected decisions. Who has access to the documentation server? Who is the document written for? What terms are used to make the knowledge discoverable from the outside? These small, innocuous decisions come together to create barriers.

These barriers disrupt the flow of information, and prevent workers from being effective and/or knowledgeable about areas that are adjacent to their own areas of expertise. In really bad cases, this hoarding creates a world in which no one focuses on the whole, but just on optimizing their small slice of the pie.

You may be wondering what all of this has to do with DevOps. How you share information is always going to be a blueprint for how you communicate as a team and how you draw the lines of responsibility and ownership. DevOps is about breaking down those silos, but those walls exist as much in our minds and in our words as they exist in our reporting structures. Being sensitive to how you hoard and protect information about your team continues to build your muscles of empathy. Self-reflection will empower you to make better choices individually and to build those choices into the cultural DNA of your team. This continues to be core of the DevOps mindset.

In this chapter, I'm going to talk to you a little bit about this idea of information hoarding, how it happens, and (hopefully) how to pivot away from it through structured activities and rituals that almost any organization can adopt.

10.1 Understanding how information hoarding happens

It's easy to view owners of systems as malevolent dictators who don't want people outside their fiefdom to understand how the systems they're responsible for managing operate. I don't want to pretend that these villains of the organization don't exist, but in my experience they're much less common than you think.

So, if it isn't some Bond-style villain sitting in the back office hording all the wiki documents, you have to ask, what is it that drives these silos of information? It's a combination of organizational structure, incentives, priorities and values, which all coalesce into a collection of empty folder structures on document repository servers.

I'd like to start with the idea that two primary types of information hoarding exist, and it's important to differentiate the two. There's intentional and unintentional hoarding. *Intentional hoarding* is what most of us are familiar with. A manager or engineer decides that information is currency and decides to hoard it for their own benefit. I'll talk about these hoarders a bit later in the book, but even their behavior is the result of organizational influences combined with poor incentives. The *unintentional hoarders* are fascinating, because they often don't even realize they're doing it! There's value in being able to recognize when you're being an information hoarder and then taking action on correcting that behavior to make engineers more effective.

10.2 *Recognizing unintentional hoarders*

Jonah has been working on a project for about two weeks now. The project is set to launch a new method for environments to register themselves with third-party services. The project, however, is a proof-of-concept and will move on to full project status only if the tool proves useful.

Like most successful proof-of-concept projects, the tool becomes way too valuable to turn off after its launch. As a result, a lot of frantic changes occur to get the application performing the way it should. Architecture and code changes are happening on a weekly basis, and the landscape of the application seems to change quite regularly. Because of the fluid nature of the project, documentation keeps getting put off until the tool reaches some poorly defined metric of "stable."

Once the changes do finally seem to settle down, the team is off to another project, and the sheer amount of documentation that's now necessary feels insurmountable. A ticket for documentation goes into the backlog of work, never to be seen or heard from again.

Some of you might find this story vaguely familiar or even a bit triggering. Some might even vilify Jonah for creating something without appropriate documentation. But Jonah is as much a victim here as he is a villain. The organization has been structured and incentivized in such a way that Jonah's actions are completely in line with the way the organization is designed and structured to behave. Documentation has been given a lower degree of importance than the other tasks on Jonah's plate. Jonah has unwittingly become an unintentional hoarder.

This is a common scenario that people see in organizations, but they often don't consider it information hoarding. The argument is that Jonah is more than forthcoming with any and all information that is asked of him. But the fact remains that Jonah is the gatekeeper of what information you receive.

Not only that, but the data that you get is always filtered through Jonah's own lens of relevance. He gets to decide on his own which information is important for your query and which isn't. If there's an extra component that Jonah feels isn't important for what you're working on, he might not mention it. This isn't about making Jonah the villain, but about the realities of how humans can have differing views on the context of a question, situation, or problem.

That doesn't even begin to address the issue of Jonah's availability for questioning around the subject. Does Jonah ever go on vacation? Attend meetings? Jonah's availability dictates access to the information stored in his brain, which is almost never a good thing. This leads us to the first of the unintentional hoarding behaviors: not valuing documentation.

10.2.1 Documentation isn't valued

I want to be specific about how I use the term "valued." Everyone thinks they value documentation, but it's not really true. People think documentation is important, but that's very different from actually valuing it. People think toilet paper is important, but it's not until it becomes a scarcity that people actually begin to *value* toilet paper. (I write this during the 2020 COVID-19 pandemic, during which toilet paper and paper towels have suddenly become the most in-demand product in every grocery and household goods store in the country.)

Here's another example of how companies value some documentation and not others. Have you ever launched a service, application, or product without any documentation around it? Most of you probably have. In organizations like that, documentation might be important. The company wouldn't stop you from providing documentation on the product and would probably even applaud you. But when push comes to shove, if you need to launch that product, a lack of documentation is definitely not going to delay deployment.

Now on the other hand, try submitting an expense report without documentation for every single reported transaction and see how far that submission gets. Probably not very far at all. You might argue that with expenses, the company is at risk of being defrauded, overpaying for non-existent expenses, and other types of financial malfeasance. But I argue that there's just as much risk of doing that with applications, technical products, and code changes.

The value of documentation is rooted in action, not rhetoric. And your systems have to be in place to treat documentation as something that's valued in the organization. If you're willing to skip documentation, then ask whether it's really something that's valued. And if it's not, that's OK. It can be hard to break a company of poor documentation habits if it's not something that the organization values.

When to write documentation

A large documentation problem that exists on teams is figuring out when to write documentation. Because of the expense and overhead of maintaining documentation, I think it's important to be careful and selective about the documentation you actually write.

(continued)

When it comes to engineering, implementation details seldom need to exist in any written documentation. Those details are a single commit away from being obsolete and in some cases potentially dangerous. One of the riskiest things in the organization is highly-detailed documentation that is out-of-date! Decisions that are made based on outdated information can have rippling effects on a project. Writing documentation on motivations, context, and strategy is far better than including specific implementation details.

In an engineering context, you often make trade-offs about code design. Sometimes no good choices exist when it comes to deciding an object hierarchy. Documenting the strategy for the chosen hierarchy, as well as the trade-offs you made, not only gives context to the existing design strategy, but also can inform future implementation choices long after the original author has moved on.

High-level design documents are also helpful in solidifying the ideas of the system in the reader's mind. Avoid getting overly detailed with things like specific software implementations or number of servers. Those change over time. Instead of documenting that you have three ActiveMQ servers running version 5.2 between the frontend and the backend servers, you might generically label it as a "message bus," which for a high-level design communicates the purpose without clouding the reader's mind with unnecessary detail. The more specific the documentation becomes, the smaller the audience is that finds it relevant.

The documentation isn't really the end goal. The end goal is the *sharing of information.* If you can get the same quality of information sharing via a different means, then it might absolutely be worth it to skip the mounds of written documentation in favor of something a little easier to manage or produce. The value of documentation must exceed the opportunity cost of producing it.

> **DEFINITION**   *Opportunity cost* is the potential loss you experience when one activity or action is chosen over another. If a developer has to spend a week writing documentation, the opportunity cost might be the week of coding progress that the developer could have been making if they weren't writing documentation.

If getting a developer moving on to the next project is more valuable to the organization than producing documentation, I argue that this is an OK choice to make. In fact, most engineers make this choice all the time. They have the intention of coming back to the documentation at a later date, but seldom do. Not prioritizing documentation is a choice, but you have to be real with yourself about when that choice is being made and try to come up with alternatives for the true goal, which is sharing information. I discuss methods beyond just written documentation later in this chapter.

Documentation isn't the only way that teams end up hoarding information. The way developers and architects design systems can cause information hoarding through a web of complexity. As one very personal example, my team's deployment automation is

The perceived value of documentation

An interesting aside that I've discovered on my career journey is that people tend to value documentation differently based on where they sit in the documentation equation. When someone else is required to create the documentation, in our minds, it becomes essential: "How could you possibly launch this without proper documentation?" But when the situation is reversed, suddenly documentation becomes expendable.

This is an important lesson in empathy and how you put yourself in the shoes of another. Instead of chastising someone for not having written documentation, think about the various factors and time pressures you've experienced on your own projects and try to approach the situation from a position of understanding instead of blamefulness.

incredibly helpful and empowering, but its obfuscation prevents other teams from contributing to it and completely understanding it. Instead, my team serves as a gatekeeper to one of the most important functions of the development process.

10.2.2 *Abstraction vs. obfuscation*

When you're designing a complex system, it's often worthwhile to deal with layers of abstraction as you attempt to solve the problem.

> **DEFINITION** *Abstraction* is the idea of treating something as independent from the various associations and implementations that the abstraction interacts with, making it easier to use and interact with. As a real-world example, regardless of the manufacturer, all cars have a gas pedal, a brake, and a steering wheel. This presentation to the user is treated separately from the detailed implementation of steering, braking, and accelerating inside the car's engine.

These abstraction layers allow you to hide a lot of the complex details that you would normally need to know. Let's take an order-taking system, for example. An order has to be fulfilled and delivered to the customer. The order could either be a pickup order or a delivery order. Without abstractions, the order system would need to know about both pickup order workflows and delivery order workflows. It would need to know about shipping details, postage costs, and a laundry list of other things. This amount of data creates a lot of burden and complexity on the order system.

But if you break the code into two parts, the order system and the fulfillment system, the order system could become completely ignorant as to *how* an order is delivered to a customer. It just needs to record a few key pieces of information and then pass that data to the fulfillment service. The fulfillment service is then aware of the particulars of order delivery. But it also is ignorant of how an order is actually taken and processed, because it just receives an order upstream and needs to get it delivered.

If you look at figure 10.1, you'll see that the order system has to be aware of the delivery mechanics and implement either a pickup order fulfillment or a delivery

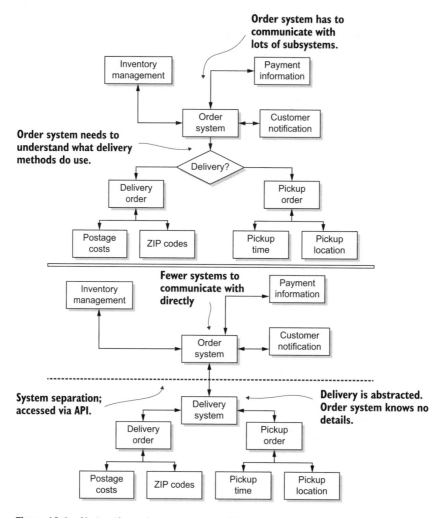

Figure 10.1 Abstraction reduces communication.

order fulfillment. In the second, abstracted diagram, the order system is interacting with just the delivery system. The specifics of delivery are handled within the abstraction, shielding the order system from the nitty-gritty details.

This abstraction is helpful when it comes to managing the complexity of a system. The problem comes in when the order team needs to know an implementation detail about the fulfillment team's process. Because these groups have created a system that allows them to be silos, documentation is further devalued: anyone who needs to know is on the team and intimately familiar with the information. The fulfillment team isn't intentionally hoarding information, but thinks that the only real audience for the documentation is themselves. Everyone else just needs to know "you give fulfillment an order and a delivery type, and we figure out the rest for you!"

But what if the order team wants to make a change and needs to ensure that the change won't impact the fulfillment team? Or if the order team runs into problems and needs to understand how the fulfillment service functions as part of its trouble-shooting efforts? This accidental silo of information can cause problems because the fulfillment team becomes ingrained in potentially mundane requests for information. There are a ton of reasons that the order team might need or want to understand how the systems they're interacting with behave. This information is often highly situational, meaning that they need to understand the system in order to deal with a specific request or problem.

Another problem with this abstraction is that it suddenly creates a firewall between the teams, which often allows for bad behaviors to fester. Think about your house for a second. I'm sure that at times your home is in a state that you would absolutely never allow visitors to come and see. It's too disorganized, too chaotic, too authentic for people to see.

I'm here to tell you that the same thing can happen with code, when the only people who will see the mess also live in the house. This scenario can breed a bit of obfuscation with the way things work or why they work the way they do. Maybe your team was experiencing a shortage of developer hours and took a shortcut to meet a deadline. Maybe your code was lacking in comments so the context gets lost. Your team might be OK living with that situation because you are all aware of the context and the opportunity costs of doing things the way you did.

But for other teams, that context is lost, and your code looks like an obfuscated, complex nightmare. Now anytime someone looks at this section of code, they need it explained to them first to make sure they're not making incorrect assumptions about a particular fundamental piece. This is why abstraction can be good but can lead to obfuscation, and in turn, accidental hoarding of information. The issue can compound over time as special cases, one-off customer requests, and bug-fix scenarios creep up and are bolted on without properly being thought about and refactored into the solution.

10.2.3 *Access restrictions*

Teams tend to have information that, for one reason or another, they feel shouldn't exist beyond the eyes of the team. This is common in operations teams that may have configuration files littered with passwords and other bits of sensitive information, for instance.

Imagine you have a project space on your wiki. That project folder contains sensitive information, so the team decides to lock it down to just their group. Over time, however, data gets added to the folder, putting more and more information behind the protective wall. But the wall has now extended well beyond its intended borders and begins to protect the highly sensitive as well as the incredibly routine pieces of information that a team might need.

Access restrictions start off with the best of intentions. But if they're not carefully monitored, they can quickly spiral into an overprotective police state. People can be divided into two types when it comes to situations like this. A few people become intellectually curious when they face a "locked door" and decide to ask for permission or poke around. But the majority of people come to a locked door and presume that whatever is behind the door isn't intended for them. They'll move about their business, presuming that what lives beyond the door either can't or won't help them. Worse, this learned behavior self-replicates through the organization.

I don't mean to imply that protecting sensitive information isn't important, because it most certainly is. But before deciding to place something in a highly secure folder area, you need to evaluate whether it really needs to be in such a locked-down area of the wiki.

Ticketing system permissions

This is a bit of a divergence, but I think it's especially prudent to mention the importance of local access restrictions in ticket-management systems. In a lot of ticketing tools, the security model allows for team-level workflows and permissions, but often the administration of those projects still exists in a centralized fashion. So much time is wasted when a team doesn't have the ability to quickly turn around access requests to their project and the subsequent tickets, reports, and filters.

If your tool allows for project- or department-level access controls, the teams that manage that project should have the ability to manage those controls and workflows. This reduces the amount of turnaround time and helps in addressing restrictions that impact the team's effectiveness.

10.2.4   *Evaluating gatekeeper behavior*

The areas I've listed aren't the only ways that people can accidentally hoard information, but they're the most common and often the most benign in their origins. I challenge you to evaluate your potential for information hoarding by looking at the sorts of gatekeeping functions that people go through to access information that you possess. Are there other methods for getting at this information that your team could provide? Are people generally looking for your subject-matter expertise, or are they looking for more general information about something you support? Does the documentation for this exist but people just don't have the access permissions necessary to get it?

This doesn't mean that you need to always have some form of documentation at the ready for every piece of information, but you should consider how you can make each request more self-service in the future. Keeping an eye on how information from your team is requested and extracted is a muscle that you'll need to continue to exercise. But if you're on the lookout for signs of accidental information hoarding, you'll quickly recognize where you're deficient and where you can improve. The next section presents specific ways to get better at documentation.

10.3　*Structuring your communication effectively*

A common mistake when it comes to information sharing is assuming that everyone intrinsically knows how to communicate knowledge effectively. Structuring the way you communicate knowledge is a core skill, regardless of the medium used to actually share information. If you have a strong method that you prefer for communicating information, then I'm by no means asking you to abandon it. Continue to use what is effective for you. But if you find yourself struggling to organize your thoughts into a cohesive message, this section offers guidance on the best way to do that.

If you've ever had a bad teacher, you know there's a large gap between having knowledge and communicating it. Scientists and psychologists have identified four primary methods of learning that people adapt to: visual, auditory, reading/writing, and kinesthetic (hands-on) activities. Many people prefer one type over another, while many thrive when there's a mixture of all the styles.

Keep in mind that not everyone will learn or prefer the same style as you when it comes to learning. Regardless of the style chosen, however, conveying information still follows a structured approach to optimize the way people process the chosen topic.

I suggest following these communication steps, which are detailed in the following subsections:

1　Define the topic.
2　Define your audience.
3　Outline your key points.
4　End with a call to action.

10.3.1　*Defining your topic*

Starting with a clear topic is the first step of communication. If you decide to give a talk about television, you have a lot of ground to cover. Are you talking about the technology that delivers television? Or the myriad of shows and entertainment that television provides? What about the societal impact it's had? These topics are all different, even though they revolve around the same subject.

You have to home in on your topic so that it structures the rest of your teaching. Defining your topic will help you to quickly identify what is in scope and what is out of scope for your communication.

When you think about defining the topic, try to also keep in mind what it is you want to be able to convey in the communication. If you set out with the goal of creating the most comprehensive billing documentation, you have to be prepared to go into every single detail of that process. But if you really just want to give people a clearer understanding of how the teams interact with each other during a billing cycle, then limiting the documentation to that specific area for your topic will help you to stay on track.

10.3.2 *Defining your audience*

Once your topic is defined, you'll want to think about who you plan to communicate this to. Every communication has to have an intended audience. Think about anything and everything you've ever watched or viewed. To communicate information effectively, you have to be able to make certain assumptions about the person receiving that information.

Those assumptions are what drives the definition of who your audience is and the level of detail that you might need to go into. If your audience is engineers, you can use the word "compiler" in your communication without the need to define it. If your audience is a fifth-grade classroom, you might need to alter your language and define what a compiler is before you begin using it in your communication. Defining your audience is a crucial step that is often overlooked when designing documentation.

Once your audience is defined, you can also begin thinking about ways to assist people who are not in your core audience group to understand the communication. Maybe you use the word "compiler" without a definition but create a hyperlink to other documentation that describes what a compiler is in greater detail, outside the specific context of your documentation.

10.3.3 *Outlining your key points*

Once you have the topic defined and your audience selected, structuring your key points is next. Your *key points* are areas of the topic that you want to communicate. They can be separated into two camps, core and color. Your *core group of points* covers information that you are absolutely committed to communicating and is essential to understanding the topic. *Color points* are areas that help enhance understanding but may not be vitally important to communicating the topic at hand. If you're writing an article on the impact of television on society, the technology of television may not be as important, relegating it to the color area. The reason for creating this separation is so that as your communication evolves, you have a specific area of focus that you can begin to trim down if necessary.

10.3.4 *Presenting a call to action*

Finally, at the end comes the call to action. What is the audience supposed to do with that information, and what are those next steps?

Your call to action might be just sharing more information with them to research a topic further, or requesting that they fill out a survey, or asking them to repeat the skills taught in the communication with their own team. But always end the communication with some form of call to action that engages the audience and keeps them moving on the journey.

This is just one method for structing your communications. Again, if you have a method that works for you already, by all means continue to use it. But if you find yourself struggling with how to effectively communicate, following this pattern is a great way to structure your messaging.

10.4 Making your knowledge discoverable

As accidental as information hoarding can be, the process of knowledge sharing needs to be as equally deliberate. *Knowledge stores* are the locations in which you collect information, data, and documentation about the company knowledge that your employees possess. This can be in the form of a wiki, SharePoint site, or even just a folder on a shared drive.

But managing these knowledge stores and setting guidelines about their structure is a problem that requires explicit attention. Documentation and knowledge transfer are other tasks in the knowledge management realm that everyone expects to be part of the daily job, but the truth of the matter is that without explicit direction and prioritization, they simply lose out to all of the other demands that teams place on their engineers.

These well-known problems tend to require quite a bit of structural change to make knowledge sharing an organizational priority. In the meantime, I'll give a few tips on how you can increase the amount of knowledge sharing that is occurring among yourself and your fellow coworkers. It all starts with rituals and habits.

10.4.1 Structuring your knowledge stores

One of the biggest problems that companies face isn't just creating good documentation, but also finding the documentation after it's been created. Wiki pages and knowledge repositories are often a disorganized mess, causing us to spend way more time searching for information than actually learning from it.

Repositories often don't do a good job of being structured for knowledge discovery instead of knowledge retrieval. Say you're looking for information about the billing process, but you have no idea where to look. Finding that information in the document repository on your own would be *knowledge discovery*. Without anyone's help, you're able to discover the information. This is very different from *knowledge retrieval*. In that case, you already know the document exists, but you just need to retrieve it from the repository. (And even that is not always an easy task.)

There are a few small actions you can take, however, to ensure that knowledge discovery can happen in your document repository:

- Use a common lexicon.
- Create documentation with a hierarchical structure, linked to one master document.
- Structure documentation around topics, not departments.

USE A COMMON LEXICON

I've been in situations where I've watched two people talk about the same process for 10 minutes without realizing they were talking about the same process. It's challenging enough when people have differing mental models about how a system behaves, but it becomes way more difficult when people have different names for the same system or process.

Naming things is one of the most difficult tasks in computer science. But effectively communicating what that name is and ensuring that everyone sticks to that name pays huge dividends. Where I live in Chicago, every freeway has two names, the actual interstate route designation and the honored name the city has bestowed upon it. The Dan Ryan Expressway is also referred to as I-90/I-94, but then splits at some point and remains just I-94. When you're describing the roads to people who are not from Chicago, it can be mind-numbingly confusing because people don't realize that I-94, I-90/I-94 and the Dan Ryan Expressway are all the same road.

Creating a common lexicon and naming strategy for business processes, services, systems, and tools isn't meant to help the 15-year veterans of the company. It's designed to help the new hires in the organization get up to speed quickly on the inner workings of the company instead of trying to figure out whether two things are, in fact, identical.

> ### Beware of project names
> When a team is working on a new product, the product will often assume the name of the project that created it. This is a common area of miscommunication, because the project is long-finished, but teams still reference the product by the name of the project as opposed to the product name. This can create a ton of confusion for people who are unaware of the project name.

CREATE A DOCUMENT HIERARCHY

When a company performs an organizational process, like a month-end billing run, the process is useful only if it runs to completion. If accounts receivable doesn't do its job, it doesn't matter whether the operations team executes the month-end close on time. It's all one process that involves the coordination of several teams and departments to deliver the final results.

If you looked at the documentation for this, however, you might think that these processes exist in a vacuum. In many organizations, nowhere is there a complete document highlighting the entire process from start to finish. Instead, each department splinters into their own groups and writes documentation that addresses their specific area or focus.

This would be an acceptable practice if the documentation across departments was structured in such a way that the whole could be derived from its parts, but it isn't. Document linking between steps in the process is almost nonexistent if the process crosses boundaries between departments or teams. If you're lucky, you might receive a passing reference to a process, but even then, you're not even guaranteed to call the process by the same name across teams. What's even more frustrating is that despite how bad things are with documentation, we already have an almost perfect real-world example of how things should be done: Wikipedia.

What makes Wikipedia such an incredible tool is not only the massive amount of content available, but the structure of its documents. Content in Wikipedia starts with a primary page that serves as the primary entry for the topic. It doesn't matter how complicated that entry might be; one primary article sets the tone for any linked articles.

Take something as broad as "Democracy" (https://en.wikipedia.org/wiki/Democracy). That entry starts with a table of contents describing the structure of the document (figure 10.2).

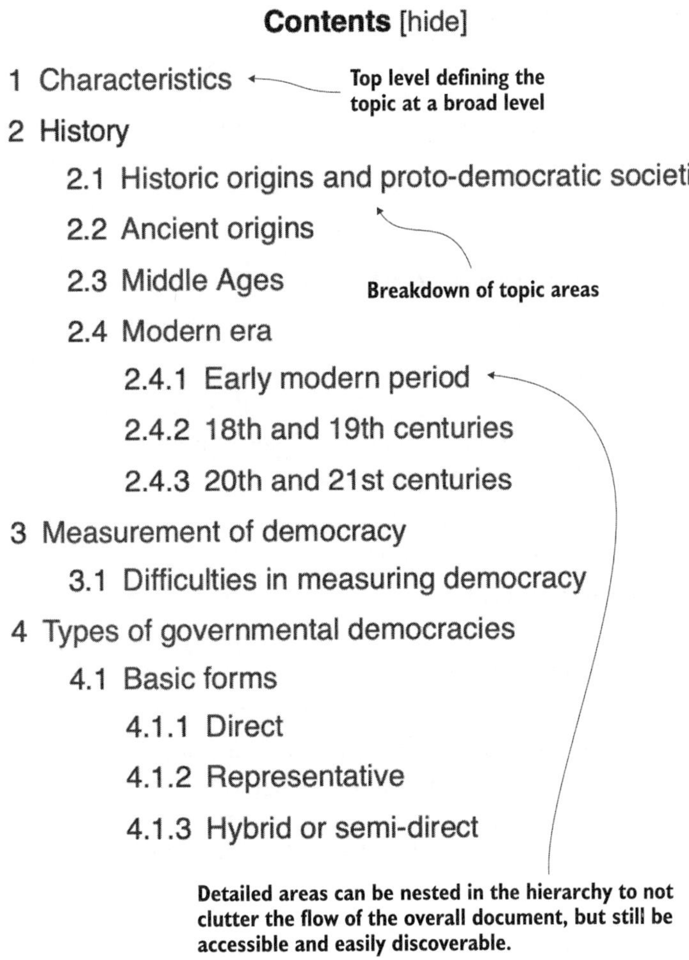

Contents [hide]

1 Characteristics ←———— **Top level defining the topic at a broad level**

2 History

   2.1 Historic origins and proto-democratic societies

   2.2 Ancient origins

   2.3 Middle Ages   **Breakdown of topic areas**

   2.4 Modern era

      2.4.1 Early modern period ←

      2.4.2 18th and 19th centuries

      2.4.3 20th and 21st centuries

3 Measurement of democracy

   3.1 Difficulties in measuring democracy

4 Types of governmental democracies

   4.1 Basic forms

      4.1.1 Direct

      4.1.2 Representative

      4.1.3 Hybrid or semi-direct

Detailed areas can be nested in the hierarchy to not clutter the flow of the overall document, but still be accessible and easily discoverable.

Figure 10.2 Structuring the document well allows for detail in one area, while still allowing for easy navigation to relevant topics.

The document has many sections that touch on aspects of the topic of democracy. A section that's broad and incredibly complicated such as "History" is still discussed in the primary article. Discussing the entire history of democracy is easily an article in itself. But because history is an important component to someone researching democracy, it's referenced in the main article. A more detailed article about the history of democracy is appropriately linked, as shown in figure 10.3.

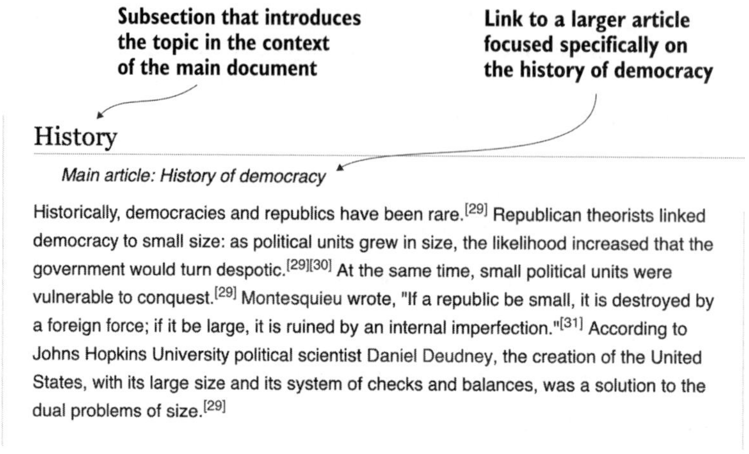

**Subsection that introduces
the topic in the context
of the main document**

**Link to a larger article
focused specifically on
the history of democracy**

History

Main article: History of democracy

Historically, democracies and republics have been rare.[29] Republican theorists linked democracy to small size: as political units grew in size, the likelihood increased that the government would turn despotic.[29][30] At the same time, small political units were vulnerable to conquest.[29] Montesquieu wrote, "If a republic be small, it is destroyed by a foreign force; if it be large, it is ruined by an internal imperfection."[31] According to Johns Hopkins University political scientist Daniel Deudney, the creation of the United States, with its large size and its system of checks and balances, was a solution to the dual problems of size.[29]

Figure 10.3 A subsection of a larger document that links to a more detailed document on the topic

Just this simple linking allows you to guide the reader in the discovery process of information related to democracy. Let's go back to our fictional end-of-month billing example to see how you might apply similar principles to a document. Our example billing process has multiple steps handled by various departments:

- Reconciliation (accounts receivable)
- Application of credits (business operations)
- New services registration (sales)
- Close of books (finance)
- Billing job execution (IT operations)
- Delivery of invoices (facilities/IT operations)

These steps are wildly different for each department, but none of the steps can really be done in isolation and still create the desired effect of sending out correct bills. When everything works correctly, team members may never need to cross over their departmental line. But when something breaks, understanding the whole process suddenly becomes incredibly important. If someone complains that they didn't receive their bill, the process could have broken down in one of a few places:

- Did the bill get mailed, or was it supposed to be an electronic delivery?
- Was a bill even generated by the billing job execution?
- If there were enough credits to make the customer's bill $0, would the billing job generate a bill?

When dealing with the unhappy path of the billing process, you realize how intertwined these steps are and just how much one affects the other. Finding a bit of information on the preceding processes might help an engineer looking into the billing job execution understand with more precision and clarity exactly how their tasks interact with other tasks. Maybe the engineer was completely unaware of how credits get applied and in which circumstances. A little bit of documentation can go a long way in helping with that.

Having the documentation referenced, even in passing, in a master document for the billing process makes it much easier for someone to find information they didn't even realize they were missing. As an engineer, if I'm unaware of the credit-granting process, how would I ever think to look for it in documentation? This is the strength of having a master document on a process that points the reader to the various areas that have more specific information.

The master document should focus on a process, application, or system and provide a jumping-off point for any specific departmental information if necessary. Documentation should be based on a hierarchical structure leading back to the master document that it covers, and that master document should be concise and specific about a topic. Having all of your documents connect to a department or team master document is ineffective because then others don't contribute to it with the understanding that the team owns that document. But when the organization has a single document called "Billing," and everything regarding billing links up to it, a much stronger sense of communal ownership of it results. Figure 10.4 is an example structure for the billing documentation.

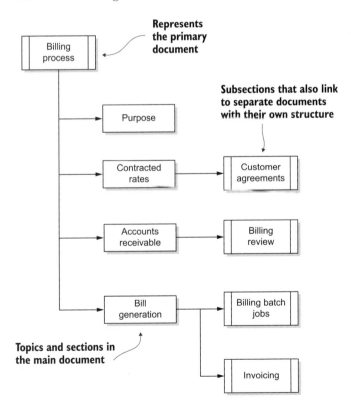

Figure 10.4 A hierarchy of documentation for the billing example

Another advantage to the master document approach is that more eyes are on it. One of the reasons documents get outdated is that fewer eyeballs see the inconsistencies and take action to correct them. When it comes to documentation, you have to consider the Pareto principle, also known as the 80/20 rule. The rule states that for most events, 80% of the effects are come from 20% of the causes. So if you have 10 people working on a wiki document, 80% of the work on that document is going to come from two people.

> **DEFINITION**   The *Pareto principle* states that for most events, 80% of the effects come from 20% of the causes.

The Pareto principle holds true in a lot of scenarios. With this principle in mind, it makes sense to maximize the number of people who see and interact with a document in order to further increase the size of that 20% grouping.

The master document strategy does require a bit more coordination and management to ensure that people are conforming to the strategy. But in truth, the lack of coordination is usually what makes wikis and documentation repositories so ineffective anyway.

STRUCTURE AROUND TOPICS, NOT DEPARTMENTS

As you create master documents, structure your documentation around topics instead of departments. If you structure around departments, information becomes splintered across various teams and areas. Although team-specific documentation (such as policies, procedures, and meeting artifacts) may have value, more often than not, broader documentation connects into processes that are of interest to people outside the team.

The operations group might have a document that outlines the network architecture of the platform, as well as the server topology used for a key application service. This seems like something that is of specific interest to IT operations, but putting it in an IT operations space would be a mistake. Someone outside the IT operations organization might have an interest in the network topology for various reasons. Maybe they're troubleshooting latency that the application is experiencing and they're trying to get an understanding of how many network hops need to happen for the application server to get to the database server. Maybe they're wondering whether two services that communicate with each other exist on the same network.

Creating documentation in such a way that people can organically discover it requires having a clear path to that documentation. A document that is linked to its related topic has a much better chance of being discovered than a lone document dangling off the root of a team-specific page. When a document is placed with other documents of the same or similar context, it increases the chance that it gets discovered organically.

10.4.2 *Creating learning rituals*

Rituals are the activities and events that an organization repeats. Rituals are an important part of culture building, and I'll dive deeper into the relationship between ritual and culture later in the book. But for now, think of a ritual as a process, activity, or event that is repeated within the organization. Some rituals might be good, some might be bad, and some might exist solely for their own existence. But when it comes to learning and knowledge sharing, you're going to create rituals that are not only valuable, but a self-sustaining part of the culture.

Before I dive into these rituals, though, I think it's important to talk about another one of the structural reasons that just a general "document more" approach doesn't work. Most topics in the organization have subject-matter experts (SMEs)—people with specialized knowledge on a particular area or topic. The problem with SMEs is that their expertise can create a self-replicating scenario. If you have only a single SME for a particular topic, all information and requests funnel through that person. They become consumed by requests related to their expertise, which puts demands on their time that are outside their regular day-to-day duties. It also pushes them into more projects than an individual can realistically support. This pattern creates further demand on their time. The solution is often to do some form of "knowledge transfer," but those transfers are usually poorly defined, poorly prioritized, and poorly structured.

> **DEFINITION** *Knowledge transfer* is the process whereby one person or organization teaches or trains another person or organization about a specific topic. Knowledge transfer aims to distribute information throughout the organization to ensure its availability to users in the event of employee attrition or an employee's change in job function.

The act of training or educating people is in itself another demand on the SME's time. Eventually, the realities of the SME's day-to-day tasks kick in, and the ability to perform knowledge transfers is abandoned. Figure 10.5 illustrates this vicious cycle of demand on the SME.

With this cycle in mind, you have to acknowledge that just adding documentation requirements doesn't fix the process. Documentation must also be prioritized, which means other tasks have to be de-prioritized in order to make progress. There might also be ways to increase knowledge transfer without the time sink of written documentation. Different people have different strengths, and what comes easy to some may not come so easily to others. Let's discuss other ways you can create knowledge-sharing opportunities, while at the same time being cognizant of this cycle that puts demands on our team members.

LUNCH-AND-LEARNS

Food is a binding agent among humans. Combine food with learning, and you have a chance to share information to a really broad audience. *Lunch-and-learns* are structured presentations given by someone to a large audience over the lunch break. The topic should be focused on a specific area without trying to educate someone on a

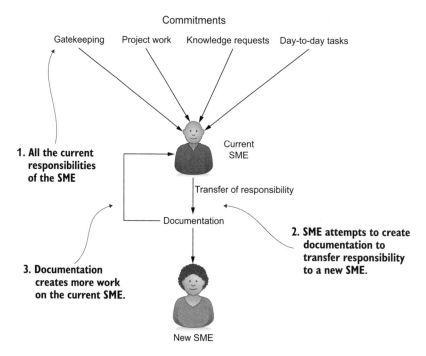

Commitments

Gatekeeping   Project work   Knowledge requests   Day-to-day tasks

Current
SME

**1. All the current
responsibilities
of the SME**

Transfer of responsibility

Documentation

**2. SME attempts to create
documentation to
transfer responsibility
to a new SME.**

**3. Documentation
creates more work
on the current SME.**

New SME

Figure 10.5   The demands of documentation feed into the lack of time for documentation.

subject in its entirety. The goal of the lunch-and-learn is to educate people on a topic at a high level and to attract interest in the area of focus. Remember the Pareto principle? At a lunch-and-learn, you're looking for people who might want to be part of the 20% who will help share and produce the knowledge on a subject.

Scheduling the event of the lunch hour can help increase participation because most people share a similar lunch time. In most offices, lunch time is generally devoid of meetings. Another great piece of the lunch-and-learn is that it's easy to make the activity available to remote employees. Other types of knowledge-transfer rituals can be difficult to complete remotely, mainly because they lack structure. But the format of a presentation, combined with a focused structure to the topic, like the model I outlined earlier, make lunch-and-learns an excellent method for sharing information.

When you schedule your lunch-and-learn, it's important to leave enough time for questions. Interaction with the audience is the key to a successful event. Encourage questions if you can by creating a safe space in which ask questions. Be sure to highlight during the lunch-and-learn the complexity of the topic. This makes people feel comfortable with not understanding a component of the topic because you've expressed its difficulty.

If a presenter says over and over again, "This is so easy. This part is simple. And then it's pretty obvious that you . . . ", people may not be willing to admit their confusion. You've spent 20 minutes talking about how simple the content is, so attendees would prefer to wallow in their ignorance than to risk looking like a fool in front of a room of people. When you get a question from an audience member, find a way to praise them: "Great question" or "I hadn't thought of that" or "Oh, excellent catch." These words of affirmation make people feel comfortable in not fully understanding the subject matter.

You'll often find that one question begets more questions, and before long, you have an avalanche of pent-up confusion rushing out at you. Embrace this! It's a good sign that people are engaging with the content and want to know more.

Finally, with a lunch-and-learn, you want to provide some sort of call to action at the end. Think about what it is you want the audience to do with the information that you've provided. Was it just general awareness? Are you looking for contributions to a project? Or maybe you're looking to share in the on-call support of a system? Think about what it is you'd like out of the group and make a specific plea to that effort at the end of your presentation. Your call to action should express at least the following:

- What it is you're looking for help with.
- How to answer the call to action. For example, send an email, visit a website, or contact the presenter.
- The deadline for the call to action. Even if your call to action isn't time-boxed, it's always best to set a timetable to create a sense of urgency around the call. Without it, people inevitably delay answering the call, even if they're legitimately interested.

LIGHTNING TALKS

Sometimes putting together a 20- to 30-minute presentation is just too much for some people. When you have a defined time window to fill, finding enough content can feel paralyzing. As a public speaker, I can tell you that some of my most terrifying moments arose from worrying that I wasn't going to have enough content to fill the allotted timeslot. This is where lightning talks really shine.

Lightning talks are brief, hyper-focused talks on a particular topic. They usually last from 5 to 10 minutes but can be as short as necessary to get the idea or content across. Lightning talks aren't ideal for complicated subjects but serve as a great mechanism for a primer into a topic or as a condensed instructional period. Lightning talks typically fall into a few categories:

- Sharing techniques for accomplishing a task
- High-level overviews of a broad topic
- Introduction of a new technology

When it comes to sharing techniques, this one is often used by technical teams. I've seen a lot of talks given by people trying to display their workflows for development—for example, what tools they use and how they leverage them to increase speed and efficiency of their iteration cycle. I imagine every organization has that technical wizard who seems to be able to do things in half the time that most other engineers do. What's their development environment setup like? What IDE do they use? How do they iterate on tests so quickly? Lightning talks are a great format to explore some of these topics and share with the audience tips and tricks of the trade.

Broad high-level overviews are also a great topic for lightning discussions. Sometimes engineers might be working with a process or organization that they don't know a lot about. For example, when I started in the ad-tech industry, a quick five-minute presentation was incredibly helpful for me to get a broad understanding of how the industry was structured, who the players were, and which way the money flowed.

While the presentation didn't answer all my questions, that was never the goal. The goal is to give attendees a rudimentary understanding of the space and to be armed with enough information so that they can form intelligent questions about it. If I asked you right now to ask me four questions about astrophysics, you might stumble a bit. If I gave you a five-minute primer on what astrophysics is, you would probably then be able to easily come up with four questions to ask. That's the goal of the lightning talk.

Introduction of new technology is another great usage of a lightning talk. Every organization has a small group of people who are experimenting with a new technology or an old technology that many people don't interact with that often. A quick five-minute presentation on that can be golden for people who are curious, but never have the opportunity to use or interact with the technology being discussed. It can also help to achieve buy-in on the technology if the lightning talk is structured in a way to explain the problems that the new technology is attempting to solve and why existing technology isn't up to the task. Again, going back to structuring information, getting an idea of what it is you're trying to convey and building your lightning talk around that is key.

Because lightning talks are short and incredibly focused, all of them should end with a slide that links people to more information about the topic. Remember, this is an introduction to the material. Pointing people to additional resources to continue their learning journey is important. Since you are the relative subject-matter expert, you have an obligation to point the audience in the right direction when it comes to finding more on the topic.

HOSTING EXTERNAL EVENTS

The industry tends to focus on the FANG companies (Facebook, Apple, Netflix, and Google) and the way they go about solving problems. But truth be told, most of you reading this book aren't facing the same types of challenges that the FANG group is. Most of us are solving the same problems over and over again en masse.

The wastefulness of this repetitive work might depress you at first, but it truly is a blessing in some ways. It means that somewhere, some organization just like yours has a working solution to your problem that you can reuse. This is where hosting external events can be beneficial.

The technology world is besieged with conferences, meetups, and networking events in pretty much every portion of the globe. If I go to meetup.com and type the word "DevOps" in the search box, I see meetups all over the world. There's probably one near you. If there isn't, I'm sure there's enough interest that starting one is an option. And don't limit your search to just DevOps, because there are many groups focused on different aspects of technology—database meetup groups, Kubernetes clubs, and coding camps, just to name a few.

Inviting these groups into your space is a great way to learn. Your team members probably have a lot of pressing obligations outside their work lives that make it difficult for them to engage with the tech community around them. But if you bring that community into your place of business, suddenly it becomes a lot easier for them to get involved, network with people outside the organization, and learn. Most of these groups are always looking for space to have a meeting hosted.

For the price of 20 pizzas and sodas, you can create not only a recruiting opportunity, but also a learning opportunity for all of your staff members. If you think about the big conferences that companies send workers to, most conference attendees will tell you the most valuable part of the conference is "the hallway track"—the organic conversations that happen between sessions and at the evening networking functions. In these informal settings, it's possible to cluster into your own groups to discuss the topics that are important to you, regardless of the conference agenda. Hosting networking events allows you to create this hallway track atmosphere without actually flying 20 engineers to a conference!

I highly suggest you look into your area and reach out to some of these groups to offer hosting. If you create an atmosphere for learning from groups outside the organization, then, through other means, individuals can share that information inside the company. Maybe after a networking event, you have a group of people perform a series of lightning talks on information they learned through their networking conversations. It's a strangely untapped resource that has tremendous upside with minimal expense.

BLOGGING

I've talked a lot about various presentation styles that people can create, but what if people aren't the presenting type? Many folks clam up in front of an audience, don't like the pressure of being in front of crowds, or generally hate creating slide decks. The blog is an often-overlooked tool for sharing information across the organization.

What's the difference between a blog and just writing internal documentation? The two are actually very closely related. To me, the difference between a blog and an official piece of internal documentation is small and lies mainly in the mind of the author. For a formal piece of documentation, mentally a business persona begins to take over. Your writing may become needlessly stiff, rigid, and formal. This transfer to a business dialect makes it difficult for some people to write documentation because it feels like contract writing. But a blog is usually much less formal, way less structured, and allows a bit of creative freedom in the writing process. If the choice is between no documentation and informally written documentation, I'll take the informal writing every time. Blog posts should still follow the teaching principles outlined previously to ensure that they're effectively communicating, but they're free of any rigid formatting requirements that might exist in a formal set of written documentation.

Another advantage to writing in a blog-style format is that it becomes easier for team members to subscribe to. With most blogging software, you can subscribe to an individual author or topic and get emailed when they make a post. Or if you still use an RSS reader, subscribing to the RSS feed is another popular option. The chronological order of blog posts is also helpful because it's more commonly accepted as a point-in-time entry. When you see documentation in a wiki or other official document repository, you may naturally assume that the documentation is up-to-date and current, because its implicit intent is to be a living, breathing document. A blog post, on the other hand, is commonly accepted as a document that was written in the moment and could suffer from some outdated information. As an example, if you saw a blog post about Donald Trump from 2004, you wouldn't be surprised that it's written outside the context of his presidency. But if you went to Donald Trump's Wikipedia page and saw no mention of his presidency, you'd be a little mystified. That's the sort of silent expectations people place on blogs versus official documentation. I might follow the commands of a wiki page without hesitation, but a blog post would cause me to verify the age of the post, whether the command is still valid, and so forth.

Blogging can be a great avenue for those who don't want to create presentations or feel paralyzed by the rigidness imposed on official documentation.

Remember to stay focused on the documentation outcome you want. The goal is about the organization having the knowledge necessary to operate, even in the face of staff disruptions or attrition. Don't become obsessed with the format in which knowledge sharing takes place. Unless the format is mandated by something external like an auditor, encourage information sharing via whatever method allows it to take place.

10.5   *Using chat tools effectively*

Chat tools are on the verge of becoming ubiquitous in most organizations. If you don't have an official chat client at your company, chances are you have an unofficial one being used by teams in an ad hoc fashion. With many chat tools offering free solutions, it doesn't take much for a small group of employees to decide that they'll be using chat with or without the company's blessing.

If used appropriately, chat tools can serve as an awesome method of sharing information across teams. But if you don't have rules in place and corporate etiquette defined, your productivity gains will quickly be absorbed by cat pictures and cupcake recipes.

10.5.1   *Establishing company etiquette*

Each company seems to use chat tools slightly differently. Some companies are dismayed when every decision doesn't appear in a chat log somewhere, and others have a point of diminishing returns, where that chat conversation moves into a physical meeting. There's no right or wrong answer on how to approach it, but it is important to have an idea about how the organization should behave. Sometimes this culture will evolve naturally and might differ from team to team. Sometimes you will need hard-and-fast rules about how people should engage. The following are a few rules that I suggest people try to help keep chat manageable.

USE SHORT-LIVED, TOPIC-FOCUSED CHANNELS

One of the really great things about using chat tools to coordinate and discuss ideas is that they're searchable. This can be an immense tool for new hires to understand the context around a decision or even for long-time employees who have forgotten a few details. But even with the power of search, people probably use the words "database failover" quite a bit. If you're searching for details on a particular database failover almost three years later, it can be almost impossible to make sense of it all.

This is where I like to use small, short-lived channels. This is particularly useful when you're discussing an issue that is being tracked in whatever work-tracking system you use. If you're using a work-tracking system, name the channel after the ticket number. This becomes a much broader identifier for conversations. Through the ticket number, you can find real-time conversations around the issue (via chat search), commits made related to the ticket (via referencing the ticket in the commit message), and even how the work ticket relates to other projects (via the ticketing system itself).

If you're not doing work that relates to a ticket, giving the channel a descriptive name can help the results pop a bit easier. You might get 200 hits on "database failure" in the "#general" chat channel but if you get one hit in a channel that was named "database_failure_20180203," chances are that's going to be a bit more relevant to you. And even if it isn't, it's probably going to be an interesting read nonetheless.

The other nice thing about creating separate channels is that it makes the end of the conversation surrounding the topic obvious. In a more general chat channel, you'll notice that some conversations tend to get resurrected hours or even days later. Those conversations now have additional conversation interleaved with the points that you care about. When you have a separate chat channel with a sole purpose, it becomes a lot easier to control a lot of the casual chit-chat that inevitably occurs in chat.

Once a conversation has completed and the task has been finished or the issue resolved, archive the channel. This will help keep your overall list of channels to a somewhat manageable level as well.

USE THE THREADING FUNCTIONALITY

Many chat tools now are beginning to offer *threading functionality*. This allows you to collapse many messages under a single message header. It prevents you from polluting the main timeline of the chat application and keeps specific conversations grouped together. But unlike creating a separate channel, this remains in the primary channel so that others who might be interested in joining the conversation can find it quickly and participate.

Threading is especially useful with larger teams, where you might have more than one conversation happening at the same time. While a small group is discussing an object model design, another group in the same chat channel can have a conversation about the latest internet meme that's going around.

The key to good thread participation is knowing when to start a thread. The best time is at the very beginning, especially when you know you're going to be soliciting feedback. Start your threading message with something obvious like "Thread discussing the new object model" and then in your first message you can expound on the problem and what you're trying to solve. This provides a clear signal to everyone that they should be responding on the thread as opposed to the general chat. It also makes it handy to search for in the future, assuming you can remember the thread name!

UPDATE YOUR STATUS REGULARLY

Every chat application allows you to update your current status. Use this as often as possible, allowing for the description to accurately reflect what's going on. I have a status that's called "Heads-down work" when I'm in Do Not Disturb mode. This is used when I have some deep thinking work that requires me to have uninterrupted bits of time. I set that status, turn off notifications, and focus for that period.

Your status absolves you of the guilt of not being constantly available. If it's an emergency, people will find other ways to get in touch with you besides chat, so don't feel like you're letting people down. You just have to take responsibility for your time.

LIMIT USE OF ALL CHANNEL NOTIFICATIONS

When users don't know who they need to focus a question to, they'll sometimes enter a channel and do a channel-wide notification or broadcast, typically done via @here, @all, or @channel depending on the tool you use. Try to discourage this as much as possible! It's the real-world equivalent of walking into a meeting and demanding that everyone answer your question right now.

Being able to tag a user in a message to draw attention to it is a useful tool to help people manage conversations that need their attention. But if people use the @here, @all, or @channel aliases, everyone will get a notification that they have a message waiting for them. Just like with noisy alarms, over time people will become desensitized to notifications generally.

In some tools, you can control who can use these aliases. Try to limit it to a select few people with clear guidelines on when they should be used.

10.5.2 *Moving beyond just chat*

Once you've become accustomed to working in chat tools, you'll quickly realize an even greater upside to using chat collaboration tools, especially around execution and automation. When you think of your chat tool as an automation command line, you can begin to open up a realm of possibilities that is incredibly powerful.

THE BENEFITS OF CHATBOTS

Tools like Hubot (https://hubot.github.com/) allow you to use your chat tool as an interface into automation frameworks. This is empowering on a few levels. For starters, it opens up where and how people can interact with systems. In my current environment at Centro, I've launched database restores from my phone while shopping for groceries. The chat interface is usually consistent across all manner of devices, opening up the types of commands you can execute that may normally have required you to log in to a computer.

Another benefit is that these commands and their outputs take place in a channel with all the other channel participants. This increases the visibility of remediation and troubleshooting efforts. So often in an incident-management type of scenario, you agree on a course of action, and someone executes the commands on their terminal, where only they see the output unless they explicitly share it. But with a tool like Hubot, the entire room sees not only the command that was executed (for repeatability), but also the output the command generates and the conversation around that output (for shared learning).

Chatbots are also a tremendous tool when you need to revisit the situation as part of a follow-up postmortem. Conversation, actions, and results are all neatly packed together in a single page. No more conversations trying to discern which commands ran in what order. All of it is laid bare in a nice timeline in the chat channel.

SHARED RESPONSIBILITY WITH CHATBOTS

Another advantage to chatbots is the idea of shared responsibility. As discussed in earlier chapters, access restrictions often prevent a broader audience from being able to use tools and automation. Even if something has been heavily automated, a user might need to log on to a production server to execute the command. With a tool like a chatbot, the interface and the automation become separated, allowing for a much broader audience to be able to use these tools.

You still need to do due diligence to make sure the commands aren't harmful when executed, or worse, when executed incorrectly. But as I outlined earlier, these are really requirements for any automation you build. Chatbots allow you to share the responsibility of certain tasks with other users who might not have as permissive a set of rights as the operations team.

The topic of chatbots is vast and deep and well beyond the scope of this book. But if your organization gets comfortable with regards to chat and working via chat, you might want to consider using a chatbot to automate more of your workflows. As I mentioned earlier, Hubot is a great place to get started, as it handles a lot of the chat components for you. Another great option to look into is StackStorm (https://stackstorm.com/). StackStorm takes a lot of the effort for chat automation and builds it into a relatively easy set of tools to begin doing your own automation. It also includes a nifty workflow engine, allowing you to tie a series of steps into an automation plan with little to no programming necessary.

Summary

- Allow knowledge sharing to occur in different formats for different types of subject-matter experts.
- Create learning rituals as an alternative to standard written documentation.
- Create structure around documentation repositories to make information retrieval easier.
- Gatekeepers to information can create accidental information hoarding.

Culture by decree

11

The *culture by decree* antipattern happens when an organization's culture is defined by a verbose statement or plaque that hangs in the main lobby but doesn't exist, in any tangible sort of way, within the organization itself. A culture must be fostered, grown, and be demonstrable in action, not just in rhetoric.

There's a single question that gets asked in almost every interview: "What's the company culture like?" The prominence of this question hints at the importance and the weight that company culture carries. But the answer that you get back from the interviewer isn't always true or demonstrable. It's a string of sentences and catchphrases that have been ingrained in workers so deeply that they may not even question what they mean or if they're even true.

If you're looking at the title of this chapter and thinking to yourself, "My company already has a Ping Pong table and beer taps; we've got culture nailed!", then you should probably read this chapter twice. Culture goes beyond the fun activities at office parties and the wide variety of gluten-free snacks provided in the break room.

Enron was named one of the "100 Best Companies to Work for in America" by Fortune magazine in 2000 (http://mng.bz/emmJ), citing its culture and amazing workforce as major contributors for its success. But it soon became apparent that Enron's actual culture was radically different from its stated culture. Greed fueled the organization from the top all the way down to the line employees. While the perks heaped upon the teams might indicate a caring, employee-first environment, the moral compass that guided the company was rotten. By December 2001, Enron was filing for bankruptcy amidst the largest financial accounting scandal in US history. I'm sure the victims of Enron's collapse took some comfort knowing they had awesome holiday parties.

Culture has become an obsession among business leaders. One of the most well-known idioms on culture comes from management guru Peter Drucker: "Culture eats strategy for breakfast." When companies go through hiring, there is an almost unhealthy obsession with ensuring that the candidate fits the organization's culture.

But why is culture so important in a DevOps organization? Because the culture sets the tone of how work gets done. It allows some behaviors while demanding others. If the emphasis of the company culture is on output and not quality, even those quality-minded employees are forced to abandon their principles in order to keep pace with team members focused less on quality and more on output.

Bad cultures eventually lead to bad outcomes. A company with a good, strong culture doesn't implode in financial scandal. A company with a culture of fear and retribution doesn't have an open and collaborative working environment. Instead, it has turf wars and kingdom builders.

In the DevOps community, culture is used to produce more desirable working environments, with teams marching toward a common goal. Culture is used to create better outcomes. To do these things, it's important to understand what culture is, how it fits into your organization, and how a bad culture could already be slowing down your teams. Culture is not immutable, but changing it takes effort and a deliberate break from the status quo.

This chapter is split into two halves. In the first half, I discuss the structure behind a company's culture and how you can help influence it. In the second half, the chapter's emphasis switches to hiring. Hiring is an important part of maintaining the culture and keeping it on a solid trajectory. Many tech organizations focus so much on algorithms during their interviews that they fail to evaluate the softer skill sets and whether a candidate possesses the human qualities needed to make the company thrive. A single bad hire can potentially wreck much of what you begin to build with regards to culture.

11.1   *What is culture?*

Culture is defined as a set of shared values, rituals, and beliefs that distinguishes one group of people from another. This macro definition encompasses all types of cultures, from teams, to entire companies, to entire countries. Values, rituals, and underlying assumptions are the three knobs that you can use to identify and change the culture inside an organization.

11.1.1   *Cultural values*

Cultural values are the principles and standards that an organization believes are essential to the way it governs and conducts itself. Cultural values are sometimes encapsulated in a company's mission statement as part of its guiding principles. Regardless of where they manifest themselves, they are supposed to serve as a written testament to the ideals that the company emphasizes. For an example, Enron's four core values were as follows:

- Respect
- Integrity
- Communication
- Excellence

These values are not completely expressive, but they give you a sense of what the company purportedly cared about with regards to the behavior of the organization and its employees.

Cultural values, however, do not exist in a vacuum. Values are just declarations without action. Cultural norms are the activities that bring cultural values into something tangible.

> **DEFINITION**   *Cultural norms* are the behaviors and activities that express an underlying value. Cultural norms are the rules or actions that a group makes to enforce their values. As an example, the cultural norm of paid family leave time is an expression of the cultural value of supporting families.

When you think of cultural norms, you should think of rules or guidelines in your organization that are designed to elicit desired behaviors. For example, your company might have a *value* around employee health and well-being. The *cultural norm* for that might be a program that reimburses employees for their gym membership. By removing the financial barrier of joining a gym, the company hopes to encourage gym membership and usage, which in turn promotes employee health.

Being able to identify cultural norms is an important process if you want to ensure that your company values are more than just a declaration. Cultural values without cultural norms are just empty platitudes.

11.1.2 *Cultural rituals*

Cultural rituals are specific ceremonies or actions that are performed within an organization. For example, a cultural ritual that exists at the company I work for is to send an introduction email to the entire technology group when a new hire starts. The email consists of the employee's preferred name, their role in the organization, their seating location, their previous job, college education, a photo, and four interesting facts about the employee (provided by the employee).

This ritual accomplishes two things. It helps new employees feel welcome. It also gives current employees an easy opportunity to introduce themselves and strike up conversation. Prompts provided by the interesting facts portion of the introduction email help avoid those awkward first few minutes of topic searching.

Cultural rituals can also exist within a larger process framework within your company. Many development organizations practice the *Agile method* of software development.

> **DEFINITION** The *Agile method* is an approach to software development whereby requirements and solutions evolve over time through collaboration among cross-functional teams.

The Agile method is filled with rituals that help support its style of work and collaboration. The most commonly encountered ritual is the *stand-up meeting.* The idea behind the ritual of stand-up meetings is to provide a forum for frequent check-ins with members of the teams in order to discuss the current assignment of work. Team members talk about what they worked on yesterday, what they plan to work on today, and any issues that are impeding them from getting their work done. The ritual is performed with all members standing to encourage a laser-sharp focus on the meeting and prevent rambling updates. But if you've ever been part of a stand-up, you know that standing isn't a deterrent for someone who loves talking to a crowd.

Rituals are reflective of the cultural values of a group. A *value* of employee well-being leads to *cultural rituals* of Monday yoga classes in the office. Without rituals, it can be difficult to bring a group of individuals to rally around a central theme or idea. Rituals, like the new hire email example, can also be used as an indoctrination into a new process. The ritual can serve as an easy, guided transition into something new for the employee. With teams that have on-call rotations, an employee taking their first on-call shift can also be used as a celebration, a rite of passage, signaling the end of a new-hire's transition period.

Throughout your organization, rituals of all shapes and sizes are taking place. Some are performed as celebrations, some as keepers of momentum, and others as rites of passage. It's important to understand the rituals in your organization and to ensure that they're promoting the beliefs or values you intend.

You may not be able to set the culture at an organizational level, but plenty of opportunities exist to tweak the culture at a more micro level. Think of all the cultural rituals and norms that are set inside a small team: practices as small as pull-request etiquette, requiring unit tests, and automation. These are all rituals and norms that exist on a team that might not be enforced organizationally but that you can help enforce within your sphere of influence. Even things as simple as the way team meetings are run can have an impact on how team members view the organization culturally.

It can be easy for a weekly status meeting to quickly devolve into a regular gripe session among peers. Blowing off steam is a favorite pastime in the office. But be wary when it starts to impact team members' long-term views on the organization and what the organization is or is not capable of. Don't miss the opportunity to recognize how the little things happening within your team are still aspects of a culture.

11.1.3 *Underlying assumptions*

The *underlying assumptions* of a group are the most limiting of factors to an organization's capabilities. If you've ever had a discussion about big changes to a company's way of working, you'll always find someone who will say, "That could never work here." That statement is an expression of an underlying assumption.

The employee feels that something about the organization—whether it's talent, capabilities, or government regulations—prevents the company from change. If enough people in your company believe this, the assumption becomes fact as people become handcuffed by the mindset. Examples of underlying assumptions are as follows:

- The company could never release twice per week because of our customers.
- Agile software development would never work here because it's not structured enough.
- There is no way for us to deploy software without taking application downtime.
- Our process is too complex to automate.

These are just a few examples, but I'm sure that you can probably add a lot more to this list. Assumptions create a culture in which questions aren't asked, and a better way of doing things is so far outside the realm of possibilities that even making the attempt seems like a fool's errand.

Underlying assumptions don't always have to be negative. In a company with a strong culture, the assumptions that employees carry around with them are part of what makes the company strong. Take these assumptions, for example:

- Management will support a well-reasoned and argued idea.
- I'm empowered to make a change if necessary.
- The organization won't accept a manual process.
- If no one is working on a fix for an issue, leadership may not be aware of it.

It doesn't take much imagination to think of the differences in behaviors that these contrasting assumptions would produce. Underlying assumptions about the organization shape the framing of a particular problem. If you're burdened by negative assumptions, breaking out of that mold and coming up with innovative fixes can become incredibly difficult.

With these three components of a culture in mind (cultural values, cultural rituals, and underlying assumptions), you have the basis for a culture's genesis. But cultures, good or bad, spread through the organization, encapsulating every corner. Understanding how culture is shared is an important aspect if you ever hope to change it.

11.2 How does culture influence behavior?

In the previous section, I discussed the three knobs that you can use to modify your company culture. But how does culture influence the way your employees perform and behave? Well, these three areas (values/norms, rituals, and underlying assumptions) create a sphere of expectations affecting anyone who is part of this culture. And an organization allows its culture to create either a positive or a negative set of expectations. I'll use an example to highlight.

Justin has just joined the development team of a financial institution named Web Capital. The company has put a tremendous amount of investment in automation, testing, and reproducibility of environments. Justin comes from a company where a lot of work was done manually, without much automation or test coverage. Even code review sessions were a hit-or-miss requirement at this former company.

Justin gets his first individual coding assignment. His requirement is to create a new feature that allows customers to make scheduled transfers to other account holders at Web Capital. When Justin submits his first code change to the team, they review it and immediately critique it because it doesn't meet their standards:

- No automated testing is present with the change.
- The feature relies on a manually executed database change to set up data.
- No log messages are generated.

Justin has never worked with automated testing before, nor has he ever had to create an automated, repeatable database change. The rest of the team members at Web Capital are resolute in their defending of values. With additional coaching and training, Justin makes the appropriate changes, resubmits the changes, and receives swift approval.

This is an example of how culture can influence behavior. If it weren't for the reviewers insisting on Justin meeting the cultural norms of the team, he could have easily slipped his substandard change into the pipeline. Someone else might come across it two or three weeks later and used it as a justification for submitting a similarly below-norms change. Eventually, this replicates and eats away at the value and its supporting norms. But the culture of the team and the enforcement of its norms created a level of conformity that keeps the standards of the group intact.

This example highlights how culture acts as a binding agent across teams and organizations. It can force high standards or allow low ones. In a 2018 letter to shareholders, Amazon CEO Jeff Bezos wrote on the teachable nature of high standards (http://mng.bz/pzzP). They are not an intrinsic quality that people either have or they don't. But teaching of standards requires discipline and requires a culture that will accept nothing less.

No one would ever dream of going to Google and submitting a coding change with no automated testing. Why is Google different from your company? Because of what they do and don't allow through their culture. It doesn't take a staff of 400 engineers to simply state what's acceptable and what's not. You just need to be deliberate about the things that are antithetical to the way you want your team to function. But before you can do that, you have to understand what exactly are the things that you and your team care about.

11.3 *How do you change a culture?*

Identifying the components of a culture has prepared you for the mother of all tasks: changing your organization's culture. The first thing to do is establish the underlying assumption that you are capable of doing this. Cultures can often have a single catalyst.

The change might start small, just inside your team, but as you learn how culture spreads, you can reach a much broader audience. Have you ever had a single person leave a company or an organization, and then had people remark on how much the culture changed after they left? "It just stopped being fun after Quintez left the company!" This is a testament to the power a single person can have on a group of people. To change a culture, though, it's important to understand how culture is transmitted through a social group.

11.3.1 *Sharing a culture*

When you think of a culture, you think about the commonalities among people who belong to that culture. *Language* is probably one of the biggest components of cultural sharing because it's the basis for communicating about your culture.

You use language to share *stories* and ideas. Through language, you organize and build institutions that further the ideals of your culture. Inside the various institutions, you build and communicate *rituals* as an expression of your shared beliefs and values. Language is at the heart of all of expressions of culture.

SHARING CULTURE THROUGH LANGUAGE

When you talk to a peer at work, what you say and how you say it reveals a lot about the environment that you work in and how you view it. Through language and the way you speak about your coworkers, you can quickly assess which teams you work well with, which teams you don't, and the level of respect you have for each.

This language, good and bad, is transmitted throughout your team as members mimic the behaviors of others in the group. If you're constantly talking poorly about the database administrators, it's not long before those around you also have a negative view of the database administrators. It's easy to conceive of the negative aspects of language, but it can also be used for positive influences.

The same way that language spreads negative sentiments, it can also spread positive interactions and influences. For a basic example, think of the simple phrase "I don't know." Being able to openly say something as simple as this can communicate numerous values or norms in the culture of your team or organization.

For starters, right on the surface, the statement communicates an acceptance of not always having the answer. This lifts a huge psychological burden off the shoulders of team members who, especially in technology fields, feel a constant compulsion to know anything and everything about their job. Being able to say "I don't know" rejects this unrealistic doctrine of technological omniscience.

Beyond the pressure of needing to know everything, being able to say "I don't know" reveals a vulnerability in a person that can be difficult to see in a work environment. That vulnerability humanizes team members in a way that makes it OK to be a mere mortal, full of mistakes, biases, and misguided assumptions. This vulnerability allows you to instill a sense of candidness about yourself and others. Suddenly, concerns like skill-set gaps can be interpreted as the innocent critique that they are, as opposed to an indictment on someone's worthiness of their station and title. To some, this may sound overly dramatic, but many others are nodding in agreement.

With just a simple phrase like "I don't know," we've explored how a culture gets shared through language. With the turn of a phrase, language can also express underlying values. The television show *New Amsterdam* on NBC features a young, bright doctor named Max Goodwin, who has been charged with turning around the failing hospital New Amsterdam. Dr. Goodwin intends to place the focus of the hospital back on patient care, and his intent is to empower the remaining staff at the hospital to focus on customer care.

New Amsterdam as a show uses language quite a bit to highlight Goodwin's underlying values of empowerment and patients first. His signature phrase in the show is "How can I help?" Whenever a staff member or a patient comes to Goodwin with a problem, his first response is almost always "How can I help?" Similar to the "I don't know" response, this phrase says a lot about an organization's culture.

First, it highlights that despite his relatively high-ranking position, Dr. Goodwin is accessible and is there to help service and facilitate his staff's needs. How much more empowered would you feel if you knew that when you brought a problem to your boss's office, they would reliably respond with offers of assistance?

Second, Goodwin's approach leaves the problem squarely in his staff's court. He doesn't relieve them of the problem or burden; it's still theirs to solve. But he does offer his experience and influence as a leader to help get the resources they need to solve the problem themselves. This is another example of how language and the way you use it can help establish your culture, but also make it spread. (As you can imagine, other characters begin using the phrase as well, leading to a spread of the culture.)

Language is a catalyst for the advance of culture because it's at the cornerstone of your social structure. Through language, you can use stories and lore to help solidify ideas and abstract concepts.

SHARING CULTURE THROUGH STORY

Humans have been telling stories in one fashion or another since the beginning. Humanity identifies with stories better than just a straight narrative, allowing us to distill numerous ideas and concepts into a form that's easily reproducible and engaging. Stories in organizations often lack the entertainment factor, but they serve a similar role.

Every company I've ever been at has someone who has been there for a considerable amount of time and is the keeper of a lot of lore. They can explain any situation with a story describing how the organization got into a particular state. The change management process may have its roots in a specific system outage that gets recounted in increasing fashion each time it's told.

But this strikes at the heart of how we spread the state of our culture through tales. For example, think of the stories of outages that happen in your company. These stories are more than just folklore. They're used as justification of current behaviors. I remember a company I worked for had a dramatic tale of how a developer once implemented a caching layer in the application, which subsequently led to an enormous amount of downtime as the caching layer didn't function quite as expected. (Cache invalidation can still be pretty tricky.)

This story got passed around until everyone feared a caching layer and removed it from the toolbox of solutions. The removal resulted in a lot of friction in the organization as people attempted to work around this deficiency. The pain gets compounded when the best tool for the job is also the most feared and prohibited.

Stories of joy can also be the bedrock of a company's culture, giving it purpose and shaping its attitude toward tackling problems. So many tech companies have started in some garage in Silicon Valley that the origin story feels like a tired trope. But for the companies that spawned from these tales, the story acts as a guiding principle throughout the building. Teams describe themselves as scrappy, inventive, experimental, whatever-it-takes kind of players—underdogs in a fight with bigger, more well-resourced competitors.

Some companies carry this culture beyond its applicability, even as they become the 800-pound gorilla of the industry. The origin story fuels their culture. It's so powerful that the narrative it creates inside the company has an impact that endures through the company's expansive growth. Stories are powerful in the way they engage people and get them to understand, empathize, and commit to a higher purpose. Stories are a perfect method to transmit your company culture.

SHARING CULTURE THROUGH RITUAL

If you think back to a positive experience in your family upbringing, chances are it centers around some sort of ritual. Holiday meals, annual summer vacations, birthday party celebrations, and even family movie nights are all examples of rituals that happen within families.

These same sorts of rituals take place inside your company and are a big part of how the company shares its values to employees. The Centro new hire email mentioned earlier in this chapter is an example of how the Centro value of employee comfort and belonging is expressed. Technology teams often express their values through code reviews and other development practices.

A good technology organization has a healthy respect for complexity. This respect is turned into a value, and that value is expressed through the ritual of pair programming. In *pair programming*, two developers work side-by-side on the same piece of code. One person writes the code, while the second, at the same workstation, reviews each line of code as it's typed. This way of working allows one person to focus on the actual act of writing the code, while the other serves as an observer and as a guide throughout the process. The developers switch roles frequently so that both have a solid understanding of the code being written.

This process gets turned into a ritual as people develop their own sets of schedules, rhythms, and communication styles. The ritual infuses the values of collaboration, communication, and constructive feedback. If you work in an environment where pair programming is a must, not only can you not escape the ritual, but you're also coerced into it by the organization's cultural norms.

A group doesn't allow its members to continue violating the cultural norms of the group. Through feedback, group social pressures, and sometimes even punishment, members of the group engage in the group's rituals. One of the hidden powers of rituals is their ability to instill conformity. But this power cuts both ways. Are your rituals producing net positive effects or magnifying the negatives? Be sure to cultivate the rituals that are creating the cultural impact your teams are looking for.

Language, stories, and ritual are three key ways in which culture is transmitted, good or bad. Now that you know the three main ways a culture spreads through an organization, you can look at how to go about changing the culture to one you can be proud of.

11.3.2 An individual can change a culture

Imagine you're at a going-away party for a colleague. She's been at the company for several years and is well-respected throughout the organization. Everyone is stopping by the party to wish her good luck with her next big adventure. These parties are always filled with coworkers sharing the sentiment that the place will never be the same without that high-caliber person. I like to describe these people as *culture chiefs*.

> **DEFINITION** *Culture chiefs* are employees who embody the cultural values of the organization. Regardless of their level in the organization, they are considered influencers in the company. They're often considered the emotional leaders of a team or group.

The culture chief has the power to completely transform the way a team or department is organized or how it functions. How can that be? Can a single person really shape the emotions of an entire organization?

When a brilliant jerk leaves the company, no one is distraught about the emotional cavity left in their wake. The brilliant jerk might be a wellspring of information and knowledge, but they fail to share the warmth that an employee who embodies the company's values brings. It's hard to quantitatively compare a brilliant jerk's 5,000 code commits to the hours that a culture chief spends encouraging debate, mentoring younger engineers, and pushing the team to do better while not completely disparaging the team's previous work. But whether you're a culture chief or a brilliant jerk, be assured that a single person can change a culture for good or ill.

THE CULTURE CHIEF

The culture chief is easily spotted in a company. They're the person embodying the cultural values that the company promotes. In teams that value collaboration and mentorship, the culture chief can be found in meetings discussing ideas, weighing the pros and cons of different approaches, and inviting dissent from their opinion.

The culture chief is a joy to work with and tries to be above the petty disputes that plague a lot of other cross-functional relationships. The culture chief has the power to change a team, department, or organization through their thoughtfulness, the shedding of ego, and their focus on the larger goal.

A brilliant jerk or a bad culture chief?

It can be easy to assume that the culture chief always is someone to be admired. But if your company doesn't have strong, positive values, the culture chief can quickly become someone who manifests the negative aspects of your culture.

In a team that values individual effort and exhibits a winner-take-all worldview, you'll find the culture chief berating someone for what they deem is a stupid mistake. But the mistake is always viewed through the experience lens of the person passing judgment and not the person who made the mistake. There is no empathy in this environment.

Does your company have a lot of brilliant jerks? If so, examine what your hiring practices are like and what's attracting the brilliant jerk personality type to the company. But you need to be certain that you're distinguishing between a brilliant jerk, and a bad set of cultural values and norms.

Your culture chief could simply represent the poor cultural norms your company has. Having a lot of brilliant jerks and a bad set of culture norms are two distinct problems with different solutions. Brilliant jerks require hiring and firing; fixing poor cultural norms is the subject of this chapter.

Every organization has at least one culture chief. It might even be you. If you're trying to make a cultural change, there's no better gift than having a well-respected culture chief be an advocate for change alongside you. Individuals can change a company culture.

It will seem like a daunting task, but culture change can be sparked as long as people know where the change is headed and what it will bring. If you feel your company is in need of a cultural shift, you're probably not alone. Your peers, all the way up the chain to your company president, probably feel that something is off. If you're not in the C-suite of offices, chances are you have an even better perspective on what's wrong than the executive team, making you better equipped to usher in the change needed.

To get started, you should examine your company's core values. If you don't know what those values are, ask human resources for a copy of your company's mission and values statement. This statement will serve as the foundation for all the changes and decisions you'll make going forward. Keep in mind, however, that these are the company's *stated* values, not their *actual* values.

But after you have the stated values, it becomes a lot easier and defensible to compare and contrast activities against the stated values. If your organization has quality as one of its core stated values, that doesn't track against cutting out the testing portion of the project. Highlighting that to leadership may not necessarily change things, but it highlights the hypocrisy. Pay close attention to how the organization deals with the misalignment of rhetoric and reality. It can tell you a lot about the company's true values.

11.3.3 *Examining your company's values*

Before you can begin, you must have a strong understanding of your company's values. When you start this journey of changing a culture, your company values will be the shield for your actions. If the company has established that these core values are important to it, setting up processes and activities that express these values can be difficult to argue against. If the company values community service, organizing a company outing to volunteer at a local food pantry should receive widespread support.

For my example company, I'll list the company's values as follows:

- Collaboration
- Candid and open conversation
- The wellness of the whole employee
- Being a part of the community

With these values in hand, you can begin thinking of the cultural norms that you can set inside your company through language and ritual. Starting with language is the easiest method because it doesn't require a ton of buy-in from others. As long as your culture chief is on board, you have a pretty good chance of making a change.

Changing the language in support of your company values can have a powerful effect among your team members. Think of the previous example regarding the TV show *New Amsterdam.* "How can I help?" was a piece of language that helped to influence the mindset of the team members. The same phrase would be extremely helpful in this example, in tying it to the collaboration value. Candid and open conversation is a value that can benefit from a change in language.

Candid conversation typically doesn't happen within teams because people fear insulting or hurting the person they're talking to. Having a poor relationship with team members can put an enormous anchor on the happiness you get from your job. Many people opt to just avoid conflict. This can lead to paralysis in your organization as people are not having difficult conversations with each other or the type of rigorous debate that produces better outcomes, better designs, and better products. Sparking this cultural change could be as simple as changing the language around having candid conversations. An example is to use language that acknowledges that your feedback is coming from your perspective, as opposed to it being a categorical truth. I'll give an example.

Kiara is a developer who has been working on a new piece of software for the company that is set to launch in the coming days. Chin is an operations engineer who is in charge of setting up all of the infrastructure for the software launch. Chin is adamant that the team perform exhaustive performance testing prior to the application's launch. Kiara, who has gauged demand for the software, feels that the effort necessary to performance-test the software now is too great when weighed against the valuable user feedback they can get by launching immediately. Chin has fears that the application design and needed infrastructure might not support any growth beyond Kiara's predictions.

Both sides make valuable points. Kiara could interact with Chin in a few ways. For example, Kiara approaches the subject and says, "We don't need to performance test now. There won't be that many users, and it's better to get feedback from users right away." From Chin's perspective, this isn't really a conversation. The language used is absolute. Where's the point of argument for Chin if everything is stated as an accepted fact?

Kiara has approached the subject as if everything stated is a universal truth. But she has merely spoken about her perspective, all of which is filtered and biased by the context in which she's operating.

This style of dialogue fuels the fire of conflict between teams. When you interact with other teams, you want to use language that does the following:

- Explicitly separates hard fact from perspectives or opinions that are drawn from that fact
- Uses phrasing that opens the floor for debate
- Establishes the end goal of your action

A better version of Kiara's statement could be, "We've done some end-user surveying, and the data suggests that we're only going to get about 50 users. From my perspective, I think the application should easily support 50 users, and if we get more, I think it's a risk worth taking. The company is betting a lot on this solution long-term, but we need to ensure we're building what the customer wants first." This version will take Kiara about 20 seconds extra to say aloud, but it takes Chin from a position of frustration to a position of debate.

Now Chin understands the background of what's being asked and why performance testing may not be needed now. In the first version, Chin is uncertain when performance testing does become important. Will it ever? Is Kiara just hostile to the extra work? A lot of reasoning needs to be made up and filled in by Chin. If you don't provide reasons or context around your messaging, the receiver of the message will fill it in. But what they use as filler may not be accurate.

This is a simple example in a single exchange, but when this pattern replicates, you begin to have more open and honest conversations widely throughout the organization. This changes the culture in support of the values you've expressed. With a change in the way we communicate, we can begin to look at how our language combined with our rituals can be the driver for the cultural norms we adopt.

11.3.4 Creating rituals

Remember previously I stated that cultural norms are the enforcers of the culture. Your cultural norms are influenced by the way you communicate and the rituals you partake in among the group.

How many times have you asked someone what their plans are for September 25th? Probably not that often, and if you asked someone this, they might be puzzled. If you asked someone what their plans are for the 4th of July, they would instantly understand the context—because Americans are part of a shared culture, and the culture has a ritual of barbecues, fireworks, and spending time with friends and family in celebration of Independence Day.

You can use the power of rituals to create sets of shared behaviors among team members. In the context of an organization, there are really two types of rituals: social and process. A *social ritual* is one you're familiar with. It takes place in a social atmosphere, and relationship is the primary motivator. An example of a social ritual is a shared meal, the annual holiday party at your office, or happy hour. *Process rituals* are rooted in coercing the completion of a task, sometimes in support of a larger task. Process rituals are things like morning stand-ups, change approval board meetings, and performance reviews.

When you approach a new ritual, you need to ask yourself a series of questions:

1 What is the goal of the ritual?
2 What style of ritual are you creating (social or process)?
3 What is the expected output of the ritual?
4 What triggers the ritual's execution?

Defining the ultimate goal of the ritual might be the most important step. Are you attempting to build better relationships among your team? Or are you trying to get teams to perform better code reviews?

The ultimate goal for the ritual will give you the context needed for how to approach the ritual, and the type of ritual it is. You don't build stronger relationships and social bonds in a change approval meeting.

Next, you'll want to define the outputs of the ritual. The outputs will help you determine the effectiveness of the ritual. For social rituals, the output is most likely going to be something intangible, like learning something new about a colleague. For process rituals, the output can sometimes be an artifact of some kind—a finished review or a detailed comment on code.

Finally, you need to define what triggers the ritual. A spontaneous ritual is one that never happens with any real consistency. Any activity that isn't triggered or prompted by an event ultimately gets lost in the shuffle of the day. It's important that you define a specific trigger for your ritual.

The trigger could be based on a date, like happy hour every second Friday of the month. It might be based on a milestone, like the employee's 100th day on the job. It might be kicked off whenever an accident in the system happens that requires support activity. Whatever you decide, just make sure that you choose a trigger for the ritual. I'll walk you through an example.

EMBRACING FAILURE WITH RITUAL

At Web Capital, everyone hates touching the caching layer code. It's a tangled mess of indirection, overengineering, and a misunderstanding of the actual constraints of the system. The problem is that the caching layer is extremely critical to the overall operation of the system. Many people who make commits to it end up taking down the system. As a result, people don't touch the caching layer; they merely code around it.

Sasha, the new engineering manager, wants to change this. She has decided to create a ritual in which failure is celebrated and knowledge is shared. She wants the team to understand that failures will happen and that the team needs to simply deal with them in the right fashion. Her goal is to produce an understanding of why the failure happened and to create work to reduce the chance that it happens again.

She categorizes this as a process ritual, but still wants to mix in some social aspects. Any time a system failure occurs in the caching layer due to a code change, the team celebrates it. She decides that the team should have some fun with the ritual. They keep a wall chart that counts the number of days since a caching layer code change failure. She orders pizza for the team, and the meeting is open to anyone who wants to attend. The developer who takes the system down gives a presentation on the following:

- The intent for the change as compared to what the change actually did.
- Why everyone involved with the change thought it would work, expressing their understanding of and mental model of the system at the time of the change. Key factors to focus on are the different areas that led to that choice. Old documentation, an obfuscated or complex method, or poorly defined requirements are a few examples that lead into our mental model of systems.
- Why the change caused a failure, and the team's new understanding of the system. Focus on what was wrong with the mental model and how those things contributed.
- A walk-through of all the things that need to change to help people better understand the caching layer for the next change.

This presentation fits nicely with the postmortem process defined previously, but sometimes the ritual is useful on a smaller scale, even if it didn't create an outage or major incident. This scaled-down version of the postmortem ritual embraces the notion of failure, accepting that it's going to happen and that wishing it wouldn't is not a viable strategy.

The ritual instills a sense of organizational safety, the idea that mistakes are not fatal to your career with the company. It expresses the company value of collaboration and candid conversation. The discussion isn't centered around the idea that the developer made a mistake, but around how they made that mistake and the shortcomings not only of the developer in this scenario, but also of the system being worked in. Failure doesn't happen in a vacuum.

This template of ritual creation can be used to create and produce an array of behavioral and cultural changes. It will require some deep thinking on your part to fully understand the scope of behavior you're trying to influence. But once you understand those behaviors, walking through the steps of ritual creation will help you on your journey to change.

11.3.5 Using rituals and language to change cultural norms

Armed with your changes to language and your new rituals, you can begin to use these tools as the backbone for your cultural norms. It's not enough to simply define these things; it's important to also express when a cultural norm has been violated. Without that, your norms really aren't universal—not accepted by the entire team—and therefore will begin to die.

Nobody wants to be the only person on the team enforcing coding standards. If nobody else cares about the standard, that particular ritual or behavior will die. Cultural norms do need collective buy-in, but remember that the norm is nothing more than an expression of the value that the group already agreed to! If your company says it values the change approval process, and creates a ritual around the change approval process, then logically it follows that people who violate the process are informed of that violation.

In technology, we have the added advantage of being able to use technology to enforce a lot of our cultural norms. If you have values around automated testing and code review, you can have your source code management tool be the cultural norm enforcer through configuration. Maybe you have your source code tool configured with rules so that nobody can merge a code commit without at least one approval and one successful passing test build.

This enforces the cultural values of collaboration, by forcing your code to be reviewed by another person; and automated testing, by forcing that reviewed change to have a successful test run. Use your tools as much as possible, because they not only enforce the norms, but also inform the new user of those norms.

Take code linting, for example. *Linting* is the process whereby code is checked and validated to ensure it meets certain stylistic standards. If your team has staked its position on the dreaded tabs versus spaces debate, instead of needing a human to remind a developer of that during code review, the linting tool can be configured to warn the user through automation. Before ever submitting a code commit for review or talking to another team member, the developer has identified a cultural norm set by your team. This is just one of many ideas that you can use your automation for.

But often you'll need to travel outside the bits and bytes of code and enforce norms in the real world. Enforcing these norms reminds team members of the company's cultural expectations. Combining our language skills and our rituals can serve as a healthy way to remind people of the cultural norm violation. I'll give you an example.

Chad is a software developer who is looking to implement new functionality into the application. To do this, he opts for a new library that is getting a lot of buzz on the internet. Chad knows that this should probably go through the code architecture review team, but he also knows that process will take more time than he has. He skips it and gets some folks to approve the code commit under the assumption that the library has already passed the code architecture review team.

When the code architecture review team finds out, they discuss it with him. "Hey Chad. We noticed on July 8th you committed some code with a new library in it. It appears to me, though, that you may have skipped the architecture review process. This process is extremely important because it allows us to evaluate new tech and to also kick off certain other tasks like updating documentation about our dependencies, adding new security scans, and so on. Did you submit to the architecture team and I missed it? If you didn't, can you just make sure that you do this in the future? Thanks!"

Again, this response is a bit long-winded, but the extra 20 seconds you spend in communication pays huge dividends with regards to long-term behavior changes. To further extend the example, Chad should discuss his own frustrations with the turnaround time of the architecture review team. There could be added value in evaluating why a review takes so long and the impact that has on the speed of development. Architecture review doesn't occur in a vacuum, either. In a sense, the slow turnaround time of the architecture review helped to create the scenario of Chad feeling pressured to circumvent it. That doesn't necessarily excuse the omission, but it does suggest that the architecture review team might not be meeting the needs of the entire organization—namely, developers. I'll give a real-world example.

One day, my team implemented new alerting across our application build servers. A team member discovered a login to a Jenkins child server, which is unusual because the team almost never logs in to those servers. Upon inspection, it was discovered that a developer had gotten access to a (Secure Shell) SSH key for the Jenkins child server. He would occasionally use it to log in and fix connectivity to the Jenkins node. Normally, this would be performed by the operations team via a support ticket, but that ticket could take a day or more before it was seen, prioritized, and processed.

Even though the developer shouldn't have had SSH access, the operations team contributed to an environment in which the developer felt this was a necessary step. After some discussion on the nature of the issue, operations created commands that he had access to that would perform the remediation steps he needed in a safe, secure way. Through conversation, the team was able to further empower developers, which led to even deeper conversations about more efficient ways of working.

Continuous violation of cultural norms

If you have someone who continuously violates cultural norms, you may want to consider some sort of repercussions for that person. Maybe they lose direct commit privileges, or perhaps their code commits undergo additional scrutiny. Even better would be automation that detects the addition of a library and automatically adds the code architecture review team to the commit review.

11.4 Talent that matches your culture

Talent is crucial to a DevOps transformation and to your company's overall success. Talent and culture are so tightly intertwined because it's talent that will ultimately define your culture.

You cannot succeed in building a DevOps culture without having the right talent in place, both from a hard and soft skills perspective. The brilliant jerk who can't collaborate with teams is no more effective than the impassioned operations engineer who is a people person but can't automate workloads.

Finding and retaining talent can be one of the toughest hurdles in the DevOps journey. It requires time, energy, a thoughtful approach, and an almost constant mindset for recruitment. This section offers a few tips and strategies on finding the right people to flesh out your teams.

11.4.1 Old roles, new mindset

As I've discussed in previous chapters, DevOps is as much about a mindset as it is about hard skills. Your teams must begin to think about the totality of what it takes to bring systems online and to production. Teams must begin to adopt some of the concerns that were previously the purview of other groups.

Operations needs to think about the pains developers face, while developers need to think about how their systems run in production and have a sense of shared ownership of those production systems. Security teams need to balance out the needs of the business, weighed against the risks to the business, and viewed through the lens of the teams that need to implement and maintain it. Empathy is the core muscle that gives DevOps its strength.

The adage "You can't understand someone until you've walked a mile in their shoes" is apt for empathy in a DevOps context. The way your team's goals or metrics are defined can prevent empathy from taking hold, because your team goals are independent from one another. But as I'll discuss in chapter 12, you can begin to build empathy by having a set of shared goals. If you're in operations, it can be easier to empathize with the frustrations of developers if you're measured by similar goals. As a developer, being called in the middle of the night when a process goes bad gives you empathy for the operators who deal with it regularly. This shared responsibility approach is a way to systematically build empathy, but often it's just as effective to find people who have performed different roles previously and can empathize with another team because they've been in the situation before.

Having interest in another team member's job is the goal when preparing teams to adopt a new mindset. That interest might stem from shared responsibilities, as I've outlined, or it might be through innate curiosity or past experiences. But developers must have concerns about the operational side of things, and operations must have a similar sense of interest in development hurdles. For some employees, this interest might already exist, but for others, you may have to develop some prompting to get that interest flowing.

SHARING PROBLEMS THROUGH CONVERSATION

Creating empathy comes through dialogue and conversation. Team members who don't share an understanding of each other's problems probably don't do a lot of communicating with each other generally. An easy way to start this sort of empathy building is by creating natural interactions for the teams to get together and communicate. This can be something as formal as a regular knowledge-sharing session or something as informal as a brown bag lunch session. Crucial pieces of information that should be shared at these kinds of events are as follows:

- Current goals of the team and what they're trying to accomplish
- Current pain points that the team is running into
- Areas where the other team(s) might be able to assist

By sharing goals and pain points, you're giving team members an idea of the challenges your team is facing. This also creates a context for how other teams might be able to assist. If you find out a team is struggling with a custom metrics solution, the operations team might have the expertise necessary to lend a helping hand in solving that problem. The operations team might also recognize they haven't done a good job of advertising their tools that could help other groups that might have this problem.

A key point is that this is not a session for the teams to exchange work and hand out additional tasks. This session is intended only to bring awareness. If teams decide to take on work to help each other out, that's great! But it should be communicated up front that this meeting is for informational purposes only.

The reason for this is simple: nobody wants a meeting that results in more work being assigned to them. Most teams are already operating at capacity, with a backlog of work waiting to get done. Any new work needs to be accepted via the team's usual methods of accepting work. The goal of these interactions at this stage is not about solving the problems, but simply generating empathy for them by team members who are not immediately impacted. But again, set the expectations up front about the goals of the meetings, or you'll quickly see participation begin to decline.

If you can't get entire teams together, bringing individual team members together for conversations can be useful as well. Creating prompts to do this can be the nudge that people need to reach out to one another. In my office at Centro, we use a Chatbot plugin called *Donut* (www.donut.com), which randomly pairs two people and encourages them to meet for a donut or coffee. It does the pairing at a regular cadence, follows up with team members to confirm they've met, and reports on the number of successful meetings that have happened. This is a great tool to generate interactions between team members and for them to learn about the various problems other groups are facing. We've also done this between remote workers as well through video chat.

Even if your company doesn't use a chat collaboration tool, replicating this sort of functionality offline is incredibly easy. A low-tech solution of putting names in different buckets based on team and then pulling one name from each team bucket to form a pair works just as well. How the interactions come to be is much less important than the fact that they happen. Creating interactions between members of different teams is an incredible tool for generating empathy and sparking curiosity about another's role.

Generating empathy among existing teams is only part of the process. At some point, you'll have to hire new team members. And that process is never easy.

11.4.2 *The obsession with senior engineers*

In my experience, companies are obsessed with senior engineers. If they can afford it, companies would rather have someone with extensive experience coming in and adding value on day one. Senior engineers are in high demand.

But how do you or your company define a senior engineer? Years of experience is a typical barometer, but does it really provide the kind of qualitative data you're looking for? You could have an engineer who's been doing the same thing for 15 years. Looking at the operations space for a moment, you could have an operations engineer with 20 years of experience. But how much of that was spent using modern approaches like configuration management? If an engineer has 20 years of manually installing operating system software packages, depending on what you're looking for, that might be very different from three years of using configuration management software to do the same job.

If you're going to hire a senior engineer, it's important that you define what makes a candidate senior. Sometimes it can be the variety of experience combined with the number of years in the field. You might weigh years of experience more heavily because of the variety of problems that engineer has seen. It's much more likely that an engineer with 15 years of experience has seen a broader range of problems than an engineer with 5 years of experience. Which definition of experience is correct?

You must ask why those years of experience are required and if time is a good measure for experience. If you're looking for exposure to an array of problems, a consultant who travels to different client sites every six months would probably generate more experience in three years than someone with the same company for 10 years.

But if you're looking for someone with experience growing and maintaining a system and dealing with all of the cruft that comes up as a result, years of experience, particularly in a single company, becomes much more prudent.

The bottom line is, you have to define what seniority looks like. This will allow you to broaden your candidate search instead of scaring off potential applicants with job requirements that you don't care about.

Once you've defined seniority, the next question should be to challenge yourself on why you need that seniority. If it's because you need a technical leader to guide the team in design choices and decision-making, that's a solid reason. But if your team already has two or three senior engineers, it is more likely that you prefer the hard skills you think a senior engineer will bring over a more junior engineer.

A typical job description has several sections, one of which is requirements, usually taking the form of a bulleted list of skills matched with the number of relevant years of experience with those skills. But the misnomer here is that years of experience translates into level of proficiency. That may be true for some people and some styles of learners. But it's undeniable that many applicants just have a natural knack for this type of work.

They can pick up concepts, theories, and ideas and turn them into functional skills in far less time than others. Their experience with a technology can almost be measured in dog years! But based on how you've structured your job description, you've either dismissed the applicant or discouraged them from even applying. The three to six months you spend looking for a candidate that checks all your boxes could be spent getting a dog-year type of candidate whose concentrated exposure with a technology or skill fills the need of the role.

REMOVING YEARS OF EXPERIENCE

Trying to get away from years of experience as the measure of proficiency can be challenging. It's easy to imagine that an operations engineer with 10 years of experience in large Linux-based infrastructure environments has dealt with things like Logical Volume Manager, package management, basic filesystem navigation, and so on. But I would say if those skills are important to have on day one, just list them individually on the job description. Once you've listed these skills, you'll quickly realize that not all of them are essential, day-one skills.

Don't be paranoid if an engineer doesn't have a skill on day one. If it's not 100% necessary, there's nothing wrong with the engineer learning it on the job. One of the biggest skills that engineers have (or should have) is the ability to learn! Separate the must-have skills from the skills that you don't normally train people on. Give concrete examples of how people might demonstrate this proficiency to you.

As an example, say you have a requirement that currently reads as "two to three years of experience working with ActiveMQ Messaging." If you tease that apart, what experience do you really need? Does it have to be with ActiveMQ? Your real core requirement is that they have experience working in an asynchronous environment using a message or event bus. This could be broken down into a much more specific bulleted list:

- Recent experience working in an asynchronous processing environment
- Recent experience designing and implementing work queues and topics
- Experience designing deduplication algorithms to prevent duplicate work from being processed

These are skills that are demonstrated and may not require the two to three years of experience you're initially looking for. Maybe your candidate has spent the last year working on a project that dealt exclusively in this problem domain. Not only does this give the applicant the opportunity to craft their résumé to highlight this experience, but it also gives you an ample source of information to draw questions from about their experience during the on-site interview process. Someone may have worked at a company that uses a message bus, but their interaction with the bus was minimal. But consider this résumé portion:

- Lead Software Engineer: DecisionTech 1999 – October 2019
  - Developed and maintained our primary Java product platform
  - Implemented asynchronous messaging using ActiveMQ

This can be difficult for a hiring team to parse. Did the candidate spend 20 years working on the ActiveMQ implementation, or was it their first nine months on the job, never to be touched again? These are questions that can get ironed out during the interview process for sure, but if the experience requirements were more explicit, the applicant could more closely tailor the résumé to your needs. Not every applicant will do that, but the ones who do will most certainly rise to the top. This will help you weed through a potentially crowded field of applicants.

Senior engineers can be a boon to your team. Defining seniority isn't always an easy task, but once you do it, you can begin to focus your search on those specific skills that you need without a disproportionate balance on years of experience.

But sometimes the length of time it takes to fill the position begins to drain on the team. Interviews take up a considerable amount of team energy. At some point, you may recognize that a senior engineer isn't a necessity. Then you may want to consider looking at more junior engineers.

HIRING A JUNIOR ENGINEER

Junior engineers can be a fantastic addition to the team for a variety of reasons. For starters, junior engineers can be easier to mold in terms of your organization's style of work. Without years of exposure to a way of doing things, the junior engineer can easily adapt to a new style of working. This is a double-edged sword, of course, because it presumes that the style of working you're placing on the junior is a good one. It's just as easy to teach a junior engineer bad habits as it is to teach them good ones.

Hiring junior engineers also offers an opportunity for your more senior engineers to mentor. This is a way to broaden the scope of responsibility of senior staff members without forcing them into a management role. Many senior engineers want to remain technical, but still have the desire to share their expertise within a formal structure.

Mentoring is a great way to give the senior engineers on your staff that opportunity while at the same time providing an excellent opportunity for learning to the junior staff member.

Junior engineers can lower the cost of getting certain tasks done. You don't typically think of an engineer in an hourly fashion, but it's valuable to do so. A senior engineer doing work that a junior engineer could do robs the organization of the value and level of contribution that the senior engineer is capable of. You would never want the head chef of a restaurant also taking orders from the customers, because that's less time the chef would spend in the kitchen, where their time is more valuable. Junior engineers give you an opportunity to offload some of the less complicated, but still valuable, work being done by senior engineers. This isn't about dumping boring work onto junior engineers, but about making sure you're getting the most valuable output from your senior staff members.

> ### The learning curve of junior staff
> There's always a learning curve for junior staff members that comes at a cost of the senior engineer's time. To my knowledge, there is no good way to avoid paying this time tax.
>
> But this time tax dissipates over time. In addition, your senior engineers gain valuable mentoring time, and are forced to look at the system through the eyes of a novice. Sometimes this different perspective helps solve problems. A design may seem second nature to a senior engineer who has been working with it for the past five years. But to a novice, it may seem overly cumbersome or confusing. Being forced to explain it to someone not attached to the emotional legacy of the design can often lead to rethinking the approach in the future.

Regardless of whether you're hiring a junior or a senior engineer, interviewing can be a daunting process. You can do a couple of things in the interview to help the process along.

11.4.3 *Interviewing candidates*

The interview process is a bit stressful for all involved. Your team members are pulled from their day-to-day activities and must assume the role of the inquisitor. The typical interview process is the most unnatural setting to assess someone's skills for a job. Depending on the candidate, they may not do well under pressure. Nerves and anxiety can cloud their ability to think clearly.

Depending on the role, this could be a good thing to glean from a candidate. If they're applying for an operations role, you want to identify whether someone can't function in high-scrutiny, time-sensitive situations. If the position is for a QA engineer, the need to function in a high-pressure accident investigation environment may not be as prudent.

When you're designing your interviews, you should take this into account. If high-pressure scenarios are part of the job, you'll want to be able to simulate that during the interview process. If not, you'll want to ensure that the interview process can mimic the traditional working environment as much as possible.

THE INTERVIEW PANEL

Interviews should be conducted by more than one person, and if possible, by more than a single team. The hire for the position will undoubtedly work across various groups and departments in order to be successful. It's useful if some of these groups are represented in the interview panel in order to provide perspective on the candidate.

Each group should interview with at least two people, as it's useful to have a pair of perspectives from the same context. You want two developers interviewing from the developer context so that they can compare notes, two analysts from product so they can compare notes, and so forth. Not all areas need to be represented, but it's important that interactions with nontechnical staff are accommodated.

The hiring manager should be part of the interview panel but can either sit in with their functional area's portion of the interview or have their own separate interview. I find it more efficient for the hiring manager to participate on another panel so that the interview the hiring manager participates in, has someone else to offer perspective. For example, if the hiring manager does their own interview, no one is there to challenge or give perspective on their observations. If the candidate "seemed to not give full answers" to a hiring manager conducting the interview alone, there's no one to give a different perspective on that observation. Two people in the same interview might have two completely different reads on an exchange.

Try to avoid having overly lengthy interview processes. As the interview process drags on, candidates can begin to fatigue, presenting a very different persona than to the earlier interview teams. Unless seeing that sort of degradation is valuable for the position you're filling, try to keep the interview to a single morning or a single afternoon. If your interview requires a lunch break, it's probably too long.

Make sure you meet with the interview panel and understand what each group will be asking of the candidate. It might be worthwhile to have some groups overlap on questions so that you can see whether the answers differed based on who was asking.

With the panel assembled, you'll want to look at structuring the interview questions so that you're sure to hit all of the areas you intended to hit.

STRUCTURING THE INTERVIEW QUESTIONS

The interview should be designed to elicit answers based around a few key areas of hiring:

- Organizational values fit
- Team values fit
- Technical capability

These categories are equally important. A strong technical hire is useless if they can't integrate with the team or if they hold beliefs antithetical to the team's beliefs. If the hire has a set of values that don't match the organization's, a constant source of friction will exist when other groups or teams need to interact with the hire, potentially giving your team a bad name to the rest of the organization.

I've seen it happen firsthand, after focusing more on the technical aspects on the hire and not enough on the organizational and team fit. The result was a cancer that spread across the team, a dip in morale across the team, and a constant push against the team's momentum. I was fortunate enough to have the hire recognize the misalignment and move on of their own accord, but the situation could have just as easily had an unfortunate resolution.

When looking at these categories, you should start by listing the actual areas in which you want to see demonstrated competence. If your organizational values are healthy conflict, write that down, creating a list of skills under each area. An example of a list of organizational values might be as follows:

Organizational values

- Healthy conflict
- Cross-department collaboration
- Employee engagement

With those values in hand, you can begin to craft questions that give the candidate an opportunity to demonstrate those values. Ask for specific examples of how the candidate may have engaged a skill. An example question for healthy conflict might be: "Give me an example of a disagreement you had with a colleague on something that was very important. How did you ultimately resolve it?" This gives the candidate an opportunity to draw on their specific experiences and shows you real-world examples of how they manage situations.

You could also modify the question a bit to see how they would handle different outcomes. An example might be: "Give me an example of when you and a colleague had a disagreement on something important, and your solution was not the chosen solution. How did you come to the resolution, and what made you accept someone else's solution?" This allows you to see how the candidate handles compromise.

You can repeat this process for each value in each category that you've outlined. Keep the questions outside the realm of yes or no answers, creating open-ended questions. On questions that you feel are of outsized importance, you may want to ask for more than one example to confirm that the behavior is repeated in different scenarios.

You also need to be sure that the interview process is as similar as possible among candidates. It can be hard to properly evaluate candidates against each other if what you're measuring changes with each interview. That's why it's important to identify your list of questions ahead of time and try to stick to those questions as closely as possible. Digging deeper on a candidate's response is perfectly fine, but don't ask the candidate an initial question that you don't intend on asking the other candidates. If the first candidate dazzles you with their response, that will leave an impression on you that the other candidates are never afforded the opportunity to make.

IDENTIFYING PASSION

At the core of every great engineer I've ever met is a passion for the craft. Never have I met someone who produced continued success in their field if they treated it simply as a 9-to-5 job. Passion can raise the ceiling on the potential of a candidate, and it's something that I try to identify as early in the interview process as possible.

Passion is something that gets conveyed more than articulated. When candidates say they have a passion for something, ask them how they demonstrate that passion. Do they read blogs? Tinker at home? Do they have an open source project that they contribute to? Passion can manifest itself in different ways, but it always manifests. If not, a passion is nothing more than an interest. Ask your candidates what it is they're passionate about. How do they express that passion?

TECHNICAL INTERVIEW QUESTIONS

Soft skill questions have their place, but they go only so far when hiring an engineer. Any engineering interview *must* have some level of technical assessment. In fact, some candidates might become wary of your company if you don't have a technical assessment. If you're not evaluating a candidate's technical capability, then it stands to reason that you didn't evaluate any of your other hires either. This could signal to the candidate that the technical proficiency in your organization could be problematically low.

When you're designing technical questions, try to avoid simple right or wrong answers. You don't want to just evaluate the candidate's memory recall. You want to be able to test how they think and reason about the types of problems that they're going to face in their new role.

Asking a candidate about the default page size of a database server doesn't exercise their knowledge of database tuning, just their ability to remember a fact. But if you asked them, "What would you do to improve performance of a read-heavy database," the mention of tuning the default page size gives you way more information about their level of proficiency. Try to avoid arcane questions of memorization and instead focus on practical, real-world scenarios that they could encounter.

Encourage the candidates to think through the problem aloud. You can learn more from a candidate talking out loud in front of a completely blank whiteboard than you would if they wrote a solution in complete silence. Did the solution come naturally to them? Have they solved this problem before? Why did they make that choice with their answer? Listening to an engineer connect the dots on their own gives you insight into their experience. I'll give an example.

DecisionTech is hiring a new systems architect. One of the questions in the technical assessment is to design an order-intake system. One candidate draws out a pretty impressive implementation, but it's really just a carbon copy from their previous job. They don't fully understand or grasp the technology choices being made, but just fall back to what they're familiar with. Meanwhile, another candidate is thinking through the problem, and although they don't know what specific technology to use, they have a solid grasp of the problem they're trying to solve:

Candidate: "*So, I'm not sure which technology to use here. But I know that when a new order arrives, I don't want to process it right away in the HTTP request response life cycle. I'd rather that be a separate concern; that way, if the process dies or something, we don't lose the order. Plus, this way it allows us to separate order processing from order intake. We can scale those concerns separately.*"

Even though this candidate doesn't have a specific answer, the thought process is spot on. In a real-world scenario, they'd never have to offer a technology choice up on the spot. They would be permitted to do research, understand the scope of the problem, and evaluate trade-offs. If you're giving them that leeway in the job, giving them the same leeway in the interview makes sense.

When giving a technical assessment, another important thing to do is challenge the choices that the candidate has made. It's worthwhile to know whether the person has considered the trade-offs being made by a decision. Challenging choices also gives you a firsthand opportunity to see how they receive feedback and criticism.

Lastly, during the technical interview, candidates should have access to the same or similar tools that they would have in the real job. How someone solves problems they don't have answers to is arguably more important than seeing them solve problems they've seen before.

If the engineer doesn't know the proper syntax for something, allowing them to use the internet to find the answer is way more productive than watching them fumble through figuring out the positional arguments for a function call. Unless they're working in an environment where the internet is simply not a tool that could be used for research, allowing them to use it in interviews can only be helpful. If they need to use the internet to answer every portion of the technical assessment, that gives you just as much information as watching them struggle through each portion. It's also much less uncomfortable for all involved.

Dividing the interview into categories of questions like career goals, technical expertise, and personality fit, creates a sense of logical flow throughout the interview process. This will help in notetaking during the interview as well. I feel that taking notes about the evaluation of a candidate needs to happen during the process, while these ideas and feelings are fresh in your mind. The more time passes, the more the nuances of the interview begin to fade, leaving you with only a handful of touchstone moments to dwell on later.

To keep the interview process flowing, I suggest an easy scoring system that allows you to quickly jot down notes and feedback on candidates. If you keep the interview structured, you can also structure your note-keeping document to match the flow of the questions. Keeping some rough notes is going to be critical when you review your experience with the rest of the interview panel. Figure 11.1 shows how you might structure your interview review document for quick access during the interview.

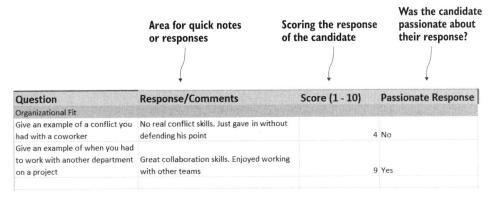

Figure 11.1   An interview structure document to keep quick notes

11.4.4 *Evaluating candidates*

Once the candidate has completed interviews with each panel, the group should convene *the same day* as the interview. This is important, again, because memories fade and begin to cluster around a handful of key moments in the interview. But the details are really in those mini micro-moments that happen throughout the interview process. The flash of brilliance or frustration, the body language around a particular question, the excitement behind discussion on a certain topic are all things that seem small in the moment but can add up to a fuller impression of the candidate. I cannot stress enough how important it is to meet and discuss a candidate's interview as soon as possible after the interview concludes.

With the interview panel all together, the participants should simultaneously reveal whether they want to hire or not hire the candidate. A simple thumbs-up or thumbs-down method works fine, so there's no need to get overly complicated on how participants reveal their choice. The key is that everyone must vote yes or no. There's no room for people being on the fence. My personal philosophy is that if I'm on the fence, then out of an abundance of caution, it's a no to initially start. But force anyone who is trying to ride the middle to vote yes or no. They'll have an opportunity to amend that vote shortly.

Now that everyone has committed one way or another, pick a team member to discuss why they voted the way they did. Ask for specific concrete examples. Do not allow people to simply report that "they have a feeling" about a person, because that doesn't give the other panelists any actionable information to sway their opinion.

This isn't to say that your gut instinct isn't important. Instincts are usually a subconscious pattern recognition based on previous experiences. This is an incredibly important part of your decision-making, but it can't be the entirety of it. Think hard to try to conceptualize the factors that are influencing your instinct so that you can share and communicate that with the rest of the group. Once the first person has finished sharing, move in a clockwise fashion to the next person and continue on until everyone has discussed why they've voted the way they did.

At this point, the panelists have the perspective of their peers on the interview. Maybe they saw something that you didn't. Or perhaps they had different questions based on their specific context that led to interesting responses. You want to allow people the opportunity to have their decisions influenced by this feedback. As you hear the feedback, try to relate the candidate's strengths and weaknesses from the other panelists to the position that you're trying to fill. At this point, each panelist should be afforded the opportunity to change their vote. Once everyone has updated their vote (if necessary), the process should go back to the hiring manager for any follow-up questions or conversations.

This process enables the panelists to offer their viewpoints, providing great feedback for the entire team, but ultimately the hiring decision still rests in the hands of the hiring manager. That person may want complete consensus for any hire being made or may just use the interview panelists' feedback as input into the decision process. But make no mistake that the hiring process is not done by committee. The hiring manager is the ultimate decision-maker.

11.4.5 *How many candidates to interview?*

In a perfect world, you'd interview candidates until you found your top candidate, the one who checks all your boxes and has the team's agreement. When you hire this way, it can sometimes avoid the entire process of comparing candidates to one another. Each candidate goes up against your list of requirements, and either they meet them and impress you or they fall short and are quickly dismissed. Unfortunately, not all of us live in a perfect world.

Hiring is tied to budget, and different organizations have different cycles to their budget. Some organizations have an unofficial time window for how long a requisition for a new position can stay open before it gets absorbed into another fiscal bucket. These policies seem antiquated, but I'm assuming that you, the reader, don't have the power to influence this at a corporate level and so are resigned to operate within these boundaries. The question then becomes, when do you stop interviewing candidates?

Mathematicians have tried to come up with algorithms for this. One is called the *optimal stopping problem*, sometimes referred to as the *secretary problem*. (For more details, see "The Secretary Problem and Its Extensions: A Review" by P.R. Freeman, in *International Statistics Review*, 1983.) The optimal stopping problem can't be used directly for hiring, in my opinion, but we can borrow from it to produce a slightly different strategy.

At the beginning of the interview process, decide how many candidates you'll interview before going into what I'll call *stopping mode*. If you don't hire a candidate, you'll continue to interview X many more candidates before your pool is exhausted. For this example, you'll use six as the stopping mode number.

If you interview the first candidate and they amaze you, hire them and stop. If they don't, interview a second candidate. If they amaze you, hire them; if not, move on to the third. Repeat this process until you get to your stopping mode number.

When you've reached that number, decide which of the six candidates you've interviewed is the best candidate. Now that you've reached your stopping mode number of candidates, continue to interview new candidates. Choose the first candidate that is better than the best candidate of your initial stopping mode batch. Figure 11.2 illustrates this point a bit further.

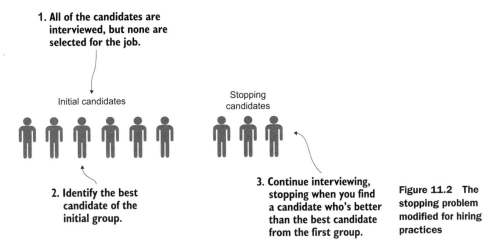

1. All of the candidates are interviewed, but none are selected for the job.

Initial candidates

Stopping candidates

2. Identify the best candidate of the initial group.

3. Continue interviewing, stopping when you find a candidate who's better than the best candidate from the first group.

Figure 11.2 The stopping problem modified for hiring practices

This strategy obviously comes with some caveats. What if all candidates of your stopping mode batch are terrible? You may want to consider retooling your screening process in that case, but it could happen. This process is less of a hard-and-fast rule and more of a way to create a system for ensuring you don't lose the head count because of a lack of movement during the hiring process.

The team is a crucial building block in building a DevOps culture. But hiring is a constant endeavor. People leave, they get promoted, they grow and become interested in other things. No matter who is on your team today, there will come a time when they won't be. Hiring is something that is never finished; it merely takes a break. Having a hiring process and philosophy can make the process a bit smoother when it does happen so that everyone has a ready-made playbook for one of the biggest decisions a team can face.

Summary

- Different components of a culture influence the overall culture of the organization.
- Modifying how we use language to communicate can bolster our effectiveness and help the spread of cultural value and norms.
- You can change a culture through language and rituals, and use those changes to enforce cultural norms.

- You must create a new mindset in team members so that they are empathetic to the other roles in the organization.
- Structure your interviews so each candidate receives the same sets of questions. This will allow you to more accurately compare candidates to each other.
- Hire with your company culture and organizational fit in mind.

Too many yardsticks

12

The power of an organization is centered on the idea of a group of people coming together to complete a task that would be impossible to complete as individuals. Organizations have the ability to direct a group of people toward a single objective, and they use *priorities* to do this. Creating a skyscraper would be incredibly difficult without a group of people, skills, and disciplines coalescing around a set of prioritized goals.

But many teams tend to not coalesce around the overall goal, but instead around their specific slice of that goal. That slice gets prioritized above the overall team goal. As the slices become more specific, so do the ways in which you measure them. Before long, you have a bunch of different means of measuring the performance of the teams, and those means may incentivize behavior that detracts from the overall goal. This is the *too many yardsticks* antipattern.

Goal setting and the process of prioritization are extremely important in DevOps cultures because they set the groundwork for putting energy behind work that has traditionally been neglected. The reason you release 30 features a quarter but can't find time to patch your servers is that one task has been prioritized and the other has not. Prioritization isn't just saying yes to a task, but also saying no to another. The time you have is finite, so simply saying something is important isn't enough. At some point, you have to say that something is *more* important than something else. This can be difficult and a bit painful, but the reality is, you're implicitly making these choices by not making the choice.

But where do priorities come from? They come from the goals and objectives you've set for yourself based on the goals and objectives of your team, department, and organization. Even though you have a to-do item to upgrade that OpenSSL library your program uses, it never gets done because you haven't prioritized it. You haven't prioritized it because it probably isn't part of a goal or objective that you're being measured by. Instead, you let other items shove their way into the front of your consciousness; because of the way tasks are packaged and presented, you accept that one task is more important than the others. This chapter aims to look at that process and force you to evaluate a task for its objective importance.

12.1   Tiers of goals

Goals are typically *tiered*, with one set of goals flowing into the next tier of goals. The organization has a set of goals for the year, whether it be revenue growth, the launch of a new product, or retaining customers. Knowing the organizational goals is necessary to create the next level of priorities, which are departmental.

Each department needs a set of goals that support the organization's goals. This gets repeated right down to the individual, whose goals are influenced by their department's goals, which in turn are influence by the organization's goals. This relationship is depicted in figure 12.1, noting the cascading nature of goals.

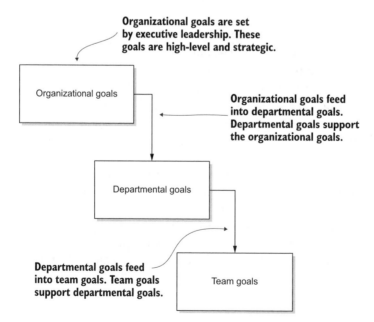

Organizational goals are set by executive leadership. These goals are high-level and strategic.

Organizational goals

Organizational goals feed into departmental goals. Departmental goals support the organizational goals.

Departmental goals

Departmental goals feed into team goals. Team goals support departmental goals.

Team goals

Figure 12.1   Goals cascade from the top of the organization.

Knowing your goals and how they factor into the larger set of organizational goals is, for many people, an influencer of job satisfaction. When your work is off on an island and nobody appreciates what you do or why you do it, you can become disconnected from the rest of the organization. As everyone marches on toward goals that get talked about in company-wide meetings, you're on the sidelines, wondering why you're doing what you're doing and if it matters at all. Understanding the organization's goals and tying your work to one of those can go a long way to helping fight that feeling.

Goals and OKRs

The goal structure that I'm laying out uses a goal-setting technique known as *objectives and key results* (OKRs). This section is not about setting goals, but about understanding how goals cascade throughout the organization. If a top-level company goal is set, it can't be achieved unless the underlying teams align their goals to meet the company goal. How those goals get set is beyond the scope of this book, but if you're interested in goal-setting techniques and OKRs specifically, I highly recommend *Radical Focus* by Christina R. Wodtke (Cucina Media, 2015) and *Measure What Matters* by John Doerr (Portfolio, 2018).

12.1.1 Organizational goals

Unless you're on the executive leadership team at your company, your organizational priorities are largely beyond your control. Because the executive team is many steps removed from the tactical details of how things get done, *organizational goals* are high-level and strategic in nature.

Mapping your tactical, engineering-specific work to these higher-level objectives can be difficult. It can require some outside-the-box thinking. Often this work is done for you by the technology senior leadership team, as they map the departmental goals to the organization's goals. Some examples of organizational goals might be as follows:

- Reduce operational spending by 15%.
- Achieve 20% year-over-year growth in subscribers.
- Increase the spending of existing customers by 10%.

From a technology standpoint, mapping your work to these goals might not be immediately intuitive, because your work is often not a straight line to the goal. For the first goal of reducing operational spending, you might be able to reduce the number of servers you're using in the infrastructure, thereby reducing your operating expense for the platform. Maybe you can identify some low-hanging automation that you can develop to assist other departments in their tasks. Achieving year-over-year growth in subscribers could be supported by tackling key features that some subscribers want, but you haven't had much luck getting into the work queue. The new features are delivered to the product team, which goes to the sales team, and the sales team dangles these new features as enticements for potential customers who have been on the fence. The same thing goes with increasing the spending of existing customers.

The point is that when you start looking at organizational goals, you can begin to look differently at your pile of work. Your team's to-do list can quickly become filtered through the lens of the organization's goals. But this is just one of the levels of goals. Your department will most likely have a specific set of goals that leadership wants that focuses on and prioritizes the things that you should be working on.

12.1.2 Departmental goals

Departmental goals are going to be a little closer to your immediate day-to-day work because they're created with an engineering context in mind by the leadership team. Mapping your team's or even your personal goals should be a pretty straightforward task.

Depending on your level in the organization, you may be involved with setting department goals. If you are, you should consider how the department goals roll into the larger work of the organizational goals. As mentioned previously, not all technology work is a straight line to an organizational goal. But being able to connect the path to the goal still has value for seeing how work is connected. This sense of connectedness for work can be a key factor in team members' job satisfaction. Table 12.1 shows how departmental goals can be defined and mapped to organizational goals.

Table 12.1   Departmental goals mapped to organizational goals

Departmental goals	Organizational goals
Launch 2.0 version of sales software	Achieve 20% YOY growth of subscribers
Rearchitect data pipeline process	Increase existing customer spending by 10%
Improve billing process performance	Reduce operational spending by 15%

Knowing that their work matters and affects people outside the organization can be an enormous team motivator.

12.1.3 Team goals

The *team goals* focus on what the individual teams inside a department will be working on. Just as departmental goals link up to organizational goals, team goals should map to departmental goals. This should be easier than mapping directly to organizational goals, because the department's goals should have been created through the lens of technology. In fact, when you look at the team goals, they are versions of the departmental goals, but with more specificity.

Team goals are more tactical versions of departmental goals. Team goals offer the specific ways that departmental goals will be achieved. "Improve billing performance" is a strategic goal set at the department level that doesn't lay out anything resembling a plan for how to achieve it. Team goals help provide the high-level strokes of how the department is going to execute on improving billing performance.

The goal might not be a single team effort, either. The goals might spread across multiple teams. Development teams might focus on different parts of the code that are known to be particularly slow, while operations teams might focus on tuning the existing hardware to squeeze out more performance. Table 12.2 gives a few examples of how team goals map to departmental and organizational goals.

Table 12.2 Multiple teams focused on a departmental goal

Team	Team goals	Departmental goals	Organizational goals
Dev team #1	Rewrite calculations billing module	Improve billing process performance	Reduce operational spending by 15%
Dev team #2	Move billing to a queue-based, multithreaded process	Improve billing process performance	Reduce operational spending by 15%
Operations team	Tune billing database server to match workload type	Improve billing process performance	Reduce operational spending by 15%

With the team goals mapped out, you can get a sense of how an individual contributor can not only have a clear understanding of what to work on, but also how it fits into the larger organizational goals. Now you're all rowing in the same direction.

12.1.4 *Getting the goals*

If you're not part of the leadership team, you might be confused about what the organizational and team goals are. Your company may not have strong communication around goal setting and planning. I assure you, though, that every company has some understanding of the organizational goals.

They may change and shift frequently, but someone at the senior level knows what they want the company to focus on. This information may just be bottled up and failing to trickle through the organization. The easiest way to solve this is simple—just ask!

Asking for goals seems overly simple, but the reason it works is straightforward: goals are one of the core tasks of any management team. Asking a manager to identify the goals for you or your team is a reasonable request. Even if your direct manager doesn't know, they certainly won't respond with, "I don't know, and I don't plan to find out." That's a completely unreasonable response. If you do get that response, a gentle prompt of, "Well, maybe you can find out for me?" should be enough to set the wheels in motion. If your company has any sort of feedback that goes back to the senior leadership team, it would be invaluable for them to know that the company's objectives and goals are not being filtered down to the individual contributors of the organization.

Some of you might be thinking of how horrible your boss is and how they'll never give you an answer on goals. For that I'd say, ask someone else's boss. The beauty of organizational goals is that they're universal for the company! I doubt that any of you risk being terminated for trying to identify the most important things to work on.

That's essentially what you're doing when you're asking for goals. You're looking to get an understanding of the most important tasks that you can be working on for the company. If you're extremely paranoid about your boss, you can phrase the question to other leaders as a way of understanding how your work connects to the larger work of the organization. Understanding how your work touches, impacts, and enhances other teams is an innocent question that will provide you with tons of additional context from other leaders.

If you're still having trouble, you could consider getting in touch with your culture chief. As described in chapter 11, a *culture chief* is typically well connected and respected throughout the organization. Chances are, they can help you understand how your work supports the larger goals of the organization.

With the goals properly defined, you can begin to look critically at the items that you and your team have been assigned to work on and be much more conscious about the way you spend your time.

12.2 *Consciousness around what you work on*

You have a countless number of demands on your time. Teams consistently have more work to do than they have the capacity to perform. To keep from being pulled in multiple directions, you need to be able to defend your choice of what you're currently working on. Your goals and priorities are the shield you use to defend your current work. Any task or item that comes into your team's work queue must be able to pierce that shield to get your current attention. Your shield is strongest when you have a clear understanding of goals and your tasks related to those goals.

Being conscious of what you work on is rooted in this idea of *commitments*. You make commitments to coworkers and to your boss. Your department makes commitments to the organization, and so it goes up the chain. When it comes to individuals, commitments are the currency of credibility. When someone commits to something, you instantly do a calculation on that person's credibility. Do they frequently deliver when they say they will? Or is this person or department consistently underestimating the time it will take to complete a task? This credibility is heavily determined by how well you manage the number of commitments that you make and their impact on each other. Once a commitment is made, it needs to be delivered or renegotiated. Once you understand that, you can begin to say yes to the important work, and no to the unimportant.

12.2.1 *Priority, urgency, and importance*

Many people confuse *importance* and *priority*. A *priority* takes precedence over other actions. But if a priority takes precedence over other actions, how can there possibly ever be multiple priorities? It can be difficult to reason about, especially as an individual contributor who is being handed multiple tasks, all of which are deemed a priority.

It is my assertion, though, that an individual can have only a single priority at a given time. That doesn't mean you don't have other important items in your to-do list, but only one of them is *the* most important thing to do. If you have an important board meeting, but right before it starts you find out a loved one was involved in a horrible accident, do you juggle multiple priorities? No, you must choose one as being more important than the other.

If you can have only one priority, you still need a mechanism for being able to categorize other work. Incoming work has two other characteristics: *urgency* and *importance.*

Urgency defines how soon a task must be performed. It might have an external deadline or may be needed as input into another process that's stuck or blocked. *Importance* relates to the significance or value of the work. A piece of work that makes life easier for a developer's workflow may be considered less important than a feature change that impacts thousands of customers. Neither item may be urgent, but one has more importance than the other.

> **DEFINITION** *Importance* of a task is its relative value or significance to the organization. *Urgency* is related to the time horizon in which a task needs to be completed. Urgency requires an objective deadline, not just the requester's preferences.

It's important to recognize that both urgency and importance are tainted by the context in which they're looked at. The requester will look at a task as important based on how it relates to other work that they need to perform. The implementer of the request may not have that same context and view the request differently. This is another reason why it's important for you to understand the goals of your team, department, and organization. The goals provide an objective lens through which to view these requests.

When a task given to you is the priority, it should become the default that you turn to when you have time to perform work. All other commitments should be looked at as it relates to the priority that you've been given. When you look at any other time commitments, the commitments should be examined through the lens of the priority. If the new commitment can impact your priority, your options are to defer the new work, attempt to elevate the new work as your priority, or renegotiate your existing priority's deadline. Consider the following:

- Will this commitment impact your ability to deliver the priority on time?
- Does this new commitment have the potential to become your new priority?
- Is this new commitment important enough that you should renegotiate your priority's deadline commitment?

These questions will help you assess whether you can take on this new time commitment—whether it's a meeting, a new project, or even just a new smaller task. If the task isn't going to impact your time commitment to your priority, accepting the new commitment is OK. If it will impact your ability to deliver on your priority commitment, you have to evaluate the relative importance and urgency of this new task. Is it important enough to become my new priority? This is a decision that you'll probably want to make in tandem with your manager or supervisor.

It is possible (and common) that a new, unexpected item that comes up is important enough to become the new priority for you. Evaluate it with your manager and decide. If it's not important enough to become the new priority, maybe it's important enough for you to renegotiate your deadline for your existing priority. Again, you'll want to have this conversation with your manager.

But enter the conversation understanding how much time this is going to add to the delivery of the priority. You can't decide on delaying a priority if you don't know how long the delay is going to be. If you absolutely cannot measure the delay, you'll want to make sure that you tell your manager. The uncertainty of the delay may impact the decision on whether to accept this new time commitment. If you cannot successfully navigate any of these options, you should reject the new time commitment.

For some of you, the idea of refusing work may sound alien. But the truth is, you and your team are already refusing work. The difference is, you tell whoever is requesting the work that you'll do it, but consistently prioritize other activities over it. If you look in any work queue, you'll find work requests that have been sitting for quite some time and have no realistic chance of getting prioritized.

Not only does this work act as an attention thief, but ignoring it is also incredibly unprofessional to the requestor. The person who requested the work probably has some hopes, dreams, or plans around what they'll do when this ticket is finally completed. But if this ticket has no hopes of every getting prioritized, you're robbing the requestor of the ability to properly plan for that reality. They could be making alternate arrangements or gaining more executive support for their tasks. Instead, they're waiting on you with the misguided belief that their work is happening soon.

PRO TIP   Refusing a task is more professional than accepting it and never doing it.

12.2.2 *The Eisenhower decision matrix*

In the previous section, I discussed an evaluation mechanism for interpreting whether a task should be accepted. This process is an informal version of the *Eisenhower matrix*. The Eisenhower decision matrix is a tool that was used by Dwight Eisenhower, the 34th president of the United States. Eisenhower was known as a shrewd decision-maker who often leveraged this tool.

The purpose of the tool is to create a four-square decision matrix and to place each task inside the matrix to determine the best way to deal with it. Figure 12.2 depicts an Eisenhower decision matrix. The y-axis boxes are labeled as *not important* and *important*. The x-axis boxes are labeled as *urgent* and *not urgent*. The four boxes inside the matrix are labeled as *do, decide, delegate,* and *delete.*

As each task comes in, you can classify it for both urgency and importance. The task is either urgent or not urgent, and it is either important or not important. Based on those assigned values, you can place the task in your matrix and know what to do with it.

I've modified the context of each box slightly to account for the fact that you may not have complete decision authority on the tasks you work on. If you're an individual contributor, you may need to clear some of these actions with your immediate supervisor or manager. The goal of the matrix is to aid you in your decision-making on what you should and shouldn't be working on.

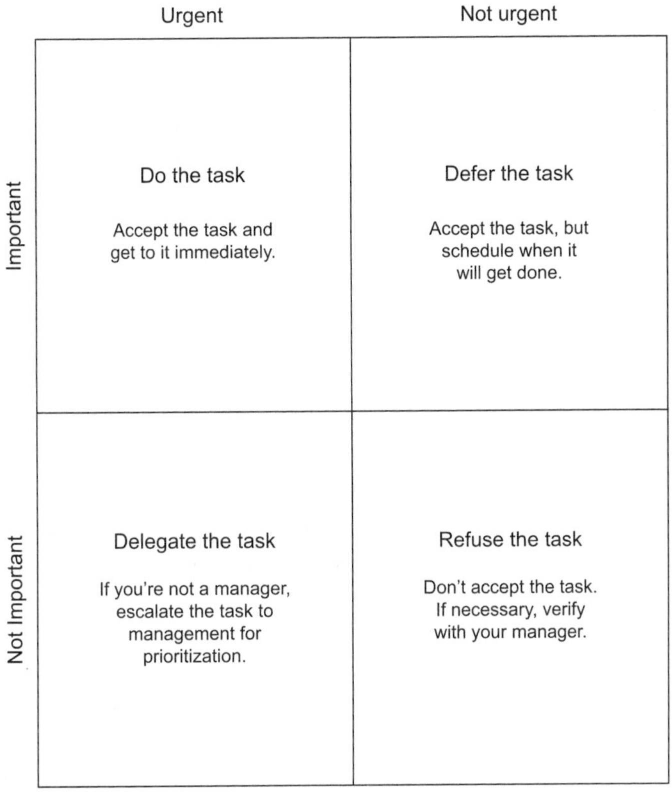

Urgent   Not urgent

	Do the task Accept the task and get to it immediately.	Defer the task Accept the task, but schedule when it will get done.
Important		
Not Important	Delegate the task If you're not a manager, escalate the task to management for prioritization.	Refuse the task Don't accept the task. If necessary, verify with your manager.

Figure 12.2 The Eisenhower decision matrix can be used to evaluate incoming work.

12.2.3 *How to say no to a commitment*

Saying no to a new commitment can be difficult, but necessary. Commitments are the currency of credibility. When you accept a commitment, you're putting your organizational credibility on the line. Saying no to new commitments that you can't meet is just another method of maintaining your credibility. Sometimes a request for a commitment isn't presented as a request but as a demand. But the work that you've done up to this point is setting you up to make saying no to new commitments not only possible, but entirely defensible. Your goals and priority are a shield against new commitments.

If your work is aligned with goals and your priority is set, then new commitments can be run through the Eisenhower matrix to see whether they should be performed. If they do need to be performed, you can run them against the following three priority questions discussed earlier:

- Will this commitment impact your ability to deliver the priority on time?
- Does this new commitment have the potential to become your new priority?
- Is this new commitment important enough that you should renegotiate your priority's deadline commitment?

With these questions answered, rejecting the new commitment is straightforward. You state that you cannot accept the new commitment because it interferes with your current priority. If the commitment aligns with your goals (hence, it is important), you can defer that work to be performed later. Confer with the requestor, and if necessary, your manager, and come to an agreement on when the task might possibly be scheduled to be worked on.

If you're an individual contributor, I highly recommend that you do not commit to a deliverable date at this point. Remember that your commitments are your credibility, and you don't set the priority; your manager does. You can commit to bringing the request to your manager for prioritization, but that's about it.

> **PRO TIP**   Unless you have complete control over how your work is prioritized, you never want to offer commitments that you may have no control over honoring. This is important not only for the requestor, but for your own personal reputation in the organization.

When a requestor is adamant about the commitment being accepted, remember that declining the work is about honoring a previous commitment, and you don't break commitments. If the requestor continues to be adamant, refer them to your manager.

You can say something simple and gentle as, "I'd love to help, but I have previous commitments that I have to meet. If you want to talk about prioritization or make a case for this being more important, you should talk to my manager, Sandra. She sets my priority and other tasks." This simple way of saying no to a time commitment is unarguable. You don't set the priority; your manager does. Just keep in mind that you've already made a commitment. You should never feel bad or pressured about accepting a new commitment that violates that.

Evaluating work as the manager

If you are the manager of a team, you have a slightly different worldview, because you set the priority. But the process isn't much different from that of the individual contributor.

You have the added ability to delegate the task to another team member. Maybe they're working on something that is less urgent and important than this new commitment that's popped up (or impacts their priority to a lesser degree).

The key is to be explicit with your team members in identifying the priority and indicating when that priority is due. If team members don't clearly understand their priority, they'll undoubtedly spend time working on the less important task.

Your manager may not have the same sense of work prioritization that you have. If your manager asks you to take on the commitment, regardless of the impact, be sure to clarify the new due date for your priority. It *must* be renegotiated.

You must be clear that accepting the new commitment conflicts with your ability to deliver the priority on time. You should also ensure and verify that the priority has not changed. Sometimes a manager may think that because they told you to do task A instead of task B, this implies a reordering of the priority. You should always clarify: "Just so I'm clear, does this change my priority?"

You'll be surprised how often a leader may not recognize that they're asking the impossible. Forcing them to choose between tasks that are competing for your priority may make them reevaluate the new commitment. Always make sure you have a clear understanding of your current priority. Also remember, you can have only one priority. Force your manager to choose a single priority for you. It can be helpful to iterate the newly negotiated priority in email as a reminder and clarification of the new expectations for everyone.

The following is an example interaction between Brian, the employee, attempting to renegotiate a priority with his manager, Sandra.

> Brian: "Hey, Sandra. Joanne just asked me to work on this ticket for the recruiting team to fix some SEO issues with the careers page. But you've got me working on the calculation module for the billing project. I can't do the SEO work and deliver the calculation changes by Thursday."
>
> Sandra: "Hmm. The SEO thing is pretty big because of the recruiting push behind this conference we're sponsoring. Go ahead and work on the SEO page."
>
> Brian: "OK, but then I can't deliver the calculations module by Thursday. The SEO work is probably going to take me a week, so I can deliver the calculation work two weeks from Thursday. Is that OK?"
>
> Sandra: "Oh, no. We need the calculations before then to make the deliverable date for user acceptance testing."
>
> Brian: "Ok. Which is my priority? The billing work or the SEO work?"
>
> Sandra: "Definitely the billing work."
>
> Brian: "OK. That means I'll work on the SEO stuff after billing. But that might mean the SEO work won't be done before the recruiting event."
>
> Sandra: "Well, the calculation work ties into our departmental goals, so you better stick with that. The recruiting event was never part of our goals or our priority, so if something has to suffer, it should be that. Maybe I can find someone else to take the SEO work."
>
> Brian: "Ok, sounds good. I'll just send a quick email summarizing what we decided. Thanks!"

This dialogue shows how knowing the goals, priority, urgency, and importance of tasks and the work that your team is doing aids in deciding what to work on. Sometimes there is no easy way out of a task. There will always be a time when your attention must immediately shift to the new task on your plate. But how you manage and control that work will help relieve the sense of powerlessness you feel against it.

12.3   *Structuring your team's work*

You and your team need a way to track both the work that you're currently executing and the work that you've made previous commitments to. I won't prescribe a specific technical solution. Your organization likely already has some sort of tool in place.

If there's wide acceptance of a tool within the organization, but your team specifically isn't using it, just adopt the tool that everyone else is using. Accepting the tool that's widely in use creates less friction; it's already approved, and makes interoperability and collaboration with other teams much easier. Something is most certainly better than nothing.

You might not have a technical solution, instead opting for pen and paper. That's fine too. The only requirement is that all outstanding work must be captured *somewhere* and made visible to the team. Work cannot be an ephemeral idea inside people's heads. Regardless of the solution you use, I'll refer to it as a *work queue system*.

> **DEFINITION**   *Work queue systems* are tools or practices that help document a team's current work. Each piece of work is known as a *work item* and is represented via a ticketing system, sticky note, or other physical or digital manifestation. This allows team members to visibly see the outstanding and in-process work for the team.

The remainder of this section discusses techniques for how to look at all the work you have before you. I'm addressing these steps to you as an individual; know that if you're a manager, these same techniques apply, just across your entire team instead of to yourself.

12.3.1   *Time-slice your work*

If you break out your list of things to do, you'll quickly become overwhelmed by the number of tasks. You always have more work than you have the capacity for. Looking at the list in its entirety is a recipe for disaster. The human mind can't focus on that many variables at any one time. A to-do list of 50 items can instantly put you in a state of analysis paralysis, preventing you from making progress on anything.

The first thing you need to do is time-slice your work. *Time-slicing* is a technique that is often used for smaller work iterations. You may sit down to work on something in 30-minute increments, giving yourself time in between to stretch, get some water, take a break, and get back into the task.

Here, I'm taking the idea of time-slicing and expanding on it. When confronted with many work items, it's best to choose a time-slice, during which you'll focus on a subset of those work items. I call these time-slices *iterations*. In the Scrum approach to the Agile methodology, this is called a *sprint*.

> **DEFINITION**   *Iterations*, or *sprints*, are time-boxed periods during which a person or team commits to deliver a defined set of work.

Many companies don't use the Agile methodology and instead opt to work in a style that breaks projects into sequential phases, with each phase providing its outputs as inputs to the next phase. This style of working is called the *waterfall model*. Either model is supported by this process, however.

For our example, I'm going to assume you're working with two-week iterations: you've committed to completing the work that you've been assigned within two weeks. In the real world, you'll need to come up with your own iteration length. It's better to keep the iterations relatively short, to allow you the ability to add or remove items without throwing off a lot of dependent tasks. You can also consider choosing your iteration length based on the cadence of project-related activities.

Do you have a status meeting every three weeks? Maybe having three-week iterations makes sense to line up with that. Maybe your company is a bit nimbler. Maybe one-week iterations make sense in that case.

The primary benefit of using iterations is it allows you to ignore the other work items that you're currently *not* working on. This is key, because the clutter of other work in your work queue system can serve not only as a distraction, but as a sense of anxiety for people who are overwhelmed when a lot of unfinished work is out there. You know you can't do it all at once, so it's better to create a laser-like focus on the items that you can do something about.

12.3.2 Populating the iteration

Now that you have defined a time-slice, you can begin looking at populating the items you plan to commit to in your time-slice. The total number of work items you commit to will be based on a mixture of factors: the number of work items on your team, the complexity of the work items, and any work that comes to your team in an ad hoc fashion. Ad hoc work is sometimes unpredictable and can force you to reevaluate work items in the current iteration. This work is referred to as *unplanned work* and is discussed in detail in the following section.

> **DEFINITION** *Unplanned work* is new work that interrupts your current set of tasks, forcing a disruption to your previously scheduled work. Unplanned work may force you to switch to the new task immediately or to complete it in the short-term, potentially jeopardizing previous commitments. An example might be a bug from a previous sprint being flagged as urgent and needing an immediate fix.

Your list of items that will influence the number of work items you can commit to will look like the following:

- The number of people working on work items on your team
- The complexity of the work items
- The amount of unplanned work that your team experiences

The number of people working on your team will be a strong influence for the maximum number of work items you should commit to. In a two-week iteration, my rule of thumb is no more than four work items per person. This number will vary from team to team, depending on the team's productivity. For the first few months, track how many work items you commit to per iteration and how many get done in that time span. Use this as an input to adjust and refine the number of work items you can realistically commit to per iteration.

The complexity of work items needs to be considered. You can have a work item count as multiple items in your iteration. This allows you to account for a task's complexity. For example, if you have a task to automate database restores, but you know that process is extremely complex, you may count it as four tasks instead of just one, leaving less room in the iteration for other tickets.

If you have a work item that simply won't fit into a single iteration, try breaking the task into smaller subtasks and scheduling those small subtasks. For example, if you had a ticket that said patch all servers to the latest version, and that's a manual task, you might not be able to do it in a single iteration. You could break the task into smaller subtasks like "patch the web servers" and "patch the database servers." Then just schedule those style of tasks across multiple iterations until you're complete.

Unplanned work is an unfortunate reality for everyone. You need to account for unplanned work your team encounters, because when it happens, it's not uncommon for those tasks to jump straight to the top of the work queue. You should continuously strive to eliminate unplanned work by applying some of the techniques mentioned earlier in the chapter. But you should keep a watchful eye on the amount of unplanned work you receive so that you can track and understand its sources.

The goal is to complete all the tasks you commit to for an iteration by the deliverable date. Sometimes that's not possible because of unforeseen circumstances, but that's OK. You'll always be confronted with unplanned work, and sometimes that work will take precedence. Sometimes a task will appear easy, but balloon into way more than you could ever possibly get done in an iteration. Just continue to strive for improvement in the accuracy of your commitments, and continue to try to reduce unplanned work.

Once you have the iteration scheduled, you now have two distinct piles of work. The first pile is iteration-planned work that you've committed to getting done during the next iteration. The second pile is a collection of work items that you've accepted but haven't yet scheduled when that work will be done. I'm going to borrow a term from the Agile community and refer to that work as *the backlog*.

> **DEFINITION**   The *backlog* is a collection of work items that have been accepted by a person or team as work under consideration, but the decision for if or when that work will be done has not been made yet.

The backlog can be a sort of mental trap for many teams. Seeing the unending pile of work items can nullify any sense of progression. Therefore, it's extremely important that teams try to focus on the current iteration of work as much as possible. The backlog can be reviewed for planning purposes for the following iteration, but the backlog itself should be hidden from the current work view. The team should be focused solely on the work that's been committed to for this iteration.

The iteration queue also has the added benefit of potentially being viewable to everyone, since your work queue system represents work either physically or digitally. This allows you to have transparency around the things you and or your team are working on.

12.4 Unplanned work

Occasionally a colleague will stop by unannounced and ask you for assistance with something. Trying to be a good coworker, you agree to help them out. What seemed like an innocent 30-second task quickly spirals into a web of misunderstanding and confusion that ultimately consumes way more time than you could have ever possibly imagined.

Once the magnitude of the intrusion settles in, you realize that your entire schedule for the day has been completely ruined. You've become the victim of *unplanned work*. Unplanned work is corrosive in its demands on your time and attention, forcing you to switch gears and focus on a brand-new task.

The problem with unplanned work is multifaceted. To start, your attention is immediately pulled away from the task you're working on. Regardless of how big or small the new task that you're presented with, there is a penalty for having to switch from one task to another. Getting back to the state of focus that you were in on your previous task is not fast or easy. This disruption is known as a *context switch*, and it can be very disruptive to the working flow of an engineer.

Context switching, and by extension unplanned work, is extremely expensive cognitively because of the amount of time it takes a person to get back into the flow of the previous task that they were working on. If you've ever been deep into a problem and then pulled away from it, you know how difficult it is to get back into the rhythm. It can take an engineer 15 to 30 minutes to get back into the previous mental state before the unplanned work.

Imagine an environment where an engineer is working on a problem and being interrupted once per day. In a five-day work week, that's at least 75 minutes per week of lost productivity! On a team of four engineers, that's almost five hours per week! You'll never eliminate unplanned work, but controlling it is extremely important.

12.4.1 Controlling unplanned work

Controlling unplanned work requires a few high-level steps:

1 Evaluate the work coming in.
2 Make a note of the sources of the work.
3 Determine whether the work is truly urgent. If it is, do it. If it's not, defer it.
4 When you've completed your focus work, evaluate the work deferred in more detail and decide when it will be worked on.

Before you can control unplanned work, you must first understand the types of unplanned work that exist in your environment and its sources. First, I'm going to talk about the kind of unplanned work that is easier to maintain: the cubicle drive-by.

COWORKER UNPLANNED WORK

Your coworkers are one of the most constant forms of unplanned work in the office. If you're not careful, their problems can become your problems without any regard for the work that you currently have on your plate. People don't do it to be rude, but in this hyperconnected world, people are accustomed to quick access to resources, information, and other people.

For some reason, many people have bought into this unofficial social contract that you always need to be available. But this mentality just makes you less productive for more hours of the day. The best way to handle human unplanned work is to make yourself less accessible during times of deep focus. Turn off your email, close down chat, put on your headphones, and just try to get deep on a task.

The idea of turning off chat and email might make you a bit nervous. You might have a fear of missing vital communication or an emergency chat that's going to require you to spring into action immediately. Chat and email exist and are leaned upon because they're easy, but they're not the end-all method of communication.

Setting expectations is another method to curtail coworker interruptions. You set up open time slots in the day for anyone who has a nonurgent need of your time. Blocking time on your calendar and making it known that you prefer ad hoc meetings to occur between 10 a.m. and 12 p.m. Monday, Wednesday, and Friday lets people know the best time to interrupt you. The key is to stick to those hours! If people visit outside those hours with nonurgent issues, gently decline, inform them of your open hours, and suggest they come back then or schedule a meeting on your calendar.

In an actual urgent situation, people will exhaust methods of communication, including but not limited to phone calls and actual desk visits. Urgency and importance seldom occupy the same space.

> *I have two kinds of problems, the urgent and the important. The urgent are not important, and the important are never urgent.*
>
> —Dwight D. Eisenhower
> Address at the Second Assembly of the World Churches,
> Evanston, Illinois, August 19, 1954

If turning off chat and email are unacceptable in your work environment, you can try turning on your out-of-office automatic reply and setting your chat status message to Away. Within these messages, you can provide an alternative method for getting in touch with you in case of a real emergency. I suspect that most people will recognize that interrupting you isn't completely necessary and can wait until you become available again.

At smaller offices, the chat and email message might be skipped entirely, and people will go directly to the desk visit. The best way to solve unplanned work at your desk is to be honest with the visitor. When people stop at your desk, they often break the ice with a question like, "Hey, Kaleed. You got a second?" An honest "no" is the best response. Let them know you're deep in a problem and that you'll catch up with them in 30 or 60 minutes.

You'll be amazed at how often this works! Remember that they're asking for your time, which means unless it's a true emergency, you can set the terms. Sometimes the interruption is warranted, and you just have to pay the context-switching cost. But being able to eliminate half of the unplanned work you experience in a given week will give you a lot of time back.

The key with this response, however, is to honor your commitment! If you said you were going to follow up, make sure you follow up. If you don't, the next time they try to interrupt you, they may not be happy with waiting until later.

Why do people interrupt us?

People who interrupt you aren't trying to be rude and usually have good intentions. They're just taking advantage of the technology, or the proximity to each other, to solve their needs as quickly as possible. It's all very subconscious.

Think about how many times you've instant-messaged someone for a relatively benign and unimportant question. Could that message have waited? Better yet, could that message have been an email, instead of forcing away someone's attention on their current task?

Humans generate unplanned work for each other because they're focused on accomplishing their own set of tasks as quickly as possible. The requestor might be trying to avoid their own context switch by getting a vital piece of information from you.

SYSTEM UNPLANNED WORK

Sometimes the systems themselves generate unplanned work for you while you're working. That system unplanned work might be something as complicated as a system outage or as mundane as an event that requires just a little bit of live investigation.

Either way, system unplanned work can be hard to ignore. It's important that you understand where your system unplanned work is coming from. It can become a constant nuisance to your overall productivity if you must frequently context-switch to deal with an automated alarm or system message.

Tackling system unplanned work starts with categorizing the sources. Any sort of automated system unplanned work should be categorized by a few axes, such as the following:

- What system generated the alert? (For example, did a user-generated action, a monitoring system, or a log aggregation tool create the alert?)
- What service or system is experiencing the problem?
- What was the date and time that the issue was detected?

As time goes on, you'll see many other bits of data that you want to be able to report on, but this is the bare minimum of datapoints you need to collect. You want to ask and answer these questions to generate more information about the alerts for classification purposes, and attempt to solve the underlying issue behind the unplanned work. With these points, you can begin to get a sense of any patterns to the unplanned work:

- Is the unplanned work coming from a system at a specific time frame?
- Does one system generate more unplanned work than the others?
- Is there a common time of day that generates a lot of unplanned work?

Chapter 6 provided a lot of tips and advice on alert fatigue, and Chapter 3 offered some ways to approach creating metrics. Once you've identified a pattern to the unplanned work, you can focus your energy on the most egregious interrupters.

This is also another opportunity to apply the Pareto principle. In this case, it would mean that 80% of the unplanned work by systems is probably caused by 20% of the systems. Finding the 20% in your unplanned work generation can lead you to massive productivity savings.

DO IT OR DEFER IT

Regardless of whether your work is human-driven or system-driven, your ability to stay on task will be determined by how fast you can figure out whether you need to handle the unplanned work immediately or can defer it. The time horizon for later might be hours or it might be days, depending on the situation. But the key is to avoid getting too deep into the weeds of understanding the new task, forcing you to context-switch from your current task.

Quickly assess whether the task requires your attention *immediately*. If it doesn't, defer the task to a later time and get your attention back on the task at hand. Once you have a clean break, you can take time to examine the task more closely and understand its impact and level of importance.

It's common for a casual desk visit to turn into a much larger request than can be handled in one easy conversation. Larger work will come in for your team from many sources. For the work that can be deferred to a later date, the next section covers how you manage all the work you've put off for later.

12.4.2 Dealing with unplanned work

Dealing with unplanned work will be an ongoing effort and struggle. There's no easy way to get rid of this type of work if you're working with other people and computers. In the previous section, I said that you should consider how much unplanned work you may receive throughout an iteration's time period.

The first thing to establish is the urgency of the unplanned work. Sometimes after minimal examination, you can determine that the work isn't nearly as urgent as it may seem. If it's not urgent, you can put the request in the backlog for consideration in the next iteration.

In some cases, it may not be urgent, but still has some time sensitivity. At that point, you can just guarantee its placement in the next iteration. This gives the requestor the peace of mind that the task will be addressed soon, and it allows you keep your previous commitments.

But this doesn't always work. Sometimes work shows up and it's urgent. With any luck, the buffer you've created for unplanned work is enough to absorb this work without impacting the commitments you've already made. But what if this unplanned work is going to take considerable effort? You must fall back on your principles of being conscious about the items you work on and commit to. This means you need to renegotiate some of your commitments.

If people are dependent on your work and potentially blocked by you failing to deliver on your commitments, you need to restructure your commitments. I suggest you always start with the person delivering the unplanned work. If they're the requestor of other work items in your queue, it makes sense to make a commitment swap. You offer up the other work items that they own in your iteration and ask them which one they'd like to remove. This forces the person who is showing up with unplanned work to prioritize their requests.

But the requestor who has unplanned work might not have other work items for you in the current iteration. Now you're forced to impact someone who isn't involved with this new work item. If you have items that you know have scheduling slack, you can reach out to the requester and try to negotiate a new commitment date. If there's flexibility in the schedule, this can be an easy affair. If there's not, the situation may need to be escalated.

Sometimes nobody will willingly volunteer their work to be rescheduled. At that point, it makes sense to get the requestors together and have each of them hash out the business case for their request. By making a business case, all of the potential stakeholders have the context necessary to evaluate the competing tasks. The following are key areas to hit:

- Why is the request important? Does it roll up to one of the defined goals?
- What's impacted by the request's delay?
- Who are the other stakeholders of the request? (For example, who else is impacted by the request's delay?)

With these three questions laid among the group, you should be able to negotiate a delay in someone's process based on importance and impact to the business. This sounds like an extremely formal process, but it can typically be done in less than 10 minutes. The work item that gets bumped should be the priority in the following iteration.

> **NOTE** You'll be tempted to consider bumping your own work for things like maintenance, patching, security, and rearchitecting. Reduce the urge to devalue your work. As a technologist, you need to protect your time for dealing with these tasks. If you offer to reschedule that work, be sure that it gets prioritized in the following iteration.

The key to managing unplanned work is to be able to identify it and its sources. Is unplanned work coming from repeated manual requests for your team? Maybe you can automate that. Perhaps testing environments require more care and feeding than they should? Whatever the reasons, you need to be able to identify unplanned work so that it can be examined later.

You can do this in many ways, depending on what you've used to implement your work queue system. Many software solutions have labels or tags that you can apply to a work item for reporting purposes. Here are few options for software solutions:

- Jira Software (www.atlassian.com/software/jira)
- Trello (https://trello.com)
- Microsoft Planner (https://products.office.com/en-us/business/task-management -software)
- monday.com (https://monday.com/)
- Asana (https://asana.com/)
- BMC Helix ITSM, formerly Remedy (www.bmc.com/it-solutions/remedy-itsm .html)

If you're using a paper-based work queue system, you might need to create a separate log or spreadsheet that tracks this information. Microsoft Excel or Google Sheets is a perfect solution for this, with many functions that can help you easily generate reports on specific fields.

Whatever method you use, just make sure it's something that can be reported on so you can identify where the unplanned work is originating from. This will be your primary insight for reducing it.

You can easily confuse difficult work with the most time-consuming. You may have some unplanned work that is incredibly burdensome but happens infrequently. Compare that to work that's easy to execute so it doesn't feel painful and is handled quickly. But if you consider three or four team members are doing it multiple times a week, it begins to add up. Being able to report on the sources of unplanned work gives you objective visibility into where the work is coming from.

How is this different from Agile or Kanban?

If you've worked in a company that practices Agile methodology, what I've outlined may sound familiar. The process borrows heavily from the Kanban style of working. I don't specifically refer to the process as Agile or Kanban, because both terms may have a lot of baggage in some organizations. In addition, Agile implementations are rife with ritual and ceremony that goes beyond the need to just get a handle on what's being worked on. If you're interested in Kanban, I highly recommend reading *Making Work Visible* by Dominica DeGrandis (IT Revolution Press, 2017).

Having a solid approach to handling work is critical to a DevOps environment. A key part of DevOps is making the time for the automation, the permanent fixes, and the internal tools that have been neglected previously. Being able to prioritize your work and defend that prioritization process is a must-have skill.

Iterations are a solid way to block out as many of the excess tasks as possible and to put focus on a small subset of tasks. When you've planned your work, being able to identify unplanned work becomes easy. When unplanned work comes to you or your team, you need to be objective about its urgency. Is this something that's truly urgent, or is it merely important? Important tasks go in the backlog to be prioritized during your next iteration. Having a firm handle on the work that you're committed to allows you to be intentional about accepting, and sometimes rejecting, new work.

Summary

- Goals cascade throughout the organization.
- Work needs to be classified and prioritized to ensure that the right tasks are getting done.
- Urgency and importance are two categories to classify work.
- Work needs to be organized so the team has insight into pending and in-process work.
- Unplanned work is disruptive and needs to be identified, tracked, and reduced as much as possible.

Wrapping it all up

You've done it. You've reached the end of this wild ride called DevOps, or at least the instruction manual. But now you have to go into your organization and put it into practice. A common question to ask at this point is, "Where do I start?" My advice is to start where it's easiest.

Remember that a DevOps culture isn't necessarily a prescribed path from A to B. Some organizations will struggle at parts that differ from the struggle that other organizations will face. Some companies don't even have all of the problems that I've discussed in this book. I've taken great care to not dictate any path as the only path because every company is different and has a different set of problems.

One piece in this DevOps movement seems universally true: there isn't just one thing that you need to do in order to unleash the power of DevOps. It'll take several changes in several areas to get teams working closer together, solving common problems, and working toward a common set of goals. Start where it's easiest—where you can deliver the most value with your own personal effort. For example, it might be easiest to start organizing lunch-and-learns to help foster and facilitate knowledge transfers. Maybe you can begin instituting the postmortem process after an incident, facilitating the conversations and helping the team to more thoroughly explore the nature of the failure.

It's tempting to dive right into tools and workflows that are touted in conferences and tech blog articles. I beg you to resist that urge—not because tools aren't important, but because they're not as important as the soft skills outlined in this book. When your company has developed those soft skills in the organization, you'll be better equipped to ask the difficult questions surrounding your technology choices, with open, honest dialogue about the needs and wants of the team members who will be using it.

Last, I recommend finding a community outside your organization to talk about DevOps with. Meetup.com is a great place to find like-minded individuals to share the burden, troubles, and triumphs of what it's like trying to make this leap to a new way of working and interacting. Being able to meet with others and see how their approach can influence your own is a lifesaver. You'll quickly find that organizations have similar personality types in them, and some knowledge gained could be widely applicable.

If there aren't any DevOps groups in your area, start one! If you're interested in DevOps, I can guarantee that there are others within a 20-mile radius who are also interested. Just start by meeting consistently, even if it's only to network and talk. If things start to pick up, you can begin creating more structured meetings with presentations from members of the community. You'd also be surprised how many companies like Datadog, PagerDuty, GitHub, and many others will fly someone to your Meetup group to present lectures. Take advantage of these opportunities.

Our interactions don't have to end with the final page of this book. I look forward to interacting with you and offering any advice I can give. The best ways to reach me are via Twitter, where I'm @DarkAndNerdy, or via LinkedIn. You can also find me at my website, https://attainabledevops.com. I wish you the best of luck in your DevOps journey!

index

Y